ecpr PRESS

Global Tax Governance

What is wrong with it and how to fix it

Edited by
Peter Dietsch and Thomas Rixen

First published by the ECPR Press in 2016

The ECPR Press is the publishing imprint of the European Consortium for Political Research (ECPR), a scholarly association, which supports and encourages the training, research and cross-national co-operation of political scientists in institutions throughout Europe and beyond.

ECPR Press
Harbour House
Hythe Quay
Colchester
CO2 8JF
United Kingdom

Typeset by Lapiz Digital Services

Printed and bound by Lightning Source

British Library Cataloguing in Publication Data

A catalogue record for this book is available from the British Library

ISBN: 978-1-785521-26-3
PDF ISBN: 978-1-785521-64-5
EPUB ISBN: 978-1-785521-65-2
KINDLE ISBN: 978-1-785521-66-9

www.ecpr.eu/ecprpress

If you are interested in taxation, you may also wish to explore the following title from ECPR Press

The Politics of Income Taxation: A Comparative Analysis
Steffen Ganghof
Marginal income tax rates in advanced industrial countries have fallen dramatically since the mid-1980s, but levels and progressivity of income taxation continue to differ strongly across countries. This study offers a new perspective on both observations. It blends theoretical inquiry with focused quantitative analysis and in-depth investigation of seven countries: Germany, Australia and New Zealand as well as Denmark, Finland, Norway and Sweden.

The Politics of Income Taxation highlights the equity-efficiency tradeoffs that structure the politics of income taxation, and analyses how income taxes are embedded in broader tax systems. It explains the limited but enduring importance of political parties and democratic institutions. Finally, the study paints a nuanced picture of the role of globalisation and thus sheds light on the pros and cons of tax co-ordination at European and international levels.
ISBN: 9780954796686

Please visit www.ecpr.eu/ecprpress for up-to-date information about new and forthcoming publications.

Table of Contents

List of Figures and Tables

Figures

Tables

List of Abbreviations

AEI	Automatic Exchange of Information
AIE	Automatic Information-Exchange
ALS	Arm's Length Standard
APAs	Advance Pricing Agreements
AuM	Assets under Management
BCG	Boston Consulting Group
BEA	Bureau of Economic Analysis
BEPS	Base-Erosion and Profit-Shifting
BIAC	Business and Industry Advisory Committee
BIS	Bank for International Settlements
CCCTB	Common Consolidated Corporate Tax Base
CFC	Controlled Foreign Corporation
CIT	Corporate Income Tax
CPM	Comparable Profit Method
CUP	Comparable Uncontrolled Price
DoJ	(US) Department of Justice
DSP	Dispute Settlement Panel
DTA	Double-Tax Avoidance
ECOFIN	Economic and Financial Affairs Council
ECPR	European Consortium for Political Research
EFD	Eidgnössisches Finanzdepartment
ETI	Extraterritorial Income Exclusion Act
EU	European Union
FA	Formulary Apportionment
FAT	Financial Activities Tax
FATF	Financial Action Task Force
FC	Financial Crisis
FFIs	Foreign Financial Institutions
FIA	Futures Industry Association
FATCA	Foreign Account Tax Compliance Act
FDI	Foreign Direct Investment
FPI	Foreign Portfolio Investment

FSB	Financial Standards Board
FSC	Foreign-Sales Corporation
FSF	Financial Stability Forum
FSI	Financial Secrecy Index
GAO	Government Accountability Office
GFC	Global Financial Crisis
GNI	Gross National Income
GSW	Global Scale Weight
HTC	Harmful Tax Competition
IAIS	International Association of Insurance Supervisors
ICC	International Criminal Court
ICJ	Court of Justice
IFRS	International Financial Reporting Standard
IFTT	International Financial Transaction Tax
IGA	Intergovernmental Agreement
IGO	Intergovernmental Organization
IMF	International Monetary Fund
IOSCO	International Organization of Securities Commissions
IPE	International Political Economy
IPOs	Initial Public Offerings
IRC	Internal Revenue Code
IRS	(US) Internal Revenue Service
ITO	International Tax Organization
KPMG	Klynveld, Peat, Marwick und Goerdeler
KSFIs	Key Financial Secrecy Indicators
KYC	Know-Your-Customer
LDCs	Least Developed Countries
LGT	Liechtenstein Global Trust
LJ	Listed Jurisdictions
LSC	Legal-entity-Specific Counter-measures
MFN	Most-Favoured-Nation
MNCs	Multinational Corporations
MNEs	Multinational Enterprises
NRAs	Non-Resident Aliens
OECD	Organisation for Economic Co-operation and Development
OFCs	Offshore Financial Centers

PTAs	Preferential Trade Agreements
PTRs	Preferential Tax Regimes
QI	Qualified Intermediary
SDA	Schweizer Depeschen Agentur
SSHRC	Social Sciences and Humanities Research Council of Canada
TIEA	Tax Information-Exchange Agreement
TJN	Tax Justice Network
TNMM	Transactional Net Margin Method
UBS	United Bank of Switzerland
UK	United Kingdom
UNCTAD	United Nations Conference on Trade and Development
UNFPA	United Nations Population Fund
US	United States
UT+FA	Unitary Tax and Formulary Apportionment
WTO	World Trade Organization
WZB	Wissenschaftszentrum Berlin

Contributors

LAURENS VAN APELDOORN is Assistant Professor in Philosophy at Leiden University, the Netherlands. His research interests include early modern political thought and contemporary political theory, and his work has been published in *History of European Ideas* and *Hobbes Studies*.

REUVEN S. AVI-YONAH is the Irwin I. Cohn Professor of Law and director of the International Tax LLM Program. He specialises in corporate and international taxation and has served as a consultant to the U.S. Department of the Treasury and the OECD on tax competition. He has published more than 150 books and articles, including the forthcoming *Advanced Introduction to International Tax* (Elgar, 2015) and *Global Perspectives on Income Taxation Law* (Oxford University Press, 2011).

KIMBERLY CLAUSING is the Thormund Miller and Walter Mintz Professor of Economics at Reed College. Her research studies the taxation of multinational firms, examining how government decisions and firm behaviour interplay in the world economy. She has received two Fulbright Research awards, and her research has also been supported by grants from the National Science Foundation, the Smith Richardson Foundation, the International Centre for Tax and Development, and the U.S. Bureau of Economic Analysis.

PETER DIETSCH is Associate Professor at the Université de Montréal. His research interests lie at the intersection of political philosophy and economics, with a particular focus on questions of income distribution as well as on the normative dimensions of economic policies. He is the author of *Catching Capital – The Ethics of Tax Competition* (Oxford University Press, 2015).

RICHARD ECCLESTON is Professor of Political Science and founding Director of the Institute for the Study of Social Change at the University of Tasmania. He works on various aspects of comparative politics and economic policy. His specific expertise is in the politics of public finance and taxation reform. His most recent books are *The Dynamics of Global Economic Governance* (2014) and *The Future of Federalism: Multi-level governance in an age of austerity* (forthcoming).

PHILIPP GENSCHEL holds a Joint Chair in European Public Policy at the Robert Schuman Center for Advanced Studies and the Political and Social Sciences Department of the European University Institute in Florence. He has published widely on issues of international taxation, global governance and European integration. His latest books include (co-edited with Markus Jachtenfuchs) *Beyond the Regulatory Polity? The European Integration of Core State Powers* (Oxford University Press, 2014) and (co-edited with Ken Abbott, Duncan Snidal and Bernhard Zangl) *International Organizations as Orchestrators* (Cambridge University Press, 2015).

ITAI GRINBERG is a professor of tax law at the Georgetown University Law Center. His research focuses on tax reform, international tax, and tax and development. Prior to joining the Georgetown faculty, he served in the Office of International Tax Counsel at the United States Department of the Treasury, and as Counsel to the President's Advisory Panel on Federal Tax Reform of 2005.

LUKAS HAKELBERG is a doctoral candidate in political science at the European University Institute in Florence, Italy. His research interest lies in international political economy, where he currently focuses on international co-operation against tax evasion and avoidance. His published work has appeared in *Journal of European Public Policy* and *Global Environmental Politics*.

LYNE LATULIPPE is a professor in the department of taxation at the Faculté d'administration of the Université de Sherbrooke. Her main research interests are the design and implementation of domestic and international taxation policy and international tax governance. She is an associate researcher for the Research Chair in Taxation and Public Finance and is responsible for studies on international taxation issues, tax evasion and avoidance and tax fairness.

MARKUS MEINZER is a senior analyst for the Tax Justice Network (TJN). He is working predominantly on the Financial Secrecy Index and Automatic Information-Exchange. He is author of the German language book *Steueroase Deutschland.* He studied development economics and political science at the Free University of Berlin and at the University of Sussex (UK).

THOMAS RIXEN is Professor of political science at the University of Bamberg. His research interests are in international and comparative political economy. He is the author of *The Political Economy of International Tax Governance* (Palgrave Macmillan, 2008) and has, among others, published in *European Journal of International Relations*, *Review of International Political Economy* and *Journal of Common Market Studies*.

MIRIAM RONZONI is Senior Lecturer in Political Theory at the University of Manchester. She works on various issues of international justice, with special focus on labour, taxation, non-domination, and supranational institutional design. Her work has been published, among others, in *Journal of Political Philosophy*, *Political Studies*, *Politics, Philosophy and Economics*, *Review of International Studies*.

LAURA SEELKOPF is a postdoctoral research fellow at the Research Center on Inequality and Social Policy at the University of Bremen. Her substantive research focus is on comparative tax and social policy, both inside and outside the OECD. Her work has been published in *New Political Economy*, *Politics & Society*, and *The Oxford Handbook of Transformations of the State*.

HELEN SMITH is a researcher at the University of Tasmania. She holds a 1st Class Honours degree in International Relations for a thesis analysing the influences of geo-strategic factors on US energy policy. She has co-authored various chapters and articles in the areas of taxation and fiscal federalism.

GABRIEL WOLLNER is assistant professor in philosophy at Humboldt University Berlin and leads the research group 'Global challenges in economic and environmental ethics' at the Integrative Research Institute for the Transformation of Human Environment Systems (IRITHESys). His work has been published in *Journal of Social Philosophy*, *Journal of Political Philosophy* and *Canadian Journal of Philosophy*.

RICHARD WOODWARD is a senior lecturer at Coventry Business School, UK and a Non-Resident Fellow at the Trends Institute, United Arab Emirates. His research interests include global governance, international organisations, offshore financial centres and small states. His books include *The Organisation for Economic Co-operation and Development* (Routledge, 2009) and (with Michael Davies) *International Organisations: A companion* (Edward Elgar, 2014).

Acknowledgements

In a world of capital mobility, the fiscal policies of states have become more and more intertwined. Understanding the mechanisms and dynamics of this process as well as their consequences is crucial to developing a model of global tax governance that is fit for the 21st century. Effective global tax governance and the fiscal sovereignty it assigns to states is a necessary condition for maintaining the model of the fiscal state as we know it, and thus for promoting the socio-economic goals it stands for: the provision of public goods, social justice, democracy, and economic efficiency.

A comprehensive analysis both of the shortcomings of global tax governance today and of potential solutions cannot be conducted from within a single discipline. Hence our idea to bring together a group of political scientists, international tax lawyers, political philosophers, and economists to discuss these issues. We were happy to be given the opportunity to convene a workshop at the ECPR Joint Sessions held at the University of Mainz in March 2013. We thank the ECPR and the local organizers in Mainz for making this possible, and the Wissenschaftszentrum Berlin (WZB) for the stimulating research environment in which the idea first germinated. We would also like to acknowledge financial support for this workshop by the Social Sciences and Humanities Research Council of Canada (SSHRC), the Humboldt Foundation, as well as the Direction des Relations Internationales of the Université de Montréal. Most of all we would like to thank all participants at this event, including those who did not end up contributing to the present volume: Gillian Brock, Kim Brooks, Allison Christians, and Peter Schwarz.

After the workshop, several rounds of mutual feedback have ensured that this is not a mere collection of papers, but a coherent body of work evolving around the main questions global tax governance faces today. We were amazed at the commitment of everyone involved in this project and the willingness to keep deadlines, even when their two editors were not always the perfect role models in that respect. We feel that our collaborative approach has allowed us to produce a result that is more than just the sum of its parts. We thank all the contributors for making this interdisciplinary dialogue such a fruitful and inspiring experience. We also benefited from the comments of anonymous reviewers on both the initial proposal as well as on the draft manuscript.

We are grateful for the support of ECPR Press throughout the publication process. Peter Triantafillou and Alexandra Segerberg supported the project as editors of the Press. Deborah Savage did a great job as copy-editor and Simon Ward guided us through the final stages of production.

Finally, we would like to thank François Letourneux for his research assistance in the process of putting the manuscript together.

Last but not least, we would like to thank Cynthia, Lena, Nora, Imke, Jesse and Till for grudgingly accepting us spending more than a few late night sessions on our notebooks. Then again, our collaboration has made it possible to bring our two families together on several occasions, which has always been fun – and had nothing to do with taxation.

Peter Dietsch and Thomas Rixen
Montréal and Bamberg/Berlin
November 2015

Chapter One

Global Tax Governance: What It is and Why It Matters

Peter Dietsch and Thomas Rixen

Until quite recently, a book with the title *Global Tax Governance* would have been unthinkable. Most social scientists interested in the then already widely used concept of global governance would have thought either that there is no such thing as global governance in the area of taxation or that it is too rudimentary to warrant any attention. This has changed.

Today, global tax governance is very high on the international and various national political agendas. There are two main reasons for this. First, in the wake of the 2008 financial crisis, many states have seen their public debt rise to high levels and, hence, can no longer afford to forgo tax revenues currently lost to international tax evasion and avoidance. Second, political initiatives are fuelled by recent tax scandals (such as Starbucks, Apple, Offshore Leaks and LuxLeaks) that have raised public awareness and guaranteed media attention.

While these events have triggered a rare public debate on international tax issues, the academic discussion, though still relatively young, goes back a little further. Apart from isolated contributions (Picciotto 1992; Palan 1998), issues of international taxation had hardly been dealt with in political science and international political economy until around ten years ago, when a small number of scholars began to address the issue (Sharman 2006; Rixen 2008; Webb 2004). Since then, a sizeable literature has developed. A similar situation pertains for normative political philosophy. While fiscal policy is regarded as an important tool by contemporary theories of justice (for example, Rawls 1999; Dworkin 2002), and while some work on the normative foundations of taxation has emerged in recent years (Murphy and Nagel 2002; Halliday 2013), normative work focused on the international dimensions of fiscal policy has been almost completely absent (but see Cappelen 2001). In recent years, however, a few contributions have emerged (Brock 2008; Dietsch and Rixen 2014; Dietsch 2015; Gaisbauer, *et al.* 2015). This book aims to take stock of the academic debate on global tax governance.

We are convinced that the recent interest in global tax governance is well justified. Since taxation is the most direct interface between the market and the state, it is the perfect policy area in which to observe the relation between, and relative power of, the two spheres. Moreover, taxation represents one of the core functions of the modern nation-state. Therefore, it should be key to an understanding of how economic globalisation affects state sovereignty and the choice and development of international institutions, as well as the effectiveness and legitimacy of both national and international institutions; these are, of course, the major themes of the literature on global governance.

Politically, the governments and international institutions involved in designing global tax governance claim that they are on track to tackle the problems created by tax competition. Soon after the financial crisis hit, the G20 and OECD revived their 'black' and 'grey' lists of uncooperative tax havens and forced them to sign bilateral tax information-exchange agreements (TIEAs). Recently, the OECD has even forged an agreement that foresees multilateral automatic information-exchange (AEI) as the new global norm. In addition, the G20 and the OECD are taking steps to control the practices of base-erosion and profit-shifting (BEPS) of multinational corporations.[1] All that being said, most experts, while admitting that these initiatives represent real progress, are less optimistic about their effectiveness.

The contributions to this volume are directly relevant to this political debate. They explain why current attempts to strengthen global tax governance are insufficient; and they propose alternatives. More specifically, this involves (1) identifying the problems that globalisation creates in the area of taxation, through tax competition in particular; (2) explaining the institutions, structures, and processes of global tax governance as well as analysing their shortcomings; (3) developing the normative foundations for an appropriate regulatory response and building on these foundations; (4) deriving proposals for the reform of institutions and policies.

This is an ambitious agenda that could not be addressed appropriately within any single discipline. It requires a thorough understanding of the economics of tax competition at the interface between markets and states; a grasp of the complex and technical legal issues involved; awareness of the geopolitical and social forces at work that might either foster or obstruct reform; and, finally, a normative framework that allows one to weigh such competing values as fiscal autonomy, distributive justice, and economic efficiency. This is why this volume brings together political scientists, lawyers, economists, and political philosophers. Each contribution has a well-defined role in producing a comprehensive assessment of the challenges facing global tax governance today. Unique in this interdisciplinary focus, the book combines theoretical and conceptual work with empirical analysis. One of the key motivations in putting together this collection is the conviction that any approach to global tax governance that is grounded in a single discipline is bound to omit important considerations, and thus will most likely fail to provide sound analysis and

1. Under the current rules of international taxation, multinational enterprises have various possibilities for shifting their profits (the tax base) to subsidiaries in low-tax countries and making sure that actuarial losses are attributed to high-tax countries. This way, the enterprise arbitrages across different tax systems in order to save taxes. The different techniques of achieving this and what could be done to avoid this, will be explained in subsequent chapters (*see* e.g. Clausing 2016, Chapter Two; Eccleston and Smith 2016, Chapter Eight; Dietsch 2016, Chapter Eleven; Avi-Yonah 2016, Chapter Thirteen; and Rixen 2016, Chapter Fifteen).

policy advice. At the same time, the volume aims to provide a comprehensible and accessible overview that may serve as an entry point to the field for non-specialists.

In this introduction we will first define global tax governance, briefly situate it in the two relevant but often separated bodies of literature on global governance and taxation, and provide a sketch of its historical development as well as of how current events fit into this trajectory (Section 1). We then detail some of the challenges that tax competition poses (for national and global governance), notably concerning state sovereignty (Section 2) and in terms of rising inequalities of income and wealth (Section 3). Section 4 contains an outline of the individual contributions to the volume and of how they fit together. We conclude with a look at some of the lessons for global tax governance that we can draw from this volume (Section 5).

1. What is global tax governance?

In the broadest sense, governance can be defined as the activity of 'organizing collective action' (Prakash and Hart 1999: 2). It covers the creation or development of institutions – defined as formal and informal principles, norms, rules, and procedures – that structure individual and collective behaviour. Such governance may be exercised by state and non-state, public and private actors. Governance is global governance if the reach of the principles, norms, rules, and procedures is global or at least international.[2] Global tax governance thus consists of the set of institutions governing issues of taxation that involve cross-border transactions or have other international implications.[3]

This definition implies that global tax governance need not, but could, involve a full or partial shift of the power to tax, that is, the right to impose taxes on citizens, to the international level. Currently, the right to tax is firmly tied to the nation-state. While global tax governance circumscribes and shapes a nation's power to tax in various ways, it exclusively consists of institutions governing the interaction among national tax systems. Whether or not a shift of some or all dimensions of a nation's power to tax to the international level would be desirable is one of the themes addressed by various contributions in this volume (*see* Ronzoni 2016, Chapter Nine; Dietsch 2016, Chapter Eleven; Wollner 2016, Chapter Fourteen; and Rixen 2016, Chapter Fifteen in this volume).

---

2. The reference to principles, norms, rules, and procedures relates to Keohane's well known definition of an international regime, an important concept in the literature on global governance (Krasner 1982: 186). While the term 'global' suggests the full inclusion of all countries in the world, in practice it is often used for any kind of international policy-making.

3. Global tax governance concerns direct and indirect taxation. Currently, most discussions of global tax governance are limited to direct taxation. This is due to the fact that under current institutional arrangements, international aspects of indirect taxes are addressed in the international trade regime. This empirical fact does not imply that the tax-related aspects of international trade should not be considered a part of global tax governance analytically. In this volume, Gabriel Wollner's proposal for a financial transaction tax (2016, Chapter Fourteen) relates to indirect taxes.

Global governance aims at the cooperative regulation of globalisation. The basic assumption/insight is that in an age of globalisation, an ever-increasing number of issues cannot be adequately governed within the nation-state. If societal interactions cross borders and create interdependencies and externalities among national societies and polities, there is a need for global governance (Dingwerth and Pattberg 2006; Zürn 2013). This has been argued convincingly for policy areas ranging from environmental protection, world trade, and financial stability to issues of health, human rights, and security (*cf.*, for example, Kaul *et al.* 2003). Until quite recently, this line of argument has been conspicuously absent in taxation.

While globalisation and its effects have been a major research field in the fiscal context since at least the 1990s, the focus has been almost exclusively on *national* political reactions. In taxation, globalisation has entered the debate as tax competition, that is, national governments competing for mobile tax bases. Political scientists and economists have asked: does tax competition lead to a race to the bottom in terms of tax rates and, consequently, in terms of revenues and public-goods provision? Does it constrain the political capacity to maintain the welfare state? A set of influential papers in political science has shown that tax revenues in industrialised countries have remained constant and concluded that, therefore, the autonomy of national tax and welfare state policy was still intact (*cf.*, for example, Swank and Steinmo 2002; Garrett and Mitchell 2001; Basinger and Hallerberg 2004). Others, building on empirical findings in economics (Devereux and Griffith 2002; de Mooij and Ederveen 2008; *see* Clausing's overview 2016, Chapter Two in this volume), disagreed. They have argued that the focus on tax revenues alone was misguided and masked important changes in the structure of tax systems. In particular, they have made the case that tax competition has undesirable distributive implications in developed countries and leads to significant revenue losses in the developing world (Genschel 2002; Ganghof 2006; Rixen 2011b; *see also* Genschel and Seelkopf 2016, Chapter Three in this volume). According to this view, tax competition seriously constrains the autonomy of national policy.

Rather than reopening this important debate, which will be taken up in detail by the three contributions in Part One of this volume, the relevant point for the purpose of this introduction is that *international* political actions were not considered by political scientists and economists. This overlooks two important aspects. First, globalisation itself, including tax-base mobility, is a political phenomenon, that is, it is the result of deliberate international cooperative efforts to liberalise international trade and investment and reduce cross-border tax distortions. It is a product of global governance. Second, national adaptation to the pressures of tax competition is not the only possible reaction. Governments could, in principle, react by establishing global governance mechanisms, or by adapting existing ones, to rein in harmful tax competition. For a long time, both aspects of global tax governance – the removal of tax obstacles and regulating tax competition – were the almost exclusive territory of international lawyers, who focused on explicating and interpreting the relevant legal rules (*cf.*, for example, Graetz 2003).[4] Meanwhile, the political and economic determinants of global tax governance have received little or no attention. It is only recently that political scientists, economists, and political philosophers have taken up the issue. It is one major purpose of this volume to present original contributions of scholars engaged in that enterprise.

The long-time neglect of global tax governance is all the more surprising as the history of global tax governance goes back to the beginning of the twentieth century and to the first wave of globalisation that was comparable in magnitude to the current one (Bordo *et al.* 1999). The original and initially sole purpose of global tax governance was to mitigate international double taxation in order to liberalise international trade and investment.[5] In response to demands by the International Chamber of Commerce (ICC), the League of Nations commissioned several reports and convened meetings that ultimately resulted in a model convention for bilateral double tax avoidance (DTA) treaties shortly before the Second World War. In parallel to these developments, several countries began to develop unilateral (domestic) laws on the taxation of cross-border activities and also drafted bilateral tax treaties. After the war, this work on DTA was briefly taken up by the United Nations before it then migrated to the Organisation for Economic Co-operation and Development (OECD), which continuously revised and modernised the model convention. Over time, due to these multilateral efforts, a remarkable homogeneity among national laws and bilateral treaties has been achieved. Today, there are about 2500 DTAs (Rixen 2008; Genschel and Rixen 2015).

As intended, the abolition of capital controls enabled increased capital mobility and the effective removal of tax obstacles through DTAs has increased the potential fiscal advantages of moving capital across borders. In this sense, globalisation in general is a political phenomenon and tax-base mobility, in particular, is the result of global tax governance. However, the specific principles and rules chosen to avoid double taxation had an unintended, albeit foreseeable, consequence. They caused the related phenomena of tax evasion and avoidance as well as of tax competition. DTA treaties aim at disentangling the transnational tax base and assigning it to different jurisdictions. Once the jurisdiction to tax has been established, a country is then free to apply its own national tax law to its share of the income. DTA rests on the mere interface-regulation of autonomous national tax systems, and governments retain almost unlimited sovereignty over their share of the transnational tax

4. A few studies from lawyers took a broader perspective and presented more political and historical analyses of the development of international taxation (e.g. Picciotto 1992; Avi-Yonah 2000) or presented analyses of the dysfunctionalities of the system (e.g. Bird 1988; Dagan 2000).

5. Double taxation stems from an overlap of jurisdiction to tax between the country in which a taxpayer lives (residence state) and the country where the taxpayer's income is generated (source state). If both countries exert to the full their power to tax, then the tax burden for international investments is higher than for national investments, causing an inefficient allocation of capital. In order to prevent this, governments engage in efforts to avoid double taxation.

base (Bird and Wilkie 2000: 91–5; Vann 1991: 102). Governments are free to underbid each other in tax rates and other relevant legislation in order to attract a larger part of the transnational tax base. This is the supply side of tax competition. On the demand side, taxpayers exploit the resulting differences in national tax systems and engage in profit-shifting and tax arbitrage, which are to a large extent, made possible by the particular legal constructs on which DTA treaties rely. In other words, the rules of DTA endogenously create tax avoidance and tax competition. Most prominently, the principle of 'separate entity accounting' and the 'arm's length standard' (ALS) facilitate various kinds of thin capitalisation and transfer-pricing manipulations, two of the techniques used to shift profits to low-tax countries and erode tax bases in high-tax countries (*see* Clausing 2016, Chapter Two and Avi-Yonah 2016, Chapter Thirteen in this volume). The sovereignty-preserving approach to the global governance of DTA provided the institutional foundation of tax competition (Rixen 2011a).

In the 1960s, many countries reacted to the problem of tax arbitrage. Following the example of the US, they began to incorporate anti-avoidance legislation in their unilateral (domestic) tax laws. The OECD participated in those efforts by trying to promote the diffusion of such legislation across its member countries. From the late 1990s it became increasingly clear that such unilateral approaches were insufficient to solve the problem. In 1998, the OECD launched its project on harmful tax competition (OECD 1998). Likewise, the EU started initiatives such as the code of conduct on business taxation (Radaelli 2003) and the Savings Tax Directive (Rixen and Schwarz 2012; Hakelberg 2014) to formulate an international answer to the problem of tax competition. While the avoidance of double taxation continues to be a topic of global tax governance, the focus has clearly shifted to tax competition. The present volume focuses mostly on this issue and on developments since the late 1990s. Since, as explained above, DTA and tax competition are intimately connected, the institutions of DTA are nonetheless part of the analysis (*see*, for example, the contributions by Dietsch 2016, Chapter Eleven; Avi-Yonah 2016, Chapter Thirteen; and Rixen 2016, Chapter Fifteen).

Without anticipating too much, the trajectory of global tax governance can broadly be understood as an incomplete adaptation of the governance structure to the fundamentally altered international tax game. In the first period of global tax governance, when governments were mostly interested in liberalisation, a bilateral approach – supported by the OECD through its dissemination of information and shared practices that all states have an interest in following – was appropriate to accommodate countries' preferences. In a nutshell: since DTA is a coordination game with a distributive conflict, the institutions needed to deal with this problem do not have to be equipped with enforcement capabilities. The soft governance mechanisms used by the OECD – non-binding recommendations, providing technical expertise, diffusion by collecting best-practice examples and so on – were adequate. In contrast, the issue of tax competition exhibits the institutionally more demanding structure of an asymmetric prisoner's dilemma.[6] This strategic structure would require a shift to hard and multilateral governance with independent international enforcement. While current events may be interpreted as struggles to react to the functional demands of this strategic structure, the required shift is not forthcoming. In part, this is due to the fact that global tax governance exhibits significant path-dependence (Rixen 2011a; Eccleston 2012).

Three key observations can be made about the current institutional trajectory. First, while it is true that there is a move towards multilateralism in the fight against tax evasion, it is not fully global and inclusive of all states. For example, the recent agreement on automatic exchange of tax information (OECD 2014), which is an important step forward, was signed by a mere fifty-one countries. The fact that the membership of the OECD consists only of developed countries may be part of the problem here, if the signatory OECD countries do not succeed in getting developing countries on board. Second, while major economic powers are increasingly willing to exert pressure on tax havens, they still rely on informal instruments such as naming and shaming (*see* Woodward 2016, Chapter Five in this volume) or, less often – but the US Foreign Account Tax Compliance Act (FATCA), under which foreign banks are required to disclose their US clients to the US tax administration, is an example – on blunt power politics (*see* the contributions by Hakelberg 2016, Chapter Six in this volume; and Grinberg 2016, Chapter Seven in this volume). So far, there has not been any attempt to institutionalise formal enforcement mechanisms. Third, it is true that states are increasingly willing to engage in administrative co-operation and information-exchange with other governments. However, they are hardly willing to delegate or pool their legislative sovereignty, that is, the authority to make national tax policy. While this would not be a problem as long as the particular issue could be effectively addressed by administrative co-operation, there are strong indications that the effective regulation of BEPS requires a sharing of legislative sovereignty, that is, the partial harmonisation of national tax laws (*see* Eccleston and Smith 2016, Chapter Eight in this volume).

In summary, global tax governance historically played an important role in creating the problem of tax competition but also holds the promise of providing a solution, albeit one it has not yet delivered. Thus, it is a significant phenomenon that warrants more attention than it has traditionally received in the social sciences.

---

6. An asymmetric prisoner's dilemma is characterised by the following strategic structure: one party (tax haven) has deadlock preferences, i.e. it not only prefers defection over co-operation in individual strategies but also prefers the outcome of collective defection over the outcome of collective co-operation. The other party (big, developed country) has prisoner's dilemma preferences, i.e. while it prefers defection over co-operation in individual strategies it prefers the outcome of collective co-operation over that of collective defection. The game is thus different from the regular (symmetric) prisoner's dilemma, in which the cooperative outcome is preferred by both parties over the uncooperative outcome. Nevertheless, in the asymmetric game, the cooperative and Pareto-optimal outcome could be achieved if, in game-theoretical parlance, big countries offered side-payments to tax havens. For a detailed derivation of the strategic structure, see Rixen (2008: 43–8). *See also* the contributions by Genschel and Seelkopf 2016, Chapter Three; and Hakelberg 2016, Chapter Six in this volume.

Before we turn to the empirical and normative analysis of global tax governance that is the central task of this book, we first need to explain why tax competition is indeed a problem. We turn to this in the following two sections.

2. Tax competition, democracy and state sovereignty

Who decides what and how to tax, and for whose benefit? Tax competition introduces an important bias into the way national fiscal systems respond to these questions. First, tax competition undermines the capacity of polities to choose the size of their public budget as well as the level of redistribution, because it compromises their ability to tax capital. Under conditions of capital mobility, attempts to tax capital will usually trigger capital flight and thus prove futile. Second, this inability to tax capital effectively means that the 'haves' are likely to enjoy a lighter tax burden compared to the 'have-nots', for the simple reason that capital-ownership tends to be concentrated among the former. This section looks at the effect of tax competition on democratic decision-making; the next section focuses on the link to inequality.

The idea that the dynamics of economic globalisation constrain the room for manoeuvre of national economic policies is neither new nor limited to fiscal policy. One poignant way to capture this phenomenon has been formulated by Dani Rodrik in what he calls the 'political trilemma of the world economy' (Rodrik 2011: 372). The basic idea is that we cannot simultaneously have democratic politics, the nation-state as the primary *locus* of political control, and hyper-globalisation, which includes the unrestricted movement of capital. Rodrik uses corporate tax competition as one of the case studies to illustrate his trilemma (Rodrik 2011: 357–60).

In response to the trilemma, so Rodrik claims, we have three options. We can compromise democracy; we can curtail the power of the nation-state by enhancing global institutions; or we might reverse some of the deregulation that has led to hyper-globalisation. Compromising democracy is clearly undesirable but note that, under the *status quo*, this is precisely what is happening. As highlighted by Streeck (2014), the frequent political appeal to TINA ('there is no alternative') policies illustrates the diminishing leverage that democratic preferences have over global economic pressures. As a consequence, national politics is increasingly emptied of its democratic substance (Crouch 2004; Mair 2013). By comparison, the two other routes out of the trilemma are more attractive. In the fiscal context, to put it simply, this confronts us with a choice between limiting the mobility of capital on the one hand and, through global tax governance, boosting the capacity of states to tax mobile capital on the other.[7] This choice is by no means a binary one: combinations of the two are possible.

7. While several commentators, including Rodrik (2011), Streeck (2014) and Mair (2013), appear to favour regulating the forces at work in globalisation over developing institutions of global governance, the contributions to this volume are open to both approaches.

Which combination should we choose? What are the relative advantages and potential drawbacks of either approach? By answering these questions, this volume wants to make a contribution to plotting our way out of the political trilemma of the world economy.

Such projects of re-embedding the market are not utopian but already inform policy-making today. The OECD and the European Union issued the European Savings Tax Directive and started their respective initiatives on eliminating harmful tax competition as well as on working towards a consolidated corporate tax-base well before the financial crisis. The events of 2008 and the years since have added to the urgency of these projects. While the financial crisis was not caused by tax competition, one can argue that the latter had an exacerbating effect: it meant that a number of financial risks were hidden offshore (Rixen 2013); moreover, it largely blocks the option of taxing accumulated corporate profits in order to reduce public deficits. One of the dangers today, which has been borne out by the response to the crisis thus far, is that governments take the inability to tax mobile capital as a parameter rather than as a policy variable they can influence. This is not the place to assess the merits of austerity as a response to the crisis[8] but, at the very least, complementing austerity with measures to ensure the effective taxation of capital seems like a promising idea. The financial crisis has opened a window of opportunity in this regard. This volume aims to contribute to the debate on how we should go about seizing this opportunity.

3. Tax competition and rising inequalities

One of the democratic decisions undermined by tax competition concerns the level of redistribution among the members of a polity. When it is hard to tax capital effectively, redistribution becomes more difficult. As Piketty and his collaborators have shown, there is a strong and significant positive correlation between the decrease in tax rates and the increase in inequality of income and wealth. Those countries with the biggest fall in the top rates of their income-tax schedule experienced the strongest increase in the share of income going to the richest 10 per cent. Likewise, the increase in capital concentration is largely driven by reductions of the capital (income) tax. As Piketty points out, the reforms to lower tax rates occurred in all developed countries over the last two to three decades and were to a significant extent driven by the pressures of tax competition (Piketty 2014; Piketty *et al.* 2011).[9]

---

8. For a critical assessment, see Blyth 2013.

9. It is worth noting that before Piketty, economic analyses of tax competition tended to neglect its distributive implications. The standard economic models focus on the criterion of economic efficiency to assess the effects of tax competition (for overviews, see Wilson and Wildasin 2004; Genschel and Schwarz 2011; and Clausing 2016, Chapter Two in this volume). One notable exception in this context is Sinn's selection principle, which not only states that competition between states will be inefficient but also underscores the link between tax competition and inequality (Sinn 2003: 60).

A political consensus has been forming that inequality needs to be reined in, but how? Piketty plausibly argues that any reversal of the trend of rising inequality will have to involve the return to a more progressive income-tax schedule. He states that 'the optimal top tax rate in developed countries is probably above 80 per cent', but emphasises at the same time that, in the US for example, 'taxes would also have to be raised on incomes lower in the distribution (for example, by imposing rates of 50 or 60 per cent on incomes above $200,000)' (Piketty 2014: 512–13) in order to have a significant impact on revenue. As he admits, only if tax competition is effectively curbed or at least dampened will nation-states actually have the required policy autonomy (sovereignty) to pass and implement such legislation effectively.

With regard to wealth inequalities, while he discusses the introduction of a global wealth tax, he is silent on other measures of tax co-operation. In particular, the return to higher income-tax rates and higher tax rates on capital will depend on an effective solution to the problems of tax evasion or tax avoidance through capital flight. Among other things, such as multilateral automatic information-exchange (which he briefly mentions in his proposal for a global register of wealth) and a general push for more transparency, any solution will have to be sensitive to the fact that corporate taxation acts as a backstop for income taxation (Ganghof 2006; *see also* Clausing 2016, Chapter Two in this volume). In this book, we provide a comprehensive treatment of the kind of tax co-operation required to make reforms *à la* Piketty possible.

In sum, tax competition tends to exacerbate inequalities in income and wealth. Conversely, global tax governance is a crucial element in the fight against increasing inequalities, which many policy-makers and experts have identified as a serious threat not only to economic stability and growth (for example, Ostry *et al.* 2014) but also to democracy (for example, Schäfer 2013; Stiglitz 2008). This last point establishes a link to the previous section. Tax competition, in addition to directly undermining the fiscal sovereignty of states in terms of their ability to tax capital, risks having a second, indirect negative impact on democracy once inequalities attain levels that bias the democratic process in favour of the rich.

4. Structure and content of the volume

The logic behind the structure of the volume is the following: Part One presents a diagnosis of the problematic aspects of international tax competition. The contributions to Part Two put forward an assessment of where current attempts to address these problems fall short. Part Three discusses the normative principles that a coherent and feasible political response to tax competition should be based on. Finally, the contributions to Part Four detail several of the institutional arrangements that are necessary to regulate tax competition in practice.

The three chapters that make up the first part of the book explain how tax competition works and what its consequences are. First, Kimberly Clausing presents an overview of the major empirical findings on the economics of tax competition (Chapter Two). She focuses on mobile multinational enterprises

(MNEs) and shows that these are tax-sensitive in their business decisions. In particular, referring to data on the micro- and macro-level, she shows that 'virtual' tax competition is much fiercer than 'real' tax competition. While MNEs tend to seek low-tax environments for their real economic activities, they are far more tax-sensitive when it comes to (paper) profits, the location of which can be manipulated through their financial arrangements. This implies that tax competition is unlikely to be a drag on growth in capital-rich countries (as aggregate capital stocks are hardly affected), yet it does adversely affect tax revenues and leads to a lighter tax burden on corporate income. This has regressive distributive implications in itself but Clausing explains that these are further amplified by the fact that an erosion of the corporate tax endangers the integrity of the larger income-tax system. Overall, the empirical evidence supports the notion that curbing tax competition would entail substantial welfare gains.

In Chapter Three, Philipp Genschel and Laura Seelkopf take up this finding and inquire why, given these potential welfare gains, tax competition persists. They take a political-economy perspective and ask who are the winners and losers from tax competition. They refine the conventional view, according to which workers lose and capital wins everywhere. Using the insights of a model of asymmetric tax competition (Bucovetsky 1991) and differentiating countries with respect to regime type (democracy *versus* autocracy), they show that in addition to capital (in all countries), the winners from tax competition include the governments and workers of small, well governed democracies. The losers are governments and workers of large countries, of less developed ones in particular, which are more likely to be autocratic and poorly governed. In contrast, large democratic countries can at least maintain large welfare states. However, since the latter are increasingly financed via debt and taxes on labour and consumption, workers in these countries also lose. Irrespective of these distributive implications, tax competition remains a negative-sum game: big countries lose more than small countries gain.

One implication of this is that the collective-action problem inherent in overcoming tax competition is worse than the conventional view suggests. If workers were the losers everywhere, and assuming that the median voter typically receives the large majority of her income from work, then all governments, at least in well functioning democracies, should be in favour of international tax co-operation. But since governments and workers in small countries profit, there is typically a political conflict of interest between big-country governments and small, tax-haven governments, which has become very obvious in recent campaigns for tax co-operation.

Nevertheless, if all the losers from tax competition identified by Genschel and Seelkopf are aware of being short-changed, does it not seem puzzling that they do not manage to overcome the collective-action problem of regulating tax competition, even in the face of resistance from tax havens? In Chapter Four, Lyne Latulippe offers a solution to this puzzle. She argues that countries internalise the logic of tax competition in their domestic policy-making, by adopting a competitiveness discourse that reinforces tax competition. To support her argument, Latulippe looks at consultation processes on international tax policy in Australia in 2002 and in Canada in 2008. Both episodes illustrate how, by blurring the line between corporate and national interests, the notion of competitiveness has emerged as a policy goal. While the Australian and Canadian consultation processes were formally open in terms of both the experts who headed the process and those who participated by submitting opinions, corporate interests were dominant, thus introducing a bias into the recommended policy options. This account implies that to the extent that developed democracies are susceptible to interest-group biases – and thus less responsive to the demands of the median voter than Genschel and Seelkopf assume – tax competition is even more likely to be a stable political equilibrium. Latulippe's analysis allows us to gain a better understanding of the way, and the extent to which, domestic interest-group influence undermines multilateral efforts towards fiscal co-operation; and to appreciate just how resilient a phenomenon tax competition is.

Building on this understanding of the economics and politics of tax competition, the contributions to Part Two analyse the current political responses to tax competition. When you fix a problem, you want to know whether the fix works. In Chapter Five, Richard Woodward argues that the lack of this ability is one of the biggest shortcomings of recent initiatives in international taxation. Given that offshore financial centres (OFCs) have repeatedly been in the line of fire of international institutions – first in the 1990s and then again in the wake of the financial crisis of 2008 – how come they are still doing so well? Woodward claims that one explanation thus far neglected in the literature is that OFCs successfully feign compliance with new international standards while not actually changing their ways. Such behaviour, dubbed 'mock compliance' by Walter (2008) and Woodward, occurs when compliance costs would be high and when it is difficult for others to detect non-compliance. Woodward argues that mock compliance is the preferred strategy of tax-haven governments, first, because they cannot afford to remain openly non-compliant due to reputational risk and the greater power of large OECD states and, second, because full compliance would cause trouble with powerful domestic business interests. Woodward presents evidence that mock compliance poses a serious problem for both past and present OECD initiatives, especially when it comes to the implementation of recent TIEAs but also with regard to the 2014 Declaration on Automatic Exchange of Information in Tax Matters.

Lukas Hakelberg (2016, Chapter Six) takes a close look at the recent move towards multilateral automatic information-exchange. He asks why this breakthrough was possible after decades of failed attempts at international tax co-operation and argues that political-science theories conceptualising international co-operation as a Pareto-improving response to market failure cannot account for this outcome, because we should then see joint gains for all countries involved. However, as explained by Genschel and Seelkopf, some tax havens are clearly worse off under the new regime. The missing piece of the puzzle of this outcome of 'redistributive co-operation' (Oatley and Nabors 1998), according to Hakelberg, is power. In this power-play, the US as the dominant financial centre in the world played a crucial but very ambiguous role. At first, the US used its financial power (measured as financial market share) to pass a unilateral, extra-territorial law that required all banks in the world to report the foreign income held by US citizens to the US government. As Hakelberg shows, this law unlocked the stalemate in the EU on automatic information-exchange and significantly contributed to the move towards AEI in the OECD. While this development may appear as an instance of ‘benevolent hegemony’ (*cf.* Kindleberger 1976; Keohane 1984), the US itself, having pressured other countries into co-operation, did not sign the OECD Declaration of AEI – thus acting as a ‘malign hegemon’, positioning itself as a haven for unreported capital.

Whereas Hakelberg focuses on the origins of automatic information-exchange, Itai Grinberg is interested in its implications for the future development of global tax governance. In Chapter Seven, he asks under what circumstances unilateral tax reforms can trigger wider multilateral tax co-operation. After the US adopted FATCA in 2010, the compliance issues raised by this legislation for financial institutions triggered a negotiation with five large European countries and, ultimately, paved the way for the Common Reporting Standard that forms the centrepiece of the OECD’s new model of automatic information-exchange. Grinberg analyses the enabling factors behind this agreement and asks whether this sequence of events – a bold unilateral initiative leading to multilateral reform – could represent a blueprint for other areas of international taxation. He argues that one of the crucial elements facilitating the trajectory from FATCA to multilateral agreement was the alignment of interests among the large OECD members who pushed this agenda: individual tax evasion hurts them all. By contrast, when considering whether the problem of base-erosion and profit-shifting (BEPS) could be tackled in a similar way, Grinberg is pessimistic because the allocation of corporate tax base represents an essentially distributive problem, thus making consensus less likely.

Richard Eccleston and Helen Smith (2016, Chapter Eight) continue the analysis on exactly this issue: BEPS. Building on the distinction between information-exchange and tax competition, they provide an analysis of the role of the G20 in post-crisis international taxation. They argue that given the non-binding character of OECD recommendations, endorsement by the G20 is vital. It provides the OECD’s policies with the necessary political clout and thus enhances compliance. G20 support has played this role in the fight for information-exchange, which is relatively uncontroversial as it is designed to counteract illegal tax evasion. But it may not suffice in the fight against the aggressive tax-planning practices of multinational corporations. To date, these practices have been legal, and measures against them require limits on a state’s sovereign right to tax. As Eccleston and Smith point out, the issue also involves more serious conflicts of interest among the powerful G20 and OECD members. Consequently, the authors are pessimistic both about the scope and substance of the BEPS action plan and about the general prospects for compliance with the BEPS initiative.

The remaining contributions to the volume develop normative principles (Part Three) and make concrete reform proposals (Part Four). The chapters in Part Three address the following question: what are the normative criteria we should appeal to in order to assess the practice of tax competition? In Chapter Nine, Miriam Ronzoni analyses tax competition through the lens of the two dominant families of contemporary theories of global justice (Barry and Valentini 2009). She argues that it is not only cosmopolitans (because they start from the premise of the equal moral status of all individuals around the globe) who have reasons to condemn tax competition; perhaps more surprisingly, internationalists, who accord substantive autonomy to national political communities, should do the same, because tax competition risks undermining this autonomy. Ronzoni thus defends the idea that we should condemn tax competition independently of which of these theories of justice we hold. Subsequently, focusing on the internationalist position, she asks what a regulation of tax competition along internationalist lines would entail. She argues that it would include three elements, namely, *some* taxation at the supranational level; the adoption of minimum tax-rates across states; and the creation of international institutions with the mandate and capacity to enforce tax standards.

Laurens van Apeldoorn, in Chapter Ten, discusses the contours of a modern understanding of the idea of fiscal sovereignty. He critically discusses recent attempts to define this sovereignty in a way that extends, at least to some extent, to the protection of the effectiveness of fiscal policy (Dietsch and Rixen 2014; Ronzoni 2016, Chapter Nine in this volume). While these accounts maintain that the mobility of tax-bases constitutes a *variable* that polities, at least to some extent, should be able to control, van Apeldoorn defends the idea that capital outflows in reaction to tax incentives elsewhere should be viewed as a *parameter* of national tax policies. As a result, his conception of fiscal sovereignty is substantially thinner than those of the accounts he criticises – Dietsch takes up this challenge explicitly in the subsequent chapter. The robust core of fiscal sovereignty that van Apeldoorn recognises is based on the idea that sovereignty, in the sense of domestic authority and control, is potentially subject to erosion. On the one hand, a state can be said to lose control when aspects of (fiscal) regulation are not respected by the citizenry and, on the other hand and perhaps more problematically, a state can be said to lose legitimacy when its regulations do not reflect democratic preferences. The latter scenario corresponds to the corporate capture of the legislature by vested interests as, for instance, in the US states of New Jersey and Delaware (Palan *et al.* 2010: 109–11).

In the final contribution to Part Three, Peter Dietsch (2016, Chapter Eleven) distinguishes between virtual and real tax competition; he makes the case that our response from an ethical and political point of view needs to track this distinction. The first, virtual type refers to cases where tax bases are mobile even though their owners stay put – think of the German citizen who does not declare capital gains in a Swiss bank account or of multinationals like Google or Volkswagen who generate a lot of income in France but book their profits in Bermuda or Luxembourg. From a legal perspective, there is a difference between these two cases – the first is considered evasion and illegal whilst the second constitutes legal tax avoidance – but from an ethical perspective, there is no difference between the two. Dietsch argues that the case for banning this type of activity, which has been called 'poaching' by the OECD, is strong. The second, real type of tax competition is more akin to a form of 'luring'. Here, the owner of the capital in question responds to tax incentives by actually relocating elsewhere, for instance, through foreign direct investment (FDI) in a low-tax jurisdiction. Dietsch points out that these cases are more complex from an ethical perspective. Instead of defending one specific normative response to them, he outlines a menu of positions one might defend, depending on one's conception of fiscal autonomy.

The final part of the volume turns to concrete reform proposals. In Chapter Twelve, Markus Meinzer, who is not only an academic but also a tax-justice activist, argues that political initiatives to counter tax havens at national and international levels have, typically, relied on arbitrary and doubtful criteria for what constitutes a tax haven. This arbitrariness is one important factor behind the failure of past and most current attempts to counter harmful tax competition. In contrast, Meinzer proposes to rely on the Financial Secrecy Index (FSI), which shifts the focus away from tax aspects on to secrecy, using transparent, verifiable criteria and data sources. The index assesses the degree to which a jurisdiction's legal and regulatory system contributes to global financial secrecy and thus facilitates corrupt practices, including those stemming from tax-abuse. The FSI, Meinzer claims, can help to shape reforms in three main ways. First, the high ranking of major OECD powers in the index (that is, their lack of transparency) underlines their need to lead through example, by enacting domestic policy reforms, before imposing changes on others. Second, once these reforms are implemented, a broad menu of specifically designed counter-measures can be adopted, targeting aspects of the financial secrecy of all jurisdictions. Third, by focusing on transparency as an intermediate step to achieving fair international tax rules, more sustained public support for reform efforts against the resistance of vested interests is likely to emerge.

In Chapter Thirteen, Reuven Avi-Yonah argues for the introduction of a system of unitary taxation and formula apportionment (UT+FA). He explains why the current system of arm's-length standard (ALS) transfer-pricing does not work properly. Among other problems, it is overly complex and allows corporations to engage in profit-shifting to avoid paying taxes. According to Avi-Yonah, the best alternative would be the introduction of full-scale UT+FA. Under such a system, corporations would have to issue a combined report on their global profits, which would then be attributed to the different jurisdictions in which the MNE is active according to a formula that relies on indicators of real economic activity, such as the number of jobs, sales, or assets in a country. He discusses a number of objections raised against UT+FA and comes to the conclusion that they can all be defeated. However, given fierce resistance from the OECD and many governments, he acknowledges that full-scale UT+FA is currently unfeasible (at least as long as the EU does not move forward to introduce such a system, which is referred to as the Common Consolidated Corporate Tax Base (CCCTB) by the EU). Consequently, he argues for an intermediate step that would use formula apportionment only in those cases where the OECD guidelines currently foresee the use of profit-split methods. These are cases where it is particularly difficult to determine ALS prices in the traditional manner and which are therefore already resolved by reference to the profits realised in different countries.

Gabriel Wollner (2016, Chapter Fourteen) analyses the role that an international financial transaction tax (IFTT) could play in the institutional arrangements of global tax governance. He presents two families of arguments that have been mobilised in favour of such a tax. First, what one might call an internal argument (James 2012: 144), namely, Tobin's idea that sand needs to be thrown into the wheels of finance in order to reduce the risk of financial instability. From this perspective, an IFTT would ensure that the risk-externalities of transactions are internalised and that those who benefit from the public good of a well functioning financial system contribute to its maintenance. As to the second, external argument, an IFTT represents an important means of promoting distributive justice. Its progressive features on the revenue side, as well as the fact that it represents an important potential source of expenditure targeted at reducing poverty, make it an attractive policy option. Finally, Wollner argues that an IFTT would promote global background justice by shoring up the effective sovereignty of states over their economic fate, for instance by increasing the transaction costs of tax arbitrage and other practices that undermine this sovereignty.

Finally, in Chapter Fifteen, Thomas Rixen proposes an International Tax Organisation (ITO). This new organisation would be responsible for the international governance of direct taxation. Rixen engages in an exercise of positively informed normative institutional design that builds on two considerations: first, an analysis of the functional requirements of the institution – what kind of collective rules are required to defeat individual states' incentives to engage in harmful, competitive behaviour? And second, which rules help to safeguard national *de facto* tax sovereignty? The answers to these two questions provide the design of the institution (and its policies), which are spelled out in detail in the chapter. The design features turn out to be similar to those of the World Trade Organization (WTO). The ITO would, for one, function as a multilateral forum for governments to negotiate the concrete rules, thus replacing the mode of bilateralism and increasingly (partial) clubs so far prevalent in international taxation. Second, and even more importantly, it should entail a legalised dispute-settlement procedure very similar to that of the WTO, in which countries can be forced to abandon tax policies that constitute harmful tax competition.

5. Theoretical and political implications

The subtitle of this volume asks a double question about global tax governance: what is wrong with it and how to fix it? In this final section, we pull together some of the main insights the contributing chapters offer to answer these questions. In doing so, we follow the logic of the four parts to the book.

A precise diagnosis is a precondition for any cure. The contributions to Part One offer a sophisticated understanding of the phenomenon of tax competition and the challenges it presents. It is worth highlighting three of them here. First, consider the relative importance of virtual *versus* real tax competition. While Clausing 2016 (Chapter Two) rightly points out that today, poaching through *virtual* tax competition is the dominant form of tax competition, a ban on this kind of activity would substantially increase the incentives of corporations to actually shift their economic activities to low-tax jurisdictions. Reform efforts will have to be alert to this substitutive relationship. Second, both the *status quo* of tax competition and potential reforms come with distributive implications. Genschel and Seelkopf (2016, Chapter Three in this volume) identify the winners and losers of tax competition and notably dispel the idea that all members of a state share the same interests in a context of tax competition. Especially in large countries, workers and governments tend to lose from tax competition. Even within the corporate sector gains and losses differ: on the one hand, multinationals benefit from being able to play different jurisdictions off against each other but, on the other hand, small and medium-size enterprises' ability to avoid paying taxes is much more limited. Third, as highlighted by Latulippe (2016, Chapter Four in this volume), one of the principal difficulties of forming a coalition among the losers of tax competition is the extent to which the competitiveness discourse has led to an internalisation of the idea that competing on taxes is in the public interest.

Building on this analysis, the contributions to Part Two point to areas in which regulation needs to do better than today. The common finding of these chapters is that international taxation, an area that only ten years ago was governed by an administrative and technocratic logic, has clearly developed into a salient issue that is on the radar of IGOs, governments, parliaments, and civil-society activists. The process of international tax policy-making has been politicised. In terms of policy outputs, the chapters also agree: the recent initiatives represent an astonishing development and significant progress when measured against the long-term historical trajectory of international taxation; they do, however, fall short when measured against what would be needed to regulate international tax competition effectively. One obstacle is the phenomenon of mock compliance in the context of initiatives on transparency and information-exchange, as discussed by Woodward in Chapter Five. Also, as argued by Hakelberg in Chapter Six, leadership by the United States in promoting automatic exchange of tax information has not been driven by benevolent motives but rather by the desire to redistribute to its own advantage. Another obstacle lies in the distinctive challenge posed by BEPS. While both tax evasion and tax avoidance through BEPS represent types of 'poaching' and are thus equally problematic from an ethical standpoint, Chapters Seven and Eight, by Grinberg and Eccleston and Smith, both underline the importance of distributive conflict in any regulation of BEPS. Whereas it has been relatively straightforward to form a coalition against individual tax evasion, the configuration of winners and losers in the case of corporate tax avoidance makes it harder to find a consensus on reform.

One of the contributions of this volume is to underscore the importance of a sound normative justification for global tax governance. The chapters in Part Three illustrate the kinds of arguments that are necessary to arrive at such a justification. First of all, we need a more nuanced understanding of such concepts as efficiency, sovereignty or fiscal autonomy, and distributive justice, which are frequently invoked in the debate on global tax governance. For instance, Chapters Nine through Eleven agree that tax co-operation can, in fact, be sovereignty-enhancing rather than sovereignty-compromising. That said, they vary in the robustness of the concept of sovereignty they adopt and thus also in the intensity of tax co-operation they advocate. Second, normative justification requires value judgements about the relative weight we should attach to the kinds of concepts listed above. For example, the extent to which one's regulatory response to tax competition includes the levying of some global taxes – *see* Ronzoni (2016, Chapter Nine) – plausibly depends on the relative weight one attaches to distributive considerations relative to sovereignty or efficiency. Likewise, as both van Apeldoorn (2016, Chapter Ten) and Dietsch (2016, Chapter Eleven) emphasise, the normative stance we adopt towards the luring of tax-base depends both on our understanding of fiscal autonomy and on its weight relative to other values.

Finally, when it comes to concrete reforms that flow from the arguments in this volume, Part Four offers a number of valuable lessons. First, a general precondition for a paradigm shift on global tax governance, as emphasised by Markus Meinzer (2016, Chapter Twelve), is the development of new and more appropriate measures to combat tax-abuse, secrecy and other problematic features of global tax governance. Second, as underlined in Avi-Yonah's (2016, Chapter Thirteen) defence of UT+FA, one of the critical drawbacks of the current OECD's efforts to 'repair' the arms-length standard (OECD 2013) lies in the fact that this perpetuates the 'cat-and-mouse' game between regulators and the tax-avoidance industry – one in which regulators always seem to be one step behind. Effective reform such as UT+FA has the potential to overcome these dynamics. The last two chapters of the volume sketch two complementary paths to reform. Wollner's (2016, Chapter Fourteen) case for an IFTT amounts to slowing down tax competition by making tax-avoidance strategies less profitable. Rixen (2016, Chapter Fifteen) more ambitiously calls for the creation of an ITO to oversee and enforce the regulation of the various forms of tax competition. Given the arguments throughout the volume with respect to the nature of tax competition as well as concerning the blind spots of the current regulatory response, this call for an international organisation is a logical conclusion. It is hard to see how anything short of an ITO could satisfy the functional requirements of global tax governance today.

References

Avi-Yonah, R. S. (2000) 'Globalization, tax competition, and the fiscal crisis of the welfare state', *Harvard Law Review* 113(7): 1573–1676.

— (2016) 'A proposal for unitary taxation and formulary apportionment (UT+FA) to tax multinational enterprises', in Dietsch, P. and Rixen, T. (eds) *Global Tax Governance: What is wrong with it and how to fix it*, Colchester: ECPR Press.

Barry, C. and Valentini, L. (2009) 'Egalitarian challenges to global egalitarianism: a critique', *Review of International Studies* 35(3): 485–512.

Basinger, S. J. and Hallerberg, M. (2004) 'Remodeling the competition for capital: how domestic politics erases the race to the bottom', *American Political Science Review* 98(2): 261–76.

Bird, R. M. (1988) 'Shaping a new international tax order', *Bulletin for International Fiscal Documentation* 42(7): 292–9.

Bird, R. M. and Wilkie, J. S. (2000) 'Source- vs. residence-based taxation in the European Union: the wrong question?', in Cnossen, S. (ed.) *Taxing Capital Income in the European Union: Issues and options for reform*, New York: Oxford University Press, pp. 78–109.

Blyth, M. (2013) *Austerity: The history of a dangerous idea*, New York: Oxford University Press.

Bordo, M. D. *et al.* (1999) *Is Globalization Today Really Different Than a Hundred Years Ago?*, Cambridge: National Bureau of Economic Research Working Paper No. 7195.

Brock, G. (2008) 'Taxation and global justice: closing the gap between theory and practice', *Journal of Social Philosophy* 39(2): 161–84.

Bucovetsky, S. (1991) 'Asymmetric tax competition', *Journal of Urban Economics* 30(2): 167–81.

Cappelen, A. W. (2001) 'The moral rationale for international fiscal law', *Ethics & International Affairs* 15(1): 97–110.

Clausing, K. A. (2016) 'The nature and practice of tax competition', in Dietsch P. and Rixen, T. (eds) *Global Tax Governance: What is wrong with it and how to fix it*, Colchester: ECPR Press.

Crouch, C. (2004) *Post-Democracy*, Oxford: Polity Press.

Dagan, T. (2000) 'The tax treaties myth', *New York University Journal of International Law & Politics* 32(4): 939–96.

de Mooij, R. A. and Ederveen, S. (2008) 'Corporate tax elasticities: a reader's guide to empirical findings', *Oxford Review of Economic Policy* 24(4): 680–97.

Devereux, M. P. and Griffith, R. (2002) 'The impact of corporate taxation on the location of capital: a review', *Swedish Economic Policy Review* 9(1): 79–102.

Dietsch, P. (2015) *Catching Capital: The ethics of tax competition*, New York: Oxford University Press.

— (2016) 'Whose tax base? The ethics of global tax governance', in Dietsch, P. and Rixen, T. (eds) *Global Tax Governance: What is wrong with it and how to fix it*, Colchester: ECPR Press.

Dietsch, P. and Rixen, T. (2014) 'Tax competition and global background justice', *Journal of Political Philosophy* 22(2): 150–77.

Dingwerth, K. and Pattberg, P. (2006) 'Global governance as a perspective on world politics', *Global Governance: A review of multilateralism and international organizations* 12(2): 185–203.

Dworkin, R. (2002) *Sovereign Virtue*, Cambridge, Massachusetts: Harvard University Press.

Eccleston, R. (2012) *The Dynamics of Global Economic Governance: The financial crisis, the OECD and the politics of international tax co-operation*, Cheltenham: Edward Elgar.

Eccleston, R. and Smith, H. (2016) 'The G20, BEPS, and the future of international tax governance', in Dietsch, P. and Rixen, T. *Global Tax Governance: What is wrong with it and how to fix it*, Colchester: ECPR Press.

Gaisbauer, H. P. *et al.* (2015) *Philosophical Explorations of Justice and Taxation – National and global issues*, Dordrecht: Springer.

Ganghof, S. (2006) *The Politics of Income Taxation: A comparative analysis of advanced industrial countries*, Colchester: ECPR Press.

Garrett, G., and Mitchell, D. (2001) 'Globalization, government spending and taxation in the OECD', *European Journal of Political Research* 39(2): 145–77.

Genschel, P. (2002) 'Globalization, tax competition and the welfare state', *Politics & Society* 30(2): 244–74.

Genschel, P. and Rixen, T. (2015) 'Settling and unsettling the transnational legal order of international taxation', in Halliday, T. C. and Shaffer, G. C. (eds) *Transnational Legal Orders*, Cambridge: Cambridge University Press, pp. 154–84.

Genschel, P. and Schwarz, P. (2011) 'Tax competition: a literature review', *Socio-Economic Review* 9(2): 339–70.

Genschel, P. and Seelkopf, L. (2016) 'Winners and losers of tax competition', in Dietsch, P. and Rixen, T. (eds) *Global Tax Governance: What is wrong with it and how to fix it*, Colchester: ECPR Press.

Graetz, M. J. (2003) *Foundations of International Income Taxation*, New York: Foundation Press.

Grinberg, I. (2016) 'Does FATCA teach broader lessons about international tax multilateralism?', in Dietsch, P. and Rixen, T. *Global Tax Governance: What is wrong with it and how to fix it*, Colchester: ECPR Press.

Hakelberg, L. (2014) 'The power politics of international tax co-operation: Luxembourg, Austria and the automatic exchange of information', *Journal of European Public Policy* 22(3): 409–28.

— (2016) 'Redistributive tax co-operation: automatic exchange of information, US power and the absence of joint gains', in Dietsch, P. and Rixen, T. (eds) *Global Tax Governance: What is wrong with it and how to fix it*, Colchester: ECPR Press.

Halliday, D. (2013) 'Justice and taxation', *Philosophy Compass* 8(12): 1111–22.

James, A. (2012) *Fairness in Practice: A social contract for a global economy*, New York: Oxford University Press.

Kaul, I. *et al*. (eds, 2003) *Providing Global Public Goods: Managing globalization*, Oxford: Oxford University Press.

Keohane, R. O. (1984) *After Hegemony: Co-operation and discord in the world political economy,* Princeton, New Jersey: Princeton University Press.

Kindleberger, C. (1976) 'Systems of international economic organization', in Calleo, D. (ed.) *Money and the Coming World Order*, New York: New York University Press.

Krasner, S. D. (1982) 'Structural causes and regime consequences: regimes as intervening variables', *International Organization* 36(2): 185–205.

Latulippe, L. (2016) 'Tax competition: an internalised policy goal', in Dietsch, P. and Rixen, T. (eds) *Global Tax Governance: What is wrong with it and how to fix it*, Colchester: ECPR Press.

Mair, P. (2013) *Ruling the Void: The hollowing of western democracy*, London: Verso.

Meinzer, M. (2016) 'Towards an international yardstick for identifying tax havens and facilitating reform', in Dietsch, P. and Rixen, T. (eds) *Global Tax Governance: What is wrong with it and how to fix it*, Colchester: ECPR Press.

Murphy, L. and Nagel, T. (2002) *The Myth of Ownership: Taxes and justice*, Oxford: Oxford University Press.

Oatley, T. and Nabors, R. (1998) 'Redistributive co-operation: market failure, wealth transfers, and the Basle accord', *International Organization* 52(1): 35–54.

OECD (1998) *Harmful Tax Competition: An emerging global issue*, Paris: OECD: http://www.oecd.org/tax/transparency/44430243.pdf (accessed 22 June 2015).

— (2013) *Addressing Base Erosion and Profit Shifting*: OECD Publishing: http://dx.doi.org/10.1787/9789264192744-en (accessed 22 June 2015).

— (2014) *Multilateral Competent Authority Agreement on Automatic Exchange of Financial Account Information*, 29 October: http://www.oecd.org/tax/exchange-of-tax-information/multilateral-competent-authority-agreement.pdf (accessed 7 May 2015).

Ostry, J. D. *et al*. (2014) 'Redistribution, inequality, and growth', IMF Staff Discussion Note 14/02: http://www.imf.org/external/pubs/ft/sdn/2014/sdn1402.pdf (last accessed 12 April 2015).

Palan, R. (1998) 'Trying to have your cake and eating it: how and why the state system has created offshore', *International Studies Quarterly* 42(4): 625–44.

Palan, R. *et al.* (2010) *Tax Havens: How globalization really works*, Ithaca, New York: Cornell University Press.

Picciotto, S. (1992) *International Business Taxation: A study in the internationalization of business regulation*, New York: Quorum.

Piketty, T. (2014) *Capital in the 21st Century*, Cambridge, Massachusetts: Harvard University Press.

Piketty, T. *et al.* (2011) 'Optimal taxation of top labor incomes: a tale of three elasticities', CEPR Discussion Paper 8675, December: http://econpapers.repec.org/paper/cprceprdp/8675.htm (accessed 22 June 2015).

Prakash, A. and Hart, J. A. (1999) 'The concepts and politics of globalization and governance', in Prakash, A. and Hart, J. A. (eds) *Globalization and Governance*, London: Routledge, pp. 1–24.

Radaelli, C. M. (2003) 'The code of conduct against harmful tax competition: open method of co-ordination in disguise?', *Public Administration* 81(3): 513–31.

Rawls, J. (1999) *A Theory of Justice*, Oxford: Oxford University Press.

Rixen, T. (2008) *The Political Economy of International Tax Governance*, Basingstoke: Palgrave Macmillan.

— (2011a) 'From double tax avoidance to tax competition: explaining the institutional trajectory of international tax governance', *Review of International Political Economy* 18(2): 197–227.

— (2011b) 'Tax competition and inequality: the case for global tax governance', *Global Governance: A Review of Multilateralism and International Organizations* 17(4): 447–67.

— (2013) 'Why reregulation after the crisis is feeble: offshore financial centers, shadow banking and jurisdictional competition', *Regulation & Governance* 7(4): 435–59.

Rixen, T. (2016) 'Institutional reform of global tax governance': a proposal, in Dietsch, P. and Rixen, T. (eds) *Global Tax Governance: What is wrong with it and how to fix it*, Colchester: ECPR Press.

Rixen, T. Schwarz, P. (2012) 'How effective is the European Union's Savings Tax Directive? Evidence from four EU member states', *Journal of Common Market Studies* 50(1): 151–68

Ronzoni, M. (2016) 'Tax competition: a problem of global or domestic justice?', in Dietsch, P. and Rixen, T. (eds) *Global Tax Governance: What is wrong with it and how to fix it*, Colchester: ECPR Press.

Rodrik, D. (2011) *The Globalization Paradox*, New York: W. W. Norton & Co.

Schäfer, A. (2013) 'Liberalization, inequality, and democracy's discontent', in Schäfer, A. and Streeck, W. (eds) *Politics in the Age of Austerity*, Cambridge: Polity Press, pp. 169–95.

Sharman, J. C. (2006) *Havens in a Storm: The struggle for global tax regulation*, Ithaca, New York: Cornell University Press.

Sinn, H.-W. (2003) *The New Systems Competition*, Oxford: Blackwell.
Stiglitz, J. E. (2008) *The Price of Inequality*, New York: W. W. Norton & Co.
Streeck, W. (2014) *Buying Time: The delayed crisis of democratic capitalism*, London: Verso.
Swank, D. and Steinmo, S. (2002) 'The new political economy of taxation in advanced capitalist democracies', *American Journal of Political Science* 46(3): 642–55.
van Apeldoorn, L. (2016), 'International taxation and the erosion of sovereignty', in Dietsch, P. and Rixen, T. *Global Tax Governance: What is wrong with it and how to fix it*, Colchester: ECPR Press.
Vann, R. J. (1991) 'A model tax treaty for the Asian-Pacific region?' (parts I and II), *Bulletin for International Fiscal Documentation* 45(3): 99–111 and 45(4): 151–163.
Walter, A. (2008) *Governing Finance: East Asia's adoption of international standards*, Ithaca, New York: Cornell University Press.
Webb, M. C. (2004) 'Defining the boundaries of legitimate state practice: norms, transnational actors and the OECD's project on harmful tax competition', *Review of International Political Economy* 11(4): 787–827.
Wilson, J. D. and Wildasin, D. E. (2004) 'Capital tax competition: bane or boon?', *Journal of Public Economics* 88(6): 1065–91.
Woodward, R. (2016) 'A strange revolution: mock compliance and the failure of the OECD's international tax transparency regime', in Dietsch, P. and Rixen, T. (eds) *Global Tax Governance: What is wrong with it and how to fix it*, Colchester: ECPR Press.
Wollner, G. (2016) 'International financial transaction taxation, public goods and justice', in Dietsch, P. and Rixen, T. (eds) *Global Tax Governance: What is wrong with it and how to fix it*, Colchester: ECPR Press.
Zürn, M. (2013) 'Globalization and global governance', in Carlsnaes, W. *et al.* (eds) *Handbook of International Relations*, London: Sage, pp. 401–25. Mair, P. (2013) *Ruling the Void: The hollowing of western democracy*, London: Verso.

PART ONE

THE PROBLEM: INTERNATIONAL TAX COMPETITION

Chapter Two

The Nature and Practice of Tax Competition

*Kimberly A. Clausing**

1. Introduction

One of the most pressing questions of modern public finance is how to reconcile the scope of economic activity with the scope of governance. In recent decades, this reconciliation has become increasingly difficult as the pace of international economic integration has accelerated, without any commensurate surge in co-operation among sovereign governments. This disconnect is particularly visible in the international taxation of multinational corporations. As corporations increasingly become global entities, while governments do not, there are pressures for governments to compete with one another to attract both real economic activity and tax revenue. This chapter will focus on the mechanisms of such tax competition.

The first section of the chapter will consider how countries compete over the corporate tax-base. Set within the context of modern tax-competition theory, it will investigate types of government tax competition, including competition over statutory tax rates, the overall corporate tax burden (or effective tax rates) and preferential tax regimes. In many, but not all, contexts, such tax competition can be harmful to welfare, as countries may harm each other's capacities to collect tax revenue and fund government services. Theoretical models have been extended to include possible favourable effects of tax competition, asymmetries between countries and other factors. This section of the chapter will also review the empirical evidence on these types of tax competition. There is substantial evidence that the path of statutory and effective tax rates has been affected by tax competition; and there is evidence of especially large tax-competition effects for small and open countries.

Section 2 of the chapter will consider how multinational corporations respond to tax competition. It will consider both the theoretical predictions of the literature as well as the empirical patterns of multinational firms' responses. There will also be some simple examples of the tax sensitivity of multinational activity taken from US Bureau of Economic Analysis survey data on US-based multinational corporations.[1] Evidence indicates that multinational corporations are particularly

* I would like to thank Vladislav Mankov for his capable research assistance.

1. While multinational firms based in other countries may conceivably behave differently, the US example allows the use of excellent survey data, which is more likely to capture the essential mechanisms at hand. Financial data suffers from differences between book- and tax-profit definitions as well as insufficient country-level reporting detail. Further, financial reporting incentives are different from tax incentives in important substantive ways.

sensitive to tax differences across jurisdictions when determining where to book their income. Yet real economic activity is less responsive to tax incentives than financial decisions, a finding that is consistent with a long-standing literature in public finance.

Section 3 of the chapter will consider the larger consequences of tax competition, focusing on the impact on tax revenues and capital stocks across countries. Evidence indicates that tax competition has particularly large effects on government revenues. However, there is far less evidence of effects on real economic activity for OECD countries; for example, capital stocks are not shown to be sensitive to tax-rate differences. In part, this insensitivity may result from tax avoidance. For example, tax avoidance by multinational firms may reduce tax burdens (and government revenues) without necessitating substantial changes in the location of economic activity. Also, the substitution between different sources of investment funding (debt-financed *versus* equity-financed, portfolio *versus* direct and so on) may reduce the tax sensitivity of the *overall* capital stock.

Finally, within this context, tax-policy design issues will be discussed, emphasising the benefits of international efforts, the importance of base-erosion protections by national governments and the essential importance of interactions between different features of national tax systems.

2. Tax competition among governments

How do countries compete?

Wilson (1999), Fuest *et al.* (2005), Wilson and Wildasin (2004), Zodrow (2003, 2010), and Keen and Konrad (2014) provide surveys of the tax-competition literature. It has long been recognised that the international mobility of capital has the potential to generate a fiscal externality, whereby when one country raises (or lowers) its corporate tax rate, it has a positive (or negative) effect on other countries, as the mobile tax base reacts to changes in the tax rate. This raises the marginal costs of public-good provision through capital taxation, implying lower levels of public-good provision and/or a shifting of the tax burden on to less mobile tax-bases, such as labour or consumption, and/or an increase in public debt.[2]

Also, it is possible that capital is misallocated internationally, with high-tax economies experiencing a sub-optimally low capital stock and a higher marginal product of capital (and lower marginal product of labour) than low-tax economies. In general, these models generate the expectation that increasing economic integration should be accompanied by fiercer tax competition. As integration

2. The loss of tax-base to other countries, alongside the associated capital mobility, generates inefficiency in the worldwide allocation of capital. It is noteworthy that some have argued that the optimal capital tax rate should be lower than the optimal labour tax rate, or even zero. However, recent studies have concluded that the optimal capital tax rate may be the same or higher than the optimal labour tax rate. *See also* Footnote 19. For a full review of evidence on this question, see Clausing 2013.

proceeds, we expect declining statutory tax rates, as well as lower corporate tax burdens, as countries compete for mobile investments and to host multinational firms with supra-normal economic profits.[3]

However, as is often the case in economic theory, more complicated models can generate contrary results. For example, some models consider tax competition as a useful constraint on the 'Leviathan' tendencies of governments seeking to maximise their own size rather than national welfare. Capital taxes can also be sub-optimally high due to tax competition, for various reasons described in Fuest *et al.* (2005), including imperfect competition in labour markets, tax exportation with foreign firm ownership and other political-economy motivations. Other models consider the interaction between taxation and public-good provision, and possible heterogeneity across countries whereby some countries specialise in producing goods that require higher levels of public-good provision (and thus taxation), and other countries the opposite, so that tax differences persist over time.

As countries vary in size or economic openness, this can also generate disparate tax rates in tax-competition models, since smaller and/or more open countries face more elastic capital-supply curves and thus choose lower tax rates in response. Baldwin and Krugman (2004), Haufler and Wooten (1999) and Borck and Pflüger (2006) have emphasised that agglomeration effects may help insulate some nations from the effects of tax competition, allowing them to set higher tax rates without losing capital.

A particularly relevant extension of this literature considers the interaction between real capital mobility and tax-avoidance practices that allow corporations to move income without commensurate movement in real activity. As Hong and Smart (2010) model, tax avoidance can reduce tax burdens on real capital in high-tax countries, increasing investment in high-tax countries over the level that would prevail absent the possibility of tax avoidance. Simply put, if multinational corporations can move the income without moving the underlying activity, income-shifting reduces the tax sensitivity of investments in a way that benefits high-tax countries. However, income-shifting behaviour makes the tax base more sensitive to tax differences across countries, even as real activities are less sensitive to tax differences.

The Hong and Smart (2010) model implies a different path of tax-rate changes under tax competition, where statutory and effective tax rates could rise with the introduction of tax havens. This contrasts with other models, such as that of Slemrod and Wilson (2009), in which the elimination or reduction of havens unambiguously improves welfare in non-haven countries.

Income-shifting between the corporate and personal tax-base (or between income in capital and labour form) also has implications for capital tax competition, since there are incentives, for example, to characterise labour income as capital

3. Economic integration could also generate lower tax rates across integrated countries due to other processes, aside from competitive pressure to attract mobile tax bases. For example, yardstick tax competition may lead countries to follow each others' tax-policy choices, or ideological or economic similarities across integrated countries may generate similar tax-policy choices.

Figure 2.1: Statutory corporate tax rates for central governments, average, OECD countries

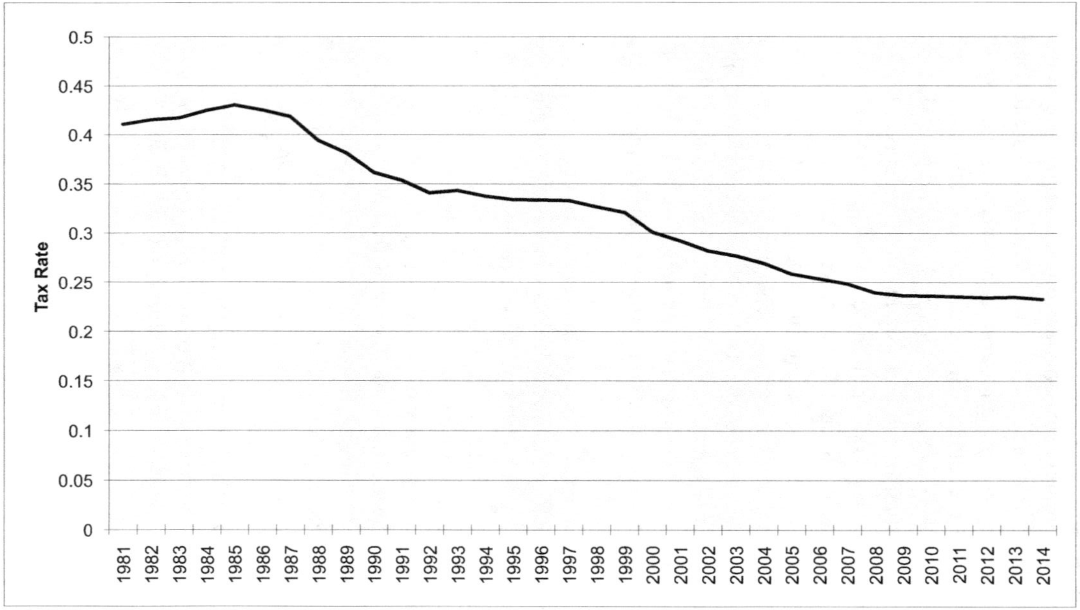

Data source: OECD Revenue Statistics Database

income as capital tax rates fall relative to labour tax rates. Gordon and Slemrod (2000), Gordon and MacKie-Mason (1995), Pirttila and Selin (2011) and Thoresen and Alstadsaeter (2010) examine these considerations. Like income-shifting more generally, this can confuse the revenue effects associated with corporate income tax changes. If a country lowers its corporate tax rate, for example, it may be compensated by increased income-shifting from abroad (or decreased outward shifting), which will attenuate negative effects on government revenues. There may also be a greater incentive (or less disincentive) to earn income in corporate form, also increasing corporate revenues. In this latter case, the additional corporate tax revenue comes at the expense of reductions in the personal income tax base.

Finally, governments increasingly compete with respect to tax-regime characteristics, although this facet of tax competition is not as well developed in the literature. Just a few examples of such tax competition include the US ‘check-the-box’ rules, discussed in Altshuler and Grubert (2005). These rules allow some entities to be disregarded for tax purposes, facilitating tax avoidance through chains of ownership that can even generate ‘stateless’ income, as described by Kleinbard (2011). Other examples include the recent UK patent-box (which gives favourable tax treatment to intellectual property), following those in Belgium, Luxembourg and the Netherlands, and the favourable rules regarding holding companies in the Netherlands. As noted above, this sort of tax competition reduces government revenue in high-tax locations; but it may have a silver lining, lessening the real response of investment to statutory tax rates.

What is the experience of international corporate tax competition?

First, consider the path of corporate tax rates in recent decades, a time that has been marked by dramatic increases in international economic integration.[4] Figure 2.1 shows the path of OECD statutory tax rates at the central government level. There is a clear decline in the average corporate tax rate, from 41 per cent in 1981 to 23 per cent in 2014. If one weights this series by the GDP of the OECD countries, the decline is less dramatic, though still present, indicating that smaller economies are lowering their corporate tax rates to a greater degree than are larger economies.

This trend also extends to effective tax rates, assuming the foreign affiliates of US multinational firms are representative of larger trends. Figure 2.2 shows the effective tax rates paid by these affiliates; it is the ratio of their actual foreign taxes paid (as a group) to their income (before foreign tax is paid) for the countries in the sample; this includes about fifty foreign countries. Effective tax rates decline steadily over this period, from 33 per cent in 1983 to 18.5 per cent in 2011. Again, it is the case that large economies have higher effective tax rates. If one regresses the effective tax rate on a time trend and GDP, one finds that effective tax rates are higher for large economies and tax rates decline over time during this period.

---

4. For an overview of relevant measures of increasing international integration, see Clausing 2013.

Figure 2.2: Average effective tax rates for foreign affiliates of US multinational firms (across 50 countries)

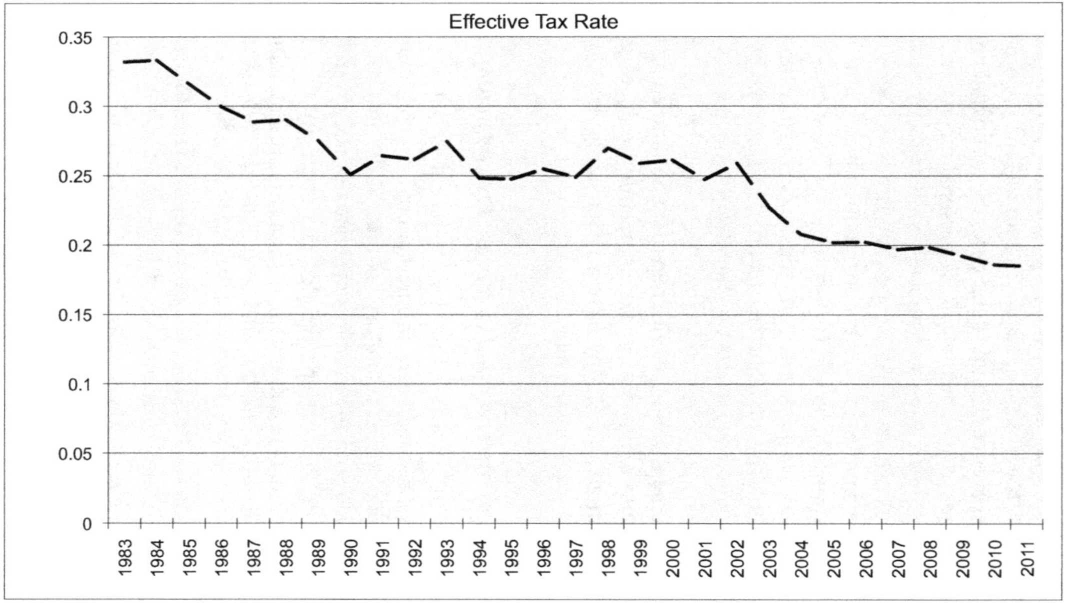

Data source: US Bureau of Economic Analysis Survey Data on Operations of US Multinational Firms

There is evidence in the literature of tax-competition pressures on tax rates. Strategic interaction in corporate tax-rate-setting is found by Altshuler and Goodspeed (2014), who examine OECD countries between 1968 and 2008. Devereux *et al.* (2008) also find evidence of strategic corporate tax-rate-setting for OECD countries between 1982 and 1999. However, Stewart and Webb (2006) find that there is little evidence of corporate tax burden convergence for OECD countries, although there is some convergence among smaller groups of countries.

Not all countries are affected by tax competition pressures equally; evidence indicates that smaller and more internationally integrated economies are more likely to set lower tax rates. For example, Mutti (2003) considers the determinants of corporate tax-rate changes over the period between 1984 and 1996; he finds that small countries and countries with higher initial rates are more likely to see larger reductions in their corporate tax rate. Azemar *et al.* (2013) also emphasise the role of country size, which is important due to market-access considerations.

Bretschger and Hettich (2002) and Rodrik (1997) find evidence that greater international integration is associated with lower corporate tax rates. Adam *et al.* (2013) consider a meta-analysis of how globalisation measures affect capital-taxation measures; studies find negative relationships between measures of globalisation flows and capital tax rates.

Davies and Voget (2008) consider the role of European Union expansion in fuelling tax-competition pressures, focusing on the period from 1980 to 2005, and they find that EU members respond more to the tax rates of other members. Clausing (2008) has a similar finding. Winner (2005) considers how tax-competition pressures affect the balance of tax burdens across capital and labour. He finds that more economically integrated countries have lower capital tax burdens relative to labour tax burdens, as do smaller countries. He focuses on OECD countries between 1965 and 2000.

Many of the above studies consider the setting of corporate tax rates in response to tax-competition pressures. Still, importantly, tax competition may also affect how much revenue a government receives for any particular tax rate; and countries may not be symmetric in this regard either. For example, a smaller or more open country may experience more tax-base erosion from a high corporate tax rate than would larger or more closed countries. This part of the tax-competition evidence will be discussed in Section 4, when the consequences of tax competition are addressed.

3. How do multinational firms respond to government tax competition?

In general, firms are expected to respond to tax differences across countries by making tax-sensitive choices regarding the location of their economic activities. For example, general-equilibrium models of corporate tax incidence in an open economy suggest that capital should move from high-tax locations to low-tax locations, equalising the after-tax return to capital across countries. Due to the tax differences between countries, higher-tax countries should experience lower capital stocks and a lower marginal product of labour, and thus lower wages, in comparison to low-tax countries. These sort of theoretical mechanisms are described in the work of Harberger (1995, 2008), Randolph (2006) and Gravelle and Smetters (2006). Still, as Gravelle (2010) notes, this mechanism need not imply that labour bears the full burden of the tax, since this will depend on several key economic parameters; the best estimates of these parameters from the literature suggest that capital will still bear a substantial portion of the burden. Further, other factors are omitted from these models that may also alter their conclusions, as explained in Clausing 2012. These factors include residence elements of the tax; dynamic considerations; the possibility of supra-normal profits; and effects on bargaining, among other things.

The tax response of the real activities of multinational firms may also depend on the possibilities for tax avoidance. In particular, if multinational firms are adept at moving economic profits across jurisdictions without a commensurate movement of the underlying economic activity, this may reduce the tax responsiveness of real economic activities. Multinational firms can shift income across locations by a variety of methods. For example, they can manipulate transfer prices on intra-firm transactions in order to make affiliates in low-tax countries appear more profitable than those in high-tax countries. This can be done by overpricing items that will be revenues for low-tax country affiliates or costs for high-tax country affiliates, while underpricing items that will be

Figure 2.3: Top income countries for affiliates of US multinational firms, 2011 (shares of total foreign profits of affiliates abroad)

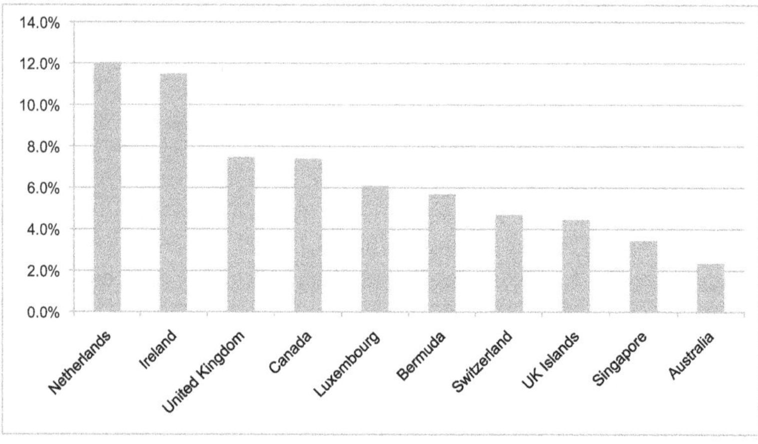

Note: Seven of these countries have particularly low effective tax rates; for Netherlands, Ireland, Luxembourg, Bermuda, Switzerland, the UK Islands and Singapore, effective rates are less than 6.5% in 2011.

Data source: Data are from the US Bureau of Economic Analysis.

Figure 2.4: Top employment countries for affiliates of US multinationals, 2011 (shares of total foreign employment of affiliates abroad)

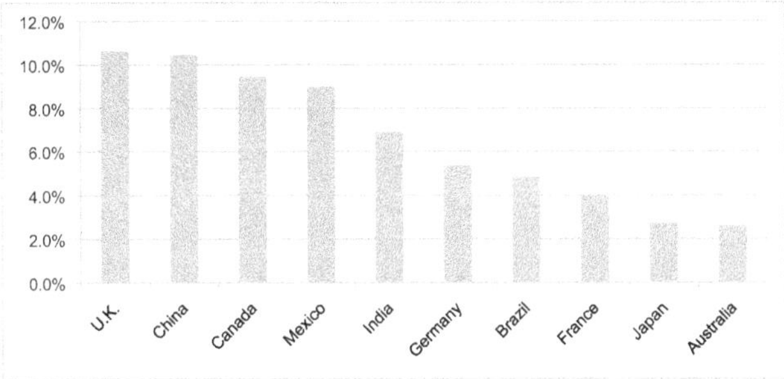

Note: None of the top employment countries have effective rates as low as the 6.5% threshold of Figure 2.3.

Data source: Data are from the US Bureau of Economic Analysis

revenues for high-tax country affiliates or costs for low-tax country affiliates. Multinational firms can also alter the structure of affiliate finance so that interest deductions are taken in high-tax countries but interest income is earned in low-tax countries. Finally, multinational firms can create complicated chains of ownership so that income becomes 'stateless income', not taxable in any jurisdiction.[5]

There is a great deal of evidence that suggests that multinational firms are tax-sensitive in their economic decisions. De Mooij and Ederveen (2003, 2008) and de Mooij (2005) provide surveys of some of this literature; there are dozens of studies demonstrating the tax sensitivity of multinational firm behaviour. Still, even simple figures illustrate that financial decisions appear to be more tax-responsive than real economic decisions. As an example, compare Figures 2.3 and 2.4, which show data for affiliates of US-headquartered multinational corporations in 2011. Of the ten destinations with the highest levels of foreign profits, seven are countries with effective tax rates of less than 6.5 per cent. These countries together account for 46.5 per cent of all foreign profits, yet they only account for 5 per cent of total foreign employment. And no wonder, since these are tiny countries, not economic powerhouses.[6]

On the other hand, Figure 2.4 shows the largest employment countries for affiliates of US multinational firms and the top ten countries do not include a single country with a tax rate below 6.5 per cent. Instead, these countries are the obvious large-market countries where one would expect US multinational corporations to have operations abroad for economic purposes.

5. Kleinbard 2011 discusses stateless income.

6. Only the Netherlands has a population in excess of 10 million and the combined population of these countries is less than that of Spain or California.

Table 2.1: Regressions explaining activity levels, 1983–2011

	(1) ln(empl)	(2) ln(sales)	(3) ln(ppe)	(4) ln(assets)	(5) ln(grossinc)
ETR	0.212	−0.000880	0.569*	−1.608*	−1.905*
	(0.233)	(0.253)	(0.263)	(0.295)	(0.285)
ln(gdp)	0.567*	0.393*	0.484*	0.300*	0.303*
	(0.0211)	(0.0229)	(0.0237)	(0.0267)	(0.0257)
ln(gdppc)	−0.0962*	0.403*	0.128*	0.531*	0.386*
	(0.0305)	(0.0330)	(0.0342)	(0.0385)	(0.0372)
ln(dis)	−0.113*	−0.103*	−0.133*	−0.138*	−0.130*
	(0.0380)	(0.0413)	(0.0429)	(0.0483)	(0.0466)
N	1338	1341	1341	1341	1342
R^2	0.38	0.35	0.31	0.32	0.28

Note: Standard errors in parentheses. Most variables are in natural log (ln) terms; empl. is employment: ppe is property, plant, and equipment: ETR is effective tax rate: gdp is gross domestic product: gdppc is gross domestic product *per capita*: and dis is the port distance between the US and the foreign country.

* $p < 0.05$

Tables 2.1 and 2.2 present a more sophisticated econometric analysis of the location of US multinational firms' employment, sales, property plant and equipment, assets and income. The data employed are from US Bureau of Economic Analysis (BEA) surveys of US multinational corporations over the period 1983 to 2011. The analysis in Table 2.1 models the scale of economic activity (employment, sales, plant/property/equipment, assets and income) as depending on the size of the economy (measured by GDP); the average income of the population (measured by GDP *per capita*); the distance between the country and the United States; and the effective tax rate paid by US affiliates. In Table 2.1, employment and sales do not show a statistically significant relationship with the effective tax rate, and property, plant and equipment are unexpectedly *positively* related to tax rates, but both assets and – especially – income, are negatively related to effective tax rates.

Table 2.2 also includes country-specific fixed effects. Country fixed effects are important, since country-specific influences are surely essential determinants of multinational firm activity, and econometric tests indicate that their inclusion is warranted. However, in these specifications, the relationships between effective tax rates and the dependent variables (which measure multinational activities) are estimated based solely on variation in tax rates *within* countries over time, since *between*-country variations in tax rates (and other matters) are captured by the country-specific fixed effects. In these specifications, real economic measures (employment, sales, and property plant and equipment) are negatively related to tax rates; but assets and income show much larger negative

Table 2.2: Fixed effects regressions explaining activity levels, 1983–2011

	(1) ln(empl)	(2) ln(sales)	(3) ln(ppe)	(4) ln(assets)	(5) ln(grossinc)
ETR	−0.393*	−0.465*	−0.482*	−2.070*	−2.383*
	(0.108)	(0.118)	(0.154)	(0.185)	(0.173)
ln(gdp)	0.00501	−0.0250	−0.0613	−0.163*	−0.0369
	(0.0294)	(0.0322)	(0.0418)	(0.0502)	(0.0472)
ln(gdppc)	0.776*	1.513*	1.349*	2.165*	1.818*
	(0.0457)	(0.0500)	(0.0650)	(0.0781)	(0.0733)
N	1356	1359	1359	1359	1360
R^2	0.41	0.67	0.47	0.64	0.64

Note: Standard errors in parentheses. Variables are defined as in Table 2.1.
* $p < 0.05$

tax effects. For example, a 1 percentage point increase in the effective tax rate reduces employment by 0.4 per cent; but it reduces reported gross income by 2.4 per cent.

The evidence in both tables is consistent with an extensive literature in the field of public finance that has emphasised a *hierarchy* of behavioural response to taxation, whereby timing and financial decisions are more tax-sensitive than real decisions about levels of economic activity.[7] While some measures of economic activity are not particularly tax-sensitive, profit rates are *very* sensitive to tax-rate differences across countries, as the regressions in Tables 2.1 and 2.2 suggest.

Further, there is also ample evidence that multinational corporations make use of special regimes that are offered by countries for certain types of income. Mintz and Weichenrieder (2010) provide a thorough discussion and related evidence on chains of ownership. The Joint Committee on Taxation (2010) also provides concrete examples of US-based multinational corporations and their tax-avoidance strategies. Indeed, many of the countries with special tax regimes are prominent in the list of top-income countries for foreign affiliates of US-based multinational corporations, as shown in Figure 2.3.

4. The consequences of tax competition

There are two essential consequences of tax competition that are likely to worry governments. First, low-tax countries may attract mobile economic activity at

7. Slemrod and Bakija (2008) and Auerbach and Slemrod (1997) summarise a vast body of research on taxation that suggests this hierarchy of behavioural response.

the expense of high-tax countries, resulting in inefficient capital allocation and changing the pattern of capital returns and wages across countries. Second, the tax-base itself is mobile, causing revenue-loss in high-tax jurisdictions relative to low-tax jurisdictions, creating concerns about fiscal externalities and possible under-provision of public goods.

Consequences for economic activity

As discussed above, the literature gives substantial support to the idea that foreign direct investment is tax-sensitive.[8] But what effect does this have on the pattern of investment and employment across countries? Even though foreign direct investment is tax-sensitive, the resulting capital stocks may be less tax-sensitive, for several reasons.

For example, clientele effects may be important. Desai and Dharmapala (2009) find evidence of substitution between foreign portfolio investment and foreign direct investment in response to tax incentives. This implies that countries that receive more foreign direct investment due to low corporate tax rates, for example, may receive less foreign portfolio investment as the returns to capital are driven down. And, in a similar fashion, increased foreign portfolio investment may compensate high-tax countries for reduced foreign direct investment.[9]

Indeed, the *financing* of particular investments may be more affected by tax incentives than the *overall level* of investment. Corporate taxation actually subsidises debt-financed investments in many cases, so a higher corporate tax rate may cause domestic investment to be disproportionately debt-financed.[10]

In general, the *type* of investment (portfolio *versus* direct, debt- *versus* equity-financed and so on) may be far more sensitive to corporate tax treatment than the overall *level* of investment that determines the resulting capital stock. If corporations are mere intermediaries in global capital markets in which a wide assortment of investors with different tax treatments invest, tax-policy changes could affect the ownership and financing patterns of assets more than they affect the aggregate level of investment in different countries.

Somewhat surprisingly, there is little cross-country evidence on the relationship between corporate tax variables and *overall* investment or capital stocks outcomes, despite the aforementioned large literature on the relationship between corporate

---

8. Again, see de Mooij and Ederveen (2003, 2008) and de Mooij (2005) for surveys.
9. While both foreign direct investment and foreign portfolio investment affect the aggregate capital stock of the economy in a similar way, there may be important differences in these types of investment in certain contexts. For example, foreign portfolio investment may respond more quickly to changes in macroeconomic conditions, exacerbating the volatility of international capital flows.
10. This is due to accelerated depreciation rules and the deductibility of debt, resulting in implicit subsidisation of debt-financed investments.

Table 2.3: Regressions explaining gross fixed capital formation/GDP

	(1)	(2)	(3)	(4)
Growth of	0.0844*	0.0980*	0.0722	0.0913*
real GDP	(0.0389)	(0.0407)	(0.0403)	(0.0406)
Unem. rate	−0.647***	−0.627***	−0.706***	−0.643***
	(0.0338)	(0.0363)	(0.0356)	(0.0378)
6 yr rel. tax	0.0451**			
(stat comb.)	(0.0166)			
6 yr rel. tax		0.000751		
(stat central)		(0.0177)		
6 yr rel. tax			0.00516	
(eff. tax rate)			(0.0164)	
6 yr rel. tax				0.4006**
(rev/GDP)				(0.1076)
Constant	0.272***	0.269***	0.276***	0.264***
	(0.00463)	(0.00494)	(0.00447)	(0.00487)
Fixed effects?	yes	yes	yes	yes
Time effects?	yes	yes	yes	yes
N	546	524	518	601
R^2	0.58	0.54	0.55	0.49

Note: Standard errors in parentheses. Variables are defined in the text.
* $p < 0.05$, ** $p < 0.01$, *** $p < 0.001$

taxation and foreign direct investment. What little cross-section evidence exists is far from conclusive.[11]

In my own investigation, I have found no systematic relationship between capital/labour ratios and corporate tax rates in OECD countries over the previous 30 years. Tables 2.3 and 2.4 excerpt tables from Clausing 2012 that consider the relationship between corporate tax rate measures (considered in a variety of ways)

11. Djankov *et al.* (2010) note a literature, to which they contribute, that suggests a relationship between corporate taxation and investment, but other studies do not typically use cross-country analysis. However, they employ a cross-section of 85 countries in 2004. They find statistically significant relationships between both statutory and effective tax rates and foreign direct investment; effective tax rates, but not statutory rates, have a statistically significant effect on overall investment. Yet the influence of effective tax rates on investment is still subject to caveats: (i) the absence of time-series variation makes it impossible to control for country-specific fixed effects; (ii) the effect loses statistical significance when a complete set of control variables is added; and (iii) the effect loses statistical significance if Bolivia is excluded from the analysis, as noted by Gravelle and Hungerford (2011).

Table 2.4: Regressions explaining ln of capital/labour ratio (K/L)

	(1)	(2)	(3)	(4)
GDP	0.0321	0.110**	−0.0295	0.0546
per capita	(.0342)	(.0351)	(.0389)	(.0404)
6 yr rel. tax	0.00980			
(stat comb.)	(0.0818)			
6 yr rel. tax		−0.253**		
(stat central)		(0.0827)		
6 yr rel. tax			0.102	
(eff. tax rate)			(0.0832)	
6 yr rel. tax				−0.553
(rev/GDP)				(0.537)
Constant	10.84***	10.06***	11.36***	10.61***
	(0.333)	(0.342)	(0.373)	(0.394)
Fixed Effects?	yes	yes	yes	yes
Time Effects?	yes	yes	yes	yes
N	601	579	582	644
R^2	0.76	0.79	0.75	0.75

Note: Standard errors in parentheses. The dependent variable is the capital/labour ratio. Other variables are defined in the text.
* $p < 0.05$, ** $p < 0.01$, *** $p < 0.001$

and capital formation (Table 2.3) and capital/labour ratios (Table 2.4), over the period 1981–2011.[12]

In Table 2.3, the dependent variable is the ratio of gross fixed capital formation to GDP. The regressions consider the impact of corporate tax variables, considering the average of the most recent six years (the current year and the five previous) of *relative* tax rates in comparison to the average of OECD countries. The specifications control for the growth of real GDP from the prior year and the unemployment rate, both proxies for the state of the macro-economy. In addition, there are both country-specific fixed effects and time-specific effects.[13]

Columns (1), (2), (3), and (4) differ only by considering the influence of four different tax-rate measures: the combined statutory rate; the central government statutory rate; the effective tax rate; and the corporate revenue/GDP ratio.

12. The table descriptions in the text are also excerpted from this source. The source provides all details regarding data-set-construction and estimation. The country and time-period selection were a result of data constraints; the most complete data are available for OECD countries over this time period.

13. The inclusion of such effects allows one to control for features of particular economies or years that may alter the typical level of the dependent variable.

Surprisingly, the only statistically significant tax coefficients are *positive*, for both the average relative statutory tax rate and the average relative corporate tax-revenue ratios. This is a puzzling finding, and I consider alternative specifications without changing the main results in Clausing 2012.

Table 2.4 examines specifications that consider how capital/labour ratios depend on corporate tax variables, controlling for the real purchasing power parity (PPP) adjusted *per-capita* GDP of countries (in order to account for the fact that capital/labour ratios tend to be higher in higher-income countries); country-specific fixed effects; and time fixed effects. Again, columns (1), (2), (3), and (4) differ only by considering the influence of the four tax rates examined above. In the case of the central government statutory rate, there is a statistically significant negative relationship between tax rates and the capital/labour (K/L) ratio; however for the other tax rate variables, the coefficients are statistically indistinguishable from zero.

What is one to conclude from the absence of clear negative effects of corporate taxation on the capital stock? It is certainly plausible that some *types* of investment or some *types* of investment finance are discouraged by high levels of corporate taxation, but that other types of investment and investment finance at least partially take their place. Such a substitution could offset much of the aggregate impact of corporate taxation on the capital/labour ratio and thus on wages.

Finally, as demonstrated in Figures 2.3 and 2.4, there has been an increased divergence between the location of economic activity (such as employment and sales) and the location of income for tax purposes. This divergence reduces the effects of relative corporate tax rates on investment, since agile firms can move income without commensurate movements of investment and jobs. Indeed, many of the most global companies have become increasingly adept at such income-shifting.[14] If firms can respond to tax differences among countries through *financial* or *organisational* decisions, this will lower the tax-sensitivity of *real* activity, thus reducing tax-induced impacts on the capital stock and wages. This is a silver lining of tax avoidance.

Consequences for revenues

Tax competition likely has important revenue effects for high-tax and low-tax countries but disentangling the precise effect on government revenues can be difficult. For example, in general, OECD countries have seen an increasing share of corporate tax revenue as a fraction of GDP, despite lowering corporate

14. The tax payments of the largest US corporations support the idea that some firms are far more global than others, and thus more adept at lowering their effective US tax burden below the statutory rate. Helman (2009) and Citizens for Tax Justice (2011) consider data from financial statements, demonstrating that effective tax rates vary widely. Globally integrated firms, like GE, Hewlett-Packard, IBM and Procter & Gamble, have far lower effective tax rates than more domestic firms, like Walmart and CVS, which have higher effective tax rates.

tax rates. This may be due to several confounding considerations: increasing corporate profitability; shifting of income from the personal tax-base to the corporate tax-base as corporate tax rates fall; and classic fiscal externality effects.

In Clausing 2007 and 2008, I estimate the relationship between the corporate tax rate and corporate revenues for OECD countries. This work models a parabolic relationship between tax rates and revenues, and the revenue-maximising rate is found to decrease as countries are smaller and more integrated with the world economy. European Union membership, an indication of greater international integration, also decreases the revenue-maximising rate.[15] These analyses demonstrate one possible mechanism for why closer economic integration fuels tax-competition pressures. At high tax rates, economic integration increases the benefit associated with lower corporate tax-rate choices, since the tax base is more responsive.

It is also likely that income-shifting has large revenue costs for high-tax countries. Simply put, if income is booked in a tax haven, it is no longer booked in a higher-tax jurisdiction and that will reduce revenues accruing to high-tax governments. Such revenue losses can be quite large. In Clausing 2009 and 2011, I estimate that income-shifting by multinational firms reduced US-government corporate tax revenue by $60 to $90 billion in 2008; given recent escalations in innovative international tax avoidance, this cost is likely higher today. This estimate is derived by using regression analysis to consider the impact of country tax-rate differences on profit rates. These regression results are then used to estimate how profit rates would change absent tax differences, and then some fraction of the resulting lower foreign profits are attributed to the US tax base.[16]

Personal capital income mobility and its consequences

Corporate income is just one form of capital income; other forms of capital income are also highly internationally mobile and sensitive to tax-competition pressures. As Zucman (2014) notes, corporate taxes typically account for about one-third of capital income taxes, with personal capital income taxes and property taxes comprising the remaining two-thirds. Increasing international economic integration has facilitated the mobility of personal capital income, as tax avoidance and evasion move personal capital income toward low-tax locations.

Unfortunately, data constraints make the tracking of offshore capital income particularly vexing. However, estimates from various sources suggest that the scale of personal capital tax avoidance and evasion is both large and increasing. Zucman

15. Of course, EU membership also entails other effects as well; and the European Court of Justice has a large impact on the ability of member-states to freely adopt policy changes.

16. The fraction is 32% in 2008 and it is based on the share of the foreign affiliates' intra-firm transactions that occur with the United States. Full details of these calculations are provided in the original papers. Gravelle (2013) reviews other studies on the magnitude of the income-shifting problem and concludes that US revenue losses are likely in the tens of billions, though there is uncertainty regarding the precise number.

(2014) calculates that, in Switzerland alone, $2.5 trillion is held by foreigners in Swiss accounts. Zucman (2013) uses balance-of-payments data to generate a lower-bound estimate of the size of global wealth held in tax havens, concluding that 8 per cent of total wealth (about $8 trillion) is located in tax havens. This number is quite similar to the $9 trillion figure calculated by Boston Consulting Group (2014), based on interviews with wealth managers.

Despite some policy efforts to reduce offshore tax evasion, including G20 efforts to bring an end to bank secrecy, evidence indicates that the problem has increased in recent years. Johannesen and Zucman (2014) indicate that bank secrecy is still alive and well, since offshore assets have been redirected in form and destination to circumvent such policy efforts. Zucman (2014) suggests that the revenue consequences of offshore wealth are quite large, with a total revenue loss for high-tax countries approaching $200 billion.

Consequences of tax competition for distribution

Since capital income is likely far more mobile than labour income, and also more highly concentrated, tax competition will also have distributional impacts. There is substantial concern regarding the indisputably large increases in income inequality in recent decades. In the United States, for example, the US Census Bureau indicates that the share of income received by the top 5 per cent of households increased by 5 percentage points between 1980 and 2010. Work by Alvaredo *et al.* (2013) indicates that these trends are particularly dramatic among the top 1 per cent of incomes in the United States. Also, this development is not unique to the United States, although it is particularly dramatic in the US case.

The distribution of wealth is typically much more skewed than the distribution of income as well. In the United States in 2010, the top 5 per cent of households received 21 per cent of income but they received 85 per cent of capital gains and 65 per cent of dividends.[17] Also, capital income is becoming more concentrated over time. For example, the 400 highest income taxpayers received 16 per cent of all long-term capital gains in 2009 and this share has been increasing since the data were first collected (in 1992), when the share of the richest 400 taxpayers was under 6 per cent of all long-term capital gains.[18]

As Piketty (2014) indicates, recent data in many countries point to an increasing importance of capital income. In the United States, three separate data sources show declining labour shares in national income in recent decades, as documented in Jacobsen and Occhino 2012. Data from the US Bureau of Economic Analysis show labour's share declining from about 67 per cent to about 64 per cent over the prior decade, data from the Bureau of Labor Statistics show the share declining from about 63 per cent to 58 per cent (from

---

17. Calculations are from data of the Tax Policy Center. See http://www.taxpolicycenter.org/T09-0490 (accessed 23 June 2015).

18. See data summarised in Burman 2012, figure 2.

the early 1980s to recently) and data from the Congressional Budget Office show labour's share of income decreasing from 75 per cent in 1979 to about 67 per cent in 2007.

This context heightens worries about tax competition, since capital income is typically deemed to be far more mobile than labour income. If countries respond to tax-competition pressures by lightening the burden on capital income relative to labour income, this will likely undermine attempts to address income inequality through the tax system. Indeed, recent tax-policy changes in many countries have tended to lower corporate and capital tax rates while raising tax burdens on labour and consumption.[19] Haufler *et al.* (2009) and Winner (2005) provide related evidence.

5. Tax competition and policy-design issues

The nature and practice of capital tax competition has important implications for tax-policy design. This section will consider implications for international efforts at greater tax-policy co-operation; implications for country decisions about corporate tax rates, rules and regimes; and implications regarding the interactions between the corporate and personal tax-bases.

International efforts

The presence of fiscal externalities across countries presents a powerful argument for greater international co-operation to address such fiscal spillovers. While there are few examples of supranational government entities capable of mediating competing concerns across countries, there is still a large potential for greater international co-operation to improve economic outcomes.

Presently, there are several efforts in this direction. In response to pressing concerns about income-shifting in OECD countries, evidenced by well publicised hearings in the US Congress and the UK Parliament, as well as priority in recent G8 and G20 meetings, the OECD has launched the BEPS project, where BEPS stands for 'base-erosion and profit-shifting'. The OECD is in the process of making concrete action recommendations to help countries address the problems of corporate profit-shifting; these will be released in phases over 2014 and 2015. This process is discussed in more detail in Eccleston and Smith (2016, Chapter Eight in this volume). The IMF has also recently issued a staff report, *Spillovers in International Taxation* (IMF 2014), which considers the nature of such fiscal spillovers and, in particular, how they affect developing countries. While these are welcome developments, there is not a consensus about their ultimate effectiveness in an environment in which tax-planners are often several steps ahead of new regulatory solutions.

---

19. This raises larger questions about the optimality of capital taxation more generally. While early models often deemed capital taxation undesirable, newer models with more realistic features have reached the conclusion that capital should not be taxed more lightly than labour. Examples are Conesa *et al.* 2009; Piketty and Saez 2012; and Farhi *et al.* 2012. See Clausing 2013 for a discussion of these papers.

Another mode of indirect international co-operation is the spread of policy ideas, as individual country 'best practices' may be adopted by 'follower' countries. Individual country efforts at corporate tax-base protection vary widely. Some countries' rules are much stricter than others and much can be learned from a more detailed examination of country experiences with base-protection rules.

One supranational effort worthy of mention is the European Union's attempt to develop a common consolidated corporate tax base (CCCTB). While this proposal is far from implementation, it is an important effort, focused on international co-operation about the definition of the corporate tax base. Under the CCCTB, it is envisaged that companies would divide their European tax base among member-states according to a system of formulary apportionment (FA). This would eliminate income-shifting among European Union member-country tax-bases, since the tax liability would be based on real factors (destination of sales, physical assets and employment/payroll), rather than where income is booked. However, the CCCTB's reach would be limited to the 'water's edge' of Europe and it was designed to be optional for companies.[20] Important related issues are discussed by Avi-Yonah (2016, Chapter Thirteen in this volume).

There are also other innovative proposals for greater international co-operation on tax policy, including Rixen (2016, Chapter Fifteen in this volume). Rixen envisages the creation of an International Tax Organization modeled in part after the World Trade Organization. An International Tax Organization could provide a forum for negotiations regarding international tax rules and work to resolve disputes regarding competing revenue claims and harmful tax competition.

Implications for national governments' tax-policy choices

In the presence of increasing international economic integration and the resulting tax-competition pressures, countries may be more tempted to lower their corporate tax rates, as lower rates will be rewarded by increased inward income-shifting (or decreased outward income-shifting). As documented above, there is substantial evidence that policy-makers respond to these incentives.

As discussed above, outward income-shifting may alleviate concerns regarding the *real* effects of high corporate tax rates but there are still substantial concerns about tax-base erosion. Measures such as strong CFC (controlled foreign corporation) laws and earnings-stripping laws may reduce the ability of multinational firms to shift income abroad with impunity. Indeed, Markle and Robinson (2012) find that countries with stronger CFC laws reduce the use of tax

20. It is also possible that individual countries adopting formulary apportionment unilaterally could lead to strong incentives for other countries to adopt formulary apportionment. The country(ies) adopting formulary apportionment would become tax havens from the perspective of other countries still using separate accounting, since income could be booked in FA countries without affecting the resulting tax liability in these countries. These incentives are discussed in greater detail in Avi-Yonah and Clausing 2008.

havens. Also, governments have substantial authority in their regulatory choices. For example, Shay (2014) describes measures that the US Treasury could take without additional legislation to stem income-shifting. In fact, the US 'check-the-box' rules were also an outcome of regulatory change, rather than legislation.

One possible concern regarding provisions that attempt to stem income-shifting is that such measures may perversely heighten real responses to tax-rate differences across countries. If mobile corporations can no longer move the income without moving the underlying activity, they may be more tax-sensitive in their real economic decisions about investment and employment. While this is a valid concern, one should also recall the longstanding finding in the public-finance literature about the greater responsiveness of financial measures (than real measures) to tax incentives. This hierarchy of behavioural response is discussed in Section 3 (and Footnote 7).

Some limited evidence is also provided by the experience of states in the US under formulary apportionment, discussed in Clausing 2014. Income-shifting is limited under formulary apportionment, since the shifting of paper profits between states does not change tax liabilities under formulary apportionment; instead, the tax base is simply apportioned to states based on their *national* income and formula factors that reflect the underlying economic activities in each state, typically sales, assets and payroll. However, while income-shifting is reduced under formulary apportionment, as found in Mintz and Smart 2004, one might be concerned about the tax-responsiveness of the formula factors themselves. Still, using the most comprehensive data and methods available, in Clausing 2014 I find that there is no evidence of large tax responses of formula factors to tax-burden differences among US states. While the applicability of the US state experience is limited, this nonetheless provides some reassuring evidence about the tax-sensitivity of real economic decisions.[21]

Implications for personal income tax

Some have suggested that more of the capital tax burden should be put on individual tax-payers instead of corporations. For example, Altshuler, Harris and Toder (2010) discuss the option of raising the tax rate on personal dividends and capital gains while lowering the corporate tax. This change would lessen international income-shifting incentives, if it is more difficult for individuals than corporations to avoid capital taxes. Still, this assumes that corporations have more opportunities for tax avoidance than individuals do. While likely, one should remember that individual income-tax avoidance and evasion is not trivial. As

21. On one hand, US states typically have lower tax rates than national economies; US state corporate tax rates averaged 7% in recent decades; this may lower the tax-sensitivity of real factors. On the other hand, tax-competition pressures are likely to be particularly heightened within countries, since competition is fiercer due to greater information flows, common currencies and common markets. Also, firms are likely more footloose within countries, since relocation across US state borders is easier and less complicated than international relocation.

discussed above, Zucman (2013) estimates that 8 per cent of the world financial wealth of households is held in tax havens, most of it unrecorded.

Also, if all taxation is done at the personal level, capital income that is held tax-free in pensions, endowments or non-profits would go untaxed. In the United States, Gravelle and Hungerford (Gravelle and Hungerford (2011) note that over 50 per cent of individual passive income is held in tax-exempt form through pensions, retirement accounts, life insurance annuities, and non-profits.

More generally, corporate tax protects the integrity of the individual income tax system, since if the corporate rate falls much below the top individual rate, the corporate form can provide tax-sheltering opportunities.[22] As discussed in Section 2, there is substantial evidence of income-shifting between the corporate/ non-corporate tax-bases, and this may confound estimates of the revenue effects of tax-rate changes. For example, lower corporate tax rates may generate more business activity in corporate form, reducing the revenue cost of the lower rate with respect to the corporate tax-base but simultaneously generating parallel revenue losses in the personal-income tax-base.

6. Conclusion

Theory predicts that national governments are likely to impose fiscal externalities on each other when setting tax rates on capital, since a relatively lower tax rate will lure mobile capital away from high-tax jurisdictions. Indeed, there is ample evidence that countries behave strategically in their tax-rate setting; that smaller and more open economies choose lower tax rates than their larger or more closed counterparts; and that corporate tax burdens, measured by both statutory and effective tax rates, have fallen substantially in recent decades, a time characterised by dramatic increases in international economic integration. Countries have also engaged in tax competition by creating favourable tax regimes, whereby some types of mobile income are more lightly taxed, or whereby tax avoidance is facilitated.

Indeed, multinational corporations are tax-sensitive in the location of their real economic activities, such as investment and employment, as well as in the arrangement of their global financial affairs in order to locate income in more lightly taxed jurisdictions. Evidence suggests that this financial responsiveness to tax-rate differences exceeds real responsiveness; tax competition has far more substantial consequences for government revenues than it does for the underlying capital stocks of countries. In part, the smaller effects on capital stocks are due to the globally integrated capital markets themselves. Tax-rate differences between countries are more likely to affect the *ownership patterns and financing* of the capital stock in particular countries than the *overall level* of the capital stock, since investment can take many forms.

22. In particular, depending on the relative tax rates of the top personal income-tax rate, the corporate tax rate and the tax rates on dividends and capital gains, business activity may be relatively tax-advantaged in corporate or non-corporate form. This point is explained clearly in Gravelle and Hungerford 2011.

However, the revenue consequences from tax competition are likely to be large and this has substantial implications for the distribution of tax revenues across countries. There are also important implications for the distributional effects of the underlying tax systems. To the extent that tax competition makes it more difficult to tax capital, it also makes it more difficult to address increases in income inequality through the tax system. Capital income is far more concentrated than labour income and tax-payers at the upper end of the income distribution are likely to have more flexibility in how they characterise their income.

This overview suggests several implications for tax-policy design. First, there are likely substantial gains from even modest international co-operation and harmonisation in elements of capital-tax policy. In particular, many countries may benefit from measures that stem corporate tax-base erosion; measures that align elements of the corporate tax base definition; and measures that reduce compliance and administrative burdens by clarifying the taxable location of corporate and capital income. Progress can be made through supranational governance in the case of the European Union, through international organisations that foster co-operation, or even through the spread of best practices in tax-policy design across countries.

Indeed, countries can take substantial measures on their own to stem tax-base erosion. For example, there is a large degree of heterogeneity regarding the strength of CFC laws, and countries with stronger CFC laws are likely to be more successful in stemming tax avoidance and the use of tax havens. Where there is political will, there is also much that can be done with legislative and regulatory measures.

Finally, it is important to remember the connection between different parts of the tax base. For example, cutting corporate rates in isolation may reduce revenue more than it appears, if it causes the corporate sector to grow relative to the non-corporate sector, since gains in the size of the corporate tax base will be offset by losses in the size of the personal tax base. Also, placing more of the tax burden on individuals is not a panacea, since individuals are also likely to engage in tax avoidance, which is especially feasible for the most wealthy individuals who hold the vast majority of capital assets. Further, a large part of capital income is held in tax-exempt form in, for example, pensions, endowments and retirement accounts. Since corporate tax is an important back-stop to individual income tax, taxing corporate income fairly and efficiently is an essential goal.

References

Adam, A. *et al.* (2013) 'The effect of globalization on capital taxation: what have we learned after 20 years of empirical studies?', *Journal of Macroeconomics* 35: 199–209.

Altshuler, R. and Goodspeed, T. J. (2014) 'Follow the leader? Evidence on European and US tax competition', *Public Finance Review* 43(4): doi: 10.1177/1091142114527781.

Altshuler, R. and Grubert, H. (2005) 'Governments and multinational corporations in the race to the bottom', *Tax Notes International* 110(8) (February): 459–74.

Altshuler, R. *et al.* (2010) 'Capital income taxation and progressivity in a global economy', *Virginia Tax Review* 30 (May): 1145–84.

Alvaredo, F. *et al.* (2013) 'The top 1 percent in international and historical perspective', *Journal of Economic Perspectives* 27(3): 3–20.

Auerbach, A. J. and Slemrod, J. (1997) 'The economic effects of the Tax Reform Act of 1986', *Journal of Economic Literature* 35(2): 589–632.

Avi-Yonah, R. S. (2016) 'A proposal for unitary taxation and formulary apportionment (UT+FA) to tax multinational enterprises', in Dietsch, P. and Rixen, T. (eds) *Global Tax Governance*, Colchester: ECPR Press.

Avi-Yonah, R. S. and Clausing, K. A. (2008) 'Reforming corporate taxation in a global economy: a proposal to adopt formulary apportionment', in Furman, J. and Bordoff, J. E. (eds) *Path to Prosperity: Hamilton Project ideas on income security, education, and taxes*, Washington, DC: Brookings Institution Press, pp. 319–44.

Azemar, C. *et al.* (2013) 'Testing tax competition': http://www.etsg.org/ETSG2013/Papers/286.pdf (accessed 23 June 2015).

Baldwin, R. and Krugman, P. (2004) 'Agglomeration, integration, and tax harmonisation', *European Economic Review* 48(1) (February): 1–23.

Borck, R. and Pflüger, M. (2006) 'Agglomeration and tax competition', *European Economic Review* 50(3): 647–68.

Boston Consulting Group (2014) *Global Wealth Report 2014: Riding a wave of growth*: https://www.bcgperspectives.com/content/articles/financial_institutions_business_unit_strategy_global_wealth_2014_riding_wave_growth/ (accessed 1 July 2015).

Bretschger, L. and Hettich, F. (2002) 'Globalisation, capital mobility and tax competition: theory and evidence for OECD countries', *European Journal of Political Economy* 18(4): 695–716.

Burman, L. E. (2012) 'Tax reform and the tax treatment of capital gains', Statement before the House Committee on Ways and Means and the Senate Committee on Finance, September.

Citizens for Tax Justice (2011) 'Corporate Taxpayers and Corporate Dodgers: 2008–2010', http://ctj.org/ctjreports/2011/11/corporate_taxpayers_corporate_tax_dodgers_2008–2010.php#.VZPYuuvyKnQ (last accessed 1 July 2015).

Clausing, K. (2007) 'Corporate tax revenues in OECD countries', *International Tax and Public Finance* 14: 115–33.

— (2008) 'Closer economic integration and corporate tax systems', *Global Economy Journal* 8(2): 1–30.

— (2009) 'Multinational tax avoidance and tax policy', *National Tax Journal* 57(4) (December): 703–25.

— (2011) 'The revenue effects of multinational firm income shifting', *Tax Notes* March 28: 1580–86.

— (2012) 'In search of corporate tax incidence', *Tax Law Review* 65(3): 433–72.

— (2013) 'The future of the corporate tax', *Tax Law Review* 66(4): 419–43.

— (2014) 'Lessons for international tax reform from the U.S. state experience under formulary apportionment', http://papers.ssrn.com/sol3/papers.cfm?abstract_id=2359724.

Conesa, J. C. *et al.* (2009) 'Taxing capital? Not a bad idea after all!', *American Economic Review* 99(1): 25–48.

Davies, R. B. and Voget, J. (2008) 'Tax competition in an Expanding European Union', Working Paper, University College Dublin, School of Economics.

de Mooij, R. A. (2005) 'Will corporate income taxation survive?', *De Economist* 153(September): 277–301.

de Mooij, R. A. and Ederveen, S. (2003) 'Taxation and foreign direct investment: a synthesis of empirical research', *International Tax and Public Finance* 10(November): 673–93.

— (2008) 'Corporate tax elasticities: a reader's guide to empirical findings', *Oxford Review of Economic Policy,* 24(4): 680–97.

Desai, M. and Dharmapala, D. (2009) 'Taxes, institutions and foreign diversification opportunities', *Journal of Public Economics* 93(5–6) (June): 703–14.

Devereux, M. P. *et al.* (2008) 'Do countries compete over corporate tax rates?', *Journal of Public Economics,* 92(5–6): 1210–35.

Djankov, S. *et al.* (2010) 'The effect of corporate taxes on investment and entrepreneurship', *American Economic Journal: Macroeconomics,* 2(3) (July): 31–64.

Eccleston, R. and Smith, H. (2016) 'The G20, BEPS and the future of international tax governance', in Dietsch, P. and Rixen, T. (eds) *Global Tax Governance*, Colchester: ECPR Press.

Farhi, E. *et al.* (2012) 'Non-linear capital taxation without commitment', *Review of Economic Studies,* 79(4): 1469–93.

Fuest, C. *et al.* (2005) 'Capital mobility and tax competition: a survey', *Foundations and Trends in Microeconomics* 1(1): 1–62.

Gordon, R. H. and MacKie-Mason, J. K. (1995) 'Why is there corporate taxation in a small open economy? The role of transfer pricing and income shifting', in Feldstein, M. *et al.* (eds) *The Effects of Taxation on Multinational Corporations*, Chicago, IL: University of Chicago Press, pp. 67–94.

Gordon, R. H. and Slemrod, J. (2000) 'Are "real" responses to taxes simply income shifting between corporate and personal tax bases?', in Slemrod, J. (ed.)

Does Atlas Shrug? The economic consequences of taxing the rich, Cambridge, Massachusetts: Harvard University Press.

Gravelle, J. C. (2010) *Corporate Tax Incidence: Review of general equilibrium estimates and analysis*, Congressional Budget Office Working Paper Series, Washington DC: Congressional Budget Office.

— (2013) *Tax Havens: International tax avoidance and evasion*, CRS Report for Congress, Washington, DC: Congressional Research Service.

Gravelle, J. G. and Hungerford, T. L. (2011) *Corporate Tax Reform: Issues for Congress*, CRS Report for Congress, Washington, DC: Congressional Research Service.

Gravelle, J. G. and Smetters, K. A. (2006) 'Does the open economy assumption really mean that labor bears the burden of a capital income tax?', *Advances in Economic Analysis and Policy* 6(1): article 3.

Harberger, A. C. (1995) 'The ABC's of corporate tax incidence: insights into the open economy case', in *Tax Policy and Economic Growth*, Washington DC: American Council for Capital Formation, pp. 51–73.

— (2008) 'Corporation tax incidence: reflections on what is known, unknown, and unknowable', in Diamond, J. and Zodrow, G. (eds) *Fundamental Tax Reform*, Cambridge, Massachusetts: MIT Press, pp. 283–307.

Haufler, A. and Wooton, I. (1999) 'Country size and tax competition for foreign direct investment', *Journal of Public Economics* 71(1): 121–39.

Haufler, A. *et al*. (2009) 'Economic integration and the relationship between profit and wage taxes', *Public Choice* 138(3–4): 423–46.

Helman, C. (2009) 'What the top U.S. companies pay in taxes', *Forbes*: http://www.forbes.com/2011/04/13/ge-exxon-walmart-apple-business-washington-corporate-taxes.html (accessed 1 July 2015).

Hong, Q. and Smart, M. (2010) 'In praise of tax havens: international tax planning and foreign direct investment', *European Economic Review* 54(1): 82–95.

International Monetary Fund (2014) *Spillovers in International Corporate Taxation*, IMF Policy Paper: http://www.imf.org/external/np/pp/eng/2014/050914.pdf (last accessed 1 July 2015).

Jacobson, M and Occhino, F. (2012) 'Labor's declining share of income and rising inequality', *Federal Reserve Bank of Cleveland Economic Commentary*, September.

Joint Committee on Taxation, staff of (2010) *Present Law and Background Related to Possible Income Shifting and Transfer Pricing*, report prepared for House Ways and Means Committee: https://www.jct.gov/publications.html?func=startdown&id=3692.

Johannesen, N. and Zucman, G. (2014) 'The end of bank secrecy? An evaluation of the G20 tax haven crackdown', *American Economic Journal: Economic Policy* 6(1): 65–91.

Keen, M. and Konrad, K. A. (2014) 'The theory of international tax competition and coordination', Working Paper of the Max Planck Institute for Tax Law and Public Finance No. 2012–06.

Kleinbard, E. (2011) 'The lessons of stateless income', *Tax Law Review*, 99–171.

Markle, K. and Robinson, L. (2012) 'Tax haven use across international tax regimes', Working Paper, November: http://www.sbs.ox.ac.uk/sites/default/files/Business_Taxation/Events/conferences/symposia/2012/markle.pdf (last accessed 1 July 2015).

Mintz, J. and Smart, M. (2004) 'Income shifting, investment, and tax competition: theory and evidence from provincial taxation in Canada', *Journal of Public Economics* 88: 1149–68.

Mintz, J. and Weichenrieder, A. (2010) *The Indirect Side of Direct Investment: Multinational company finance and taxation*, Cambridge, Massachusetts: MIT Press.

Mutti, J. H. (2003) *Foreign Direct Investment and Tax Competition*, Washington, DC: Institute for International Economics [Peterson Institute].

Piketty, T. (2014) *Capital in the Twenty-First Century*, Cambridge, Massachusetts: Harvard University Press.

Piketty, T. and Saez, E. (2012) *A Theory of Optimal Capital Taxation*, National Bureau of Economic Research Working Paper No. 17989, April.

Pirttila, J. and Selin, H. (2011) 'Income shifting within a dual income tax system: evidence from the Finnish tax reform of 1993', *Scandinavian Journal of Economics* 113(1): 120–44.

Randolph, W. C. (2006) *International Burdens of the Corporate Income Tax*, Congressional Budget Office Working Paper Series, August, Washington, DC: Congressional Budget Office.

Rixen, T. (2016) 'Institutional reform of global tax governance: a proposal', in Dietsch, P. and Rixen, T. (eds) *Global Tax Governance*, Colchester: ECPR Press.

Rodrik, D. (1997) *Has Globalization Gone Too Far?*, Washington DC: Institute for International Economics.

Shay, S. (2014) 'Mr. Secretary, take the tax juice out of corporate expatriations', *Tax Notes*, 144(473): http://papers.ssrn.com/sol3/papers.cfm?abstract_id=2473192 (accessed 1 July 2015).

Slemrod, J. and Bakija, J. (2008) *Taxing Ourselves*, Cambridge, Massachusetts: MIT Press.

Slemrod, J. and Wilson, J. D. (2009) 'Tax competition with parasitic tax havens', *Journal of Public Economics* 93(11–12): 1261–70.

Stewart, K. and Webb, M. (2006) 'International competition in corporate taxation: evidence from the OECD time series', *Economic Policy* 21(45): 153–201.

Thoresen, T. O. and Alstadsæter, A. (2010) 'Shifts in organizational form under a dual income tax system', *FinanzArchiv: Public Finance Analysis* 66(4): 384–418.

Wilson, J. D. (1999) 'Theories of tax competition', *National Tax Journal* 52(2): 269–304.

Wilson, J. D. and Wildasin, D. E. (2004) 'Capital tax competition: bane or boon?', *Journal of Public Economics* 88(6): 1065–91.

Winner, H. (2005) 'Has tax competition emerged in OECD Countries? Evidence from panel data', *International Tax and Public Finance* 12(5): 667–87.

Zodrow, G. R. (2003) 'Tax competition and tax coordination in the European Union', *International Tax and Public Finance* 10(6): 651–71.

— (2010) 'Capital mobility and capital tax competition', *National Tax Journal* 63(4): 865–901.

Zucman, G. (2013) 'The missing wealth of nations: are Europe and the U.S. net debtors or net creditors?', *Quarterly Journal of Economics* 128(3): 1321–64.

— (2014) 'Taxing across borders: tracking personal wealth and corporate profits', *Journal of Economic Perspectives* 28(4): 121–48.

Chapter Three

Winners and Losers of Tax Competition

Philipp Genschel and Laura Seelkopf

1. Who wins from tax competition?

The growing integration of the world's economies since the 1970s, progress in trade liberalisation and capital decontrol and rapid innovations in information, communication and transport technologies have made it easier to move goods, services, capital and jobs across national borders and, hence, more difficult to subject them to national taxes. Taxpayers can, in many cases, avoid or evade domestic tax by shifting the tax base to a lower-tax country. Exit has become a viable option, a credible implicit threat. Just think of the recent tax avoidance scandals involving General Electrics in the US or Starbucks in the UK (Walsh 2015). Governments can no longer turn a fiscal profit on mobile assets and activities – most importantly, real, financial and human capital – but have to vie for it through low tax rates. The result is a competitive race to the bottom in taxation that produces many losers and few winners: national governments lose to international markets; labour loses to capital; poor loses to rich. This, at least, is the conventional wisdom that informs much public and academic debate on the distributive consequences of economic globalisation.

While this conventional wisdom has a certain intuitive plausibility, it is quite puzzling from a political-economy perspective. If tax competition does indeed produce few winners and many losers, how can it be stable? Why don't the many losers gang up against the few winners to stop the competition? Their chances of success should be good – at least in democracies, where numbers count. Here the wage-earning majority with little or no capital income should be able to pressure the government into both keeping capital tax rates up and seeking international tax co-operation. Since all governments would be subject to the same domestic pressure, intergovernmental agreement should be easy. Yet, it is not. The story of international co-operation on tax competition is long and unhappy (see Genschel and Schwarz 2011: 359–63 for a short review). Even in the EU, joint action to stop tax competition is largely elusive. Why?

In this chapter, we argue that tax competition is resilient because its distributive effects are more ambiguous than the conventional wisdom assumes. We note two ambiguities in particular. First, even though tax competition undermines the revenue-raising capacity of the group of competing states as a whole, it may actually increase the revenue-raising capacity of some group members. Second, while tax competition decreases labour (net) income across the group of competing states as a whole, it may increase labour income in some competing states. Obviously, those governments that win in fiscal terms, and those workers who win in income terms, have little incentive to support high capital taxation nationally or internationally. This helps explain the political stability of tax competition even in a world in which big capital has little immediate control of the capital tax rate.

Granted the distributive effects of tax competition are ambiguous, when will it benefit governments and workers and when will it harm them? We argue that the probability of winning or losing varies due to two country-specific factors.[1] On the one hand, it depends on a country's structural position in the international economy and, more specifically, on country size. As the standard economic model of tax competition (Bucovetsky 1991; Kanbur and Keen 1993) shows, there is a structural 'advantage of "smallness"' (Wilson 1999: 278) in tax competition that privileges governments and workers in small countries over governments and workers in large countries. Second, regime differences matter. Governments and workers in well governed democracies are more likely to gain from tax competition if their country is small, and more likely to cope with the reverse effects of tax competition if their country is large, than governments and workers in poorly governed autocracies.[2] In short, then, next to big capital, the winners of tax competition include the governments and workers of small, well governed democracies. The losers are workers in large countries, especially if their countries are autocratic and poorly governed.

Section 2 provides the conceptual basis of this analysis. Sections 3 to 5 trace the fiscal and distributive effects of tax competition in three country-groups: the advanced welfare states of the OECD area; tax havens; and the group of least developed countries. Section 6 concludes.

2. Tax competition with differences in country size and regime type

The phrase 'tax competition' refers to an intergovernmental bidding contest for an internationally mobile tax base. In its starkest form it resembles a 'standard prisoner's dilemma' (Hallerberg 1996: 328) with two countries sharing one mobile tax base ('capital'). The tax policies of both countries are interdependent: high taxes in country A swell country B's revenues by pushing a larger share of the mobile tax base towards B; low taxes in A depress B's revenues by poaching elements of the tax base from B. These interdependencies ('fiscal externalities') trigger a 'race to the bottom' in taxation as each country tries to appropriate a disproportionate share of the mobile capital tax base. In equilibrium, tax rates

1. There are of course also other factors such as culture, language, legal heritage, or partisanship, which influence tax-rate choices. Yet country size and political regime are in our view the two most important drivers, which is why we focus on them.

2. Obviously, regime type (democracy and autocracy) and the quality of government are different variables. A more thorough investigation would analyse their effect separately. However, as we will argue later, both variables are highly correlated. Democratic countries are significantly more likely to be well governed than autocracies. Hence, for convenience, we treat the quality of government as an aspect of regime type here.

are lower in both countries than they would otherwise be, resulting in lower tax revenues and/or a shift of the tax burden to immobile tax bases (*see* Clausing 2016, Chapter Two in this volume, for a brief review of the theoretical literature).

The normative implications of the baseline model are controversial (see Edwards and Keen 1996). Some argue that the competitive race to the bottom increases efficiency and equity by constraining the capacity of predatory governments to over-tax domestic societies. Others fear that tax competition undermines efficiency and equity by constraining the ability of benevolent governments to supply optimal levels of tax-financed public goods and to adjust the tax burden of capital and labour to majoritarian preferences.

The baseline model has been extended in various ways. We highlight two: country size and domestic regime type. Consider country size first (see, for example, Bucovetsky 1991; Kanbur and Keen 1993). In a symmetric setting of same-sized countries, all countries face the same incentive to cut taxes and all countries suffer equal welfare losses in the noncooperative equilibrium. In an asymmetric setting, however, the smaller country faces stronger incentives to cut tax rates than the larger country and suffers a smaller welfare-loss in the competitive equilibrium. Indeed, if the difference in country size is large enough, the smaller country is better off under tax competition than in its absence. There is a structural 'advantage of "smallness" ' (Wilson 1999: 278) in tax competition.

Why is small size a competitive advantage? Intuitively, in pondering capital tax cuts governments have to weigh the costs in terms of lost revenue from domestic capital against the benefits associated with capital inflows from the other country. In a small country with a narrow domestic capital tax base and lots of foreign capital to attract, the cost–benefit ratio is more likely to be favourable than in a large country with lots of domestic capital to lose and little foreign capital to win. Hence, all else equal, the small country has a stronger incentive to cut taxes. In the noncooperative equilibrium, it undercuts the large country's tax rate and ends up with a disproportionately large share of the mobile capital tax base. This does not necessarily imply higher capital tax revenues (because the small country's capital tax rate is low and possibly close to zero). But it potentially stimulates investment, pushes up the capital–labour ratio, increases labour demand and raises employment and wages; and thus it indirectly fuels tax revenues from labour and consumption. In this way, it is not only capital that profits from tax competition; the government also gains in terms of fiscal revenue and labour gains in income terms (through higher employment and wages) – but only in the small country. The bill is paid by the government and the workers of the large country. They suffer twice from the tax-driven capital flight to the small country: first in terms of less tax revenue from the reduced domestic capital stock; second in terms of depressed investment, labour demand and tax revenues.

As a first empirical cut, Figure 3.1 compares the corporate tax rates of 110 countries in 2010. The rates are significantly related to country size, as the baseline model predicts: small countries like Cyprus and Ireland undercut the rates of large countries such as Japan and the United States. However, the correlation is far from perfect because some small countries such as Fiji and Libya have substantially

Figure 3.1: Corporate tax rates and country size across the world, 2010

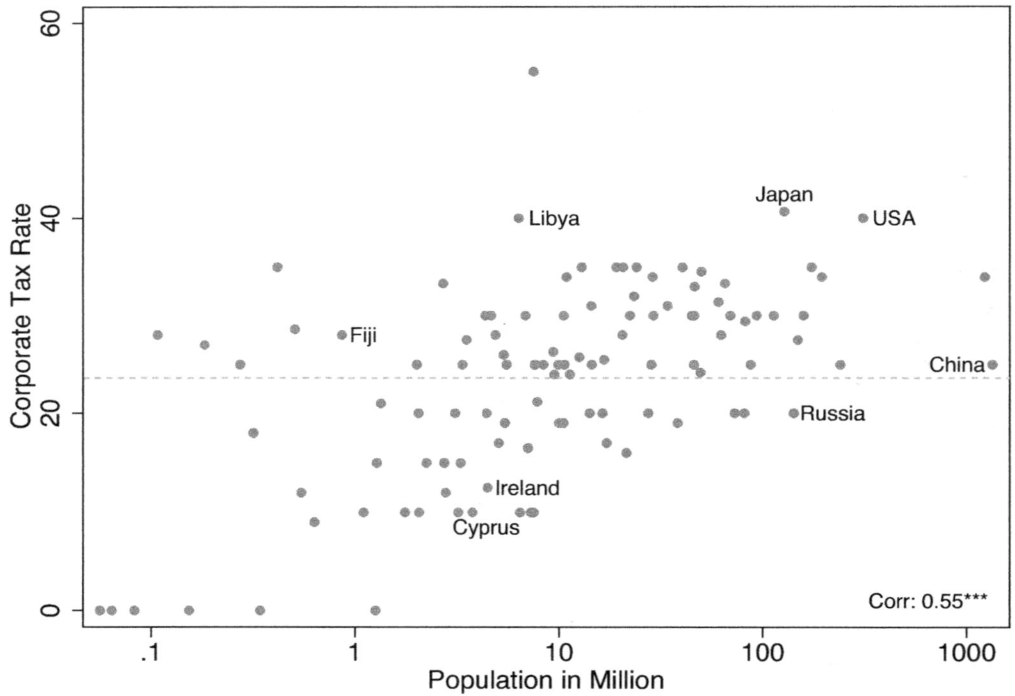

Data sources: KPMG and World Bank.
Note: The dotted line represents the average tax rate.

higher rates than much larger countries such as China and Russia. Why do not all countries follow the logic of the baseline model? The answer, we argue next, is because of differences in regime type.

The baseline model implicitly assumes competing countries to be well governed democracies. Yet, obviously, a fair number of countries world-wide are neither democratic nor well governed. This matters for tax competition because autocracies are generally less willing, and poorly governed countries less able, to compete (Genschel *et al.* 2015; Bucovetsky 2014).

Consider the willingness to compete first: democracy is government 'of the people, by the people, for the people', in Lincoln's famous definition. Political leaders who want to stay in power in a democracy have to serve the interests of the majority of the people as represented, under a range of plausible conditions, by the median voter. The median voter is usually poorer than average and derives most of her income from wages. Since the baseline model predicts that the median voter can profit from tax competition if the country is small but will suffer from tax competition if the country is large, the willingness of democratic leaders to engage in competitive tax-cutting varies systematically by country size: it is high in small democracies like Ireland and Cyprus; it is low in large democracies like the United States and Japan. Autocracy, by contrast, is government of the elite, by the elite, for the elite. Political leaders who want to stay in power have to serve elite interests, irrespective of what the implications for the median voter are. The ruling elites' preference for capital taxation is not systematically related to country size. Small autocracies may want to keep capital taxes high because dictators prefer an immediate pay rise for the military to higher long-term economic growth (as in the case of Fiji), or because high capital taxes are a handy instrument for rewarding loyal capital owners through selective tax exemptions (Dharmaphala and Hines 2009). Large autocracies may want to cut taxes because this benefits state-owned capital (Russia and China) or because the rulers depend on foreign capital (Kazakhstan). Depending on the structure of the winning coalition, an efficient adjustment to international tax competition may simply be politically unattractive for autocratic governments. This reduces the general willingness of autocracies to compete.

Turn to the ability to compete next. Well governed countries score low on corruption and have a fairly effective tax administration operating under the rule of law. Poorly governed countries lack these features and, as a consequence, can offer fewer guarantees to investors against the future expropriation of their assets, including indirectly through arbitrary tax hikes, corruption or embezzlement. This reduces the ability of these countries to attract capital inflows through low taxation because capital-owners engaging in cross-border tax avoidance and evasion tend to be risk averse. This is not only because cross-border evasion and avoidance involves inherently risky investments: direct investments in location-specific production facilities; direct investments in service operations acting as receiving ends of international profit-shifting within multi-national corporations (holding companies, financial services companies, headquarters services, sales centres and so on); as well as portfolio investments that investors conceal from tax authorities at home and therefore cannot easily repatriate. It is also because tax avoiders and

Table 3.1: Fiscal and policy characteristics of LDCs, OECD20 and tax havens, 2010

	LDCs[5]	OECD20[5]	Tax havens	Rest of world
Corporate tax rate[1]	32.4	28.7	14.9	23.9
Population in millions[2]	19	45	1	46
Voice and accountability[3]	-0.7	1.3	0.7	-0.1
Quality of government[3]	-0.8	1.3	0.7	-0.1
GDPpC in constant USD (2000er)[2]	672	26,590	13,496	4,654
Government expenditure (% of GDP)[4]	29	48	36	33

[1] KPMG's corporate and indirect tax rate surveys 2007–11.
[2] World Bank: http://data.worldbank.org/indicator.
[3] World Bank: http://info.worldbank.org/governance/wgi/index.aspx#home. Quality of government reflects the mean of all indicators with the exception of 'voice and accountability'.
[4] IMF *World Economic Outlook*.
[5] Please note that countries which are considered to be tax havens and, at the same time, LDCs or OECD members are counted as tax havens only for the purpose of this table.

evaders usually cannot count on the assistance of the home country they defraud if their host country, in turn, defrauds them. Given the risk-averseness of tax-avoiding or -evading capital, poorly governed economies have to offer larger tax cuts in order to attract the same volume of inflow (or to retain the same amount of mobile domestic capital) than well governed countries (Li 2009). As a consequence, tax competition is more costly and less rewarding for them. At any country size and tax level, poorly governed countries gain less in terms of capital inflows and suffer more in terms of capital outflows. As empirical analyses show, well governed jurisdictions attract significantly more inward investment than less well governed jurisdictions with similar tax levels (Dharmaphala and Hines 2009: 1065).

Obviously, the form and the quality of government are not perfectly related. Yet, in one respect at least, democracies tend to be better governed than autocracies. The rule of law is a constitutive element of democratic government but is alien to autocratic government because, in an autocracy, everything is ultimately at the discretion of ruling elites. This tends to increase the credibility of property-rights guarantees in democracies and to reduce the credibility of autocratic guarantees. This is why even capricious dictators like Mobuto Sese Seko (dictator of former Zaire, now Democratic Republic of Congo) prefer keeping their loot in sober democracies like Switzerland to entrusting it to other capricious dictators. In fact, the World Bank's 'voice and accountability' and 'rule of law' indicators are highly and significantly correlated (0.81*** for our country sample in 2010). Also a broad index of government quality (including measures of corruption, rule of law, political stability, and government effectiveness) is highly correlated with the regime-type measure of 'voice and accountability' (*see* Table 3.1). This allows us to treat government quality as an aspect of regime type in this chapter.

Figure 3.2: Corporate tax rate and country size by regime type, 2010

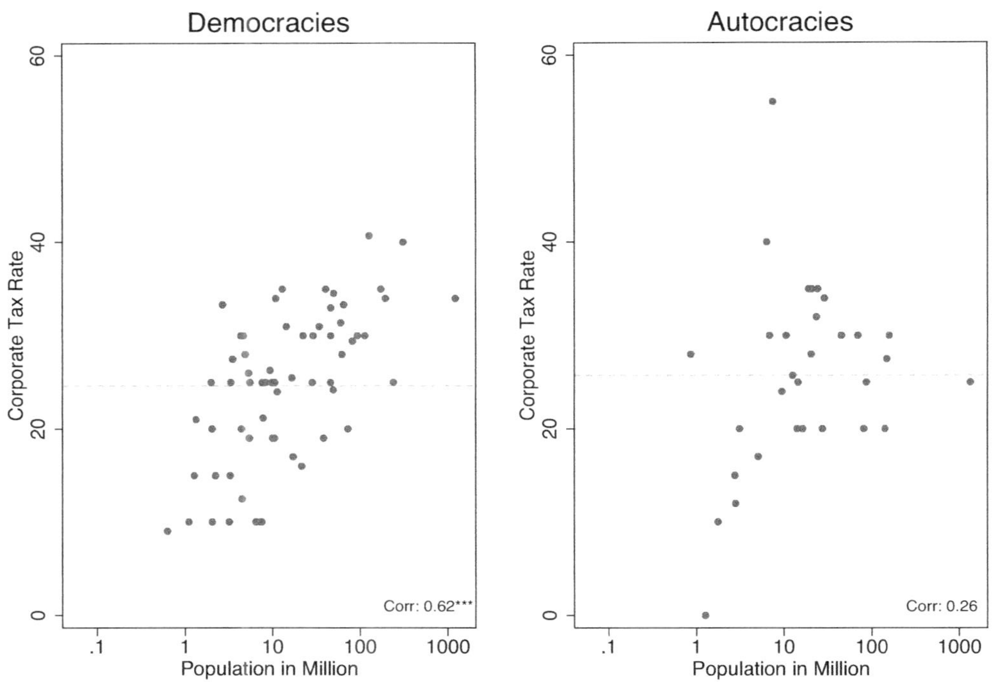

Data sources: KPMG, World Bank, and Polity IV Project.

Figure 3.2 provides some preliminary evidence for the influence of regime-type differences on competitive behaviour. It shows that corporate tax rates are strongly and significantly associated with country size in (more often than not well governed) democracies. In (often poorly governed) autocracies, by contrast, there is no significant correlation. Dictators don't compete.

3. Does tax competition undermine the welfare state in OECD countries?

While obvious differences exist between OECD countries[3] in terms of variety of capitalism (liberal *versus* co-ordinated), welfare regime (residual, Christian-democratic, social-democratic, southern) or system of democracy (parliamentary *versus* presidential; federal *versus* unitary), they all have important features in common: they are rich, they are democratic and fairly well governed and they have a large welfare state.

The question that came to preoccupy important strands of the political economy literature in the 1980s and after was whether the rich, tax-heavy welfare states of the OECD area will survive in an integrated international economy. Simplifying greatly, there are two views on this issue (for brief reviews, see Garrett and Mitchell 2001; Genschel 2004; Busemeyer 2009). On the one hand, there is the so-called *efficiency thesis*, which claims that economic integration gradually pulls the fiscal rug from under national welfare states: as rampant international tax competition eats into national tax revenues, governments lose the fiscal wherewithal to fund extensive welfare programmes. This leads to cutbacks and permanent austerity. Workers are stripped of their social protection, including protection against the negative income risks associated with globalisation and tax competition. On the other hand, there is the so-called *compensation thesis*. This thesis doubts that capital and other tax bases are as mobile as the proponents of the efficiency thesis suppose. Competitive constraints on governments' revenue-raising capacity are mild at best. Also, more importantly, to the extent that economic globalisation actually exposes workers to negative income and employment risks, they are hypothesised to use their voting power to demand additional social protection from the welfare state. Governments are forced to defend or even expand their revenues. Thus, rather than undermining national taxation and welfare policy, economic globalisation buttresses it. Globalisation and tax competition can only unfold if, and to the extent that, the welfare state compensates wage-earning median voters for their real or perceived losses.

While both theses contain important elements of truth, they suffer from the same defect. They neglect the conditioning effect of country size and therefore conceive of economic globalisation and international tax competition only as a

3. In our analysis we focus on 23 core OECD countries: Australia, Austria, Belgium, Canada, Denmark, Finland, France, Germany, Greece, Iceland, Ireland, Italy, Japan, Luxembourg, the Netherlands, New Zealand, Norway, Portugal, Spain, Sweden, Switzerland, United Kingdom and the United States. Please note that Ireland, Luxembourg and Switzerland also appear on the tax-haven list (*see* Section 4).

Figure 3.3: Size matters: corporate tax rate, corporate tax revenue, social-security expenditure and net lending/borrowing in the OECD over time, weighted and unweighted averages

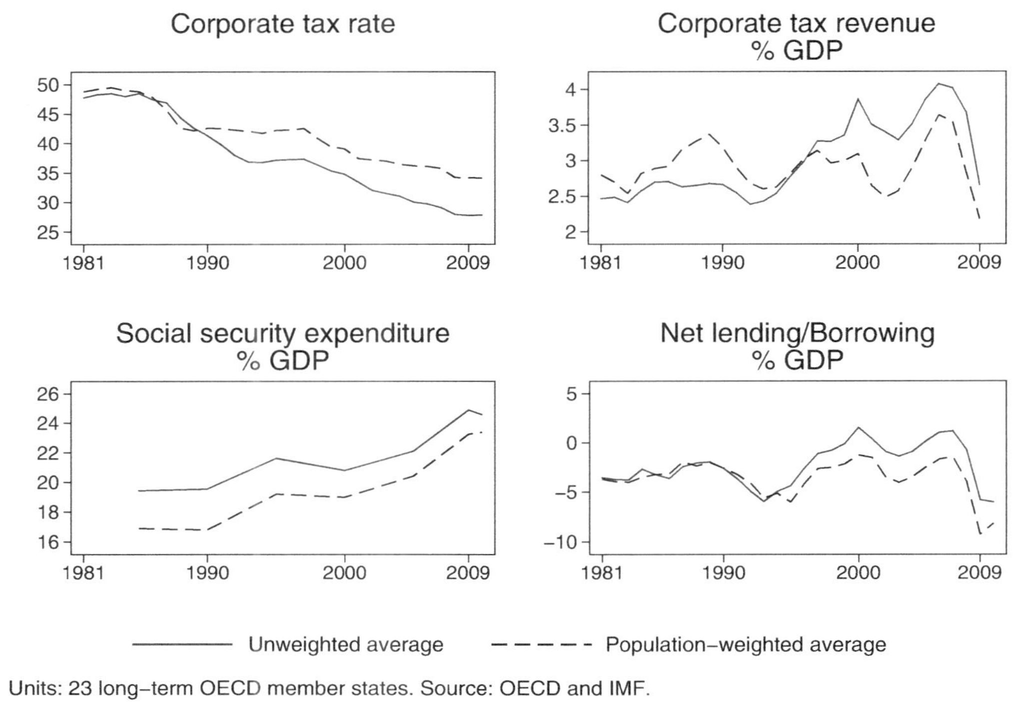

Data sources: OECD and IMF

source of problems for the welfare state – restricted revenues (efficiency thesis) and/or increased expenditure requirements (compensation thesis) – but not as a potential solution. Yet, as the economic baseline model suggests, tax competition may actually unburden the welfare state in small countries by increasing revenues (*contra* the efficiency thesis) and reducing the need for social compensation (*contra* the compensation thesis). Figure 3.3 provides some simple statistics to support this view.

As the top-left graph in Figure 3.3 shows, corporate tax rates have fallen sharply in OECD countries over the past 30 years. While the spread of neo-liberal ideas of 'market-conforming' taxation certainly fuelled this trend (Steinmo 2003; Swank 2006), there is little doubt that corporate tax competition was the main driver. There is extensive evidence that foreign direct investments and, even more so, corporate paper-profits have become highly mobile and sensitive to cross-country tax differentials (*see* Clausing 2016, Chapter Two in this volume). There is also evidence that governments strategically compete for corporate tax base (see, for example, Genschel and Schwarz 2011 for a review of the empirical literature). Finally, the diverging trends in the unweighted and the population-weighted average OECD corporate tax rate[4] testify to the influence of tax competition (Figure 3.3). While these averages hardly differed during the 1980s, suggesting that country size had no effect on corporate-tax-rate choice during that time, the unweighted average has fallen consistently faster since the 1990s and is now substantially lower than the weighted average: small OECD countries undercut the corporate tax rates of large OECD countries, as the economic baseline model would predict. There is a general race to the bottom in corporate tax rates (in line with the efficiency thesis) but the small countries race faster.

Yet, despite their substantially lower corporate tax rates, the small OECD countries realise substantially higher corporate tax revenues. As the top-right graph of Figure 3.3 shows, the unweighted average increased from roughly 2.5 per cent of GDP over the 1980s to about 3.5 per cent of GDP over the 2000s; the population-weighted average remained essentially unchanged at 2.9 per cent.[5] This is in line with the economic baseline model: tax competition enhances the revenue-raising capacity of small countries and constrains that of large countries.[6] Yet it is at odds with the efficiency thesis because it suggests that small countries may even gain from international competition in fiscal terms.

4. In the unweighted average, the corporate tax rates of the United States and Luxembourg count equally. In the population-weighted average, the rate of the United States counts much more than that of Luxembourg.

5. A similar picture emerges if corporate tax revenues are scaled by total tax revenues rather than GDP.

6. Why doesn't the weighted average actually fall? Various factors have propped up corporate tax revenues, including a substantial increase in the size of the underlying macro-economic tax base (share of profit income in national income) since the 1980s (Bassanini and Manfredi 2012) and a partial 'cannibalisation' of the personal income tax. Since corporate tax rates have generally fallen faster than top personal income tax rates since the 1980s, the incentive for domestic tax-base-shifting from the personal to the corporate sector has increased. In part, at least, the resilience of corporate tax revenues is due to the anaemia of personal income taxation (e.g. de Moij and Edeveen 2008).

Social-security expenditures have risen substantially since the 1980s (Figure 3.3, bottom-left graph) as the compensation thesis would lead us to expect in an era of increased economic openness. Interestingly, however, the population-weighted average has grown more rapidly, gradually decreasing its difference from the unweighted average. Put differently: the larger OECD member-states have increased their social spending relatively faster than their smaller peers. Arguably, the positive knock-on effects of tax-induced capital inflows on growth and employment mitigate the demand for additional social compensation. In other words, small OECD countries have profited from increased integration and tax competition, not only in fiscal terms but also in terms of a relatively lower problem-load on the welfare state (at a given level of openness).

The bottom-right graph of Figure 3.3 corroborates this view. It shows that large OECD member states have run consistently higher budget deficits than small OECD member-states for the past 20 years (the unweighted average of the budgetary balance is consistently higher than the weighted average). Apparently, the latter were better able to fund their spending requirements by tax revenue than the former. Arguably, tax competition was an important factor behind this discrepancy. Statistical evidence suggests that high corporate tax revenues are significantly associated with low deficits in OECD countries (Genschel and Schwarz 2013: 72). Higher corporate tax revenues did not only prop up revenues. Small countries also profited from the positive effect of inward capital flows on employment, wages and asset prices and the associated increase in non-capital tax revenues and relative decrease in demand for social compensation. As Hannes Winner has shown, small OECD countries have lower capital *and* labour taxes than large ones, all else equal (Winner 2005).

We draw two preliminary conclusions. First, tax competition has constrained national tax-rate choice in corporate taxation. Second, the constraint was fiscally beneficial for small countries but fiscally detrimental for large countries. The former profited from an expansion of the domestic tax base and a relative reduction of the demand for social compensation; the latter suffered from the reverse effects. The evidence does not allow for any clear-cut inferences about the distributive consequences of tax competition for labour. Our argument would suggest that small-country labour profited through higher employment levels and wages at the expense of labour in large countries. This view is corroborated by anecdotal evidence that aggressive corporate tax-cutting policies often enjoy support from left-of-centre parties in small countries like Austria, Denmark or Ireland (Genschel *et al.* 2015: 15). Labour in large OECD countries loses from the competition. However, the relatively steep increase in social-security expenditure in these countries suggests that these losses are at least partly compensated by the welfare state.

In conclusion, tax competition does not fatally undermine the welfare state in OECD countries. For small countries, the competition is actually a boon and large countries are able to cope with the adverse consequences by raising more revenue from alternative sources (including government debt and taxes on labour and consumption).

4. Does tax competition make tax havens rich?

One crucial assumption underlying our argument so far is that capital stimulates economic activity in the country of (source) taxation. This assumption is unproblematic as long as countries compete over real investment in productive assets. It is less straightforward, however, when the competition is about financial assets (bonds, bank claims, equity, corporate paper-profits, intangible assets and so on) that are not directly and physically tied to economic activity (*see* Clausing 2016, Chapter Two in this volume). High-tax countries would still lose in revenue terms (because domestic corporations evacuate their profits through international tax-planning) but they would not necessarily lose real investment (because as long as corporations can move profits to low-tax countries, they do not have to move the underlying profit-generating activities). Low-tax countries would attract financial capital. But it is unclear to what extent they can profit fiscally (because their capital taxes are low) or economically (because the booking of financial claims for tax purposes generates little economic activity). Can small countries still gain from this type of competition? Our hunch is that they can if only they are small enough.

To explore this hunch we focus on the group of roughly forty countries that are usually considered to be tax havens by academics and international institutions (see, for example, Dharmaphala and Hines 2009; Palan *et al.* 2010: 41–4)[7]. These tax havens share three important characteristics. First, they are very small. On average, they have a population of only 1.18 million people. The median size is even smaller, at only slightly over 100,000 people. The smallest tax haven, Niue, has a population of just 1260 people. Second, most tax havens are democratic and fairly well governed. On average, they score significantly higher than the rest of the world on the World Bank's indictors of 'rule of law', 'regulatory quality', 'government effectiveness' and 'control of corruption'. Also, perhaps more surprising, tax havens do significantly better than the rest of the world in terms of 'political stability' and 'voice and accountability'. Tax havens are not usually autocracies, Singapore notably excepted. Third, tax havens focus primarily on attracting paper profits and financial assets, simply because they are too small to absorb significant real investment.

Tax havens compete mostly on low income and wealth taxes. Some, such as Bermuda and the Cayman Islands, levy no corporate or personal income taxes at all. Others combine high statutory rates with generous preferential tax regimes for

7. These are Andorra, Anguilla, Antigua and Barbuda, Aruba, Bahamas, Bahrain, Barbados, Belize, Bermuda, British Virgin Islands, Cayman Islands, Channel Islands, Cook Islands, Cyprus, Dominica, Gibraltar, Grenada, Hong Kong, Ireland, Isle of Man, Jordan, Lebanon, Liberia, Liechtenstein, Luxembourg, Macao, Maldives, Malta, Marshall Islands, Mauritius, Monaco, Montserrat, Nauru, Netherlands Antilles, Niue, Panama, Saint Kitts and Nevis, Saint Lucia, Saint Vincent and the Grenadines, Samoa, San Marino, Seychelles, Singapore, Switzerland, Tonga, Turks and Caicos Islands, Vanuatu and the Virgin Islands (US). Due to data limitations, not all tax havens listed here could always be included in the analysis. *See* Meinzer 2016 (Chapter Twelve) for a discussion of the use of tax-haven lists.

Figure 3.4: Growth and income across tax havens, OECD countries and rest of world

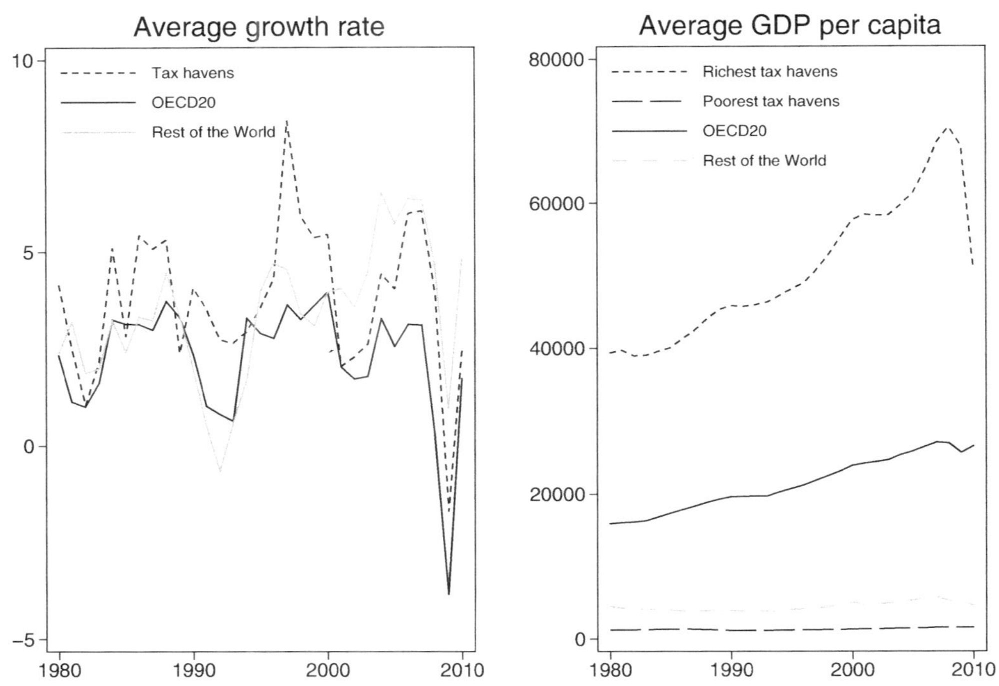

Notes: OECD-20 refers to the OECD-23 countries listed in Footnote 3, minus Ireland, Switzerland and Luxembourg, which are counted as tax havens for the purposes of this figure. The five richest tax havens are Switzerland, Luxembourg, Bermuda, Liechtenstein and Monaco. The five poorest tax havens are Liberia, Vanuatu, Samoa, Tonga and Jordan.

Data source: World Bank

foreign investors. Malta, for instance, complements a corporate rate of 35 per cent with extensive tax preferences for foreign-owned holding and shipping companies. On average, tax-haven corporate tax rates are only half of what they are in OECD countries – 15 as compared to 29 per cent (2010). Many tax havens also compete on secrecy: they adopt stringent secrecy provisions in order to assist foreign tax-evaders in concealing their tax-haven income at home, such as, for instance, banking secrecy legislation as in Switzerland, Singapore or the Cayman Islands, or investment vehicles designed to disguise the identity of the beneficial owner, as in the cases of the Liechtenstein trust, the Panamanian foundation or the St Kitts and Nevis bearer-share business company.

Various empirical studies find that tax havens are very successful in attracting mobile foreign capital. According to the United Nations Conference on Trade and Development (UNCTAD), these countries receive almost a third of global foreign direct investment – most of it, of course, just being routed through (Palan *et al.* 2010: 53). The reported profits of tax-haven subsidiaries greatly exceed those of companies in high-tax economies, indicating their use for profit-shifting operations out of high-tax locations. James Hines finds, for instance, that tax havens account for 30 per cent of the foreign income of US companies even though they only represent 0.8 per cent of the world population outside the United States (Hines 2004: table 1). Based on IMF data, Gabriel Zucman (2013) estimates that 8 per cent of global household net financial wealth is held unrecorded in tax havens. Other estimates suggest that the world's 'high net-worth individuals' hold up to a third of their wealth in tax havens (Palan *et al.* 2010: 62).

Does the flow-through of financial capital increase economic activity in tax havens? At the very least, it boosts demand for financial services. Financial services are associated with highly skilled jobs, contribute to human-capital formation and are subject to considerable agglomeration economies. If countries are very small, as tax havens typically are, this effect alone may be enough to improve growth significantly. There is data to support this view.

According to Hines (2004), tax havens enjoy a significant growth dividend. Indeed, as Figure 3.4 shows (left graph), tax havens have grown consistently faster than OECD countries over the past thirty years. It also shows, however, that tax havens have lost their growth advantage over non-OECD countries. Since the early 2000s, the average growth of tax havens is consistently lower than that of the non-OECD rest of the world, due perhaps to increased competition between them and/or to increased intra-OECD tax competition reducing the relative tax advantage of tax havens. As Figure 3.4 also shows, there is huge variance in the tax-haven experience. While the five richest tax havens for which time-series data is available have seen their *per capita* GDP (GDPpC) increase rapidly since the mid-1980s, to more than twice the OECD average in the late 2000s, the five poorest havens remain stuck in poverty. One important reason is that they lack the strong governance institutions that are necessary to attract tax-shy foreign capital and wealth. Note also that the rich tax havens suffered from a more dramatic collapse of GDPpC in the wake of the financial crisis that began in 2007 than did other countries.

Being a tax haven is no panacea for economic misery. This does not imply, however, that better growth strategies are available for small, remote island economies such as Vanuatu or Tonga, or that better strategies for recovery are available for crisis-hit havens such as Ireland or the Cayman Islands. Indeed, international organisations often encourage small, resource-poor LDCs to embrace tax-haven strategies as a means for accelerating development (see, for example, UNCTAD 2012). And in rich but crisis-stricken havens there is little support for a change of tack. In Ireland, for instance, a broad political coalition rejected Franco-German proposals to make a European bail-out contingent on an increase in the Irish corporate tax rate (Irish Government 2010: 100). Likewise, the Cayman Islands rejected calls from the UK government to introduce income taxes to meet revenue shortfalls (Ogier 2012). The staunch domestic support for aggressive low-tax strategies reflects the logic of asymmetric tax competition: tax-haven labour has more to gain from inflows of foreign capital than from redistribution of domestic capital. The costs of this strategy are externalised on the governments and wage-earners in large countries. The losses for these actors are potentially large. Kim Clausing (2016, Chapter Two in this volume) estimates, for instance, that profit-shifting by multinational firms has reduced the corporate tax revenues of the United States by as much as 60 to 90 billion USD in 2008.

In conclusion, tax competition does indeed seem to be a strategy for making very small, reasonably well governed and democratic countries rich. Unfortunately, less than 1 per cent of the world's population live in tax havens and benefit from this effect. Many more people live in poor countries. The group of least developed countries (LDCs) alone accounts for 14 per cent of the global population. How does tax competition affect the governments and citizens of these countries?

5. Does tax competition keep the least developed countries poor?

Least developed countries[8] (LDCs) are poor, often non-democratic and usually badly governed. Poverty makes these countries potential winners from tax competition: given their capital scarcity, they are small players in global capital markets; given their abundant labour supply, they should profit greatly from tax-induced capital inflows. Bad and non-democratic government, by contrast, makes them potential losers from tax competition. It makes them unattractive for tax-shy capital from abroad. It makes them fiscally dependent on easy tax handles such as the corporate tax – corporate profits are usually concentrated in a small number of

8. According to the UN definition (*see* http://unohrlls.org/about-ldcs/criteria-for-ldcs/) the list of least developed countries includes Afghanistan, Angola, Bangladesh, Benin, Bhutan, Burkina Faso, Burundi, Cambodia, Central African Republic, Chad, Comoros, Democratic Republic of the Congo, Djibouti, Equatorial Guinea, Eritrea, Ethiopia, Gambia, Guinea, Guinea-Bissau, Haiti, Kiribati, Lao People's Democratic Republic, Lesotho, Liberia, Madagascar, Malawi, Mali, Mauritania, Mozambique, Myanmar, Nepal, Niger, Rwanda, Samoa, São Tomé and Príncipe, Senegal, Sierra Leone, Solomon Islands, Somalia, Sudan, Timor-Leste, Togo, Tuvalu, Uganda, United Republic of Tanzania, Vanuatu, Yemen, Zambia. Due to data limitations, not all countries could always be included in the analysis.

large, conspicuous corporations – and thus constrains their ability to offer low tax rates to foreign investors. And it obstructs their capacity to cope with the negative consequences of tax competition. They cannot effectively monitor and counteract tax evasion by rich individuals and tax avoidance by multinational firms and, given the low monetisation of the domestic economy, they cannot easily compensate for revenue losses from capital through higher taxes on domestic labour and consumption. We briefly review whether and how least developed countries engage in tax competition and then assess the economic and fiscal consequences.

Following the global trend, statutory corporate tax rates have fallen in LDCs – down from roughly 40 per cent on average in 1980 to roughly 32 per cent in 2010. However, rates are still high by international standards – almost 4 percentage points higher than the OECD average, even though LDCs are significantly smaller in terms of population (Table 3.1). Even within the LDC group, rates are unrelated to country size: Unlike OECD countries, small LDCs do not seem to have significantly lower corporate tax rates than large LDCs. Also unlike the OECD experience, the process of rate-cutting was not accompanied by a broadening of the statutory tax base. To the contrary, while OECD countries made collective efforts to rein in preferential corporate tax regimes,[9] such regimes, including tax holidays, tax-free zones, investment tax credits and so on have proliferated among LDCs (Keen and Simone 2004; Keen and Mansour 2010; Norregard and Khan 2007).

Why do LDCs compete more heavily on preferential tax regimes than on general statutory tax rates? Two explanations are offered in the literature, both having to do with low governance capacity. The first argues that low governance capacity makes governments vulnerable to interest-group pressure, especially from multinational firms: 'Companies use their muscle to get the best tax deals possible' (Christian Aid 2008: 3). Given their institutional weakness, LDC governments have little power to resist these pressures (see also Keen and Simone 2004: 1321). The other explanation highlights the role of corruption: corrupt governments can extract higher bribes from potent taxpayers by offering targeted tax preference rather than general rate reductions (Dharmapala and Hines 2009: 1063; Christian Aid 2008). Finally, to the extent that LDCs are resource-rich, high statutory rates allow them to tap into location-specific rents associated with resource-extraction (Dharmapala and Hines 2009: 1063).[10]

Most observers agree that LDCs suffer from tax competition economically and fiscally (see Rixen 2011 for a summary). In contrast to tax havens, where low capital taxation has been a major driver of economic growth, there is little reason to suppose that LDCs' rate-cut-*cum*-base-narrowing policies were a cause of their

9. Preferential tax regimes are special perks offered to particular corporate forms or activities (foreign-held corporations, corporations located in special business areas, holding companies or corporate headquarters, etc.). Preferential regimes narrow the corporate tax base by allowing privileged corporations to partly or complete escape the general corporate tax.

10. Perversely, however, resource-extraction often benefits from preferential tax regimes, for instance, in Tanzania (Christian Aid 2008: 11).

growth performance over the 2000s (UNFPA 2011). Despite high growth rates, LDCs did not manage to increase tax revenues significantly. At around 13 per cent of GDP on average, tax collections are only about a third of what they are in OECD countries and far below what most experts consider an adequate level of funding for basic welfare and development needs (Bahl and Bird 2008: 281). Corporate tax revenues, by contrast, seem to have increased from 13 per cent of total tax revenue over the 1990s to about 21 per cent over the 2000s. Given lower rates and narrower statutory tax bases, this increase is 'something of a puzzle' (Keen and Mansour 2010: 1). Analysts warn that the increase could be mostly cyclical, reflecting the mid-2000s boom in economic growth and commodity prices (Norregard and Khan 2007: 10). Given slower growth and lower commodity prices since 2008, there is fear that corporate tax revenue may erode again.

While the revenue effect of corporate tax competition on LDCs is unclear, the effect of tax competition for individual savings and investment is clearly negative. Given their low quality of government, LDCs cannot compete for the savings and investments of foreign tax-evaders and cannot prevent domestic tax-evaders from moving their capital to tax havens or OECD countries. Partly as a result of this, revenues from individual income taxation scarcely exceed corporate tax revenues in LDCs. In OECD countries, by contrast, revenues from individual income taxation are four times larger than corporate tax revenues. Tax evasion also has a regressive distributive effect. Political and economic elites in weakly governed LDCs can abuse their power, first to appropriate wealth illicitly and then to shield their wealth from taxation illicitly by moving it abroad. One study finds, for instance, that increases in oil and gas rents in autocratic countries significantly increase the value of bank deposits held by nationals of these countries in tax havens. Purportedly, autocratic elites appropriate between 6 and 10 per cent of these rents and hide them abroad (Andersen *et al.* 2013; see also Shaxson 2011: chapter 8).

In summary, there is evidence to suggest that LDCs are seriously constrained by tax competition. In contrast to the two other country-groups, these constraints are unambiguously negative for revenue-raising capacity and redistribution. Due to their weak governance capacity, LDCs can neither profit from tax competition nor effectively compensate competition-induced revenue shortfalls in capital taxation from other sources.

6. Will tax competition last?

Not only capital wins from capital tax competition. The governments and workers of small countries can also profit, especially if their country is democratic and well governed. Given that most countries are small – the global median country size is just 6 million, that is, slightly smaller than Switzerland and considerably smaller than the global average size of 32 million (World Bank 2013) – this helps to explain the stability of tax competition.

Yet, while most countries are small, most people live in large countries. This implies not only that large countries – and the majority of their citizens – are the prime victims of tax competition but also that they have most power to stop it. Intuitively, if a large country decides to cut (or not to cut) its taxes, this increases (or relieves) competitive pressures on other countries much more than if a small country makes the same decision. As various authors have argued, it was the US tax reform of 1986 that triggered the global downward competition in corporate tax rates (Hallerberg and Basinger 1998; Swank 2006). An equally dramatic tax cut by, say, Norway, would never have had the same dramatic effect.

To be sure, the United States and the other large G20 member-states have recently used their power to talk – or bully, depending on perspective – reluctant small states into agreement on stricter standards on information-exchange (to hinder tax evasion) and corporate profit-shifting (to rein in corporate tax avoidance) (see, for example, Hakelberg 2014). Yet they carefully skirted the more fundamental issue of whether and at what level capital should be taxed. Given the structural advantage of smallness, one-size-fits-all tax harmonisation is not a politically viable option in a system of consensual or near-consensual international decision-making. Hence, if the scope for capital taxation is to be defended, the large states have to take the lead. They have to keep their capital taxes up in order to allow smaller states to cut their capital taxes by less. This, of course, would come at a cost. Large countries would not only have to accept being exploited by small countries externally; they would also have to renounce the freedom to cut corporate taxes for purely internal reasons, such as, for instance, to stimulate domestic economic activity during recessions. Yet this is exactly what many sizeable European economies, including Germany, Italy, Spain and the UK did during the recent financial crisis (Lierse and Seelkopf 2015). Thus 'tax leadership' would preserve more tax-policy options for all countries but at a cost for the large countries. Benevolent hegemony is not for free.

References

Andersen, J. J. *et al.* (2013) 'Petro rents and hidden wealth: evidence from bank deposits in tax havens', University of Copenhagen: EPRU Working Paper Series 2013-03.

Bahl, R. W. and Bird, R. M. (2008) 'Tax policy in developing countries: looking back and forward', *National Tax Journal* 61(2): 279–301.

Bucovetsky, S. (1991) 'Asymmetric tax competition', *Journal of Urban Economics* 30(2): 167–81.

Busemeyer, M. R. (2009) 'From myth to reality: globalisation and public spending in OECD countries revisited', *European Journal of Political Research* 48: 455–82.

Christian Aid (2008) *Death and Taxes: The true toll of tax dodging*: http://www.christianaid.org.uk/images/deathandtaxes.pdf (accessed 23 October 2014), pp. 27–54.

Clausing, K. A. (2016) 'The nature and practice of capital tax competition', in Dietsch P. and Rixen, T. (eds) *Global Tax Governance: What is wrong with it and how to fix it*, Colchester: ECPR Press, pp. 27–54.

de Mooij, R. A. and Ederveen, S. (2008) 'Corporate tax elasticities: a reader's guide to empirical findings', *Oxford Review of Economic Policy* 24(4): 680–97.

Dharmapala, D. and Hines, J. R. (2009) 'Which countries become tax havens?', *Journal of Public Economics* 93: 1058–68.

Edwards, J. and Keen, M. (1996) 'Tax competition and Leviathan', *European Economic Review* 40(1): 113–34.

Garrett, G. and Mitchell, D. (2001) 'Globalization, government spending and taxation in the OECD', *European Journal of Political Research* 39: 145–77.

Genschel, P. and Schwarz, P. (2011) 'Tax competition: a literature review', *Socio-Economic Review* 9(2): 339–70.

— (2013) 'Tax competition and fiscal democracy', in Streek, W. and Schäfer, A. (eds) *Politics in the Age of Austerity*, Cambridge: Polity Press, pp. 59–83.

Genschel, P. *et al.* (2015) 'Dictators don't compete: autocracy, democracy and tax competition', Open Forum CES Paper 22, Harvard University.

Hakelberg, L. (2014) 'The power politics of international tax co-operation: Luxembourg, Austria and the automatic exchange of information', *Journal of European Public Policy*, doi: 10.1080/13501763.2014.941380

Hallerberg, M. (1996) 'Tax competition in Wilhelmine Germany and its implications for the European Union', *World Politics* 48(3): 324–57.

Hallerberg, M. and Basinger, S. J. (1998) 'Internationalization and changes in tax policy in OECD countries: the importance of domestic veto players', *Comparative Political Studies* 31(3): 321–52.

Irish Government (2010) *The National Recovery Plan: 2011–2014*, Dublin: Stationery Office: http://www.budget.gov.ie/The%20National%20Recovery%20Plan%202011-2014.pdf (accessed 8 September 2015).

Kanbur, R. and Keen, M. (1993) 'Jeux-sans-frontieres – tax competition and tax coordination when countries differ in size', *American Economic Review* 83(4): 877–92.

Keen, M. and Mansour, M. (2010) 'Revenue mobilisation in sub-Saharan Africa: challenges from globalisation I – trade reform', *Development Policy Review* 28(5): 553–71.

Keen, M. and Simone, A. (2004) 'Is tax competition harming developing countries more than developed?', *Tax Notes International* 28 June: 1317–25: http://www.taxjustice.net/cms/upload/pdf/Keen_TNI_copyright_tax_competition_developing.pdf (accessed 8 September 2015).

Li, Q. (2009) 'Democracy, autocracy, and expropriation of foreign direct investment', *Comparative Political Studies* 42(8): 1098–1127.

Lierse, H. and Seelkopf, L. (2015) 'Capital markets and tax policy-making: a comparative analysis of European tax reforms since the crisis', *Comparative European Politics*, doi: 10.1057/cep.2014.48

Meinzer, M. (2016) 'Towards an international yardstick for identifying tax havens and facilitating reform', in Dietsch, P. and Rixen, T. (eds) *Global Tax Governance: What is wrong with it and how to fix it*, Colchester: ECPR Press.

Norregaard, J. and Khan, T. S. (2007) 'Tax policy: recent trends and coming challenges', IMF Working Paper 274, Washington DC: IMF Fiscal Affairs Department: http://www.imf.org/external/pubs/ft/wp/2007/wp07274.pdf (accessed 8 September 2015).

Ogier (2012) 'Cayman Islands: Cayman in calm waters', *Mondaq* http://www.mondaq.com/caymanislands/x/89478/offshore+financial+centres/Cayman+In+Calm+Waters (accessed 8 September 2015).

Palan, R. *et al.* (2010) *Tax Havens: How globalisation really works*, Ithaca, New York: Cornell University Press.

Rixen, T. (2011) 'Tax competition and inequality: the case for global tax governance', *Global Governance* 17: 447–67.

Shaxson, N. (2011) *Treasure Islands: Tax havens and the men who stole the world*, London: Bodley Head.

Steinmo, S. (2003) 'The evolution of policy ideas: tax policy in the 20th century', *British Journal of Politics and International Relations* 5(2): 206–36.

Swank, D. (2006) 'Tax policy in an era of internationalization: explaining the spread of neoliberalism', *International Organization* 60(4): 847–82.

UNCTAD (United Nations Conference on Trade and Development, 2012) 'Vulnerability profile of Vanuatu': http://www.un.org/en/development/desa/policy/cdp/ldc/profile/vulnerability_profile_vanuatu_2012.pdf (accessed 22 October 2014).

UNFPA (United Nations Population Fund, 2011) 'Population dynamics in the Least Developed Countries: challenges and opportunities for development and poverty reduction': http://unfpa.org/webdav/site/global/shared/documents/publications/2011/CP51265.pdf (accessed 22 October 2014).

Walsh, B. (2015) 'The international tax system is "repulsive and inequitable". Here's a way to fix it', Huffington Post, 20 August 2015: http://www.huffingtonpost.com/entry/multinational-corporations-taxes_55d4baede4b055a6dab265d9 (accessed 8 September 2015).

Wilson, J. D. (1999) 'Theories of tax competition', *National Tax Journal* 52(2): 269–304.

Winner, H. (2005) 'Has tax competition emerged in OECD countries? A panel data approach', *International Tax and Public Finance* 12(5): 667–87.

World Bank (2013) 'Total population (in number of people)': http://data.worldbank.org/indicator/SP.POP.TOTL (accessed 28 August 2013).

Zucman, G. (2013) 'The missing wealth of nations: are Europe and the US net debtors or net creditors?', *Quarterly Journal of Economics*, doi: 10.1093/qje/qjt012

Chapter Four

Tax Competition: An Internalised Policy Goal

*Lyne Latulippe**

1. Introduction

Research on tax competition, viewed as an exogenous force driven by globalisation, is often conducted from a macro-level perspective (Genschel and Schwarz 2011). These studies are concerned with evidence of the existence of tax competition and its consequences among numerous countries considered at a global level. Their results show that corporate tax rates have declined globally over the last decades. Tax competition not only influences decisions about statutory corporate tax rates but also prompts a series of changes to the international taxation system. Some research demonstrates that the research agenda needs to address what is going on in the 'black box' (Radaelli 2004) –that is, the circumstances in which these decisions have been made. While domestic political and economic conditions modulate tax competition (Basinger and Halleberg 2004; Swank 2006, among others), I argue that the competitiveness discourse exacerbates the effect of globalisation on domestic policies (Conley 2004). Recent studies have analysed the concept of competitiveness in the formulation of taxation policy (Gravelle 2012; Slemrod 2011; Toder 2012) but few contain any detailed analysis of this competitiveness discourse at the domestic level and its impact in relation to tax policy.

The objective of this chapter is to address how tax competition is embedded in the policy-making process through the concept of competitiveness; how this internalisation is operationalised; and how it constrains the outcome. The purpose is neither to reject the influence of external pressures on domestic tax-policy decisions nor to address the role of other domestic factors, such as political parties. The chapter takes a different and complementary look at tax competition. It focuses on how countries internalise the discourse of competitiveness; studying one important phase of the policy-making process – consultation – reveals the impact of this internalisation on policy decisions. According to studies of public consultation, more public consultation should improve the 'quality and legitimacy of decisions in government' and also would have the 'potential to address the

* The author thanks Peter Dietsch, Richard Eccleston, Helen Smith and Laurens van Apeldoorn for their helpful comments. An earlier version of this chapter was presented at the 2013 ECPR Joint Sessions Global Tax Governance', University of Mainz, 12–14 March 2013, and also at the Société québécoise de science politique, Annual Conference in Montreal on 27–28 June 2013. The author is grateful for the comments received from participants at these events.

"democratic deficit"' and to build 'community capacity and social capital' (Barnes *et al.* 2003: 379). Public consultations provide useful cases for studying the openness of the policy process to ideas. The usual studies concerned with global tax competition disregard the potential reinforcement of this phenomenon within countries. I argue that this needs to be taken into account to fully apprehend the dominance and resilience of tax competition.

The arguments in this chapter are based on findings from the study of two public consultations addressing international tax policy, findings that uncover the impact of the competitiveness discourse from within countries. While comparing two cases of consultation processes in two comparable countries (Australia and Canada) may not allow us to generalise about other countries, this comparative methodology nevertheless produces stronger conclusions than those that could be reached with a single case (Yin 2003). Furthermore, when divergences are identified, comparison allows us to refine the conclusions that can be drawn from these cases. The analytical power of the study is increased because Australia and Canada may represent 'less likely' cases, since they are not usually seen as aggressive tax competitors.

After a brief presentation of the context of the consultation processes studied in Section 2, the remainder of the chapter will be separated into four sections. For each section, theoretical claims will be explained and then findings from the case studies supporting or refining these claims will be discussed. First, I elaborate on the intertwined meanings of tax competition and competitiveness for firms and countries. Second, I address how competitiveness becomes a dominant tax-policy goal and what it implies for policy-making. Third, I illustrate how a government's competitiveness discourse restricts participation in the policy process and therefore reinforces the influence of private actors. Finally, I address how the competitiveness discourse undermines multilateral tax co-operation efforts to protect the tax base. The chapter then concludes on the impact of the prevailing competitiveness discourse in domestic policy processes.

2. Consultation processes in Australia and Canada

Australia: Review of International Taxation Arrangements in 2002

In the 1980s, Australia was concerned about the competitiveness of its corporate tax rate. Since its goal of providing a competitive rate was complemented by the objective of revenue neutrality (Ganghof and Eccleston 2004), the subsequent rate reduction was combined with a broadening of the tax base, as had been done in most OECD countries. The government changed some legislation it had previously regarded as good policy (for example, accelerated depreciation) as a way to compensate for the revenue loss caused by rate reductions (Ganghof and Eccleston 2004); as a result, the Australian corporate tax rate fell from 49 per cent in the late 1980s to 30 per cent in 2002.

The tax rate is merely one feature of the corporate tax system, albeit the most visible. In 1998, Australia launched a comprehensive review of business taxation to improve the competitiveness of the business-tax system as a whole. The resulting report (the 'Ralph Review': Ralph 1999) recommended the reduction of the corporate tax rate from 36 to 30 per cent, placed other features of the tax system under the microscope and left international taxation arrangements for further consideration (Eccleston 2007).

Before the election in 2001, John Howard, then Prime Minister of Australia, reiterated his government's competitiveness goal for the business sector.[1] On 5 May 2002, Treasurer Peter Costello announced a review of international tax arrangements and drafted a Consultation Paper (henceforward 'Australian Paper') that was made public in August 2002 (Australian Government 2002c). A Board of Taxation ('Board') was appointed to undertake public consultations, to report the outcome, and to make recommendations to the Treasurer by the end of 2002.

The consultation pertained to four main areas of international taxation: taxation of dividends paid out from foreign-source income; taxation of foreign-source income; taxation of foreign income passing through an Australian entity to non-resident shareholders; and tax-treaty policy and negotiation issues. Other issues included taxation of foreign expatriates working in Australia and taxation of financial services centres.[2]

The Australian Paper presented options for attracting equity capital for the offshore expansion of firms and for increasing Australia's attractiveness as a location for multinational headquarters. It described a potential bias in existing tax rules toward investment in firms that earn income in Australia, because a higher rate of return may be generated due to the tax system applied to dividends paid out of domestic income.[3] Its assessment of the competitiveness of the corporate tax system therefore extended to the impact of the tax system on investors and the prediction of a possible increase in the cost of capital. While the Treasurer presented a mixed view of the existence of such a problem, the Board argued in its report ('Australian Report') (Board of Taxation 2003b) that current taxation policy was causing a genuine problem for Australian corporate expansion abroad and that a solution was needed. The Treasurer issued a mixed response to the Australian Report submitted by the Board and did not agree with all of the Board's recommendations.[4]

---

1. 'My government remains firmly of the view that Australian companies can successfully compete on the global stage while remaining based in Australia. But to achieve this, we need internationally competitive taxes and taxation systems.' (Prime Minister of Australia 2001). The coalition won the election in November 2001 and John Howard remained Prime Minister.
2. While these issues merit inclusion in a study of global competitiveness and tax competition, the current study did not consider the consultation process on these more specific issues.
3. In this situation, taxes paid at the corporate level reduce taxes paid on the dividend at the shareholder level.
4. For example, the Treasurer did not agree to extending exemptions for repatriated profits to dividends received from a subsidiary's income earned in any country, whether corporate taxes were paid in the other country or not.

Canada: Review of Canada's system of international taxation in 2008

As was the case in Australia, the Canadian international tax system was reassessed after a review was conducted of the general corporate tax system and tax-rate reductions had been announced.[5] In 2006, the Canadian government committed to creating a Canadian advantage: 'To improve the business environment, *Advantage Canada* will lower business taxes, reduce regulatory and administrative burdens, enhance competition, ensure our capital markets are globally competitive and encourage free trade and foreign investment' (Canadian Government 2006). The 2006 budget announced that the corporate tax rate would fall from 21 per cent to 18.5 per cent by 2011. The following year's budget announced the creation of the Canadian Tax Advantage programme, which highlighted the importance of low corporate tax rates as an advantage that a tax system should offer.

With fairness and competitiveness in mind, the government announced its programme for a more equitable international tax system that would ensure that all parties paid their fair share of taxes while allowing businesses to remain competitive. In essence, the government was announcing that while certain tax-planning opportunities would be eliminated with the objective of improving the fairness of the tax system, other policies would be adopted to increase its competitiveness. The option for corporations to finance a foreign subsidiary and claim a deduction for the same financing expense in two countries ('double-dip planning') was to be eliminated. In addition, the government would increase the competitiveness of Canadian corporations by extending the benefits of doing business in a treaty country to countries with which Canada has signed a Tax Information-Exchange Agreement (TIEA).

On 30 November 2007, the Minister of Finance established a temporary Advisory Panel on Canada's System of International Taxation (Panel) 'to study and recommend measures to further improve the competitiveness, efficiency and fairness of this system' (Canadian Government 2007b). Whereas in Australia the Treasurer prepared the consultation document, in Canada the panel was mandated to prepare the consultation paper ('Canadian Paper'), which was released in April 2008 (APCSIT 2008a), asking for submissions by 15 July 2008.

The Canadian Paper identified issues to be addressed through consultations with the business community: the tax treatment of foreign income such as dividends from affiliated subsidiaries and capital gains; the treatment of foreign investment in Canada; withholdings on payment to non-residents; the administration of transfer-pricing rules; and other administrative issues. The panel did not specifically refer to the announced restriction of double-dip planning in the Canadian Paper. However, in its report published after the consultation process ('Canadian Report'), the Panel pointed out the following:

5. Broad studies of the Canadian taxation system, including corporate taxation, were done previously; for example, the Carter commission (1969) and the Mintz report (1998) (Slaats and Woolford 2010).

> Interest deductibility was raised as an issue at every consultation meeting and in many submissions to the Panel. Members of the business community strongly oppose any restriction on interest expenses incurred to invest in foreign affiliates (APCSIT 2008b: 53).

The panel recommended not restricting interest deductibility to finance foreign affiliates, even if the income generated by the borrowed funds was exempt from taxation in Canada.[6]

After the Canadian Report was published on 10 December 2008 (APCSIT 2008b), the government did not react to each of the recommendations, nor did it make public statements on all of them. It offered a mixed response to the recommendations, revealing its views publicly little by little in the ensuing annual budgets or in press releases. However, the government lost no time in repealing the restriction on double-dip planning. At the time of the consultation, the international financial crisis also constrained the possibility of adopting a policy that would further affect the financing activities of businesses. Since double deduction results in a single deduction in more than one country, it is difficult to eliminate this type of tax-planning without the co-operation of other countries. It is therefore almost impossible for an individual country to prevent this sort of international tax-planning from eroding the global tax base.

The government did not follow up on the panel's recommendation to expand the exemption regime for dividends received from any foreign affiliate or the exemption of capital gains on their shares. Canada's extensive bilateral tax-treaty network makes the application of the exemption regime to treaty countries less restrictive. The government also argued that keeping the exemption system for treaty countries and countries that have signed a TIEA encourages other countries to sign agreements. Internationally, Canada had committed to helping tax havens engage in signing exchange-of-information agreements, with a view to ensuring the trend spreads to all tax havens (Canadian Government 2007c). While this goal is consistent with the global discourse *against* tax havens, favourable tax treatment of capital repatriation from these countries promotes the use of tax havens as a way to reduce businesses' global taxation liabilities and enhances tax competition.

3. Theoretical and empirical consequences of the competitiveness discourse

Tax competition and competitiveness

While 'the idea of competitiveness became a routine component of political vocabulary in the 1970s' (Rosamond 2002: 165), Krugman (1994: 44), questioning

6. 'The Panel recognizes that permitting a deduction for interest expense to earn exempt foreign dividend may not be consistent with the matching principle. Nonetheless, for competitiveness reasons, the approach of permitting the deduction has been accepted within the Canadian system for many years.' (APCSIT 2008b: 49). 'Canadian businesses must compete in global markets at all times; however to hobble their ability to compete and invest in the future at the worst of times would not be consistent with the principles guiding our analysis.' (APCSIT 2008b: 50).

reliance on competitiveness as a policy goal, concluded the following: 'So let's start telling the truth: competitiveness is a meaningless word when applied to national economies. And the obsession with competitiveness is both wrong and dangerous'.[7] To understand the constraining effect of competitiveness at the domestic level, the relationship between competitiveness in taxation policy and competition, particularly tax competition, needs to be discussed first.

In the dominant globalisation discourse, liberalisation of trade and investment is key to global economic growth. Countries seek to benefit from global economic growth and compete to attract scarce and mobile resources. In the OECD's view (1992: 97), a country's competitiveness is 'the degree to which it can, under free and fair market conditions, produce goods and services which meet the test of international markets, while simultaneously maintaining and expanding the real incomes of its people over the longer term'. Owens (2011) somehow dissociates taxation from competitiveness, based on the argument that a country with the fundamental competitive conditions to promote investment should be able to tax it appropriately and further reinvest tax revenues to strengthen these fundamentals. Given this argument, lower taxes should not be associated with increased competitiveness, whereas in fact the tax system is often considered to be a competitive feature of a country, as illustrated by the Global Competitiveness Report published annually by the World Economic Forum (Schwab 2012). A competitive economy is also defined by what it can achieve in terms of the real income of its citizens, taking into consideration the characteristics of its competitors, including their tax system. This definition illustrates the stress on domestic policy-making caused by the taxation policies of other countries (Slemrod 2011).

More specifically, Knoll (2012: 372) distinguishes between the 'ability of companies to compete against one another' and the 'ability of a country to compete to attract capital'. Competitiveness discourse blurs the distinction between countries and private firms. Under the global-liberalisation paradigm, countries attach their own competitiveness to that of private firms. Porter's view about the competitiveness of a location is 'defined as the productivity that companies located there can achieve' (Ketels 2006: 116). In this paradigm, the goal is to enhance the country's competitiveness through the competitiveness of its firms.

When policy-makers compare their tax system to other more favourable tax systems, it creates pressure to change their system to be at least as favourable as, or more favourable than, those of their competitors. Cerny notes that within the competition state, 'state actors and institutions are themselves promoting new forms of complex globalisation in the attempt to adapt state action to cope more effectively with what they see as global "realities"' (1997: 251). The competition state embodies a global dimension and presupposes that global economic growth,

7. More recently, Gravelle (2012: 347) reaffirms this statement: 'It is important that public discourse move away from meaningless concepts such as international competitiveness and instead focus on what tax policies might be optimal, in that they fulfil the more appropriate objective of "better off".'

achieved through the liberalisation of markets, is beneficial for both the state and its citizens.

Given the underlying assumption about the benefits of liberalisation, variations in corporate taxation are seen as a distortion that needs to be removed for the purposes of global economic efficiency. For many economists, the most efficient corporate tax system features a low rate with a broad base (Slemrod 2011). Reliance on the competitiveness discourse within this paradigm does not allow for any nuance about the provision of public goods and the necessary financing of goods that may be valuable for multinational corporations, such as infrastructure and an educated workforce.[8] It furthermore assumes that taxation is a determining factor in the location of investments or firms, even if many recognise that other factors are of greater importance, particularly in the case of direct investment (Arnold and McIntyre 2002). Tax policy becomes a commodity, the price of which should be determined by the market.

According to Knoll (2012), economists have not defined 'competitiveness' as an economic principle of policy-making with regard to taxation. Yet the use of this term by policy-makers and market actors has elevated competitiveness to the status of a principle. Economic theories support the idea that global economic growth is enhanced if capital and firms are free to go wherever their investment will be most productive. From this perspective, countries wish to attract investment and firms and to benefit from economic growth within their borders, while preventing other countries from enjoying these benefits. In order to be successful, a country can be expected to reduce its taxes on inbound investments in order to have an advantage over other countries with higher taxes.

However, in the name of competitiveness, countries also promote investment abroad by resident firms through favourable tax treatments, for example by exempting foreign income from the firm's tax base. This reasoning is paradoxical. While countries often behave as though competition were a zero-sum game, policy-makers' encouragement of resident corporations to invest abroad suggests that they consider that both countries (resident and source) can benefit from the investment. Although tax rates are usually the main feature studied, other characteristics, such as exempting foreign income from taxation, may also be influenced by competition among states. This type of policy fits well into the competitiveness discourse, because it presumably increases the competitiveness of domestic firms abroad. Tax competition therefore affects both the residence- and source-based rules of corporate taxation systems.

The analysis of the Australian Paper shows that the competitiveness of the tax system is measured by the benefits it offers to the business community. The underlying principle of the consultation was that a competitive tax system is necessary for a competitive domestic business community, which in

8. Jensen (2012: 1007) found no relationship between lower tax rates and increased FDI and states 'If these high rates provide for an educated workforce, a well-developed infrastructure, or other public goods, multinational corporations may choose high tax countries rather than low tax countries as an investment location.'

turn is essential to national economic growth. The consultation was based on this assumption but no further information was provided to substantiate this assumption. The Australian Paper viewed the general goal of supporting the competitiveness of the domestic business community as an actual taxation policy goal.[9] The Board made the point even more directly:

> The basic competitive unit in the global marketplace is the corporation. Hence, a key focus of the Board's consideration has been the ability of Australia's corporations to compete in that marketplace. Australia has a small population and limited capital. It must be able to attract capital from overseas, and its businesses must be able to earn the best possible return on Australian's [sic] savings (Board of Taxation 2003b: 29).

The Australian Report also elaborated on the direct relationship between a competitive business community and national economic growth. The Chairman of the Board stated 'Both I and the Board believe that, if implemented, the Board's recommendations will provide reforms which will greatly benefit Australia's ability to compete globally and, by doing so, increase Australia's GDP and national income' (Board of Taxation 2003b: xiv).

However, the Board repeatedly recognised that it would be difficult to quantify any benefits the community might receive from implementing its recommendations. In the dominant paradigm, evidence of these benefits is not required since reducing corporations' tax burden will necessarily lead to an increase in the well-being of the community as a whole. The current rules were described as obstacles and threats to the maintenance of benefits to Australia.[10] For example, the focus on business competitiveness led to discussions about reducing the cost of capital, as though that initiative were a stated taxation-policy goal. Furthermore, even if participants in the consultation recognised that tax does not determine investment decisions, they emphasised the importance of having a regime as favourable as that of other countries, thus positing competitiveness as a policy goal.

The Canadian Panel also conducted its work within the liberalisation paradigm, emphasising competitiveness:

> The work of the Competition Panel and our Panel is based on the same premise: outward investment by Canadians in foreign markets and investment by residents of other countries into Canada are critical to Canada's long-term growth and development (APCSIT 2008b: 2).

9. 'Furthermore, ensuring the international competitiveness of locally based companies and managed funds is an important government policy goal.' (Australian Government 2002c: 91–2).

10. 'While the priority afforded to domestic taxation is understandable, the failure to deal with the international taxation rules has left distortions and impediments. Unless removed, they could inhibit Australian companies from competing on the world stage with a strong Australian base. This in turn will reduce the benefits which could flow to Australia through further integration into the global economy.' (Board of Taxation 2003b: 9).

Whereas the Canadian Paper mentioned the national benefits of outbound investment (growth and productivity) and inbound investment (jobs and technology) only briefly,[11] the Canadian Report justified its recommendations with frequent references to studies that provide evidence of these benefits.

The Canadian Paper begins with the statement that 'Canada's tax policy is important to the country's ability to sustain and improve its competitiveness in the changing global environment' (APCSIT 2008a: 1). It thereby not only positioned competitiveness as a tax-policy goal[12] within the liberalisation paradigm but also described tax policy as an instrument for improving competitiveness. In using the expression 'tax advantage', the government equated tax competition with the delivery of tax relief to businesses to ensure their competitiveness. Both the Canadian Paper and the Report made marginal references to other tax-policy goals.

In summary, countries address their own competitiveness through the competitiveness of firms, which they equate with domestic economic growth. In the global-liberalisation paradigm, competitiveness discussed in relation to tax policy can only support corporate-tax reduction.

4. Constraining domestic policy options

Taxation policy usually relates to fundamental principles of efficiency, neutrality and equity (Li *et al.* 2006). These principles are often in tension with one another and, depending on the dominant ideas about taxation, some become more influential than others – as in the case of efficiency over equity (Steinmo 2003). Globalisation adds a dimension through which these principles are evaluated and compared with the concept of competitiveness. Each country ascertains the competitiveness of its taxation regime by comparing it to those of other countries. This way of addressing the problem leads to identifying 'competitiveness' as an underlying and overriding policy goal in the development of tax policy, making other fundamental goals merely subsidiary. Competitiveness may be superseding other policy goals instead of being measured along with them (Toder 2012; Slemrod 2011).

In fact, competitiveness should not be a fundamental issue in policy decision-making, because competitiveness as a policy objective overlooks the possibility that allowing a corporation to be more competitive may not lead to any national or global economic growth. Policies that increase efficiency or welfare gains should

11. For example: 'Like other taxes, withholding taxes can be expected to adversely affect economic activity' (APCSIT 2008a: 38).

12. Also, 'Economists have identified three economic principles as possible guides to setting international tax. Nevertheless, the Panel has highlighted competitiveness as a predominant principle. While competitiveness is not a well defined economic principle in the context of international taxation, the Panel firmly believes that it should be a fundamental consideration in developing Canadian tax policy. The Panel also believes that a focus on maintaining a globally competitive tax system is appropriate to a small open economy such as Canada's' (APCSIT 2008b: 13).

be adopted without referring to competitiveness (Hassett *et al.* 2011). Developing policies within the competitiveness discourse makes other aspects of the tax system seem less relevant. As one constructivist analysis argued, 'Government leaders confronting either real or perceived threats from globalization, such as capital flight, are potentially capable of constructing their own policy straightjackets [*sic*], reflecting prevailing discourses about the impacts of globalization' (Bell 2012: 662).

Both the Australian Paper and the Australian Report briefly alluded to tax policy goals other than competitiveness – but almost always in conjunction with competitiveness. The Australian Report identified competitiveness and efficiency as priority policy goals.[13] Some brief references were made to neutrality, although more as a general principle. Concerning the delicate balance among export, import, and national neutrality, the Treasurer concluded in the Australian Paper:

> While benchmarks provide a useful conceptual framework for examining issues, they point to conflicting policy directions and cannot give definitive policy guidance. Practical considerations of compliance and administration, Australia's national interest in protecting its share of taxing rights, and international obligations and consensus (to the extent it exists) constrain the adoption of any one benchmark (Australian Government 2002c: 91–2).

After putting neutrality benchmarks into perspective, the Australian Paper stated that existing tax policy applied to dividends paid out of foreign income respected one form of neutrality, the national neutrality benchmark. Therefore, the decision to reconsider this policy suggests that competitiveness and international trends[14] may be more imperative considerations than national neutrality. After saying that the Board considered neutrality to be an important policy goal,[15] the Australian Report implied that some neutrality benchmarks could be set aside to benefit business competitiveness on the international level:

> The Board acknowledges, however, that there are winners and losers from virtually any reform. In particular, the Board's proposal for tax relief for dividends paid out of FSI (see Chapter 2) may not benefit every company.

13. 'Therefore, the Board's recommendations, and any policy action that might emerge from them, need to be seen as part of a continuous process of ensuring that Australia's taxation system does not hinder business decisions, and that it promotes competitiveness and international integration' (Board of Taxation 2003b: 31).

14. For example, 'Adopting a system of shareholder relief, with no link between Australian company tax paid and the shareholder relief received, would be more consistent with recent overseas trends (Appendix 2.1). A shareholder relief mechanism along these lines could be simpler for business and reduce any shareholder level tax bias against direct investment offshore' (Australian Government 2002c: 17).

15. 'A prime design criterion for the Board's recommendations has been neutrality. The recommendations are intended to ensure that Australia's taxation system does not unduly hinder business decisions. In particular, the Board's recommendation on shareholder relief for dividends paid out of FSI is designed to alleviate the present bias against Australian investment offshore, and the related bias against offshore investment into Australia' (Board of Taxation 2003b: 51).

> Those that are and remain domestically-oriented will not be able to access equity capital as easily as they can under the current arrangements, and this could be reflected in their share prices. On the other hand, internationally-oriented Australian companies will benefit. The Board believes that overall, there will be net benefits to the Australian community, and that they will increase over time (Board of Taxation 2003b: 36).

The Board viewed economic efficiency as directly related to competitiveness and stated that the neutrality principle 'complements the efficiency principle' (Board of Taxation 2003b: 31). From this perspective, both the efficiency and neutrality principles support the competitiveness goal, again blurring the distinction between the competitiveness of countries and of firms within them. Equity as a policy goal was relegated to a supporting role and presented in conjunction with capital-export neutrality.

Conversely, compliance costs and complexity were seen as more fundamental and important in the analysis of international taxation arrangements, probably because of their more direct connection to competitiveness. Many tax features are undeniably complex, as demonstrated quite eloquently by controlled foreign corporations (CFC) rules. Complex rules often arise from the fact that firms use tax-planning to get around other, less complex, rules. However, in a competitiveness discourse, the need to alleviate avoidance possibilities is superseded by the need to reduce complexity or compliance costs. In a competitiveness discourse, the government often must choose between complexity and prevention of avoidance. The Board's report focused less on preventing avoidance than did the Australian Paper, viewing complexity and compliance costs as major concerns.[16]

In the Canadian case, while the Minister referred to fairness and economic efficiency along with competitiveness, the announcement also referred to the department's description of the Canadian Tax Advantage in the 2007 budget as a programme 'providing relief in every way the government collects taxes' (Canadian Government 2007b: n/a). The budget furthermore stated that, 'lowering taxes is not enough. The tax system must also be fair, ensuring that tax considerations do not unduly influence business and investment decisions.' (Canadian Government 2007b: n/a).

---

16. This is illustrated by its recommendations on three topics:

    1. 'Submissions universally concluded that the complexity and compliance costs involved in applying the CFC rules, as well as the changes in the international environment, demonstrate the need for urgent reform' (Board of Taxation 2003b: 80).
    2. Concerning the determination of corporate residence, even though the Board acknowledges that a US rule similar to its recommendation presented integrity problems, it concludes: 'The incorporation test would provide greater certainty and reduce complexity. Integrity issues associated with this recommendation are expected to be minimal. Of course, any change will need transitional measures' (Board of Taxation 2003b: 110).
    3. 'For ease of administration, the Board prefers a system that provides the relief without the need to trace foreign tax paid offshore' (Board of Taxation 2003b: 69).While this is indeed easier to administer, it also facilitates the earning of income in low-tax countries, so reducing Australia's taxation nevertheless.

Although this sentence confused fairness with neutrality or economic efficiency, the government was also concerned with fairness in its usual sense, as demonstrated by the announcement of the elimination of double-dip planning. The fairness objective seems to have influenced the Panel's work to some extent. The Canadian Paper referred to the challenge of protecting the tax base against erosion[17] and the Canadian Report discussed the potential need to develop specific anti-avoidance provisions, given that some new or current rules offered undesirable tax-planning opportunities. Nonetheless, the document pointed out that 'any compliance and administrative costs that may impede the ability of Canadian companies to compete in global markets' (APCSIT 2008b: 37) should be considered.[18] The Panel invited 'businesses to be reasonable in their tax planning and for tax administrators to be less suspicious' in a 'spirit of co-operation and mutual respect' (APCSIT 2008b: 18). Businesses were encouraged to help Canada's tax system stand apart and enhance the country's international tax advantage (APCSIT 2008b: 18). In addition, the Panel noted that 'Businesses, their advisors and the CRA all have a responsibility to ensure that our self-assessment system works effectively' (APCSIT 2008b: 79).

The Canadian Paper appeared to base the concept of neutrality on a lowest common denominator. For example, it used cases of non-taxation (dividends from foreign affiliates) to rationalise applying the exemption regime to other situations (capital gains on shares of foreign affiliates). Broadening capital-gains exemptions was recommended, although the Paper also acknowledged that this treatment cannot be considered neutral with regard to the sale of shares of domestic corporations subject to Canadian taxes. The fact that taxing capital gains may prompt taxpayers to reduce their capital gains by paying exempted dividends was also presented to justify the exemption.

Even fairness was explained in terms of competitiveness: 'This view of fairness is consistent with the principles noted above and may be summarized as follows: ... Canada's rules regarding the taxation of outbound investment should be competitive vis-à-vis the outbound tax rules of other major countries' (APCSIT 2008a: 5). This quotation illustrates how co-ordination efforts to achieve fairness are set aside. The Panel rather suggests that some form of international horizontal equity can be achieved unilaterally, by being competitive and emulating the policies of other countries by offering similar or even better tax treatment for Canadian firms that invest abroad.

---

17. In the Canadian Paper: 'Issues to consider are its ongoing effectiveness in supporting the competitiveness of Canadian Businesses operating abroad as well as safeguards against erosion of the tax base.' (APCSIT 2008a: 15). However, the Panel also adds, 'Achieving these objectives should not come at the expense of complex rules that create difficulties in compliance for taxpayers and administration for the CRA.' (APCSIT 2008a: 15) and 'complexity should be avoided except, for example, where it is necessary to protect tax revenues' (APCSIT 2008a: 5).

18. Also, to further illustrate the opposition between preventing avoidance and the competitiveness of firms: 'The appropriateness of base erosion rules is being debated in a number of countries, particularly as many of them have the stated policy objective of increasing the global competitiveness of their domestic corporations' (APCSIT 2008b: 40).

Both the Australian and Canadian consultation processes have led to similar participation and recommendations about favouring outbound investment, reducing residence taxation (by exempting dividends and capital gains) and reducing withholding rates. In both cases, the consultation processes resulted in propositions for incremental changes to an existing regime. The two countries differed, however, in their recommendations for inbound investment and on the government's response. While in Australia little was said about the need to prevent avoidance techniques for inbound investments, the Canadian Panel was far more vocal on the issue, asking for specific anti-avoidance measures to apply to inbound investment. The competitiveness argument is more prevalent for domestic companies investing abroad than it is for foreign companies investing in Canada.[19] Canada's geographic and economic proximity to the United States, and the resulting competition between Canadian firms and American firms, may explain this concern. It can also be explained by the fact that the government had indicated up-front its intention to protect the integrity of the tax system, for example, by prohibiting double-dip planning. The Panel tried to answer this concern and underlined the need to develop anti-avoidance measures affecting tax-planning by foreign investors in order to protect the Canadian tax-base. The concerns and preferences of firms are not identical in every country and they may be influenced by domestic market conditions as well as by the policy-making environment.

5. Reinforcing the power of private actors

Economic ideas influence the identification of problems and the development of solutions. According to the global-liberalisation paradigm, global economic growth relies on productivity in the private sector, which is increased when capital is free to move wherever it will provide the best rate of return. Any distortion affecting businesses' decisions should be alleviated. According to this view, private-sector preferences should prevail in determining domestic policy. For Rosamond (2002: 168), competitiveness has been 'seized upon by US and European policy elites as an exogenous rationale for neoliberal policy solutions'. Cerny (2010) notes that a transnational elite linked with multinational corporations has formed and that 'they are said to have a common interest in the spread of a neo-liberal model of globalising capitalism' (2010: 15).

Krugman indicated that emphasising competitiveness reduces the quality of economic discussion and policy-making: 'If top government officials are strongly committed to a particular economic doctrine, their commitment inevitably sets the tone for policy-making on all issues, even those which may seem to have nothing to do with that doctrine' (1994: 42). Furthermore, embedding the issue of the international tax system in concerns about competitiveness supports the

19. 'One guiding principle regarding inbound tax policy is to ensure the proper measurement and taxation of business income generated from Canadian sources' (ACPSIT 2008b: 28).

perception that any measures beneficial to the business sector are necessarily good for the community.

Private firms compete in the international arena, where being competitive means increasing productivity. Therefore, from their perspective, anything hindering their productivity should be eliminated. Taxation is perceived as just another cost for corporations. Because it is a policy directly under governmental control, when governments ask what can be done to increase the productivity (and competitiveness) of businesses, private actors respond by asking for lower taxation in order to reduce their costs. According to this reasoning, tax competition also leads to the development of policies that reduce the costs indirectly incurred by firms, such as the cost of capital. This would, for example, mean that reducing taxes on active business income may not be sufficiently beneficial to improve firms' competitiveness. Governments should also consider reducing taxes on passive investment income. The argument is that higher taxes on dividends or interest increase the cost of capital for active business, because its investors will request a higher return on their investment.

As Bell (2012) notes, structural explanations for the power of business are inadequate. The manner in which policy-makers and private actors construct their interactions must be examined in order to understand how businesses get power. The level of mobilisation of business interests, which sometimes grows in the face of previous reform failures, may lead to the adoption and implementation of reforms (Eccleston 2000). Bell demonstrates that policy-makers can mediate or reduce the structural power of business through their ideas and current institutions. Policy-making processes based on a discourse of firm competitiveness restrict participation to a limited group within the business community, that is, private actors directly affected by the policies under review.

In Australia, the Board of Taxation was established in August 2000 based on a recommendation, following the Ralph Review, to provide a way for businesses to comment on the design of tax laws that pertained to them.[20] The government widened the Board's mandate to include the perspectives of the broader community.[21]

20. At this time, the Board was allowed a budget of $2 million annually to operate (Board of Taxation 2003a).

21. Jordan (2002) notes that the mandate of the Board is dual, namely to report on the consultation and to make recommendations. 'The Board is conscious of its responsibility in RITA consultation processes to make balanced recommendations that benefit the community as a whole. For example, a change may be very desirable in increasing Australia's competitiveness but may have an associate revenue impact. At the same time, revenue impacts are important to governments and the community seeking to maintain vital services.' Therefore, the recommendations do not have to be in total accordance with the findings in the submissions. Criticism of the non-autonomous status of the Board of Taxation were raised within the business community because the Board's secretariat was staffed from within the Treasury: 'To be effective in promoting better tax law outcomes for Australia, it is essential that our community stakeholders work closely with us and not get sidetracked into peripheral debates about whether the board should be statutory, have an independent secretariat and other such issues. Let's get on the tasks that matter' (Warburton 2001: 77).

Following the publication of the consultation paper in August 2002, anyone interested in preparing a submission had until 31 October 2002 to do so. While the consultation was open to the public in general, the tight deadline made it difficult for non-experts in international taxation to evaluate taxation policy options and write submissions. After publicly announcing the consultation process, the Board invited key stakeholders to comment. These stakeholders were (Jordan 2002: 6):

a. residents engaged in international business, or who would engage in international business under more favourable taxation arrangements;
b. non-residents who invest in Australia, or who might invest under more favourable taxation arrangements;
c. providers of capital to these two classes of companies;
d. providers of professional services to these three groups;
e. organisations that represent industry groups; and
f. the administrators of the taxation system.

Although the Board's mandate was broad and it sought to include a community as well as a business perspective on tax reforms, its members were mainly from the business sector. Out of the ten members, seven were appointed by the government on the basis of their ability to contribute to the development of the tax system. For the review process in 2002, the Board comprised two members appointed from the business community, four from law or accounting firms, and one from the broader community. The composition was rounded out by three *ex officio* members: the heads of the Treasury, the Australian Taxation Office, and the Office of Parliamentary Counsel.

The Board members relied on experts to help them understand the issues and solutions presented during the consultation process and to assist them in producing their report. The six key experts acknowledged in the Board's report were two partners from accounting firms, two consultants, and two law professors. The Board also created a high-level advisory panel to assist with its general work. Among these twenty-two experts in 2002, nine were from accounting firms and six from law firms. To conduct the review and take care of its day-to-day work, the Board created a working group composed of three Board members: two partners from law firms and one partner in an accounting firm. This structure created an entry barrier for analysis from people outside the business sphere. Eccleston notes that some insiders claimed that the premature resignation of the only member representing the wider community 'was partly motivated by the lack of resources to scrutinize many of the technical submissions' (2004: 168) that the resigning member received during the consultation.

The Board received fifty written comments. With very few exceptions, submissions were made by private firms, tax advisers and business or professional associations. Professional firms specialising in international taxation and their associations or institutes contributed lengthy submissions, representing 41 per cent of the material submitted. After receiving the submissions and holding group discussions and a consultative seminar, the Board released its report on 28 February 2003 (Board of Taxation 2003b).

In Canada, the Panel was composed of three members from the business sector, three tax professionals (two accountants and one lawyer) and one economist. The Panel indicated that its members all 'share[d] the goal of ensuring our international taxation system makes our country's businesses more competitive for the benefit of all Canadians' (APCSIT 2008a: iii).

The Panel received thirty-three written submissions, including seventeen from businesses or business associations. Professionals from law and accounting firms and professional associations provided ten submissions, but contributed the most lengthy and detailed material. The Panel asked experts to prepare reports on specific features of the international tax system that either provided a comparative analysis of different domestic options or compared these domestic options with features of tax systems in other countries. Out of the eighteen expansive expert reports submitted, ten were from professionals and eight from academics.

Our analysis shows that international accounting firms contributed lengthy submissions to consultation processes in both countries and also provided consulting services for other organisations or firms submitting documents. In addition, they provided expert opinions to the committees that conducted the consultations; and sometimes their partners were members of the committee itself. These multiple points of entry into the consultation process, as participants as well as experts, reinforce the influence tax professionals had on the policy outcome.

These findings expose the prevalence of private actors' participation and the influence of their ideas throughout the consultation process. The framing of the process could not allow for any real input by other actors who might have provided diverging policy recommendations.

6. Undermining multilateral co-operation efforts to protect the tax base

The concepts of competitiveness and co-operation are difficult to reconcile. The prisoner's dilemma that hinders co-operation efforts (Rixen 2008) is exacerbated by the goal of offering a competitive tax system. Unilateral measures are more suited to improving the relative competitiveness of a country even if 'one country alone cannot achieve efficiency' (Gravelle 2012: 338). To give domestic firms a competitive edge, or to attract foreign capital, policy-makers do not seek global co-operation. At best, policies may be crafted bilaterally and the bilateral tax-treaty network based on the OECD model is a component of the international tax regime (Avi-Yonah 2004). Multinational firms ask countries individually to provide the conditions they need to be globally competitive. Firms prefer co-operation among countries to alleviate double taxation; but competition, rather than co-operation, is more efficient at reducing their overall tax burden.

When the competitiveness of a country and of its firms are conflated into one single concept, a deeper tax-policy analysis is precluded and policies regulating capitalism are diluted. (Rosamond 2002). A form of tension is then created and exacerbated by the fact that firms are no longer considered to be attached to only one country. Countries individually strive to adopt policies to help their firms be competitive in an international environment; but since these firms also ask for the same support from other countries, a competitive rather than a cooperative climate becomes entrenched.

In the Australian Paper, the Treasurer scarcely mentioned multilateral co-operation on fiscal policy between countries and the Board's Report ignored the issue altogether. Co-ordination was somehow expected from unilateral policies, which offered relief to corporations earning income in countries with tax systems similar to Australia's. While unilateral policies can lead to a form of co-ordination to reduce double taxation with a credit method, it is of limited use in the exemption method, since two countries rarely impose the same corporate rates. The policies would also need constant monitoring to ensure that countries with similar policies do not offer new incentives for foreign investment, leading to double relief (double non-taxation).

The Australian Paper discussed bilateral tax treaties, but more as an instrument of tax competition than as a method to protect tax-bases. Tax competition sparked a trend of reduced corporate-taxation rates (residence-based taxation), with the effect also radiating to treaties through the reduction of withholding rates on income paid to non-residents (source-based taxation) as well as to unilateral measures such as credit/exemption policies. Bilateral tax treaties were therefore not seen as a co-ordination effort to offset tax competition but rather a tool for increasing competition. The Australian Report recommended a more residence-based approach to treaties and advocated changing the benchmark for the residence-determination test to place of incorporation only.[22] Also, the Board argued that source-based taxation should be reduced in order to gain symmetrical concessions by treaty partners and relief for Australian corporations investing abroad, among other benefits.[23] The prevention of double taxation through exemption or credit methods seems to be seen as insufficient. This position could intensify the effects of tax competition and promote double non-taxation instead of preventing double taxation.

The Australian Paper referred to international co-operation in connection with preventing avoidance but, again, usually in the context of bilateral tax treaties.[24] It therefore appears that it did not view international co-operation as the

---

22. The combination of both recommendations could offer possibilities for corporations not to be treated as resident in Australia and also not to support withholding taxes as non-resident, since these rates would be low. 'As many submissions stated, this approach would facilitate outward and inward investment from and to Australia. A tax treaty policy based on residence taxation, like the OECD Model, would achieve this goal and make renegotiation of major treaties much easier' (Board of Taxation 2003b: 94). Therefore, the Board is arguing for a more residence-based taxation but with a reduced test to determine corporate residence.

23. 'The source-based DTA policy has detrimental impacts on Australian firms investing offshore, because it exposes them to high taxes in tax treaty partner countries' (Board of Taxation 2003b: 90).

24. Except for one reference to multilateral discussions: 'Changes in trade patterns, the increasing importance of services and intangibles in economic activity, more sophisticated tax planning and use of tax havens, improved communications technology and electronic commerce all pose challenges to the application of current residence and source rules. How to deal with these challenges is the subject of multilateral discussions, in which Australia actively participates, through the OECD and other international forums' (Australian Government 2002c: 84).

proactive co-ordination of tax systems to protect the tax base but rather as a reactive co-ordination effort to ensure conformity with existing national tax systems.

Just as in the Australian case, neither the Canadian Paper nor the Report considered the need or relevance of international co-operation. However, the Panel repeatedly advocated comparing and benchmarking the Canadian system with other tax systems. In its analysis, the Panel relied on detailed comparisons with current systems and reviews underway in other countries in the following terms: 'To ensure Canada's international corporate and withholding tax regimes remain competitive, they should be benchmarked regularly against international norms and should anticipate global trends and changes' (ACPSIT 2008a: 5). In addition, 'Canada's tax policy must anticipate continuous change in the global tax environment and have the flexibility to adapt accordingly' (ACPSIT 2008a: 4). This competition hinders international co-operation to protect national tax-bases and creates a movement of international harmonisation focused on lower business taxation. This movement is circular: 'In fact, some aspects of Canada's system have become a model for other countries seeking to improve the tax treatment of business and investment income flowing across their borders' (APCSIT 2008a: 12).[25]

The Panel viewed bilateral tax treaties, which could be considered a form of international co-ordination, simply as tools for greater competitiveness. It argued for a reduction of residence-based taxation – for example, by recommending the adoption or broadening of the dividend exemption system.[26] Exemption is identified as an international trend to 'boost the competitiveness of its businesses that operate in global markets' (APCSIT 2008a: 6), as opposed to using a credit method to prevent double taxation.[27] Moreover, the Panel supported more limited source-based taxation and recommended bilateral reduction of withholding rates, through treaties to benefit Canadian corporations investing abroad.[28]

---

25. Also, policies that are described as compelling are set aside, because 'no member country of the OECD or the European Union (EU) employs this system in its purest sense for taxing foreign business income' (APCSIT 2008a: 12).

26. The exemption regime applies to active income earned in a country with which Canada has a treaty. Canada's tax-treaty network comprised 86 bilateral tax treaties in 2008. The exemption regime reduces the global tax burden for Canadian corporations earning active business income abroad in countries with lower tax rates than Canada's. The announcement made prior to the consultation, that Canada will offer similar benefits to countries that have signed a TIEA with Canada, increases such possibilities of double non-taxation. At this time, Canada had not signed any TIEAs. By 2012, Canada had signed 18 TIEAs and 12 more were under negotiation.

27. The Paper recognises the benefit of a credit method; however, it says that an exemption system is simpler to comply with and to administer and that it increases the repatriation of profits. The simplicity argument is a truism: not taxing is necessarily simpler. The argument about the increase in repatriated profits only demonstrates that an exemption system would benefit dividend received from foreign affiliates in low-tax countries. Since a credit is offered for foreign taxes, then it is only in the case where foreign taxes paid are lower than the Canadian taxes that corporations would choose not to repatriate profits.

28. The Panel nevertheless states that if, for revenue purposes, the government had to choose between further reductions in corporate tax rates or reduced withholding rates, the business community prefers reduced corporate tax rates.

While emulating tax rules from other countries can lead to policy convergence, this form of co-ordination embedded in competitiveness needs to be distinguished from co-operation that allows the protection of the tax base. Whereas co-ordination through bilateral tax treaties has been used to prevent double taxation, these treaties are now used as a tool for further tax competition and even double non-taxation. Both residence and source taxation are viewed as needing even further reduction to boost national competitiveness. Adopting a unilateral taxation relief provided under a territorial system, such as an exemption regime, inhibits co-ordination between two or more countries to protect against the erosion of the tax base. This trend furthers tax competition and the reduced taxation of multinational corporations.

7. Conclusion

The study of the Australian and Canadian consultation processes on the international tax system confirms the theoretical claims about the impact of framing a public consultation in a competitiveness discourse – namely, that doing so shapes both participation and subsequent policy recommendations. It is clear that the policy options considered in both of the consultation processes were within the economic-liberalisation paradigm, according to which liberalisation produces global economic growth and tax creates a distortion. In order to increase growth and wealth, it is necessary to reduce the taxation of businesses, particularly those with international activities. Arguments within this paradigm frequently assert that countries should engage in tax competition not only as a way to participate in global economic growth but also to gain an edge and to benefit in the short term from the national economic growth that results from a temporary tax advantage. This reasoning alters the tenor of the global-liberalisation paradigm. Governments do not refer to competitiveness in policy-making for the purpose of global economic growth, as expected by the global-liberalisation paradigm. They rely instead on the idea of competitiveness to generate national economic growth.

It can also be concluded that competitiveness overrides other taxation policy goals. Neutrality, efficiency and equity are set aside or seen as secondary to competitiveness. Simplicity and the reduction of compliance costs become prevalent policy goals because of their direct association with competitiveness.

In both the Australian and Canadian cases, we saw that businesses (mainly large corporations) and tax professionals are the main participants in consultations on highly technical and complex international taxation policies. Arnold noted some time ago that, 'Tax has become the preserve of the specialist' (1990: 382) and this applies even more to the complex area of international taxation. Making competitiveness the centrepiece of consultation makes it easier for businesses and tax professionals to express their preferences. Although not all of their recommendations are followed, any recommendation adopted is favourable to businesses and represents a reduced tax burden to some extent. Consultations on very specific international taxation measures that are informed by competitiveness considerations also contribute to having a limited number of convergent policy recommendations, since the interests of the participants do not vary significantly. It creates a false impression of broad consensus. It also allows corporations that might benefit from these measures to make their voices heard, even if their recommendations might create a bias against other interests, such as those of domestic corporations. Nevertheless, concerns about redistribution, the level of tax revenues, or potential political costs may partially explain why governments in both cases did not accept all of the recommendations.

The current study sheds some light on the role of tax advisers, and particularly of global accounting firms, in the development of taxation policy through their participation in consultations. Furthermore, the experiential knowledge of tax professionals may also limit the innovative character of recommendations (Smith-Merry 2012). More research could be conducted in the form of a network analysis to explain relationships among participants in consultation processes in one or several countries.

Designing a consultation around the issue of competitiveness may also help policy-makers to justify policies they would have adopted in the absence of consultation. The argument that governments construct their own policy straitjackets is also confirmed. This suggests that countries are not merely pushed into tax competition but also, at least in part, make choices that lead them down this path. On the contrary, when governments open up discussions outside the realm of competitiveness, it allows other policy options to be addressed, as was the case with Canada's concern with fairness.

Countries are compelled to co-ordinate their domestic international tax system with international trends to avoid double taxation. However, at the domestic level, international co-operation for the protection of the tax base is not addressed as an option for the development of international tax policy. The competitiveness discourse in international tax policy-making creates a rift between efforts at the international level to stop the erosion of the tax base and the policies adopted at the domestic level. Tax co-operation is alluded to only for enforcement purposes.

As Hay and Rosamond (2002: 148) state, 'policy-makers acting on the basis of assumptions consistent with the hyperglobalisation thesis may well serve, in doing so, to bring about outcomes consistent with that thesis.' The analysis reveals the consequences of embedding the policy-making process into a competitiveness discourse. This has the effect of creating a filter for ideas and participants, favouring mainly representatives from the business sector and tax professionals, thus restricting the range of policy options discussed and recommended as well as favouring international tax competition. The result is less taxation of international businesses.

The analysis in this chapter highlights the need to return to the fundamental goals of taxation – to raise revenue, redistribute and regulate (Avi-Yonah 2006) – and the principles relevant to achieving these goals. When competitiveness takes priority over other principles it can only support less corporate taxation or the development of opportunities to reduce the global tax burden for multinational firms. Further studies could investigate how the domestic policy process and the international development of norms could address international tax-policy issues, while putting into perspective the principle of competitiveness within the broader framework of the goals of tax policy.

References

APCSIT (Advisory Panel on Canada's System of International Taxation, 2008a) *Enhancing Canada's International Tax Advantage. A consultation paper issued by the Advisory Panel on Canada's System of International Taxation*: http://publications.gc.ca/collections/collection_2009/fin/F2-184-2008E.pdf (accessed 23 July 2015).

— (2008b) *Final Report–Executive Summary: Enhancing Canada's International Tax Advantage*: http://publications.gc.ca/collections/collection_2009/fin/F2-184-2-2008E.pdf (accessed 23 July 2015).

Arnold, B. (1990) 'The process of tax policy formulation in Australia, Canada and New Zealand', *Australian Tax Forum* 7: 379.

Arnold, B. and McIntyre, M. J. (2002) *International Tax Primer*, 2nd edn, Den Haag: Kluwer Law International.

Australian Government, The Treasury (2002a) 'Review of international tax arrangements', media release no 021, 2 May: http://ministers.treasury.gov.au/DisplayDocs.aspx?doc=pressreleases/2002/021.htm&pageID=003&min=phc&Year=2002&DocType=0 (accessed 23 July 2015).

— (2002b) 'Board of Taxation Advisory Panel', media release no 9, 9 July: http://www.taxboard.gov.au/content/Content.aspx?doc=publications_and_media/media_releases/009.htm&pageid=008 (accessed 23 July 2015).

— (2002c) Review of International Taxation Arrangements, A consultation paper prepared by the Commonwealth Department of the Treasury, August 2002: http://www.taxboard.gov.au/content/reviews_and_consultations/international_taxation_arrangements/consultation_paper/downloads/international_taxation_arrangements_consultation_paper.pdf (accessed 23 July 2015).

— (2003a) 'Review of international taxation arrangements', media release no 032, 13 May: http://ministers.treasury.gov.au/DisplayDocs.aspx?doc=pressreleases/2003/032.htm&pageID=003&min=phc&Year=2003&DocType=0 (accessed 23 July 2015).

— (2003b) 'Budget 2003–2004, Statement 1: Fiscal Strategy and Budget Priorities': http://www.budget.gov.au/2003-04/bp1/download/bst1.pdf (accessed 23 July 2015).

— (2007) 'RITA measures and issues – state of play': https://www.archive.treasury.gov.au/documents/940/PDF/SOP_Jul07.pdf (accessed 21 June 2013).

Avi-Yonah, R. S. (2004) 'International tax as international law', *Tax Law Review* 57(4): 483–502.

— (2006) 'The three goals of taxation', *Tax Law Review* 60(1): 1–28.

Barnes, M. *et al*. (2003) 'Constituting "the public" in public participation', *Public Administration* 80(2): 379–99.

Basinger, S. J. and Hallerberg, M. (2004) 'Remodeling the competition for capital: how domestic politics erases the race to the bottom', *American Political Science Review* 98(2): 261–76.

Bell, S. (2012) 'The power of ideas: the ideational shaping of the structural power of business', *International Studies Quarterly* 56(4): 661–73.

Board of Taxation, the (2003a) *2002–2003 Annual Report*: http://www.taxboard.gov.au/content/publications_and_media/reports/annual_reports/2003/downloads/Annual_Report_02_03.pdf (accessed 23 July 2015).

— (2003b) *International Taxation–A Report to the Treasurer, vol. 1, The Board of Taxation's Recommendations*: http://www.taxboard.gov.au/content/reviews_and_consultations/international_taxation_arrangements/report/downloads/international_taxation_arrangements_report_volume_1.pdf (accessed 23 July 2015).

— (2003c) *International Taxation–A Report to the Treasurer, vol. 2 The Board of Taxation Consultation with the Community: Summary of Submissions*: http://www.taxboard.gov.au/content/reviews_and_consultations/international_taxation_arrangements/report/downloads/international_taxation_arrangements_report_volume_2.pdf (accessed 23 July 2015).

Boidman, N. and Darmo, M. (2011) 'How are multinationals faring under Canada's incomplete international tax reform?', *Tax Notes International* 62(11): 901–14.

Canadian Government (2006) *Advantage Canada: Building a Strong Economy for Canadians*, Ontario: Department of Finance: https://www.fin.gc.ca/ec2006/pdf/plane.pdf (accessed 23 July 2015).

— (2007a) Economic statement, 30 October 2007: http://www.collectionscanada.gc.ca/webarchives/20071115081956/http://www.fin.gc.ca/ec2007/pdf/economicstatement2007_e.pdf (accessed 23 July 2015).

— (2007b) 'Government establishes Advisory Panel on Canada's system of international taxation', media release 2007-092, 30 November: http://www.fin.gc.ca/n07/07-092-eng.asp.

— (2007c) 'International tax avoidance and "tax havens"': http://www.fin.gc.ca/n07/data/07-041_2-eng.asp (accessed 23 July 2015).

— (2011) 'Government of Canada releases draft foreign affiliate rules', media release 2011-070,19 August: http://www.fin.gc.ca/n11/11-070-eng.asp (accessed 23 July 2015).

Cerny, P. G. (1997) 'Paradoxes of the competition state: the dynamics of political globalization', *Government and Opposition* 32(2): 251–74.

— (2010) 'The competition state today: from raison d'État to raison du Monde', *Policy Studies* 31(1): 5–21.

Conley, T. (2001) 'The domestic politics of globalisation', *Australian Journal of Political Science* 36(2): 223–46.

— (2004) 'Globalisation and the politics of persuasion and coercion', *Australian Journal of Social Issues*, 39(2): 183–200.

Eccleston, R. (2000) 'The significance of business interest associations in economic policy reform: the case of Australian taxation policy', *Business and Politics* 2(3): 309–25.

— (2004) *The Thirty Year Problem: The politics of Australian tax reform*, Australian Tax Research Foundation, Research Study no 42, Sydney: Australian Tax Research Foundation.

— (2007) 'The Howard government, capital taxation and the limits of redistribution?', *Australian Journal of Political Science*, 42(2): 351–64.

Ernst & Young (2012) 'Canada's Federal budget 1012: significant international tax reforms', *International Tax Alert*, 30 March.

Ganghof, S. and Eccleston, R. (2004) 'Globalisation and the dilemmas of income taxation in Australia', *Australian Journal of Political Science* 39(3): 519–34.

Genschel, P. and Schwarz, P. (2011) 'Tax competition: a literature review', *Socio-Economic Review*, 9(2): 339–70.

Gravelle, J. (2012) 'Does the concept of competitiveness have meaning in formulating corporate tax policy?', *Tax Law Review* 65(3): 323–47.

Hassett, K. A. *et al.* (2011) 'Rethinking competitiveness', paper presented at American Enterprise Institute Conference entitled 'Is Competitiveness Worth Defending?', 29 September.

Hay, C. and Rosamond, B. (2002) 'Globalization, European integration and the discursive construction of economic imperatives', *Journal of European Public Policy* 9(2): 147–67.

Jensen, N. M. (2012) 'Fiscal policy and the firm – do low corporate tax rates attract multinational corporations?', *Comparative Political Studies* 45(8): 1004–26.

Jordan, C. (2002) 'Driving the review of international taxation arrangements', paper presented at The Taxation Institute of Australia International Masterclass entitled 'First Class Ticket to Cross Border Taxation', Sydney, 14 October.

Knoll, M. S. (2012) 'The connection between competitiveness and international taxation', *Tax Law Review* 65(3): 349–73.

Ketels, C. H. M. (2006) 'Michael Porter's competitiveness framework – recent learnings and new research priorities', *Journal of Industry, Competition and Trade* 6: 115–36.

Krugman, P. (1994) 'Competitiveness: a dangerous obsession', *Foreign Affairs* 73(2): 28–44.

Li, J. *et al.* (2006) *International Taxation in Canada*, Markham, Ontario: LexisNexis.

OECD (1992) *Technology and the Economy: The key relationships*, Paris: OECD.

Owens, J. (2011) 'David H. Tillinghast Lecture: Tax competition: to welcome or not', *Tax Law Review* 65(2): 173–98.

Prime Minister of Australia (John Howard, 2001) 'Securing Australia's prosperity', media release, 15 October.

Radaelli, C. M. (2004) 'The puzzle of regulatory competition', *Journal of Public Policy* 24(1): 1–23.

Radcliffe, S. (2010) 'Non-rational aspects of the competition state – the case of policy consultancy in Australia', *Policy Studies* 31(1): 117–28.

Ralph, J. T. (1999) *A Tax System Redesigned: More certain, equitable and durable. Report of the Review of Business Taxation*, Canberra: Commonwealth of Australia: http://www.rbt.treasury.gov.au/publications/paper4/ (accessed 23 July 2015).

Rixen, T. (2008) *The Political Economy of International Tax Governance*, Basingstoke: Palgrave Macmillan.

Rosamond, B. (2002) 'Imagining the European economy: "competitiveness" and the social construction of "Europe" as an economic space', *New Political Economy* 7(2): 157–77.

Schwab, K. (2012) *The Global Competitiveness Report 2012–2013*, Geneva: World Economic Forum: http://www3.weforum.org/docs/WEF_Global CompetitivenessReport_2012-13.pdf (accessed 8 July 2015).

Slaats, S. and Woolford, P. (2010) 'The evolution of the international tax rules', *Canadian Tax Journal* 58(5) (supp.): 225–42.

Slemrod, J. (2011) 'Competitive tax policy', paper presented at American Enterprise Institute Conference, 23 September.

Smith-Merry, J. (2012) 'Experiential knowledge in action: consulting practitioners for policy change', *Policy and Society* 31(2): 131–43.

Steinmo. S. (2003) 'The evolution of policy ideas: tax policy in the 20th century', *British Journal of Politics and International Relations* 5(2): 206–36.

Swank, D. (2006) 'Tax policy in an era of internationalization: explaining the spread of neoliberalism', *International Organization* 60(4): 847–82.

Toder, E. (2012) 'International competitiveness: who competes against whom and for what?', *Tax Law Review* 65: 505–29; and also Washington, DC: Tax Policy Center Urban Institute and Brookings Institution, 12 January 2012: http://www.urban.org/research/publication/international-competitiveness-who-competes-against-whom-and-what (accessed 8 July 2015).

Warburton, R. (2001) (Chairman of the Board of Taxation), 'On Board', Australian CPA (November 2001): 76–7.

Yin, R. K. (2003) *Case Study Research Design and Methods*, 3rd edn, Thousand Oaks, CA: Sage Publications.

PART TWO

SHORTCOMINGS OF THE CURRENT REGULATORY FRAMEWORK AND INITIATIVES

Chapter Five

A Strange Revolution: Mock Compliance and the Failure of the OECD's International Tax Transparency Regime

Richard Woodward

During the 1990s, the international community's acquiescent attitude towards offshore financial centres (OFCs) and tax havens underwent a dramatic transformation. Previously ignored, or even extolled as development models or exemplars for the virtues of free markets, OFCs were now pilloried as the 'parasites' (Palan and Abbott 1996) or 'pariahs' (Hampton and Christensen 2002) of the international financial system. The leniency of their fiscal and regulatory regimes and the opacity of their financial instruments and institutions were denounced for triggering or amplifying financial crises, permitting the laundering of the proceeds of criminal activity and monies linked to terrorist conspirators and eroding the tax bases of developed states by allowing rich individuals and corporations to flee their resident tax authorities. Since then, as part of a wider thrust to design standards to promote financial stability, OFCs and tax havens have been under sustained pressure from advanced industrialised countries, and the international organisations they dominate, to hoist their fiscal and regulatory regimes up to internationally agreed standards; or risk being 'blacklisted' and denied access to major markets. Unable to resist these developments, OFCs appeared to be facing retrenchment or closure. Compliance with these standards would squeeze OFCs because it would necessitate eroding or ending the practices that gave them their competitive edge. Non-compliance would also squeeze OFCs, either because of the reputational damage induced by blacklisting or because of counter-measures that would prohibit or seriously raise the costs of transacting business in those jurisdictions.

Most OFCs chose the former path and, by the mid 2000s, reforms initiated by OFCs seemed to have drawn the sting from these international initiatives. By the end of 2006, only Andorra, Liechtenstein, the Marshall Islands and Monaco remained on the international blacklists drawn up by the Financial Stability Forum (FSF) (concerned with regulation), the Financial Action Task Force (concerned with money laundering) and the Organization for Economic Co-operation and Development (OECD) (concerned with harmful tax practices). International Monetary Fund (IMF) (2006) and FSF (2007) reviews of OFCs' application of international standards and codes revealed that OFCs were generally compliant and, in many cases, outshone their onshore counterparts (*cf.* Findlay, Nielsen and Sharman 2014). The IMF subsequently (in 2008) announced that improvements in the regulatory standards of OFCs were sufficient to render the offshore/onshore distinction meaningless and that its work in this area would be merged with its Financial Sector Assessment Programme. The onset of the global financial crisis breathed new life into these seemingly moribund efforts, however. Although they were not directly incriminated in the causes of the crisis, the feeling persisted that offshore practices hastened its arrival, through tax breaks that encouraged the build-up of debt and intensified the initial credit crunch because impenetrable structures prevented financiers from rapidly and accurately assessing the creditworthiness of their counter-parties (Palan *et al.* 2010; Shaxson 2011). At their London Summit in April 2009, the G20 leaders pledged action to 'end the era of banking secrecy' by accelerating and deepening OECD's existing work to promote international tax transparency (G20 2009). In September 2009, reforms to the OECD's Global Forum on Transparency and Exchange of Information for Tax Purposes were agreed that would expand its membership, intensify its peer-review process and speed up the negotiation of agreements to exchange information.

By August 2014, 121 countries plus the European Union had become members of the Global Forum, thereby making commitments to meet its standard to exchange information upon request and subject themselves to peer review. Moreover, 143 peer reviews had been completed and reports agreed and over 1,200 tax information-exchange agreements (TIEAs) had been signed (OECD 2014b). OECD Secretary-General, Angel Gurría, has repeatedly boasted of the OECD's orchestration of a 'revolution' (OECD 2009b) in global tax transparency. Once again, OFCs appeared to be in the invidious position of needing to choose between conformity and resistance, both of which were likely to undermine the viability of their business model. Aside from a few token casualties, however, OFCs seem to have withstood this latest regulatory onslaught. Indeed, many appear to be in rude health (*Economist* 2013), with evidence that despite compliance with various international standards, assets stashed offshore are stable or growing (Datamonitor 2013).

Several explanations for this apparent paradox have been offered. One is that conformity with international standards attracts investors because additional compliance costs are outweighed by the reputational benefits of association with an obedient jurisdiction. A second is that OFCs are being propped up by demand for offshore financial services by clients from emerging markets (Woodward 2011; Sharman 2012). Elsewhere it has been argued that the OECD's project is fundamentally flawed. For example, Meinzer (2012) denounces the 'creeping futility' of the OECD project, suggesting that an effective clampdown on tax dodgers requires tougher standards grounded in automatic information-exchange. Similarly, the complexity of the OECD project is being exploited by the fertile minds of tax-planning professionals, to launch new products that remain within the rules but which perpetuate secrecy (Woodward 2006).

This chapter offers an early sketch of research into another possible explanation, grounded in the literature on compliance in international relations. Although they disagree about the reasons, most theoretical approaches to compliance predict that smaller, weaker states (like many of those hosting OFCs) will be forced to adopt international standards, not least because of the material or reputational costs of defiance mentioned at the end of the opening paragraph. Increasingly these predictions are being confounded by empirical research revealing considerable variation not only in *levels* of compliance with international financial standards (IMF 2011a) but also in its *quality*. This chapter is mainly concerned with the quality of compliance and, in particular, what Andrew Walter (2008) has termed 'mock compliance', in which states adopt the form but not the substance of compliance. For example, as the chapter discusses further below, a state might enact an elaborate legislative and regulatory framework to enable the exchange of information on tax matters but this framework might then lie dormant. Mock compliance is most likely to arise in situations in which states recognise that outright defiance of international standards would result in serious repercussions but in which full compliance would impose significant costs on powerful domestic groups and actors (such as the financial-services industry) and where it is difficult for third parties to ascertain and expose non-compliance. This chapter argues that the OECD initiative has been dogged throughout by mock compliance; moreover, revisions to the initiative announced since 2009 do not really address, and indeed might exacerbate, the problem. Initially the enhanced peer-review process seems to raise the costs of non-compliance further, in a way that might convince states to railroad domestic groups into submission and allow third parties better insight into whether compliance is more apparent than real. Simultaneously, however, the reforms necessary to avoid the OECD's wrath will inflict considerable extra compliance costs on private actors and, even if the peer-review process is more intrusive, there is no guarantee their contents will be used by third parties or that they will be sufficiently rigorous to expose mock compliance. Therefore, the chapter predicts that states with OFCs will continue to adopt mock-compliance strategies in order to reconcile the competing demands of international institutions and markets with their domestic veto-players. The chapter concludes by considering whether the OECD's recent adoption of a new international standard predicated on automatic information-exchange will alter this calculation.

1. Compliance in international political economy

In the interregnum between the Asian financial crisis and the onset of the global financial crisis (GFC), international political economy (IPE) was awash with literature examining the emergence and efficacy of the international financial architecture. Much of this writing was highly critical, suggesting that the predilection for awarding greater freedom to private actors to manage risks would exacerbate financial instability. Nevertheless, no IPE scholar predicted the timing or the specifics of the GFC (*see* Helleiner 2011), which has inevitably led to much soul-searching about the shortcomings of the discipline and the sketching out of a post-crisis research agenda. One strand of this is to re-examine our understanding of the roles played by interstate power relations, domestic politics and transnational actors in the creation, strengthening and implementation of international financial standards (Helleiner and Pagliari 2011).

Much of the IPE literature on compliance (defined here as situations in which the behaviour of actors subject to a rule conforms to its prescriptions) predicts that states and private actors will apply international financial standards, albeit for very different reasons. Rationalist accounts stress the role of material incentives, suggesting that states choose courses of action that maximise their gains (or minimise their losses) and thus comply if the benefits of doing so exceed the costs. These approaches suggest that compliance is best achieved by offering tangible inducements (or punishments for non-compliance) that alter the cost-benefit calculation. Simmons (2001) and Drezner (2007) suggest that standards are often developed by the most powerful states, who then use their dominant market position to foist them upon others. For example, states that do not obey the rules might face restrictions or be completely denied access to major markets, something the US is exploiting to promote compliance with its Foreign Account Tax Compliance Act (FATCA) (*see* Eccleston and Smith 2016, Chapter Eight in this volume). Alternatively, and an increasingly popular tactic in global financial governance, recalcitrant territories are 'named and shamed', signalling to private financial institutions and credit-ratings agencies that they are perilous investment climates which ought to be shunned (Sharman 2009). Either way, the costs of disobedience would be significant, making compliance the probable outcome.

Alone, the rationalist explanation is problematic. For example, accurately estimating the costs and benefits of different courses of action is almost impossible and it does assume a binary distinction between compliance and non-compliance. Moreover, if straightforward power was the sole determinant we would not expect to see the variations in the levels and quality of compliance referred to in the introduction.

Constructivist accounts of IPE argue that compliance can be explained by reference to shared norms and legitimacy. Transgovernmental networks (Slaughter 2004) and epistemic communities of regulators (Porter 2005) have a prominent role in global financial governance. These narratives emphasise the socialising role played by these bodies and how the desire of participants to sustain their reputation persuades them to push compliance with regulations reflecting their shared norms. Keck and Sikkink (1998) go on to suggest that political elites can be pressured by these transnational forces to implement these norms. If these norms are successfully internalised, the issue of compliance is reduced to the status of a technical rather than a political problem. That is to say, non-compliance is not explained by reference to a deliberate strategy flowing from an appreciation of costs and benefits but is the outcome of technical issues surrounding possible ambiguities in the rules and insufficient institutional capacity. The first problem with this explanation is that the secrecy of these networks makes norms and social learning difficult to observe. Secondly, as Finnemore and Sikkink (1998) have observed, norms only become internalised late in their 'life-cycle'. Initially, new norms compete and coexist with their predecessors and, often, face domestic resistance from those not party to the rarefied atmosphere of the international regulatory networks. Indeed, while international networks offer fertile conditions for social learning, including tight groups of professionals with similar outlooks, regular interaction over long periods, and relatively de-politicised arguments, these conditions do not pertain to the domestic contexts in which such policies are implemented.

The previous point serves to highlight a more general complaint levelled at the compliance literature, namely, that it tends to accentuate the *international* dimension, where codes and standards are negotiated, to the detriment of the *domestic* dimension where codes and standards are ultimately implemented and applied. At the negotiation stage, direct power or the power of expert authority may mean weaker countries feel compelled to enlist in an initiative; but they are also freer to do so because, often, domestic interests who might oppose these developments are absent. However, domestic actors are vital at the implementation stage, enabling them to mobilise to resist compliance with international initiatives. Investigations by comparative political economists have revealed the many ways in which domestic political institutions and interests mediate the impact of external compliance pressure (Mosley 2010). Singer (2007), for example, has argued that in order to understand the implementation of international standards it is vital to examine the preferences of the regulators. Far from being passive receptors of instructions from international bodies, domestic regulators are bureaucratic agents whose desire to maintain their autonomy, prestige and future employment requires them to pacify local institutions and actors. To take a crude example from tax-information-exchange, revenue authorities are balancing demands from politicians to close tax loopholes to help plug fiscal gaps while trying not to undermine the competitiveness of the financial-services industry upon which, especially in small states, their jobs depend. In other words, while states may be committed to an international initiative, administrative forbearance might prevent its full implementation.

Walter's (2008) notion of 'mock compliance' also assigns a leading role to domestic sources of compliance. Unlike Singer, who restricts his focus almost entirely to regulators, politicians and the financial services industry, Walter focuses on a wider range of domestic actors relevant to the compliance debate, including taxpayers, civil-society organisations, non-financial firms and government ministries. While not dismissing the international factors identified in mainstream IPE debates, his explanations for non-compliance are rooted in the institutional and structural features of the domestic political system. He argues that existing understandings overlook the nature of compliance: in particular, that compliance is often superficial. Borrowing from Raustalia and Slaughter (2002) he draws a distinction between implementation and compliance. Implementation involves the transposition of international standards into domestic law but it does not follow that private and bureaucratic behaviour will immediately correspond to these requirements. For instance, compliance may be thwarted by governments introducing changes gradually, waiting for their main competitors to institute equivalent changes or agreeing only to share the benefits of compliance with selected counterparts; by bureaucracies looking to sabotage certain elements of an agreement or, especially in developing states, lacking the resources to ensure widespread compliance; and by private companies seeking to minimise their regulatory burden. Although the threats arising from non-compliance are often more imagined than real, governments, bureaucrats and private actors all have incentives to adopt the *form* of compliance but not the *substance*. In other words, while actors give the outward appearance of compliance to the international community they are concurrently engaged in behaviour at considerable variance from it. It is this lack of substantive compliance that is dubbed 'mock compliance'.

The conditions under which mock compliance is more likely include, first, where substantive compliance would immediately impose high additional costs on discrete private-sector groups. In these circumstances, states are liable to encounter very strong resistance from affected groups. Likewise, the obvious solution of introducing grave punishments for non-compliance may be politically impossible, especially where an industry makes a substantial economic contribution. Whereas the benefits of substantive compliance are often diffuse, long-term and uncertain, the costs are visible, immediate, concentrated and calculable, facilitating the advocacy of their case by coalitions hostile to reform (*cf.* Helleiner 1994). Second, mock compliance is likely if the costs of obvious non-compliance are high. If actors believe that international markets and international financial institutions will respond to explicit non-compliance by significantly raising its cost, the effect may be to shift the balance of domestic forces behind a solution that conforms, ostensibly at least, to international expectations. For OFCs, whose business model is overwhelmingly reliant on external capital, the imminent threat of expulsion from particular markets could have serious repercussions. Finally, mock compliance is likely under conditions where monitoring by a third party is difficult or costly. Many of the aforementioned costs associated with non-compliance will only be incurred if outsiders can expose it. In practice, ascertaining wrongdoing with any degree of accuracy is exceedingly difficult. The frequent portrayals of international organisations, who police many international financial standards, as omnipotent bodies with endless resources and tentacles capable of poking into the dimmest recesses of domestic policy-making are considerably at odds with reality. As the IMF's (2011b) experience with the Reports on the Observance of Standards and Codes reveals, international organisations often have to undertake this work on shoestring budgets, with few staff, and they are overwhelmingly reliant on participant countries to supply them with the requisite information. Thus, while international organisations may help to provoke initial commitments, their ability to monitor the substance of compliance is restricted, especially in cases where states and the private sector collude to conceal their failings. Furthermore, there is no guarantee that international investors or states will take notice of the findings or adjust their behaviour (IMF 2011b). For example, there is no compulsion for private actors to use compliance with international standards as criteria in investment decisions.

2. 1998–2009: mock compliance with the OECD's tax-transparency regime

The OECD's initial forays into tax transparency left some important legacies, such as the Tax Information-Exchange Agreements (TIEAs) and the Global Forum, now at the heart of the contemporary process, and mock compliance with this first initiative sheds important light on the second stage of the OECD'S, work in the period since 2009.

Following a request from the G7 in 1998, the OECD produced a report in which it argued that many jurisdictions were engaging in 'harmful tax practices'. Essentially, harmful tax practices consisted of efforts to lure non-residents' capital by combining low or non-existent rates of taxation with opaque corporate structures or secrecy provisions that prevented overseas revenue authorities from identifying the owners of these assets and taxing them accordingly. The report defined a set of criteria that constituted harmful tax practices and announced that jurisdictions would be assessed against them. While OECD countries meeting the criteria were trusted to extinguish their own harmful tax practices, non-OECD countries that were found to meet the criteria were placed on a blacklist that appeared in the OECD's follow-up report in 2000. Countries on this list were told that they must make a commitment to eradicate harmful tax practices by July 2005. Failure to do to so would result in them being placed on a revised blacklist of 'uncooperative tax havens' that would face 'defensive measures' (including withholding taxes, enhanced auditing and refusal to enter or even terminating existing tax treaties) by OECD countries. Fearing the reputational and material repercussions of blacklisting, the majority of jurisdictions made commitments.

Initially this does not look a very promising background for mock compliance. The litany of defensive measures appeared to make the costs of blatant non-compliance excessive, especially given that the OECD was proposing a peer-review system (to be pursued through a new OECD Global Forum on Taxation) that looked capable of exposing shortcomings. Furthermore, while the costs of compliance would fall disproportionately on private financial institutions that had politically privileged positions, in many OFCs these were trumped by the threat of countermeasures by OECD countries, which could effectively excommunicate these places from the global financial community. Whatever they did, the competitive position of OFCs would be damaged. If OFCs denuded their secrecy provisions to avoid counter-measures, they would lose clients who invested for those reasons; if they stood firm they would invite sanctions that would significantly raise the material and reputational costs of transacting business. Indeed, the fact that some jurisdictions complied before the OECD's 2000 report, and that many more did so shortly afterwards, suggests that the material and reputational costs of non-compliance were very high indeed for places heavily dependent on their financial sectors – possibly terminally (Mistry and Sharman 2008).

Fortunately for these jurisdictions, the transnational tax-planning industry and battalions of free-market pressure groups rallied to their aid, seeking to de-legitimise the initiative by demonstrating how it ran counter to existing norms and lacked a level playing field for OECD and non-OECD countries (Webb 2004; Sharman 2006). In particular, they pointed to Switzerland and Luxembourg's abstention from the two OECD reports, which meant, unlike their other OECD counterparts, they had not made formal commitments to eliminate their harmful tax practices. The real turning point, however, was the withdrawal of US support for key elements of the process, which prompted a serious moderation of the harmful tax-competition initiative. The prime objective of extinguishing 'harmful tax practices' was superseded by vaguer references to promoting transparency in tax affairs through the exchange of information. The scope of activities that would constitute *prima facie* evidence of harmful tax practices was slimmed down, not least by excluding issues connected with corporate actors and focusing exclusively on individuals. Finally, the OECD conceded that counter-measures against non-OECD jurisdictions would not commence prior to those against OECD countries. This last indulgence brought the initiative to an impasse. It meant that non-OECD countries with OFCs could make a commitment to promote tax transparency, and thus escape being tarnished by blacklisting, safe in the knowledge that their commitment would not be activated because of the continued intransigence of OECD members.

The OECD's programme limped on but its momentum had vanished. The Model Agreement on Exchange of Information on Tax Matters agreed in 2002 established what remained, until April 2013, the international standard for tax-information-exchange, that is, that countries should have the power to obtain tax information from those operating in their jurisdiction and ensure that the information was available to be exchanged in a timely manner upon request in circumstances 'foreseeably relevant' to the enforcement of the requesting country's tax laws. The model also became the basis upon which TIEAs, bilateral instruments to underpin effective information-exchange, were negotiated. The OECD's botched process had engendered the perfect conditions for tax havens to engage in mock compliance. The costs of TIEAs would still fall on entrenched private interests; however, all talk of defensive measures had been dropped and peer reviews remained perfunctory. Against this background, states engaged in classic mock-compliance behaviour. Safe in the knowledge that no counter-measures would be forthcoming, those states that had committed to the OECD either did not sign TIEAs (only twenty-three TIEAs were negotiated between 2000 and 2007) or failed to ratify them, thus denying them legal effect (OECD 2010b).

3. 2009–present: post-GFC compliance with the OECD's tax-transparency regime

Precisely why the G20 seized upon the OECD's tax work in the aftermath of the GFC is still a matter of debate. The agential entrepreneurship of the OECD Secretary-General, the growth of government deficits in many G20 economies, and that the OECD had a ready plan for a G20 desperate to demonstrate it was doing something to respond to the financial imbroglio probably all played a part (Eccleston 2013). In March 2009, the OECD countries that had previously objected to the organisation's tax-transparency initiative removed their reservations, thus activating the commitments previously entered into by non-OECD members. At the G20 London Summit the following month, the OECD unveiled a 'progress report' detailing the position of countries and territories *vis-à-vis* the international tax standard (OECD 2009a). Jurisdictions that had signed twelve or more TIEAs were placed on a 'white list' of those who had 'substantially implemented' the standards. Those that had made commitments but not signed twelve TIEAs (or Double Tax Agreements containing equivalent information-exchange articles) were placed on a 'grey list' of countries that had 'committed but not substantially implemented' the standard. Finally there was a 'blacklist' of countries that had not made a commitment. The London Summit also announced the readiness of G20 countries to take action against non-compliant states, presenting a "toolbox" of countermeasures reminiscent of those in the 2000 Report, something the September 2009 Pittsburgh Summit confirmed could start from March 2010 (G20 2009a, 2009b). Suddenly, non-OECD jurisdictions returned to a situation similar to that of 2000, in which failure to make a commitment and take significant steps towards implementation would see their reputations tainted by blacklisting; and they would suffer the material repercussions of counter-measures. Unsurprisingly, there was a flurry of activity. By January 2010, all jurisdictions had been expunged from the blacklist through making commitments and more than 300 TIEAs had been signed (although twenty-three jurisdictions remained on the grey list, having not yet reached the twelve-TIEA threshold).

There were also important changes to the resuscitated regime. In September 2009, the Global Forum, now endorsed by the G20, was reformed and reconstituted as the Global Forum on Tax Transparency and Information-Exchange. Its job would be to oversee an enhanced version of the earlier peer-review process, designed to evaluate implementation and compliance with the internationally agreed tax standard. The OECD (2010c) identified ten criteria against which jurisdictions would be assessed. The criteria revolve around whether states were ensuring that the requisite tax information was available (that it was being collected by private actors); that it could be accessed (that domestic authorities had the power to obtain information held by financial institutions); and that it could be exchanged (that there were mechanisms in place to allow information to be exchanged with competent bodies overseas). The peer-review process would have two stages, called phases. Phase one would simply assesses whether a jurisdiction had in place the legal and regulatory framework to enable tax-information-exchange. Under the pre-2009 peer-review system, this is where the OECD's interest ceased. However, phase two of the peer-review process would investigate whether that legislative framework was effectively complied with in practice. In other words, peer reviewers would now be scrutinising whether jurisdictions expeditiously exchanged tax information in practice. Once approved by the Forum's Peer Review Group, reports on the jurisdiction's performance would be placed in the public domain.

The outcomes of the reviews would also be more nuanced. For instance, rather than merely deeming countries compliant or non-compliant, first-phase reviews examine each of the range of recommendations, stating whether each element is 'in place', 'in place but needs improvement' or 'not in place' (OECD 2011a). Second-phase reviews now have four categories: compliant; largely compliant; partially compliant; not compliant. This more subtle approach has much to commend it, although it does raise problems for analysis. For example, the guidance notes that underpin the work of the Global Forum's expert team of assessors recognise 'that the rating of Compliant as a general matter is not to be viewed as requiring perfection' (OECD 2013a: 59). In other words, a jurisdiction may receive a compliant rating despite not having all of the required elements in place. Likewise, should a country deemed 'largely compliant' by the Global Forum be considered to meet the international standard?

Initially these reforms appear to have vitiated the conditions for mock compliance in a manner identical to that identified in the period 1998–2001. Until 2009, tax information standards in many, especially non-OECD, countries were rudimentary. Various types of information were not collected; and even if they were, would certainly not be shared. Thus, the new requirements that information should be available, accessible and transferable impose substantial additional costs on private actors. Ordinarily 'where local financial institutions benefit from the continuation of existing rule structures – and stand to lose from the adoption of new, internationally derived regulations – the process of compliance is unlikely to move forward' (Mosley 2010: 726). However, in this instance, the penalties appear very serious. Non-compliance might reduce the cost of collecting information – but at the expense of overwhelming reputational damage from blacklisting and material damage inflicted by sanctions from states in the G20. Normally, the high cost of outright resistance would similarly be a factor encouraging mock compliance. However, the more intrusive peer-review system, specifically designed to investigate the application of the regulatory framework rather than just its existence, means mock compliance should be detected and exposed through the publication of detailed reports. Moreover, the practical use of TIEAs means the effectiveness of a jurisdiction's information-exchange regime is under constant scrutiny. If competent authorities from overseas regularly find their requests for information rebuffed on spurious grounds, their complaints will soon reach the public domain. With the G20 countries poised to mete out sanctions, states may reluctantly conclude that mock compliance is as risky and costly a strategy as straightforward non-compliance. The alacrity with which jurisdictions have adopted TIEAs, despite the costs they impose and the major overhauls of domestic laws they have required, is, arguably, the best evidence of this.

4. Mock compliance with phase two of the OECD's tax-transparency regime

By August 2014, the Global Forum had published sixty-four phase-two reports assigning compliance scores to assessed jurisdictions (OECD 2014b). The achievements of the Global Forum's peer reviews appear impressive. Four-fifths of the Global Forum membership has now undergone at least one phase of the peer review and 818 recommendations to implement the international tax standard have been issued. Moreover, the Global Forum provides evidence that these peer reviews are having the desired result of shaming errant jurisdictions into reform. Eighty-five jurisdictions have provided subsequent testimony that they intend to introduce – or have already introduced – legal changes to address almost half of these recommendations. Eighteen supplementary reviews of jurisdictions reveal that seventy-eight Global Forum recommendations have been fully adopted, resulting in forty-nine upgrades to the original peer reviews' determinations (see OECD 2014a: 62). The phase-two reports lend credibility to the Global Forum's assertion that 'it has effectively improved transparency and exchange of information between jurisdictions' (OECD 2014a: 54). Of the sixty-four reports undertaken twenty jurisdictions were found 'fully compliant', thirty-two 'largely compliant', eight 'partially compliant' and four 'non-compliant'. Importantly, there was considerable evidence of improvements in tax transparency between the phase-one and phase-two reviews. In the first fifty jurisdictions that underwent phase-two or supplementary reviews, the proportion of the elements of the tax-transparency standard that were 'not in place' fell to 3 per cent, compared with 15 per cent at the end of their phase-one reviews. Equally, the proportion of elements in place rose from 58 to 82 per cent (OECD 2013a: 31). All fifty jurisdictions were fully compliant with the standard in regard to availability of banking information; while 95 per cent were fully compliant in regard to rights and safeguards in TIEAs. Finally, the implementation of TIEAs had produced a spike in information-exchange requests. In 2012, in the twenty-three jurisdictions for which comparable data is available, almost 3,000 information-exchange requests were made, an 81 per cent increase since 2009 (OECD 2013a: 33–4). Furthermore, these requests were responded to in a timelier manner than before. The proportion of requests responded to in less than ninety days rose from 47 per cent in 2009 to 73 per cent in 2012; while the number of requests taking over a year to receive a response fell from 28 per cent to 1 per cent (OECD 2013a: 32).

Nevertheless, these headline figures disguise the continued prevalence of mock compliance with the OECD regime. Successive OECD reviews reveal that non-compliance is slowly tapering off but, nevertheless, the 'broad variation in the level of implementation of standards' noted in one of the OECD's (2010d: 1) earliest summaries of the post-2009 regime endures. The OECD's 2012 Progress Report to the G20 (OECD 2012a) observed that 'the [compliance] situation is diverse' and while the Global Forum's Annual Report declares that there is 'a good level of compliance' it concedes that there are 'a number of unresolved deficiencies' (OECD 2012b: 5, 32). These problems are amply demonstrated by the first phase-two peer reviews. Under one-third of the jurisdictions assessed to date have mustered a fully compliant score; while almost one-fifth were deemed non- or partially compliant. The wider synopsis of assessed jurisdictions reveals a similar pattern. The 2012 Progress Report showed that of the eighty-eight places reviewed, thirty-four had elements 'not in place' and only fourteen countries had arrangements for the availability, access and exchange of information that did not require improvement (OECD 2012b). In 2013, the picture had slightly improved, with thirty-four out of 100 jurisdictions now possessing elements not in place and thirty-two with arrangements for the availability, access and exchange of information that did not require improvement (OECD 2013b). The deficiencies of eleven countries remain sufficiently severe that they have not been permitted to progress to the second phase of peer review (there being little point in reviewing the effectiveness of a tax-information-exchange framework that does not exist). As noted above, the OECD has trumpeted the 818 defects in tax-transparency regimes uncovered by peer reviews and the seventy-eight that have so far been addressed. Another way of looking at that statistic is to note that less than 10 per cent of the peer-review reports' findings have so far been implemented.

A similar story attends the steady improvement in the quality and effectiveness of TIEAs. In its most recent progress report, the OECD (2014c: 29) notes that Global Forum members have now signed 1633 bilateral TIEAs, 1280 of which meet the international standard. Moreover, the number of tax-information-exchange initiatives has boomed, owing to countries signing the OECD/Council of Europe Multilateral Convention on Mutual Administrative Assistance in Tax Matters. Global Forum members are now bound by 3340 tax-information-exchange agreements, 2987 of which meet the international standard. However, as Johannesen and Zucman (2014: 70) point out, this is still a long way short of a full network of tax treaties; and this number is inflated by a number of essentially meaningless agreements. This is a legacy of the OECD's original demand that to escape blacklisting, jurisdictions needed only to sign twelve TIEAs. Many jurisdictions responded by concluding the minimum number of treaties and doing so predominantly with micro-states, meaning it was unlikely the arrangements would ever be exercised (Tax Justice Network 2009). The peer reviews continue to unearth classic examples of mock compliance, regularly observing that the information-exchange process is littered with administrative obstacles that ensure it is protracted (OECD 2012a: 46). Doubts also persist about whether levels of administrative co-operation will be sufficient or whether the rapid expansion in the number of TIEAs will overwhelm the administrative capacity of many smaller jurisdictions.

That so much mock compliance lingers reflects the persistence of conditions that encourage such behaviour. First, despite the threat of material sanctions having vanished (for instance, there is currently no talk of the four jurisdictions considered non-compliant after their phase-two review being punished with counter-measures), potential reputational damage seems to have convinced most territories of the excessive costs of outright defiance of the OECD regime. As non-OECD countries learnt during the first period of the OECD campaign, 'the bark is the bite' where blacklisting is concerned (Sharman 2009). In other words, blacklisting, whether justified or not, inflicts reputational damage that prompts some business to depart. Equally, there is little incentive to comply fully if this means extensive additional compliance costs and the piercing of the cloak of secrecy scares investors away. As a regulator from one small island tax haven concludes:

> It is expensive to be a bad citizen but it is even more expensive to be a good citizen because of the extraordinarily high costs of compliance. Those opting for pure compliance will encounter extra costs without any extra benefits – especially in a world where capital mobility allows money to flee to places that might be applying international rules in a more flexible manner (author interview, quote in Eccleston 2013).

Thus, non-OECD countries seem to have once more opted for a mock-compliance strategy, whereby they signal their compliance with the standards of transparency and exchange of information for tax purposes through participation in the Global Forum process but, in practice, are continuing to indulge in proscribed practices.

That they are able to do so reflects the presence of the second ingredient in the mock-compliance 'recipe': the difficulties of exposing wrongdoing in a way that might elicit opinion-shifts in domestic interests that would make them more supportive of compliance. The 'comprehensive and in-depth' reviews of members promised by the OECD (2010a) are compromised by the tight timetable and meagre resources. In 2013, the Global Forum's 122 members were attended by a staff of twenty-seven, controlling a budget of €3.9m (OECD 2013a: 14), who manage a congested peer-review timetable. The phase-one reviews have been extremely reliant on 'desk-based' appraisals of questionnaires supplied by the relevant territories. Phase-two reviews involve a two–three day on-site visit by an OECD peer-review group (OECD 2011a) but worries that these reviews barely scratch the surface are regularly expressed. This is reinforced by the OECD's acceptance that while the system is supposed to be flexible and ongoing, resource constraints mean that it 'will not be in a position to re-evaluate jurisdictions immediately' (OECD 2010d: 5).

The shortcomings of the peer-review process also extend to the TIEAs. Requests made under TIEAs are a further way in which compliance with the tax-transparency regime is checked. In order to stop overseas tax authorities embarking on speculative enquiries – so-called 'fishing expeditions' – TIEAs require them to know almost everything about their prey, something that secrecy provisions will almost certainly preclude. As a result, as one frustrated tax inspector explains 'you already have to have pretty much all the information you're after to get the last piece. It's a Catch-22' (quoted in *Economist* 2013). There is therefore 'significant scope for an uncooperative jurisdiction to obfuscate and stonewall while still complying with their obligations under a TIEA' (Eccleston 2013: 155; *cf.* Sheppard 2009). For example, the OECD's (2011b) peer review of Switzerland noted that it was obeying the letter but not the spirit of the standards, by negotiating extremely narrow interpretations of identity requirements for an exchange-of-information request. Furthermore, because the exchange of information between competent tax authorities must be done on a confidential basis, the OECD's peer-review groups will be unable to examine specific examples of information-exchange in practice (OECD 2011a). Many offshore tax havens are happily collecting the necessary information, and may even be more rigorous in doing so than their onshore counterparts, but they are collecting it safe in the knowledge that it will never have to be exchanged.

The final factor that persists as an obstacle to full compliance with the OECD regime is its high cost for the private sector. Swiss negotiation of very tight identity requirements for information requests, and its position that it will not respond to information requests deriving from whistle-blowing activity, reflected strong domestic pressures to obstruct effective information-exchange

(Eccleston 2013; Tax Justice Network 2013). Finance lobbies retain considerable weight in many countries but this is accentuated in places recognised as tax havens, especially smaller states in which financial activities comprise a substantial share of GDP and where very tight and well connected financial communities exert considerable political clout and may have effectively 'captured' the state (Shaxson and Christensen 2013). The attractiveness of offshore financial services is not purely down to secrecy but, nonetheless, the need to comply with secrecy provision is a substantial burden. The effects are keenly felt by OFCs that work with thin operating margins, for example, those who generate income from licensing fees, where relatively small changes in compliance costs can undermine profitability. The financial-services industry in tax havens must now collect and curate a lot of information that it previously did not; states are passing some of the costs of making their own institutions more robust on to private providers or even demanding payment from their overseas counterparts before information will be exchanged (Tax Justice Network 2010).

Unlike other areas of financial regulation, in which, at times, sharp divisions have emerged between different parts of the industry (Helleiner and Pagliari 2011), the transnational tax-planning industry has remained relatively cohesive. While in large, developed states the domestic sands are being shifted by regular tax-avoidance scandals that have mobilised groups wanting an end to tax secrecy, they have much less traction in tax havens. For the moment, in places heavily reliant on offshore financial services, the power of the pin-stripe infrastructure overwhelms domestic opponents looking for a tax-haven clampdown.

5. Conclusion

If the rhetoric of the G20 and OECD is to be believed, offshore financial centres and tax havens face a bleak future. Either they will be forced to dilute the secrecy that gives them a critical competitive edge or they can maintain their secrecy but face blacklisting and countermeasures that will destroy their reputation as appropriate places to invest. The decision by 122 states to participate in the Global Forum process and the negotiation of over 1200 TIEAs appear to signify that many states have concluded that flagrant non-compliance would be a dangerous and counterproductive strategy. This paper has argued that states seem to be opting instead for a strategy of 'mock compliance', whereby they make a commitment to the initiative and adopt the form of compliance to avoid blacklisting and sanctions but then fail to implement the substance of the initiative, thereby enabling them to retain features of their regulatory regime that make them an attractive investment location. From the outset, the OECD's tax-transparency and information-exchange initiative has cultivated ideal conditions for mock compliance: the costs imposed on entrenched domestic interests are moderate but significant; the costs of brazen defiance are, seemingly, considerable; and third-party monitoring costs of compliance are high. Superficially, the post-2009 reforms seemed to address these problems. Harsh sanctions on territories that are not fully compliant combined with a more invasive system of peer review should have raised the cost of mock compliance and softened domestic opposition to implementation. In practice, this has yet to happen, because of shortcomings in the peer-review regime; and the absence of sanctions against non-compliant regimes has limited the costs of mock compliance.

In April 2013, the G20 finance ministers endorsed the principle of automatic exchange of tax information as the new international standard. By September 2014, sixty-five jurisdictions, including all OECD members, had committed to the OECD Declaration on Automatic Exchange of Information in Tax Matters, forty-seven of which have committed to early adoption (by the end of 2016). This new, third phase of the OECD's tax-transparency regime is considered a game-changer by advocates and opponents of OFCs alike, not least because automatic information-exchange removes the 'Catch-22' that has limited the effectiveness of rules based on information-exchange on request. Nevertheless, because it imposes significant additional costs on financial institutions, automatic information-exchange may exacerbate the problems of mock compliance. Indeed, there is already substantial evidence that financial institutions are lobbying their governments to garner exemptions and delay implementation (see, for example, *Australian Financial Review* 2014). Moreover, there is no indication that the OECD will beef up the peer-review system by granting it extra resources to smoke out examples of mock compliance or imposing material sanctions to deter wayward jurisdictions. Tax-justice campaigners also point out that the effectiveness of automatic information-exchange is also compromised by the absence of public registers of beneficial owners of trusts and companies (Knobel and Meinzer 2014a, 2014b). In short, although automatic information-exchange marks a step-change in the campaign to limit offshore financial practices, the danger of this regime's effectiveness being diminished by mock compliance remains high.

References

Australian Financial Review (2014) 'Big banks stall on global tax evasion crackdown': http://www.afr.com/p/business/financial_services/big_banks_stall_on_global_tax_evasion_KUurnKuqx7NMlYgpgcH2yM (accessed 24 July 2015).

Datamonitor (2013) *HNW Offshore Investment: Key trends and motivations*: http://www.datamonitor.com/store/Product/hnw_offshore_investment_key_trends_and_motivations?productid=CM00213-007 (accessed 23 February 2013).

Drezner, D. (2007) *All Politics is Global: Explaining international regulatory regimes*, Princeton, New Jersey: Princeton University Press.

Eccleston, R. (2013) *The Dynamics of Global Economic Governance: The financial crisis, the OECD, and the politics of international tax governance*, Cheltenham: Edward Elgar.

Economist (2013) 'Special report: offshore finance', 16 February.

Findley, M. G., Nielsen, D. I. and Sharman, J. C. (2014) *Global Shell Games: Experiments in transnational relations, crime and terrorism*, Cambridge: Cambridge University Press.

Finnemore, M. and Sikkink, K. (1998) 'International norm dynamics and political change', *International Organization* 52(4): 887–917.

FSF (Financial Stability Forum, 2007) 'Financial Stability Forum review of its offshore financial centres initiative': http://www.financialstabilityboard.org/wp-content/uploads/pr_070926b.pdf?page_moved=1 (accessed 24 July 2015).

G20 (2009a) 'London Summit – Leaders' Statement, 2 April 2009': https://www.imf.org/external/np/sec/pr/2009/pdf/g20_040209.pdf (accessed 24 July 2015).

— (2009b) 'G20 Leaders' Statement: The Pittsburgh Summit': http://www.g20.utoronto.ca/2009/2009communique0925.html (accessed 24 July 2015).

Hampton, M. and Christensen, J. (2002) 'Offshore pariahs? Small island economies, tax havens and the reconfiguration of global finance', *World Development* 30(9): 1657–73.

Helleiner, E. (1994) 'Freeing money: why have states been more willing to liberalize capital controls than trade barriers?', *Policy Sciences* 27(4): 299–318.

— (2011) 'Understanding the 2007–2008 global financial crisis: lessons for scholars of international political economy', *Annual Review of Political Science* 14: 67–87.

Helleiner, E. and Pagliari, S. (2011) 'The end of an era in international financial regulation? A postcrisis research agenda', *International Organization* 65(1): 169–200.

IMF (2006) *Offshore Financial Centres: The Assessment Program – A progress report*: http://www.imf.org/external/np/pp/eng/2006/020806.pdf (accessed 24 July 2015).

— (2008) 'IMF Executive Board integrates the Offshore Financial Centre Assessment Program with the FSAP': http://www.imf.org/external/np/sec/pn/2008/pn0882.htm (accessed 24 July 2015).

— (2011a) '2011 Review of the Standards and Codes Initiative – background paper': http://www.imf.org/external/np/pp/eng/2011/021611a.pdf (accessed 24 July 2015).

— (2011b) '2011 Review of the Standards and Codes Initiative': http://www.imf.org/external/np/pp/eng/2011/021611.pdf (accessed 24 July 2015).

Johannesen, N. and Zucman, G. (2014) 'The end of bank secrecy? An evaluation of the G20 tax haven crackdown', *American Economic Journal: Economic Policy* 6(1): 65–91.

Keck, M. E. and Sikkink, K. (1998) *Activists Beyond Borders: Advocacy networks in international politics*, Ithaca, New York: Cornell University Press.

Knobel, A. and Meinzer, M. (2014a) '"The end of bank secrecy"? Bridging the gap to effective automatic information-exchange: an evaluation of OECD's Common Reporting Standard (CRS) and its alternatives': http://www.financialsecrecyindex.com/PDF/TJN2014_AIE-Technical-Report.pdf (accessed 24 July 2015).

— (2014b) 'OECD's Automatic Information-Exchange Standard: a watershed moment for fighting offshore tax evasion?': http://www.internationaltaxreview.com/pdfs/TJN2014_OECD-AIE-Report.pdf (accessed 24 July 2015).

Meinzer, M. (2012) 'The creeping futility of the Global Forum's peer reviews': http://www.taxjustice.net/cms/upload/GlobalForum2012-TJN-Briefing.pdf (accessed 27 June 2014).

Mistry, P. S. and Sharman, J. C. (2008) *Considering the Consequences: The development implications of initiatives on taxation, anti-money laundering and combating the financing of terrorism*, London: Commonwealth Secretariat.

Moschella, M. (2010) 'Back to the drawing board: the international financial architecture exercise', *Review of International Political Economy* 17(1): 155–71.

Mosley, L. (2010) 'Regulating globally, implementing locally: the financial codes and standards effort', *Review of International Political Economy* 17(4): 724–61.

OECD (1998) *Harmful Tax Competition: An emerging global issue*, Paris: OECD.

— (2000) *Towards Global Tax Co-operation: Progress in identifying and eliminating harmful tax practices*, Paris: OECD.

— (2009a) 'A progress report on the jurisdictions surveyed by the OECD Global Forum in implementing the internationally agreed tax standard': http://www.oecd.org/ctp/42497950.pdf (accessed 24 July 2015).

— (2009b) 'OECD Global Forum consolidates tax evasion revolution in advance of Pittsburgh': http://www.oecd.org/newsroom/oecdglobalforumconsolidatestaxevasionrevolutioninadvanceofpittsburgh.htm (accessed 24 July 2015).

— (2010a) *The Global Forum on Transparency and Exchange of Information for Tax Purposes*, Paris: OECD.

— (2010b) 'Promoting transparency and exchange of information for tax purposes': http://www.oecd.org/newsroom/44431965.pdf (accessed 24 July 2015).

— (2010c) 'Terms of reference to monitor and review progress towards transparency and exchange of information for tax purposes': http://www.oecd.org/ctp/44824681.pdf (accessed 24 July 2015).

— (2010d) 'Note on assessment criteria': http://www.oecd.org/ctp/44824732.pdf (accessed 24 July 2015).

— (2011a) 'Revised methodology for peer reviews and non-member reviews': http://www.oecd.org/ctp/44824721.pdf (accessed 24 July 2015).

— (2011b) *Peer Review of Switzerland – Phase 1: Legal and Regulatory Framework*, http://www.oecd.org/tax/transparency/peerreviewreportofswitzerland-phase1legalandregulatoryframework.htm (accessed 10 July 2015).

— (2012a) 'Progress Report to the G20, Los Cabos, Mexico, June 2012': http://www.oecd.org/ctp/exchangeofinformation/G20_Progress_Report_June_2012.pdf (accessed 24 July 2015).

— (2012b) 'A progress report on the jurisdictions surveyed by the OECD Global Forum in implementing the International Agreed Tax Standard': http://offshore.infinity-group.ru/doc/g20.pdf (accessed 11 August 2015).

— (2013a) 'Tax transparency 2013 report on progress', Paris: OECD.

— (2013b) 'Global Forum on Transparency and Exchange of Information for Tax Purposes, Jakarta, Indonesia 21–22 November 2013, Statement of Outcomes', http://www.oecd.org/tax/transparency/ENG%20Jakarta%20Statement%20of%20Outcomes.pdf (accessed 10 July 2015).

— (2014a) 'OECD Secretary-General Report to the G20 finance ministers and central bank governors, Sydney, February 2014', http://www.g20.utoronto.ca/2014/OECD_Tax_report_to_G20_Finance_Ministers.pdf (accessed 24 July 2015).

— (2014b) 'Global forum releases new compliance ratings on tax transparency for 10 jurisdictions': http://www.oecd.org/tax/global-forum-releases-new-compliance-ratings-on-tax-transparency-for-10-jurisdictions.htm (accessed 24 July 2015).

— (2014c) 'Tax transparency 2014: report on progress', http://www.oecd.org/tax/transparency/GFannualreport2014.pdf (accessed 10 July 2015).

Palan, R. *et al.* (2010) *Tax Havens: How globalisation really works*, Ithaca, New York: Cornell University Press.

Palan, R. and Abbott, J. P. (1996) *State Strategies in the Global Political Economy*, London: Pinter.

Porter, T. (2005) *Globalization and Finance*, Cambridge: Polity Press.

Raustiala, K. and Slaughter, A.-M. (2002) 'International law, international relations and compliance', in W. Carlsnaes, T. Risse, and B. A. Simmons (eds) *The Handbook of International Relations*, Thousand Oaks, CA: Sage, pp. 538–58.

Sharman, J. C. (2006) *Havens in a Storm: The struggle for global tax regulation*, Ithaca, New York: Cornell University Press.

— (2009) 'The bark is the bite: international organisations and blacklisting', *Review of International Political Economy* 16(4): 573–96.

— (2012) 'Canaries in the coal mine: tax havens, the decline of the West and the rise of the rest', *New Political Economy* 17(4): 493–513.

Shaxson, N. (2011) *Treasure Islands: Tax havens and the men who stole the world*, London: Vintage Books.

Shaxson, N. and Christensen, J. (2013) *The Finance Curse: How oversized financial centres attack democracy and corrupt economies*, http://www.taxjustice.net/cms/upload/pdf/Finance_Curse_Final.pdf (accessed 24 July 2015).

Sheppard, L. (2009) 'Don't ask, don't tell, Part 4: ineffectual information sharing', *Tax Notes* 23 March: 1411–18.

Slaughter, A.-M. (2004) *A New World Order*, Princeton, New Jersey: Princeton University Press.

Simmons, B. A. (2001) 'The international politics of harmonization: the case of capital market regulation', *International Organization* 55(3): 589–620.

Singer, D. A. (2007) *Regulating Capital: Setting standards for the international financial system*, Ithaca, New York: Cornell University Press.

Tax Justice Network (2009) *Tax Information-Exchange Arrangements*, http://www.taxjustice.net/cms/upload/pdf/Tax_Information_Exchange_Arrangements.pdf. (accessed 24 July 2015).

— (2010) 'OECD: peer reviews and pitfalls': http://taxjustice.blogspot.de/2010/10/oecd-peer-reviews-and-pitfalls.html (accessed 24 July 2015).

— (2013) *Financial Secrecy Index – Switzerland*, http://www.financialsecrecyindex.com/database/Switzerland.xml (accessed 24 July 2015).

Walter, A. (2008) *Governing Finance: East Asia's adoption of international standards*, Ithaca, New York: Cornell University Press.

Webb, M. (2004) 'Defining the boundaries of legitimate state practice: norms, transnational actors and the OECD's project on harmful tax competition', *Review of International Political Economy* 11(4): 787–827.

Woodward, R. (2006) 'Offshore strategies in global political economy: small islands and the case of the EU and OECD harmful tax competition initiatives', *Cambridge Review of International Affairs* 19(4): 685–99.

— (2011) 'From boom to doom to boom: offshore financial centres and development in small states' http://papers.ssrn.com/sol3/papers.cfm?abstract_id=1879298 (accessed 13 November 2015).

Chapter Six

Redistributive Tax Co-operation: Automatic Exchange of Information, US Power and the Absence of Joint Gains

Lukas Hakelberg

1. Introduction

A progressive income-tax system requires the state to tax its residents in accordance with their ability to pay. High-income earners are thus supposed to contribute relatively more to the financing of the state than low-income earners. Yet tax authorities have found it increasingly difficult to put such a system to work, as they lack an accurate overview of their residents' worldwide income. This is due to the abolition of capital controls, making it easy for taxpayers to evade their obligations by shifting capital income to tax havens. These jurisdictions abet the tax evasion strategies of non-residents by offering low or no taxes on capital income as well as anonymity, through banking secrecy or interposed legal entities like trusts and shell corporations. Owing to such services, and according to the most conservative estimate, tax havens hosted $5 trillion in undeclared financial wealth in 2013, representing 8 per cent of the world's households' total financial wealth (Zucman 2014). As a result, the ability of non-tax-haven economies to make the owners of this financial wealth contribute to its financing is eroded, while the effective tax burden shifts to labour (Genschel and Schwarz 2013). As low incomes usually have a bigger labour component than high incomes, the evasion of taxes on capital income is thus likely to turn a progressive into a regressive income-tax system.

The ideal remedy for tax evasion would be an automatic exchange of information (AEI) on non-residents' capital income between banks and tax authorities, backed up by a requirement for banks to look through corporate structures that might conceal the identity of the actual beneficial owner of an account. Yet the establishment of such a system requires a very high level of international co-operation, which states have so far been unable to achieve. In fact, tax havens have staunchly defended the banking secrecy and incorporation schemes that earned them a large influx of capital, thriving financial sectors, high wages and additional tax revenue. Examples include the longstanding refusal of Switzerland, Liechtenstein and other havens to grant foreign tax authorities administrative assistance, in accordance with OECD standards for information-exchange, upon request (Emmenegger 2014); and Luxembourg and Austria's non-participation in the EU-wide AEI on non-residents' interest income established by the Savings Directive (Hakelberg 2014). The inability of other states to pressure tax havens into compliance with international standards, analysts suggest, was due to an actual or perceived weakest-link problem. That is, politicians in non-tax-havens believed that pursuing one tax haven under conditions of capital mobility would only displace illicit activity to other jurisdictions, until the point where the last remaining noncooperative state was benefiting so much from its monopoly in offshore services that it would become extremely costly either to sanction it or pay it off. Hence, they perceived the cost of enforcing effective tax co-operation as exceeding its benefits (Genschel and Plumper 1997; Sharman 2008).

Against this background, it is quite astonishing that fifty-one jurisdictions, including most major offshore centres, signed a multilateral agreement in October 2014 that provided for comprehensive AEI on non-residents' capital income from September 2017. The agreement requires banks to look through interposed legal entities when identifying account-holders and establishes a peer-review process for the monitoring of its national implementation (OECD 2014a). Unsurprisingly, the deal 'was hailed by finance ministers as a watershed in the fight against tax dodgers'. But even critical NGOs like the Tax Justice Network suggested that 'finance ministers [were] right to claim historic progress' (Vasagar and Houlder 2014). *Why was this breakthrough possible after decades of failed attempts at international tax co-operation?* Theories conceptualising international co-operation as a Pareto-improving response to market failure cannot account for this outcome. They would expect tax co-operation to produce joint gains for all parties involved. However, countries that need to replace financial secrecy with routine reporting of foreign-held assets, like Switzerland and Luxembourg, are clearly worse off under the new regime. Their financial sectors face important adjustment costs and their attractiveness to hidden capital is reduced, which is likely to depress their wage levels and tax revenue (*see* Genschel and Seelkopf 2016, Chapter Three in this volume). Therefore, I argue that the multilateral AEI agreement is an instance of 'redistributive co-operation' rather than a mutually beneficial deal: it 'intentionally reduces at least one other government's welfare compared to the status quo' (Oatley and Nabors 1998: 36).

Redistributive co-operation in tax matters is the result of a credible threat of economic sanctions issued by the United States through its Foreign Account Tax Compliance Act (FATCA). Passed by Congress in 2010, this act obliges all foreign financial institutions (FFIs) doing business in the US financial market to automatically report capital income earned by US account-holders, or pay a 30 per cent withholding tax on their US-source revenue (Grinberg 2012). By November 2014, the US had reached bilateral agreements based on the act with 112 jurisdictions, including all major offshore centres (US Treasury 2014a). These agreements then unlocked multilateral negotiations on AEI, because some signatories were bound by most-favoured-nation (MFN) clauses to offer greater co-operation to third countries as well, whereas others responded to financial-sector preferences for a single set of global tax rules (Hakelberg 2014). The main beneficiary of the resulting international tax regime is the US, which receives data on US account-holders and their capital income from across the world but does not fully reciprocate this exchange under FATCA (Christians 2013) and has not signed the multilateral AEI agreement (Vasagar and Houlder 2014). As a result, the US has become attractive to capital previously hidden in other secrecy jurisdictions.

In contrast to Grinberg (2016, Chapter Seven in this volume), I thus argue that FATCA and the AEI regime it entailed do not benefit the international community as a whole. Rather, they advantage the US at the expense of less powerful jurisdictions with secrecy provisions. In complement to Grinberg's discussion of US and OECD/G20 dynamics, I also provide an account of bargaining over AEI at EU level and discuss the distributive consequences of AEI by means of several quantitative indicators. Section 2 of this chapter briefly reviews theories of tax competition and international co-operation, before presenting my hypothesis. Section 3 explains why the US is the only great power in international tax matters. Section 4 describes the emergence of the international AEI regime, while Section 5 analyses its distributive effects. Section 6 concludes.

2. Redistributive tax co-operation

Most analysts view tax competition as an asymmetric prisoner's dilemma (*see* Clausing 2016, Chapter Two in this volume). Whereas the competitive equilibrium benefits small countries, it harms large countries. This is because small countries find it easier than large countries to replace revenue lost to a tax cut on their domestic tax base with revenue generated from incoming foreign tax base. Relative to their small domestic capital stock, they simply have more foreign capital to attract than large countries. Therefore, small countries are likely to end up with lower tax rates, disproportionate shares of worldwide capital and higher tax revenues; all at the expense of large states (Bucovetsky 1991; Kanbur and Keen 1993; Genschel and Plumper 1997). In contrast, tax co-operation that removes secrecy, and thus prevents large-country residents from reaping tax benefits from moving capital to small countries, is likely to reverse the flow of capital observed in the competitive equilibrium. Owing to their higher tax rates, large countries would even gain more revenue from this reversal than small countries would lose. In theory, large countries could thus compensate small countries for their forgone gains from competition and strike a mutually beneficial deal (Sharman 2006). This solution would be perfectly in line with theories of international co-operation that view joint gains as a prerequisite for agreement. According to this literature strand, governments create international institutions to remove information or transaction costs that hamper mutually beneficial agreements. Without joint gains, regimes would be undermined by defecting governments, if the prospect of widespread defection did not already undermine countries' willingness to carry the cost of regime-building (Keohane 2005). As in the compensation scheme, larger or more powerful countries may secure larger benefits from co-operation than others; but all involved parties need to be at least as well off as under the *status quo* to stabilise the regime (Krasner 1991).

However, the scope for such a Pareto-improving solution is slim. Bribing small countries to abstain from tax-poaching is a tough political sell for large countries

(Genschel and Schwarz 2011), and most likely costlier than a credible threat of economic sanctions that does not require any monetary commitment. Large countries powerful enough to issue such a threat therefore have no incentive to offer compensation to small countries. As a result, bargaining over competition versus co-operation in tax matters is more likely to resemble a zero-sum than a positive-sum game. If small countries mange to resist large countries, they continue to benefit from tax competition at the expense of large countries. Yet if large countries are powerful enough to coerce small states into co-operation, they are most likely to establish a regime that benefits them at the expense of small countries. This account resonates with theories of international financial regulation arguing that a dominant financial centre can impose its preferred international rules on other governments, even if this makes them worse off than the *status quo* (Helleiner 2002; Oatley and Nabors 1998; Simmons 2001; Singer 2007). It achieves this by making access to its financial market conditional on implementation of its preferred rules (Helleiner 2002). The content of these rules is determined by domestic politics in the dominant financial centre rather than by joint gains (Simmons 2001). Therefore, their impact 'sometimes will be intentionally redistributive' (Oatley and Nabors 1998: 37), in that they are conceived by politicians in dominant financial centres to shift the cost of regulation away from domestic financial institutions and on to FFIs. Such redistributive co-operation is, I argue, what we have recently observed in international tax matters. Or, in more formal terms: *a dominant financial centre will only enforce international tax co-operation if this creates a competitive advantage for its domestic (financial) industry.*

To test my argument, I will first justify in brief terms why I consider the US the dominant financial centre and how this status gives it leverage in bargaining over international tax co-operation. Second, I will demonstrate how the US triggered and sustained the political process resulting in the multilateral AEI agreement of 2014. Third, I will analyse the (likely) distributive consequences of the newly established international AEI regime, to underline the absence of joint gains. Evidence comes from official statistics and documents, press articles and several expert interviews.

3. US dominance in international tax matters

In terms of stock-market valuation, interbank transactions and trade in options and futures, the US has repeatedly been identified as the biggest financial market in the world (Simmons 2001; Singer 2007). Measured by market capitalisation of listed companies, the US stock market was three to five times the size of the second-largest market between 2008 and 2012 (World Bank 2013). Between 2009 and 2012, the value of transactions processed by interbank funds-transfer systems and clearing houses located in the US was by far the highest among all reporting countries (BIS 2013). Moreover, the Futures Industry Association (FIA) reports that 37 per cent of worldwide derivatives contracts were traded and/or cleared in North America, compared to 34 per cent in Asia-Pacific and 20 per cent in Europe (FIA 2014). The extent of international participation in the American market is reflected in statistics on foreign portfolio investment (FPI). As the International Monetary Fund (IMF) reports, 19 per cent of worldwide FPI goes to the US, compared to 8 per cent going to the runner-up, the United Kingdom (IMF 2015). Hence, the US is also the preferred FPI destination for all but one of the top-five offshore centres on the financial secrecy index, which ranks countries according to the effort they put into concealing account-holder identities (*see* Table 6.1; *see also* Meinzer 2016, Chapter Twelve in this volume).

The centrality of its financial infrastructure, and its importance as a destination for FPI, including from offshore centres, is a crucial power source for the US in negotiations over tax co-operation. This is because regulation against tax evasion essentially targets banks, the custodians of hidden wealth. They need to be obliged to identify their customers correctly and report that information to tax authorities, for any type of information-exchange to work. As FFIs depend on the US financial infrastructure, and receive substantial revenue from their portfolio investment in the country, the US has several ways to make them comply with its regulatory demands. It could threaten to exclude them from interbank settlement or clearing mechanisms, which would cut them off the international capital circuit; or it could withhold their US-source revenue. The risk of FFIs divesting in response is low, as the American share in worldwide capital demand is too big to allow for smooth absorption of US-bound FPI in third countries. Indeed, it is hard to imagine that any FFI would readily abandon its business on Wall Street.

We can thus safely consider the US the dominant nation-state in bargaining over financial transparency and information-exchange; but what about the European Union (EU) as a whole? As Table 6.1 indicates, the single market, when treated as a whole, absorbs even more FPI from three out of the five top secrecy jurisdictions than the US. Owing to its size, the number of analysts considering the EU a great power in international economic and financial affairs has also recently been on the rise (Drezner 2008; Leblond 2011; Posner 2009). Indeed, there is evidence of the EU's ability to impose its regulatory preferences on third states (Bradford 2012).

Table 6.1: Portfolio investment of top-5 secrecy jurisdictions in US and in main FPI destinations inside EU (% of total)

	Destinations						
	US	UK	FR	DE	NL	LU	EU 5
Switzerland	16	7	8	7	7	14	43
Luxembourg	21	8	9	10	5	-	32
Hong Kong	7	6	1	1	1	4	13
Cayman Islands	44	1	1	1	1	1	5
Singapore	27	5	2	3	2	2	14

Sources: IMF (2015); TJN (2014).

In international tax matters, however, the EU has been unable to translate market size into power. This is because decisions on sanctions and taxation require unanimity in the Council of Ministers. As a result, EU members profiting from financial secrecy, essentially Luxembourg and Austria, were able not only to refuse participation in intra-EU AEI on interest payments but also to block mandates for Commission negotiations on the matter with Switzerland. Whereas Switzerland could resist AEI with the EU by referring to the non-participation of Luxembourg and Austria, Luxembourg and Austria could justify their non-participation with potential capital flight to Switzerland, simultaneously blocking progress at the EU and international levels. Large member-states, in turn, were unable to coerce Luxembourg and Austria into participation – due to single- market legislation providing for non-discrimination and the free movement of capital (Hakelberg 2014). In sum, the EU was more or less paralysed at the outset of international negotiations on AEI.

4. The emergence of a multilateral AEI regime

Early AEI initiatives: the Qualified Intermediary programme and the Savings Directive

The first AEI programmes were conceived in the late 1990s. At the time, tax co-operation was high on the international agenda, owing to the 1994 IMF and 1995 OECD reports quantifying financial flows routed through tax havens for the first time. Influenced by these reports, the Clinton administration initiated discussions on tax co-operation in the G7, which then tasked the OECD to develop recommendations for fighting harmful tax competition (Eccleston 2012: 63–4; Kudrle 2003; Rixen 2008). In parallel, the Clinton administration started working on the Qualified Intermediary (QI) programme, which entered into force in 2000. This programme offered FFIs exemption from withholding on their US investments, if they agreed to routinely report the US-source capital income of their American clients to the US Internal Revenue Service (IRS) (GAO 2007).

Likewise, the European Commission proposed the Savings Directive in 1998, providing for AEI on interest payments to non-resident EU citizens between member-states (Genschel 2002). The Council of Ministers adopted the Directive in 2003 but, to reach consensus, its proponents had to concede to Luxembourg, Austria, and Belgium the right to levy a withholding tax on interest payments to non-residents, instead of collecting information on behalf of EU partners. This meant some additional tax revenue for the rest of the EU but account-holders in these countries remained anonymous (Rixen and Schwarz 2012). The opt-out should have ended once Switzerland and other non-EU states started to report information on EU account-holders upon request (European Community 2003: Art. 10). Yet, as expected by Luxembourg *et al.*, they merely accepted the same withholding option in their Savings agreements with the EU, postponing EU-wide AEI to the indefinite future (Council of Ministers 2004; Johannesen 2014).

When the Bush administration entered office in 2001, it immediately withdrew US support from the OECD initiative on harmful tax competition, owing to complaints from US multinationals over its impact on allegedly legitimate tax-planning opportunities; and to criticism from libertarian lobby groups, hailing tax competition as an efficiency-enhancing corrective to wasteful government policy (Levin and Lieberman 2001). Instead, the Bush Treasury refocused the OECD's work on information-exchange upon request, a standard that requires tax authorities to present substantiated suspicions of tax evasion against particular individuals before they can seek administrative assistance from their foreign counterparts. Moreover, this standard excluded requests about groups of investors and was not backed up by a threat of sanctions in case of non-compliance. Switzerland, Luxembourg and other offshore centres could thus uphold reservations against its administrative-assistance requirements without any consequences (Rixen and Genschel 2015; Rixen 2008). Despite its hostility towards multilateral tax co-operation, the Bush administration did not repeal the unilateral QI programme, most likely because it created reporting obligations only for FFIs and not for US banks and had little political salience. AEI under the Savings Directive also began in 2005, notwithstanding the loss of momentum at OECD level, but was constrained by the opt-outs of Luxembourg, Austria and Belgium (Rixen and Schwarz 2012).

Public scandals and the identification of loopholes in AEI programmes

The first AEI schemes had been put in place. However, towards the end of the 2000s it became clear that international banks circumvented reporting requirements by exploiting a loophole that the QI programme and Savings Directive had in common: the lack of an effective look-through approach, obliging banks to identify the actual beneficial owners of managed accounts. From 2006, Senate investigations pushed forward by Democrat Carl Levin uncovered that FFIs had evaded their reporting obligations under the QI programme by hiding the identities of their US clients behind trusts and other shell corporations (Levin and Coleman 2006, 2008). This was possible because QI regulations allowed FFIs to 'accept documentation declaring corporations' ownership of income at face value, unless they [had] "a reason to know" that the documentation [was] invalid' (Government Accountability Office 2007: 22). As a result, foreign corporations had formally received 70 per cent of US-source capital income in 2003 (GAO 2007: 22). However, Senate investigations demonstrated that United Bank of Switzerland (UBS), Liechtenstein Global Trust (LGT) and other FFIs had created or purchased many of these offshore corporations for the sole purpose of hiding client identities (Levin and Coleman 2008). Hence, they had every reason to know that their corporate creations were not the actual recipients of US-source capital income. The perception, fostered by public Senate hearings, that FFIs had made a business out of evading US regulations triggered the so-called UBS scandal in July 2008 (Hässig 2010).

In parallel, EU-internal debate on the shortcomings of the Savings Directive was fostered by the LGT scandal. With the consent of social-democratic Minister of Finance Peer Steinbrück, German intelligence had bought stolen data on clients of LGT in July 2007 (Kellner and Strunz 2008; *Spiegel* 2012). A prominent figure in the data was the CEO of Deutsche Post, Klaus Zumwinkel. Following a tip-off from the federal Ministry of Finance, his temporary arrest in February 2008 was broadcast live on TV, triggering a public debate on tax evasion (Brambusch 2013; Jäger 2014). Steinbrück seized the opportunity to put a revision of the Savings Directive on the agenda of the March 2008 Council on Economic and Financial Affairs (ECOFIN) (Mussler 2008). With the support of his French and Italian counterparts, he encouraged the Commission to speed up the Directive's review and called for a 'material and geographic extension' of its AEI mechanism (BMF 2008: 31; European Commission 2008a). The Commission presented a corresponding report in autumn 2008, conceding that investors could circumvent the Directive by either hiding behind interposed legal entities or investing in equity rather than interest-producing debt securities (European Commission 2008b).[1] As remedies, the report advocated a look-through approach, obliging banks to use information obtained through know-your-customer (KYC) due diligence when determining account ownership; and an extension of the Directive's scope to securities that investors might consider equivalent to debt in terms of their risk profile (European Commission 2008c). In contrast, the Commission did not propose changes to the AEI opt-out granted to Luxembourg *et al.*

Political reaction and attempts at reform

The political reaction to the uncovered shortcomings was swift in the US but sluggish in the EU. In response to the UBS scandal, senior bureaucrats in the US Department of Justice (DoJ) and IRS began to pressure Switzerland for data on US account-holders. Beginning in July 2008, the IRS issued John Doe Summonses,[2] prompting UBS and other Swiss banks to deliver US client files or be subject to civil penalties in the US. In parallel, the DoJ threatened the same banks with indictment for the criminal offence of defrauding the United States. As indictment would have meant withdrawal of their US banking licences, most likely resulting in bankruptcy, the Swiss government, which was heavily invested in UBS and other banks in the aftermath of the financial crisis, had no choice but to surrender requested client data, in violation of its own banking-secrecy laws (Emmenegger 2014; Hässig 2010). The incoming Obama administration then introduced a concomitant legislative response to the Senate investigations by

1. Research by academics and journalists later revealed that Swiss and Luxembourgish wealth-managers had created or purchased a massive number of mostly Panamanian corporations on behalf of their clients, just after the Savings Directive and Agreement entered into force in 2005 (Johannesen 2014; Brinkmann *et al.* 2015).

2. The IRS uses these summonses to request information from a third party on unknown taxpayers with potential tax liabilities. The unknown person is referred to as John Doe.

including corrective measures to QI loopholes in its budget proposal for 2010 (US Government 2009). These measures were introduced to Congress as the FATCA bill, which passed as a financing mechanism attached to a stimulus package in March 2010. The act obliges FFIs to use KYC due diligence when determining beneficial ownership of an account; and also to routinely report account balances and all capital income of their US clients to the IRS. If an FFI is deemed non-compliant, the IRS may impose a 30 per cent withholding tax on its US-source revenue (Grinberg 2012).

Instead of swift and sweeping legislation, Germany, France and other large EU members favouring a revision of the Savings Directive received what Luxembourgish Prime Minister Jean-Claude Juncker had already announced at the March 2008 ECOFIN meeting: 'many years of fascinating debate' (Mussler 2008). While the Commission was preparing the revised draft of the Savings Directive, and a proposal for an Administrative Co-operation Directive providing for a phase-in of AEI on all types of capital income (European Commission 2009), France and Germany tried to increase pressure on secrecy jurisdictions in- and outside the EU by reanimating multilateral efforts against tax evasion. To this effect, they held an intergovernmental conference in Paris in October 2008, calling on the OECD to draft a new blacklist of countries incompliant with its upon-request standard. This time, the list should include OECD members Switzerland, Luxembourg and Austria (Bouilhet 2008; Hall 2008). More importantly, however, France and Germany put the issue of tax transparency on the agenda of the Group of 20 (G20) at its first crisis meeting in November 2008.[3] As a result, and despite its disputed connection to the outbreak of the financial crisis, heads of state and government declared in Washington that 'lack of transparency and a failure to exchange tax information should be vigorously addressed' (G20 Information Centre 2008). In March 2009, the OECD circulated the requested draft blacklist of countries not abiding by its information-exchange standard, including Switzerland, Luxembourg and Austria (Emmenegger 2014). To underline its importance, G20 leaders took note of the list at their second meeting in April 2009, declaring that 'the era of banking secrecy [was] over', and threatened to 'deploy sanctions to protect [their] public finances' (G20 Information Centre 2009).

In reaction to international pressure, Luxembourgish Finance Minister Luc Frieden had invited his Austrian and Swiss opposite-numbers to Senningen castle in March 2009, to agree a co-ordinated response (Israel 2009). To appease the OECD and G20, they decided to drop their reservations against Article 26 of the OECD Model Tax Convention, fixing administrative assistance duties under the upon-request standard. Moreover, they pledged to update at least twelve of their bilateral tax treaties accordingly, thus fulfilling an OECD requirement for removal from the blacklist (*see* OECD 2009; Woodward 2016, Chapter Five in this volume). This concession came at relatively low cost because of the conditions linked to the provision of administrative assistance upon request. Treaty partners

3. Interviews on 6 March 2014, 14 November 2014 and 28 January 2015.

needed to provide substantial preliminary evidence against particular individuals. Most often, however, the information needed to do so was exactly what treaty partners were *seeking* from Switzerland *et al.* Hence, they only lodged a handful of requests under the new standard (Rixen and Genschel 2015; Palan *et al.* 2010). Moreover, the low number of updated treaties required by the OECD for removal from the blacklist allowed Switzerland *et al.* to make agreements mostly with other offshore centres, from whom they did not expect any actual information requests (Johannesen and Zucman 2012). More importantly, however, it was most likely at Senningen that Luxembourg, Austria and Switzerland devised a strategy to frustrate EU attempts to achieve a material and geographic extension of AEI under the Savings Directive.

During the next four years, Council presidencies made six attempts at passing a revised draft and a mandate for Commission negotiations with Switzerland over a corresponding Savings agreement (European Council 2009; 2010; 2011a; 2011b; 2012a; 2012b). Every time, Luxembourg and Austria refused to agree, arguing that a level international playing field had to be established ahead of their consent. That is, Switzerland had to first signal its willingness to practise AEI with the EU. Otherwise, capital flight from the single market was the likely result (SDA 2009; SDA 2010a; SDA 2011a; SDA 2011b; SDA 2012a; Council 2012b). In turn, Switzerland used the non-participation of Luxembourg and Austria in intra-EU AEI to justify its unwillingness to do just that (Naegeli 2010). Interestingly, however, it offered to update its Savings Agreement with the EU in accordance with the OECD upon-request standard (Naegeli 2011). Yet Swiss politicians knew that the Savings Directive's transition clause made this the crucial condition for a removal of the transitory withholding option (European Community 2003: Art. 10), which gave Luxembourg and Austria an additional reason to block any mandate for Commission negotiations on a revised Savings Agreement. Owing to the unanimity requirement in tax matters, there was little to nothing that large EU-members could do to break this arrangement (Hakelberg 2014).

The only item related to intra-EU co-operation in direct taxation that passed during this period was a severely stripped down version of the Administrative Co-operation Directive. The Commission had made a corresponding proposal, in 2009, to phase in AEI on all types of capital income. It foresaw that the Commission, assisted by a committee of national tax experts, should define the income-types subject to AEI, as well as the conditions under which information should be exchanged (European Commission 2009: Art. 8). That way, cumbersome Council procedures could have been circumvented in the future. Unsurprisingly, however, Luxembourg and Austria opposed such annulment of their *de facto* veto-power in tax matters. As a result, the final version of the Directive agreed in December 2010 left everything as it was. AEI became an option for future administrative assistance but the income-types covered had to be agreed in subsequent Council decisions (European Union 2011: Art. 8). Moreover, the Luxembourgish and Austrian finance ministers could celebrate the codification of the availability principle. That is, even if the Council decided to practice AEI on capital income other than interest, tax authorities only needed to transmit data readily available to them. Data they did not collect domestically was thus excluded from EU-internal exchange in any case (European Union 2011: Art. 3; SDA 2010b). Ultimately, the Directive served only to transpose the OECD upon-request standard into EU law, including a customary MFN clause obliging member-states to extend any greater co-operation offered to a third country also to each other (European Union 2011: Art. 19). This MFN clause seemed benign in December 2010, and thus passed without debate. But the US would soon turn it into a Trojan Horse, breaking Austrian and Luxembourgish opposition to intra-EU AEI.

Decisive US action: FATCA becomes intergovernmental

Congress had conceived FATCA as a domestic law with extra-territorial reach, establishing a direct regulatory link between FFIs and the IRS. When it passed in March 2010, no intergovernmental approach was envisaged. Indeed, its predecessor, the QI programme, had worked in exactly the same way, creating obligations for foreign banks, not foreign governments. As Tanenbaum (2012: 623) puts it, FATCA 'was steamrolling down on a unilateral basis without any immediate serious attention being given to the pursuit of bilateral or multilateral alternatives'. This changed only after the IRS had published the first guide to and timeline for FATCA-implementation, in August 2011 (IRS 2011). At this point, many FFIs realised that the act's reporting requirements would collide with data-protection and banking-secrecy legislation in their home countries, leaving them between a rock and a hard place. They had either to break domestic law to be FATCA-compliant or accept the 30 per cent withholding tax due in case of non-compliance (Dion Global Solutions 2012; Eccleston and Gray 2014). Therefore, they began to lobby the US as well as their home governments for an intergovernmental solution to the collision of laws.

In response, Assistant Secretary of the Treasury Emily McMahon announced, in December 2011, that the US 'was committed to entering into bilateral and multilateral agreements that would allow financial institutions to comply with FATCA without violating local law' (Grinberg 2012: 25). To this effect, the Obama administration began negotiations with France, Germany, Italy, Spain and the UK (EU G5), announcing in February 2012 that they had agreed a 'common approach to FATCA implementation' (US Treasury 2012d: 2). This declaration was followed by a model intergovernmental agreement (IGA) in July (US Treasury 2012a) and a first, signed bilateral treaty with the UK in September 2012 (US Treasury 2012b). In parallel, the US negotiated an alternative model agreement with Switzerland, providing for direct reporting of client information from Swiss banks to the IRS. Following a joint statement on FATCA-implementation in June (US Treasury 2012e), Switzerland and the US signed a bilateral deal in December 2012 (US Treasury 2012c). After four years of pressure from the US, major fines imposed on Swiss banks, repeated legally disputable transmissions of client data and one actual bankruptcy of a Swiss private bank following its indictment in a US court, the Swiss government's opposition to far-reaching tax co-operation was broken (Emmenegger 2014). Accordingly, the Swiss banking and fund industries greeted the FATCA deal with relief, underlining its provision of legal certainty rather than imposed costs in their initial reactions (SDA 2012b; SDA 2012c).

FATCA deals facilitate multilateral agreement

FATCA deals struck over the course of 2012 were only the beginning. In the following months, the US implemented its declared goal of making FATCA the international standard for tax co-operation (Grinberg 2012), striking bilateral agreements with 112 jurisdictions including all major offshore centres (US Treasury 2014a). This profoundly changed the dynamic of international negotiations, leading to intra-EU agreement on comprehensive AEI and a multilateral AEI treaty sponsored by the OECD. At EU level, intergovernmental FATCA deals in combination with the Administrative Co-operation Directive's MFN clause proved to be the game-changer. Shortly after Switzerland had signed its deal with the US, Luxembourgish Finance Minister Luc Frieden announced that his country would enter negotiations on a bilateral FATCA agreement and extend equivalent co-operation also to EU partners (Valda 2012). A few months later, Prime Minister Juncker made the underlying reasoning explicit in his state-of-the-nation speech:

> If we now modify our position, we do it because the Americans do not leave us a choice. They restrict their financial operations to countries which accept automatic exchange of information. If we do not comply with this condition, there won't be any financial operations with the USA. Yet, an international financial centre cannot cut itself from the American financial circuit. ... We cannot refuse to also extend to the Europeans the concessions that we have to make to the Americans within the context of a bilateral treaty (Juncker 2013: 16–17, cited in Hakelberg 2014: 12).

Likewise, Austria entered FATCA negotiations with the US in January 2013, albeit without announcing equivalent co-operation with European partners (*Standard* 2013). Yet a joint letter from EU G5 finance ministers, urging effective application of the MFN clause (EU G5 Finance Ministers 2013), apparently exerted enough pressure on the country to finally make it agree to a mandate for Commission negotiations on a revised Savings Agreement with Switzerland in May 2013. In addition, EU finance ministers decided that the revised Savings Directive should be passed, once Switzerland signalled its willingness to practise AEI with the EU in these negotiations (Council of Ministers 2013).

In parallel, the intergovernmental implementation of FATCA had also put AEI on the agenda of the G20 and of OECD. Following agreement on the model IGA between the US and EU G5, G20 leaders called on all countries to adopt this practice in June 2012 (G20 Information Centre 2012). A year later, after the first US-induced breakthrough at EU level, they endorsed AEI as the new global standard, calling on the OECD to develop a framework for its coherent worldwide application by mid-2014 (G20 Leaders 2013). Under pressure from this renewed momentum, an expert group created by the Swiss finance minister recommended, in June 2013, that Switzerland should also practice AEI with the EU and other countries, to avoid parallel standards and thus minimise compliance costs for Swiss banks (Brunetti 2013). In response, the finance ministry acknowledged that AEI would be the new global standard for tax co-operation, pledging active participation in its development (EFD 2013). Eventually, the OECD modelled its AEI standard on the FATCA inter-governmental agreement (IGA) agreed between the US and the EU G5, to avoid double regulation and ensure a level international playing field. With the Swiss vote, the standard passed the OECD Committee on Financial Affairs in February 2014.[4] Tax Comissioner Semeta could thus report to EU finance ministers that Switzerland was seeking agreement on AEI based on the new global standard (Semeta 2014).

After six years of fascinating debate, ECOFIN finally reached agreement on the revised Savings Directive in March 2014 (European Union 2014). Moreover, the subsequent European Council ordered finance ministers to adopt a revised Administrative Co-operation Directive by the end of 2014, now intended as a vehicle for transposing the OECD AEI standard into EU law (European Council 2014). Owing to the newly established consensus, work went ahead quickly and ECOFIN adopted the Directive in October 2014. It codifies comprehensive intra-EU AEI on all types of capital income, starting on 1 January 2017, with Austria joining a year later on 1 January 2018 (Council of Ministers 2014). Two weeks later, fifty-one countries signed a multilateral competent-authority agreement in Berlin, committing signatories to begin exchanging bank data among each other based on the OECD AEI standard from 1 September 2017, or 2018 (OECD 2014a), including Switzerland, Luxembourg, Austria, and the Cayman Islands (OECD 2014b). An additional fifty countries expressed support for the standard, including Hong Kong and Singapore (SDA 2014) (*see* Table 6.2). However, after imposing FATCA on 112 jurisdictions, breaking deadlock in EU negotiations and putting AEI on the G20 agenda, the creator of the new multilateral regime, the United States of America, was missing from the list of signatories (Vasagar and Houlder 2014). As a result, what finance ministers and activists alike celebrated as a historic breakthrough for international tax co-operation suffers from a major equity problem: the lack of reciprocal exchange of information from the US.

The lack of US reciprocity[5]

Neither FATCA agreements nor the multilateral treaty legally bind the US to reciprocate information-reporting. The US is thus receiving data on American account-holders from most jurisdictions but does not disclose equivalent information on non-residents to treaty partners (Christians 2013, 2014; Eisenring 2014). In fact, the US government only pledges to reciprocate information-reporting on non-resident account-holders in one variant of FATCA treaties,

4. Interviews on 4 and 6 March 2014.

5. The following subsection is a shortened version of a section in Hakelberg 2015.

Table 6.2: Adoptions of AEI among top-25 secrecy jurisdictions

Jurisdiction	FATCA Agreement (date of formal signature)	OECD AEI Standard	
		Signed MCAA* (agreed AEI start)	Political endorsement (pledged AEI start)
Switzerland	YES (14 Feb 2013)	YES (September 2018)	
Luxembourg	YES (28 Mar 2014)	YES (September 2017)	
Hong Kong	YES (13 Nov 2014)	NO	YES (September 2018)
Cayman Islands	YES (29 Nov 2013)	YES (September 2017)	
Singapore	YES (12 Sep 2014)	NO	YES (September 2018)
USA	No full reciprocity	NO	NO
Lebanon	NO	NO	NO
Germany	YES (31 May 2013)	YES (September 2017)	
Jersey	YES (13 Dec 2013)	YES (September 2017)	
Japan	YES (11 Nov 2013)	NO	YES (September 2018)
Panama	YES (not yet signed)	NO	NO
Malaysia	YES (not yet signed)	NO	YES (September 2018)
Bahrain	YES (not yet signed)	NO	NO
Bermuda	YES (19 Dec 2013)	YES (September 2017)	
Guernsey	YES (13 Dec 2013)	YES (September 2017)	
UAE	YES (not yet signed)	NO	YES (September 2018)
Canada	YES (5 Feb 2014)	NO	YES (September 2018)
Austria	YES (29 Apr 2014)	YES (September 2018)	
Mauritius	YES (27 Dec 2013)	YES (September 2017)	
British Virgin Islands	YES (30 Jun 2014)	YES (September 2017)	
United Kingdom	YES (12 Sep 2012)	YES (September 2017)	
Macao	YES (not yet signed)	NO	YES (September 2018)
Marshall Islands	NO	NO	YES (September 2018)
Korea	YES (not yet signed)	YES (September 2017)	
Russia	NO	NO	YES (September 2018)

Sources: OECD (2014b); OECD (2014d); TJN (2014).

**Multilateral Competent Authority Agreement*

the reciprocal IGA agreed with the EU G5. Yet, as Christians (2013; 2014) shows, even this IGA does not provide for full reciprocity, given that the US lacks the domestic regulations to collect all the data from US financial institutions that it requests from FFIs, including non-residents' account balances, non-US-source dividends and beneficial ownership of interposed legal entities. Accordingly, Model 1 IGAs feature the following qualificatory clause:

> The United States acknowledges the need to achieve equivalent levels of reciprocal automatic information-exchange with [FATCA Partner]. The United States is committed to further improve transparency and enhance the exchange relationship with [FATCA Partner] by pursuing the adoption of regulations and advocating and supporting relevant legislation to achieve such equivalent levels of reciprocal automatic exchange (US Treasury 2012a).

The Obama administration has, indeed, included requests for full FATCA reciprocity in its 2013 and 2014 budget proposals (Office of Management and Budget 2013; US Treasury 2014b). However, no corresponding bills have been introduced to Congress. As practitioners and lobbyists suggest, this is due to the 'likely entrance of U.S. financial industry into the fight' over reciprocity (Garst 2014; see also Newman 2014). As mentioned above, US banks can still circumvent the reporting of foreign clients and their capital income by divesting their portfolios of US and debt securities or hiding their identities behind sham corporations. Without reciprocity, FATCA not only spares US banks the costs of regulation: it also provides them with a competitive advantage over FFIs in the attraction of hidden capital (Christians 2013; Eisenring 2014; Newman 2014). Accordingly, they have a strong preference for the *status quo*, as evidenced by the ABA's criticism of an IRS-imposed reporting requirement for interest payments to non-resident aliens (NRAs):

> these proposed regulations will further strain banks' information technology staff and budgets, *for the sole purpose of providing information to the IRS*, especially when there is the risk that many banks will lose billions of dollars in deposit funds due to the resulting loss of many of their NRA customers (Mordi 2011: 2).

Unlike the reporting requirement for interest payments, which the IRS could push through on its own, the establishment of full reciprocity requires legislation at federal and state level (Christians 2013; 2014). It is thus easier to block, especially since Republicans, who have regained majorities in both chambers of Congress, are sympathetic to the ABA's concerns. Senator and 2012 vice-presidential candidate Paul Ryan, for instance, stated in 2011 that 'we need to have a tax system that makes America a haven for capital formation. Let's make this country a tax shelter for other countries instead of having other countries be a tax shelter for America' (Gabor 2011). Florida Senator Marco Rubio even introduced a bill to kill the IRS's interest-reporting regulation (*Economist* 2014), claiming elsewhere that

> forcing banks to report interest paid to nonresident aliens would encourage the flight of capital overseas … place unnecessary burdens on the American economy, put our financial system at a fundamental competitive disadvantage, and would restrict access to capital when our economy can least afford it (Rubio 2011, cited in Christians 2013: 6–7).

Despite its pledges to provide reciprocity in the future, the Obama administration is thus highly unlikely to obtain the requisite domestic regulation before the end of its term. Owing to the lobbying effort of US financial institutions, their competitive advantage in the attraction of hidden capital created by FATCA is here to stay.

Against this background, it was consistent for the US administration to enable but not sign the multilateral AEI agreement that provides for reciprocal exchange of information. For the US, having all other major economies exchange information on non-residents' capital income, while not participating itself, removes two potential competitive disadvantages at the same time. First, it reduces the risk of American investors, who have so far profited from offshore arrangements, being disadvantaged *vis-à-vis* other investors. Owing to the multilateral agreement, investors in the fifty-one signatory states are just as likely to be subject to the reporting of their offshore capital income as American investors under FATCA. Second, the risk of FFIs divesting from the United States to circumvent reporting requirements is minimised, as similar obligations will be in place from 2017 across all major economies. There are thus few alternatives available to recalcitrant FFIs (OECD 2014a, 2014c; US Treasury 2012a).

5. The redistributive effect of multilateral but non-reciprocal AEI

The last section demonstrated how the US used its financial-market power to enforce AEI in its bilateral relations. Thereby, it unlocked international negotiations at EU level, and beyond, leading to a multilateral AEI regime, codified in the OECD's common reporting standard and multilateral competent-authority agreement. Yet the US refuses to enter into reciprocal AEI itself, creating a competitive advantage for US banks in attracting hidden capital. Although it is difficult to establish causality this way, trends in the international distribution of deposit liabilities to non-residents, assets under management (AuM) and foreign holdings of fiduciary deposits suggest that countries like Switzerland, Luxembourg and Austria have recently had to suffer important losses. In contrast, the US has seen substantial gains. If we compare trends for the main antagonists in the above story in this way, a dynamic of redistributive co-operation seems at least more plausible than an account of joint gains.

At the outset of negotiations on tax co-operation, Switzerland was the world's biggest and most proficient provider of offshore wealth-management services (Zucman 2014). Likewise, Luxembourg and Austria were the biggest recipients of non-resident deposits from within the euro area (Hakelberg 2014). Given the strong correlation between secrecy and incoming foreign wealth (Johannesen 2014; Johannesen and Zucman 2012), their fierce opposition to financial transparency is not surprising. As Figure 6.1 illustrates, Swiss banks' deposit liabilities to foreign non-banks had twice the value of reporting US banks' liabilities between 1998 and 2000. That is, before the QI programme took effect. Although the value of liabilities continued to grow in both countries until the height of the financial crisis, the US rapidly overtook Switzerland in 2003. Liability values then declined in both countries over the course of 2008. However, the US saw quick stabilisation in 2009

Figure 6.1: Banks' deposit liabilities towards non-resident non-banks: United States and Switzerland (US$ millions)

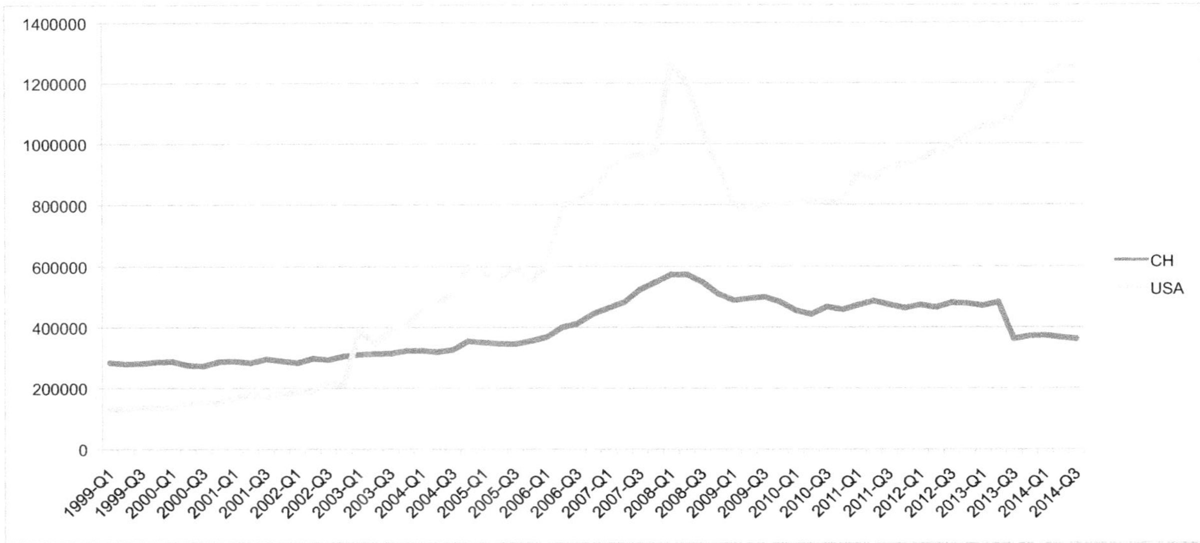

Data source: BIS (2015)

and another period of strong growth from 2011. In contrast, Swiss banks reported stable values between 2009 and 2012, followed by another rapid decline between the first and third quarter of 2013. This decline coincided with the signature of the Swiss–American FATCA agreement and Swiss acknowledgment of AEI as the new global standard (*see* Section 4). Data on foreign deposits is readily available and internationally comparable. It covers a large fraction of offshore wealth but ignores holdings of debt, and equity securities. However, looking at all assets managed by Swiss banks on behalf of foreigners, a similar picture emerges. As Figure 6.2 shows, the value of AuM held by foreign households and commercial clients[6] dropped by 36 per cent during the financial crisis, followed by a glimpse of recovery in 2009 and further decline after that. The large influx of foreign deposits into the US suggests that American banks had good reasons to oppose the reporting requirements considered by the Obama administration. In contrast, the decline in deposits and AuM recorded in Switzerland, despite the strong growth of worldwide financial wealth after the crisis (Piketty and Zucman 2014), suggests that the country has lost competitiveness in the wealth-management business, most likely due to reinforced tax co-operation.

Data on Luxembourg and Austria provides a less extreme picture but the trend seems to go in the same direction. When looking at deposit liabilities of Luxembourg's banks to euro-area households, and non-profits investing on behalf of households, we observe a strong decline after 2003, the year the Savings Directive passed ECOFIN (Figure 6.3). Deposits produce interest, which Luxembourg had to start taxing due to the Directive. The connection seems straightforward and is confirmed by Johannesen (2014), who estimates that Luxembourg lost between 15 and 30 per cent of deposits held by EU citizens because of the Directive. However, given the stability of its overall deposit liabilities to non-residents during the same period (Figure 6.4), it seems that a big part of these losses only exists in official statistics. As recent revelations suggest, Luxembourgish wealth-managers reacted to the Directive by hiding EU client identities behind Panamanian shell corporations (Brinkmann *et al.* 2015). As a result, counter-party location changed on paper but actual deposits and beneficial owners remained where they were. The value of deposit liabilities to foreign non-banks therefore developed in parallel to that reported by German banks, peaking in the first quarter of 2008, falling rapidly during the crisis and growing moderately again from 2011. Luxembourg's statistics bureau attributes the decline at the very end of the observation period to the parallel breakthrough in negotiations on intra-EU AEI (Adam 2014). Moreover, it expects AEI to cause a 5 per cent decline in AuM, producing a 5 to 10 per cent reduction in added value from the financial sector and a loss of up to 2800 jobs in the entire economy (Adam 2014).

Data on Austria suggest that the country was far from joining the global wealth-management league dominated by the likes of Switzerland and Luxembourg. Still,

6. I included commercial clients because the Swiss National Bank records AuM held by foreign private organisations without purpose of gain, that is, foundations, in this category.

Figure 6.2: Banks' deposit liabilities towards non-resident non-banks: Austria, Germany and Luxembourg (US$ millions)

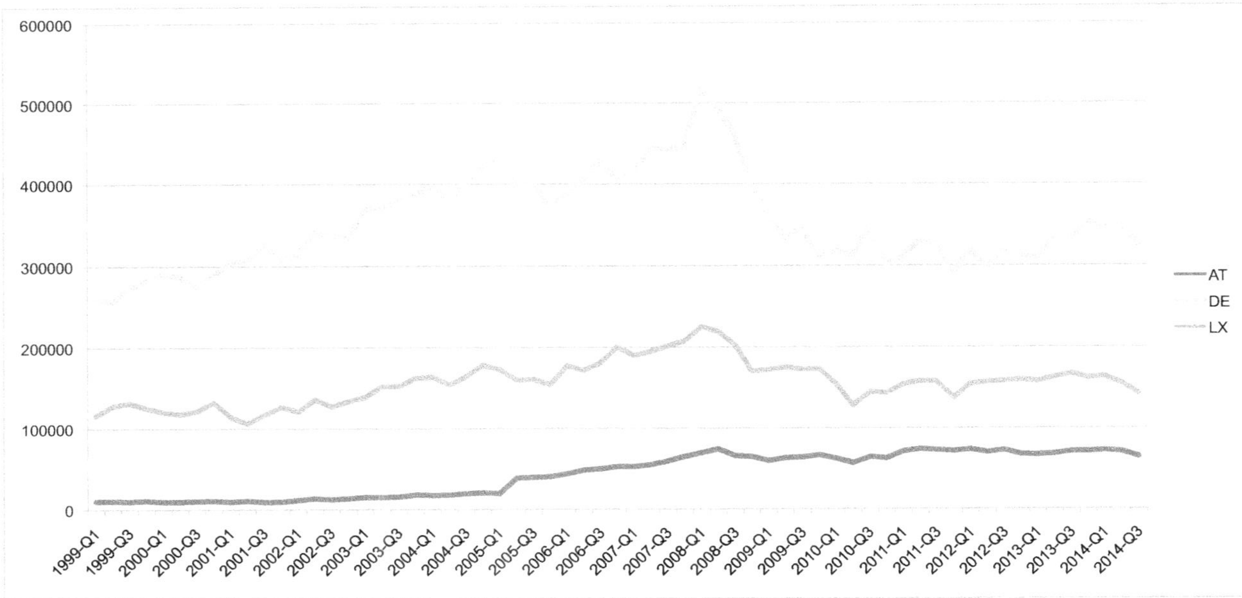

Data source: BIS (2015).

Figure 6.3: Asset-holdings of non-resident households and commercial clients with Swiss banks (CHF billions)

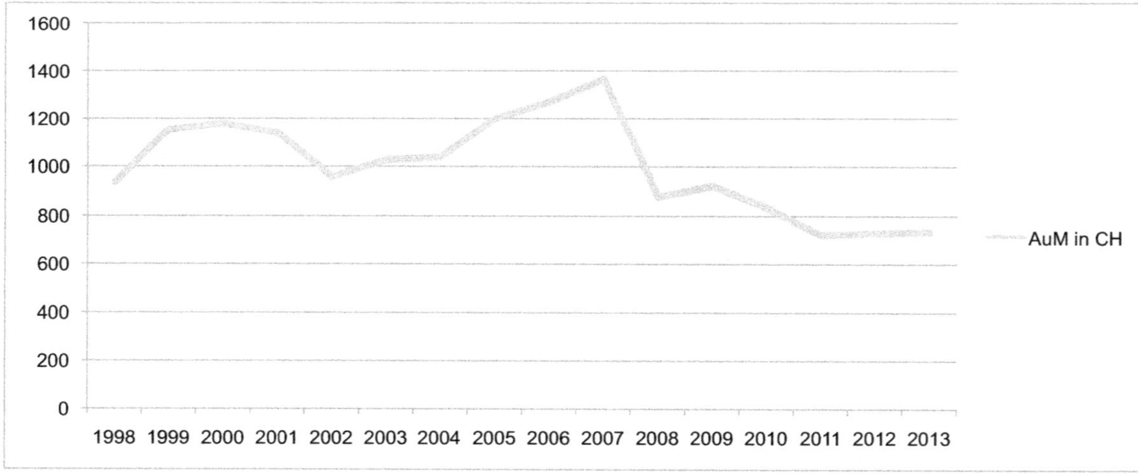

Data source: SNB (2014).

Figure 6.4: Banks' deposit liabilities towards non-resident eurozone households and non-profit organisations acting on behalf of households (€ millions)

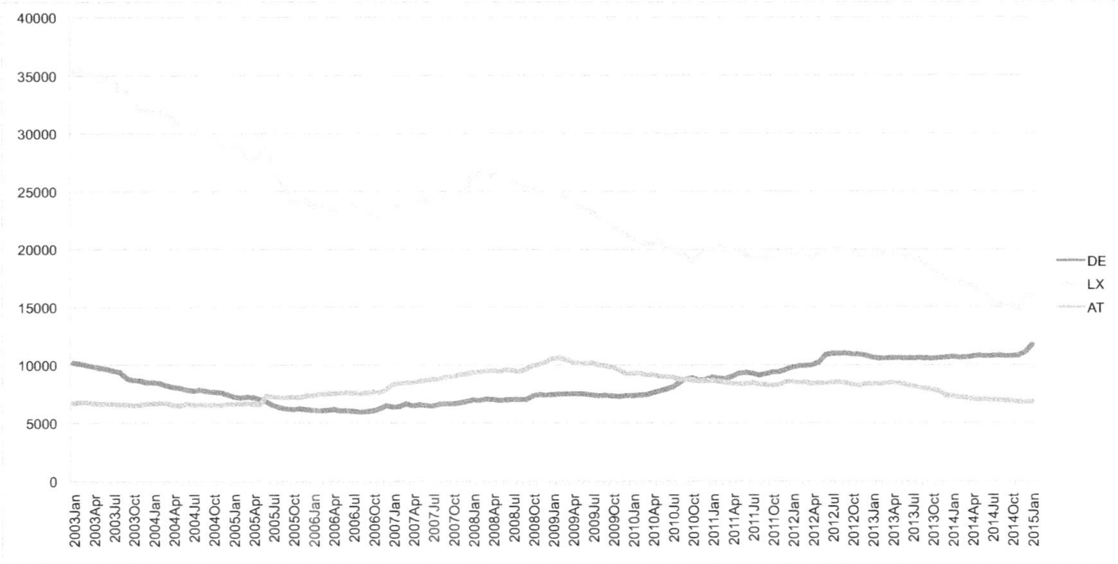

Data source: ECB (2015).

its banks reported higher deposit liabilities to non-resident euro-area households than German banks during much of the observation period (Figure 6.3), despite Austria being only one-tenth the size of Germany in terms of population. Unlike Luxembourg, however, it did not see a decline in the value of deposit liabilities before the Savings Directive came into force in 2005. Rather, its AEI opt-out seems to have been rewarded afterwards by an influx of deposits held by euro-area households. To be sure, Austrian banks also made large acquisitions in Central and Eastern Europe at the time, which may account for the jump in deposit liabilities observed in 2005. It is, however, unclear how many euro-area households actually had deposits with the acquired Eastern European banks. Moreover, the trend also continued after the jump. At the end of the observation period, we see an accelerated decline that coincides with the material and geographic extension of intra-EU AEI. Unfortunately, we cannot say whether the parallel stability in deposit liabilities to non-banks in the rest of the world is due to concealment schemes similar to those applied in Luxembourg or to a euro-area deposits being replaced by newly acquired deposits from other world regions. This is because the BIS keeps data on bilateral deposit holdings confidential. Moreover, interview data suggests that Austria's resistance to AEI was motivated to a lesser degree by a desire to defend the financial sector than Switzerland's and Luxembourg's. Rather, right-wing populists claimed, ahead of federal elections in 2013, that concessions on AEI would undermine politically sacrosanct banking-secrecy for residents, and was another sell-out of national sovereignty to Brussels. The conservative Finance Minister thus had to act tough as much for electoral as for economic reasons.[7]

Although we cannot exactly determine the destination of funds leaving Switzerland, Luxembourg and Austria, at least the first two have clearly suffered a decline in their exports of financial services. In contrast, US banks have benefited from a massive inflow of foreign-held deposits before and after the financial crisis. Given that secrecy is strongly correlated to stocks of foreign assets (Adam 2014; Johannesen 2014; Johannesen and Zucman 2012), it is highly likely that these changes are due to the establishment of AEI as the almost-global standard for tax co-operation.

6. Conclusion

From 2008, US regulators and legislators have exploited the dominance of their country's financial market to impose new reporting requirements on foreign banks. FATCA, the centrepiece of their efforts, obliges FFIs to routinely report data on US account-holders and their capital income to the IRS, imposing a 30 per cent withholding tax on their US-source revenue in case of non-compliance. To avoid conflict of laws, the US administration embedded unilateral imposition of these requirements in a network of 112 bilateral treaties, obliging foreign governments either to collect requested information on US account-holders from domestic

7. Interviews on 7 March, and 8, 9, and 16 July 2014.

banks and transmit it to the IRS or instruct domestic banks to transmit the data directly. Signatories include all major economies and offshore centres, which constitutes a step-change in US bilateral tax co-operation. Moreover, concessions offshore centres had to make to the US also enabled unprecedented levels of tax co-operation at EU and multilateral level. After concluding FATCA agreements with the US, an MFN clause also forced Luxembourg and Austria to concede AEI on all types of capital income to EU partners, ending fifteen years of successful resistance. At the same time, US progress in the imposition of AEI led the G20 to endorse it as the new global standard for tax co-operation, providing the key impetus for the establishment of a corresponding multilateral agreement also signed by many important offshore centres. After financial institutions in these jurisdictions had been forced to build infrastructure for the implementation of AEI with the US, practising the same standard with third countries simply reduced compliance costs compared with having to comply with two different standards.

Next to creating important adjustment costs for financial institutions, the multilateral AEI regime probably also induced a decline in foreign financial wealth managed in previously financially opaque jurisdictions. This decline is likely to also depress value added by financial sectors, wages, and employment, leaving these countries substantially worse off than under the *status quo* of tax competition (*see* Genschel and Seelkopf 2016, Chapter Three in this volume). In contrast, the US, which neither grants fully reciprocal AEI through FATCA nor signed the multilateral agreement, has seen a massive influx of foreign deposits before and after the financial crisis. Instead of providing joint gains, multilateral co-operation in AEI thus seems to redistribute global financial wealth to the benefit of the United States (Oatley and Nabors 1998). In terms of equity, this outcome is highly ambiguous. It enables the US to protect the effective progressivity of its tax system, increasing the chances of a distribution of the tax burden in accordance with the ability-to-pay principle. At the same time, it undermines the chances of other jurisdictions achieving just that. In fact, by forcing traditional secrecy jurisdictions to become transparent, and preserving its own financial opacity at the same time, the US simply reduces competition for those American financial institutions interested in hosting hidden wealth.

References

Adam, F. (2014) 'Impact de l'échange automatique d'informations en matière de produits financiers: une tentative d'évaluation macro-économique appliquée au Luxembourg', *Economie et Statistiques: Working papers du STATEC*, Nr. 73: http://www.statistiques.public.lu/catalogue-publications/economie-statistiques/2014/73-2014.pdf (accessed 10 July 2015).

BIS (Bank for International Standards, 2013) 'Comparative tables': http://www.bis.org/cpmi/publ/d116p2.pdf (accessed 12 August 2015).

— (2015) 'Locational banking statistics': http://www.bis.org/statistics/bankstats.htm?m=6%7C31%7C69 (accessed 12 August 2015).

BMF (2008) *Monatsbericht des BMF - März 2008*. Berlin: Bundesministerium der Finanzen: http://www.bundesfinanzministerium.de/Content/DE/Monatsberichte/Publikationen_Migration/2008/03/000_a_mb_maerz.pdf?__blob=publicationFile&v=3 (accessed 12 August 2015).

Bouilhet, A. and Crouzel, C. (2008) 'Paradis fiscaux: la Suisse au banc des accusés', *Figaro* 22 October: http://www.lefigaro.fr/impots/2008/10/22/05003-20081022ARTFIG00303-paradis-fiscaux-la-suisse-au-banc-des-accuses-.php (accessed 12 August 2015).

Bradford, A. (2012) 'The Brussels effect', *Northwestern University Law Review,* 107(1): 1–68.

Brambusch, J. (2013) 'Was ist denn hier passiert?', *Capital*, 1 June.

Brinkmann, S. *et al.* (2015) 'Ermittlungen wegen Steuerhinterziehung: Wie Fahnder gegen das System Luxemburg losschlagen', *sueddeutsche.de*, 25 February: http://www.sueddeutsche.de/wirtschaft/ermittlungen-wegen-steuerhinterziehung-wie-fahnder-gegen-das-system-luxemburg-losschlagen-1.2366065 (accessed 12 August 2015).

Brunetti, A. (2013) *Regulatorische Herausforderungen für die grenzüberschreitende Schweizer Vermögensverwaltung und strategische Optionen*, Bern: Eidgenössisches Finanzdepartement: http://www.news.admin.ch/NSBSubscriber/message/attachments/31569.pdf (accessed 12 August 2015).

Bucovetsky, S. (1991) 'Asymmetric tax competition', *Journal of Urban Economics* 30(2): 167–81.

Christians, A. (2013) 'What you give and what you get: reciprocity under a model 1 intergovernmental agreement on FATCA', *Cayman Financial Review*, April, and SSRN Scholarly Paper ID 2292645, Rochester, NY: Social Science Research Network: http://papers.ssrn.com/abstract=2292645 (accessed 12 August 2015).

— (2014) 'IRS claims statutory authority for FATCA agreements where no such authority exists', *Tax, Society & Culture*, 4 July: http://taxpol.blogspot.com.au/2014/07/irs-claims-statutory-authority-for.html (accessed 12 August 2015).

Clausing, K. (2016) 'The nature and practice of capital tax competition', in Dietsch, P. and Rixen, T. (eds) *Global Tax Governance: What is wrong with it and how to fix it*, Colchester: ECPR Press.

Council of Ministers (2004) 'Agreement in the form of an exchange of letters between the European Community and the Swiss Confederation Providing for Measures Equivalent to Those Laid Down in Council Directive 2003/48/EC on Taxation of Savings Income in the Form of Interest Payments', *Official Journal* vol. L: 351–85.

Dion Global Solutions (2012) 'Intelligent compliance: finding a solution to FATCA and all that follows': http://www.link.pt/upl/%7B330ec3f7-c551-4bc1-8bca-064f5145a1ff%7D.pdf (accessed 12 August 2015).

Drezner, D. W. (2008) *All Politics Is Global: Explaining international regulatory regimes*, Princeton, New Jersey; Woodstock: Princeton University Press.

ECB (European Central Bank) (2015) Statistical Data Warehouse – Monetary statistics – MFI balance sheets – National tables – National tables: euro area: http://sdw.ecb.europa.eu/reports.do?node=1000003158 (accessed 12 August 2015).

Eccleston, R. (2012) *The Dynamics of Global Economic Governance: The OECD, the global financial crisis and the transformation of international tax regulation*, Cheltenham: Edward Elgar Publishing.

Eccleston, R. and Gray, F. (2014) 'Foreign Accounts Tax Compliance Act and American leadership in the campaign against international tax evasion: revolution or false dawn?', *Global Policy* 5(3): 321–33.

Economist (2014) 'Putting the squeeze on Miami vice', 18 January: http://www.economist.com/blogs/schumpeter/2014/01/banks-and-tax evasion (accessed 12 August 2015).

EFD (Eidgnössisches Finanzdepartment, 2013) 'Weiterentwicklung der Finanzmarktstrategie', Bern: Eidgenössisches Finanzdepartement: https://www.news.admin.ch/message/index.html?lang=de&msg-id=49287 (accessed 12 August 2015).

Eisenring, C. (2014) 'Amerika will viel und gibt wenig: Informationsaustausch über Bankkunden', *Neue Zürcher Zeitung*, 7 March: http://www.nzz.ch/wirtschaft/wirtschafts-und-finanzportal/amerika-will-viel-und-gibt-wenig-1.18257621 (accessed 12 August 2015).

Emmenegger, P. (2014) '"A nut too hard to crack": Swiss banking secrecy and automatic exchange of information in tax matters', paper presented at the: Annual Conference of the Swiss Political Science Association, Bern: https://www.alexandria.unisg.ch/publications/231925 (accessed 12 August 2015).

EU G5 Finance Ministers (2013) 'Letter to Commissioner Algirdas Semeta', Bundesfinanzministerium: http://www.bundesfinanzministerium.de/Content/EN/Pressemitteilungen/2013/2013-04-09-g5-joint-action-to-combat-tax evasion-pdf.pdf?__blob=publicationFile&v=3 (accessed 12 August 2015).

European Commission (2008a) 'Questions arising from the first analysis of the comments on the Working Document prepared by the Commission services on 14 July 2007 for the Expert Group on Taxation of Savings': http://ec.europa.eu/taxation_customs/resources/documents/taxation/personal_tax/savings_tax/savings_directive_review/workdoc_gt4_080401_doc2_en.pdf (accessed 12 August 2015).

— (2008b) 'report from the Commission to the Council in accordance with Article 18 of Council Directive 2003/48/EC on taxation of savings income in the form of interest payments': http://ec.europa.eu/taxation_customs/resources/documents/taxation/personal_tax/savings_tax/implementation/com%282008%29552_en.pdf (accessed 12 August 2015).

— (2008c) 'Proposal for a Council Directive amending Directive 2003/48/EC on taxation of savings income in the form of interest payments COM(2008) 727 final': http://ec.europa.eu/taxation_customs/resources/documents/taxation/personal_tax/savings_tax/savings_directive_review/com(2008)727_en.pdf (accessed 12 August 2015).

— (2009) 'Proposal for a Council Directive on administrative co-operation in the field of taxation': http://eur-lex.europa.eu/LexUriServ/LexUriServ.do?uri=COM:2009:0029:FIN:EN:PDF (accessed 12 August 2015).

European Community (2003) 'Council Directive 2003/48/EC of 3 June 2003 on taxation of savings income in the form of interest payments', *Official Journal of the European Union* vol. L(157): 38–47: http://eur-lex.europa.eu/LexUriServ/LexUriServ.do?uri=OJ:L:2003:157:0038:0048:en:PDF (accessed 12 August 2015).

— (2009) 'Provisional agenda 2981st meeting of the Council of the European Union': http://data.consilium.europa.eu/doc/document/ST-16689-2009-INIT/en/pdf (accessed 12 August 2015).

— (2010) 'Provisional agenda 2990th meeting of the Council of the European Union': http://data.consilium.europa.eu/doc/document/ST-5311-2010-INIT/en/pdf (accessed 12 August 2015).

— (2011a) 'Provisional agenda 3088th meeting of the Council of the European Union': http://data.consilium.europa.eu/doc/document/ST-10035-2011-INIT/en/pdf (accessed 12 August 2015).

— (2011b) 'Provisional agenda 3105th meeting of the Council of the European Union': http://data.consilium.europa.eu/doc/document/ST-12505-2011-INIT/en/pdf (accessed 12 August 2015).

— (2012a) 'Revised version no 1 to the provisional agenda 3167th meeting of the Council of the European Union': http://data.consilium.europa.eu/doc/document/ST-9817-2012-REV-1/en/pdf (accessed 12 August 2015).

— (2012b) 'ECOFIN report to the European Council on Tax Issues': http://data.consilium.europa.eu/doc/document/ST-16327-2012-INIT/en/pdf (accessed 12 August 2015).

— (2013) 'Press release 3238th Council Meeting Economic and Financial Affairs': http://www.consilium.europa.eu/uedocs/cms_data/docs/pressdata/en/ecofin/137122.pdf (accessed 12 August 2015).

— (2014) 'Council Directive amending Directive 2011/16/EU as regards mandatory automatic exchange of information in the field of taxation, Interinstitutional File: 2013/0188 (CNS)', Council of the European Union: http://data.consilium.europa.eu/doc/document/ST-14425-2014-INIT/en/pdf (accessed 12 August 2015).

European Council (2014) 'Conclusions 20/21 March': https://www.consilium.europa.eu/uedocs/cms_data/docs/pressdata/en/ec/141749.pdf (accessed 12 August 2015).

European Union (2011) 'Council Directive 2011/16/EU of 15 February 2011 on administrative co-operation in the field of taxation and repealing Directive 77/799/EEC', *Official Journal of the European Union* vol. L(64): 1–12: http://eur-lex.europa.eu/legal-content/en/ALL/?uri=CELEX:32011L0016 (accessed 12 August 2015).

— (2014) 'Council Directive 2014/48/EU of 24 March 2014 amending Directive 2003/48/EC on taxation of savings income in the form of interest payments', *Official Journal* vol. L111(50): http://eur-lex.europa.eu/legal-content/EN/TXT/?uri=OJ:JOL_2014_111_R_0013 (accessed 12 August 2015).

FIA (Futures Industry Association, 2014) 'FIA Annual Volume Survey 2013': http://futuresindustry.org/downloads/FIA_Annual_Volume_Survey_2013.pdf (accessed 12 August 2015).

G20 Information Centre (2008) 'Declaration of the Summit on Financial Markets and the World Economy', Washington, DC, 15 November: http://www.g20.utoronto.ca/2008/2008declaration1115.html (accessed 12 August 2015).

— (2009) 'Global plan for economic recovery and reform', G20 Leaders' London Summit statement ('London Declaration'): http://www.g20.utoronto.ca/2009/2009communique0402.html (accessed 12 August 2015).

— (2012) G20 Leaders Declaration, Los Cabos Summit: http://www.consilium.europa.eu/uedocs/cms_data/docs/pressdata/en/ec/131069.pdf (accessed 12 August 2015).

— (2013) G20 Leaders' Declaration, St Petersburg Summit: https://g20.org/wp-content/uploads/2014/12/Saint_Petersburg_Declaration_ENG_0.pdf (accessed 12 August 2015).

Gabor, G. (2011) 'Inside the budget battle with Congressman Paul Ryan', *American Business Magazine*, 1 August: http://www.americanbusinessmag.com/2011/08/inside-the-budget-battle-with-congressman-paul-ryan/ (accessed 12 August 2015).

GAO (Government Accountability Office, 2007) 'Tax compliance: Qualified Intermediary program provides some assurance that taxes on foreign investors are withheld and reported, but can be improved': http://www.gao.gov/products/GAO-08-99 (accessed 12 August 2015).

Garst, B. (2014) 'Don't expect U.S. FATCA reciprocation any time soon', Center for Freedom and Prosperity: http://freedomandprosperity.org/2014/featured/dont-expect-u-s-fatca-reciprocation-any-time-soon/ (accessed 12 August 2015).

Genschel, P. (2002) *Steuerharmonisierung und Steuerwettbewerb in der Europäischen Union*, Frankfurt-am-Main and New York: Campus.

Genschel, P and Plumper, T. (1997) 'Regulatory competition and international co-operation', *Journal of European Public Policy* 4(4): 626–42.

Genschel, P. and Schwarz, P. (2011) 'Tax competition: a literature review', *Socio-Economic Review* 9(2): 339–70.

— (2013) 'Tax competition and fiscal democracy', in Streeck, W. and Schäfer, A. (eds) *Politics in the Age of Austerity*, Cambridge: Polity Press.

Genschel, P. and Seelkopf, L. (2016) 'Winners and losers of tax competition', in Dietsch, P. and Rixen, T. (eds) *Global Tax Governance: What is wrong with it and how to fix it*, Colchester: ECPR Press.

Grinberg, I. (2012) 'Beyond FATCA: an evolutionary moment for the international tax system', Georgetown Law Faculty Working Papers 160, January: http://scholarship.law.georgetown.edu/fwps_papers/160 (accessed 12 August 2015).

— (2016) 'Does FATCA teach broader lessons about international tax multilateralism?', in Dietsch, P. and Rixen, T. (eds) *Global Tax Governance: What is wrong with it and how to fix it*, Colchester: ECPR Press.

Hakelberg, L. (2014) 'The power politics of international tax co-operation: Luxembourg, Austria and the automatic exchange of information', *Journal of European Public Policy* 22(3): 409–28.

— (2015) 'The domestic politics of international tax co-operation: how party ideology and competitive advantage determine the use of American power', paper presented at ECPR Joint Sessions, 29 March–4 April, Warsaw.

Hall, B. (2008) 'Berlin calls for Swiss to be on tax blacklist', *Financial Times*, 21 October: http://www.ft.com/intl/cms/s/0/1f8a19ba-9f9f-11dd-a3fa-000077b07658.html?siteedition=intl (accessed 12 August 2015).

Hässig, L. (2010) *Paradies perdu: Vom Ende des Schweizer Bankgeheimnisses*, Hamburg: Hoffmann und Campe.

Helleiner, E. (2002) 'The politics of global financial regulation: lessons from the fight against money laundering', in Eatwell, J. and Taylor, L. (eds) *International Capital Markets: Systems in transition*, Oxford and New York: Oxford University Press: 177–204.

IMF (International Monetary Fund, 2015) 'IMF Data – Coordinated Portfolio Investment Survey – Slide 1': http://data.imf.org/?sk=B981B4E3-4E58-467E-9B90-9DE0C3367363 (accessed 12 August 2015).

IRS (Internal Revenue Service, 2011) *Internal Revenue Bulletin* 2011 (32), Notice 2011-53, 'Chapter 4 Implementation Notice': http://www.irs.gov/irb/2011-32_IRB/ar09.html (accessed 12 August 2015).

Israel, S. (2009) 'Gemeinsame Flucht vor schwarzen Listen', *Tages-Anzeiger*, March.

Jäger, S. (2014) *Realitäts-Check: Die Fahnderin - Plusminus – ARD Das Erste*, Plusminus, DasErste.de: http://www.daserste.de/information/wirtschaft-boerse/plusminus/sendung/mdr/fahnderin100.html (accessed 12 August 2015).

Johannesen, N. (2014) 'Tax evasion and Swiss bank deposits', *Journal of Public Economics* 111(March): 46–62.

Johannesen, N. and Zucman, G. (2012) 'The end of bank secrecy? An evaluation of the G20 tax haven crackdown', HAL: Sciences de l'Homme et de la Société: http://halshs.archives-ouvertes.fr/halshs-00665054 (accessed 12 August 2015).

Kanbur, R. and Keen, M. (1993) 'Jeux sans frontières: tax competition and tax coordination when countries differ in size', *American Economic Review* 83(4): 877–92.

Kellner, B. and Strunz, K. (2008) 'Peer Steinbrück: Ich senke die Steuern, wenn alle ehrlich zahlen!', *BILD.de*, 27 August: http://www.bild.de/geld/wirtschaft/wenn-alle-ehrlich-zahlen-3845802.bild.html (accessed 12 August 2015).

Keohane, R. O. (2005) *After Hegemony: Co-operation and discord in the world political economy*, Princeton Classic edition, with new Preface by author, Princeton, New Jersey: Princeton University Press.

Krasner, S. D. (1991) 'Global communications and national power: life on the Pareto frontier', *World Politics* 43(03): 336–66.

Kudrle, R. T. (2003) 'Hegemony strikes out: the U.S. global role in antitrust, tax evasion, and illegal immigration', *International Studies Perspectives* 4(1): 52–71.

Leblond, P. (2011) 'EU, US and international accounting standards: a delicate balancing act in governing global finance', *Journal of European Public Policy* 18(3): 443–61.

Levin, C. and Coleman, N. (2006) *Tax Haven Abuses: The enablers, the tools, and secrecy*, Washington, DC: US Government Printing Office: http://www.hsgac.senate.gov/download/report-tax-haven-abuses-the-enablers-the-tools-and-secrecy (accessed 12 August 2015).

— (2008) 'Tax haven banks and U.S. tax compliance', Washington, DC: US Government Printing Office.: http://www.gpo.gov/fdsys/pkg/CHRG-110shrg44127/html/CHRG-110shrg44127.htm (accessed 12 August 2015).

Levin, C. and Lieberman, J. (2001) 'What is the U.S. position on offshore tax havens?', Washington, DC:U.S. Government Printing Office.

Meinzer, M. (2016) 'Towards an international yardstick for identifying tax havens and facilitating reform', in Dietsch, P. and Rixen, T. (eds) *Global Tax Governance: What is wrong with it and how to fix it*, Colchester: ECPR Press.

Mordi, F. (2011) 'Re: IRS proposed regulations on reporting interest paid to nonresident alien individuals', *American Bankers Association*: http://www.aba.com/aba/documents/news/NRaliens4811.pdf (accessed 12 August 2015).

Mussler, W. (2008) 'EU-Steuerpolitik Steinbrücks Feldzug', *Frankfurter Allgemeine Wirtschaft*, 9 March: http://www.faz.net/aktuell/wirtschaft/eu-steuerpolitik-steinbruecks-feldzug-1510780.html (accessed 12 August 2015).

Naegeli, K. (2010) 'Merz bekräftigt Nein zu automatischem Informationsaustausch', *SDA - Basisdienst Deutsch*, February SWI: swissinfo.ch: http://www.swissinfo.ch/ger/merz-bekraeftigt-nein-zu-automatischem-informationsaustausch/8296868 (accessed 12 August 2015).

— (2011) 'EU sucht Lösung im Streit um automatischen Informationsaustausch Schweiz und weitere Drittstaaten dienen als Manövriermasse', *SDA–Basisdienst Deutsch*, January.

Newman, N. (2014) 'Explaining the wormy morass of Obama's FATCA tax evasion law', *Forbes*: http://www.forbes.com/sites/realspin/2014/05/30/explaining-the-wormy-morass-of-obamas-fatca-tax evasion-law/ (accessed 12 August 2015).

Oatley, T. and Nabors, R. (1998) 'Redistributive co-operation: market failure, wealth transfers, and the Basle accord', *International Organization* 52(1): 35–54.

OECD (2009) 'A progress report on the jurisdictions surveyed by the OECD Global Forum in implementing the internationally agreed tax standard': http://www.oecd.org/ctp/42497950.pdf (accessed 12 August 2015).

— (2014a) 'Multilateral competent authority agreement on automatic exchange of financial account information: http://www.oecd.org/ctp/exchange-of-tax-information/multilateral-competent-authority-agreement.pdf (accessed 12 August 2015).

— (2014b) 'Signatories of the multilateral competent authority agreement and intended first information-exchange date': http://www.oecd.org/tax/exchange-of-tax-information/MCAA-Signatories.pdf (accessed 12 August 2015).

— (2014c) *Standard for Automatic Exchange of Financial Account Information in Tax Matters*, Paris: OECD Publishing, http://www.keepeek.com/Digital-Asset-Management/oecd/taxation/standard-for-automatic-exchange-of-financial-account-information-for-tax-matters_9789264216525-en#page1 (accessed 12 August 2015).

— (2014d) 'AEOI: Status of commitments', Paris: OECD: http://www.oecd.org/tax/transparency/AEOI-commitments.pdf (accessed 12 August 2015).

Office of Management and Budget (2013) *Fiscal Year 2014: Analytical Perspectives Budget of the U.S. Government* Washington, DC: US Government Printing Office: http://www.whitehouse.gov/sites/default/files/omb/budget/fy2014/assets/spec.pdf (accessed 12 August 2015).

Palan, R. *et al.* (2010) *Tax Havens: How globalization really works*, Ithaca, New York: Cornell University Press.

Piketty, T. and Zucman, G. (2014) 'Capital is back: wealth-income ratios in rich countries, 1700–2010', *Quarterly Journal of Economics*, May: doi:10.1093/qje/qju018.

Posner, E. (2009) 'Making rules for global finance: transatlantic regulatory co-operation at the turn of the millennium', *International Organization* 63(04): 665–99.

Rademacher, I. (2013) 'Tax competition in the eurozone: capital mobility, agglomeration, and the small country disadvantage', Max Planck Institut für Gesellschaftsforschung Discussion Paper 13/13: http://www.mpifg.de/pu/mpifg_dp/dp13-13.pdf (accessed 12 August 2015).

Rixen, T. (2008) *The Political Economy of International Tax Governance*, Basingstoke and New York: Palgrave Macmillan.

Rixen, T. and Genschel, P. (2015) 'Settling and unsettling the transnational legal order of international taxation', in Shaffer, G. and Halliday, T. (eds), *Transnational Legal Orders*, Cambridge: Cambridge University Press, pp. 154–84.

Rixen, T. and Schwarz, P. (2012) 'How effective is the European Union's Savings Tax Directive? Evidence from four EU member states', *JCMS: Journal of Common Market Studies* 50(1): 151–68.

Schweizer Depeschen Agentur (SDA) (2009) 'EU-Finanzminister: Kein Entscheid im Steuerpaket Auf Schweiz wartet am Ende automatischer Informationsaustausch', *SDA – Basisdienst Deutsch*, December.

— (2010a) 'In den Steuerstreit innerhalb der EU kommt Bewegung', *SDA – Basisdienst Deutsch*, January.

— (2010b) 'Informationsaustausch: EU-Finanzminister einig bei Amtshilfe EU-Steuerkommissar sieht Bankgeheimnis zurückgebunden', *SDA – Basisdienst Deutsch*, December.

— (2011a) 'Italien blockiert Einigung im EU-Steuerstreit – fordert Sanktionen Tremonti: "Die EU ist der Schweiz beigetreten"', *SDA – Basisdienst Deutsch*, May.

— (2011b) 'Schwierige Lösungssuche im EU-Steuerstreit Vorerst keine Verhandlungen zwischen EU-Kommission und Schweiz', *SDA – Basisdienst Deutsch*, July.

— (2012a) 'Weiterhin keine Verhandlungen EU-Schweiz zu Zinsbesteuerung', *SDA – Basisdienst Deutsch*, May.

— (2012b) 'Schweiz und USA streben Erleichterungen bei Finanzsteuer FATCA an', *SDA – Basisdienst Deutsch*, June.

— (2012c) 'Schweiz und USA einigen sich auf Abkommen zu FATCA', *SDA – Basisdienst Deutsch*, December.

— (2014) '51 Staaten einigen sich auf automatischen Austausch von Steuerdaten', *SDA – Basisdienst Deutsch*, October.

Semeta, A. (2014) Letter to Mr Yannis Stournaras, Minister of Finance of the Hellenic Republic, Ref. Ares(2014)574281, Brussels: European Commission: http://ec.europa.eu/archives/commission_2010-2014/semeta/headlines/news/2014/03/ares(2014)574281.pdf (accessed 12 August 2015).

Sharman, J. (2006) 'Norms, coercion and contracting in the struggle against "harmful" tax competition', *Australian Journal of International Affairs* 60(1): 143–69.

— (2008) 'Regional deals and the global imperative: the external dimension of the European Union Savings Tax Directive', *JCMS: Journal of Common Market Studies*, 46(5): 1049–69.

Simmons, B. A. (2001) 'The international politics of harmonization: the case of capital market regulation', *International Organization* 55(3): 589–620.

Singer, D. A. (2007) *Regulating Capital: Setting standards for the international financial system*, Ithaca, New York: Cornell University Press.

SNB (Schweizerische Nationalbank) (2014) 'Die Banken in der Schweiz 2013': http://www.snb.ch/de/iabout/stat/statpub/bchpub/stats/bankench (accessed 12 August 2015).

Spiegel (2012) 'Schweiz, Luxemburg, Liechtenstein: Wie der Fiskus mit Steuer-CDs Millionen macht', *Spiegel Online*, 4 December. http://www.spiegel.de/wirtschaft/soziales/ein-ueberblick-ueber-die-cds-mit-daten-deutscher-steuersuender-seit-2000-a-870946.html (accessed 12 August 2015).

Standard (2013) 'Bankgeheimnis wackelt; US-Steuergesetz setzt Österreich und Schweiz zu', 10 January.

Tanenbaum, E. (2012). 'Here they come: FATCA intergovernmental agreements', *Tax Management International Journal,* 41(11): 623–25.

TJN (Tax Justice Network, 2014) 'Financial Secrecy Index – 2013 Results': http://www.financialsecrecyindex.com/introduction/fsi-2013-results (accessed 12 August 2015).

US Government (2009) *A New Era of Responsibility: Renewing America's Promise – Budget of the United States Government, fiscal year 2010*: Washington, DC: US Government Publishing Office: http://www.gpo.gov/fdsys/search/pagedetails.action?granuleId=&packageId=BUDGET-2010-BUD&fromBrowse=true (accessed 12 August 2015).

US Treasury (2012a) 'Model intergovernmental agreement to improve tax compliance and to implement FATCA': https://www.treasury.gov/press-center/press-releases/Documents/reciprocal.pdf (accessed 12 August 2015).

— (2012b) 'Agreement between the Government of the United States of America and the Government of the United Kingdom of Great Britain and Northern Ireland to improve international tax compliance and to implement FATCA': http://www.treasury.gov/resource-center/tax-policy/treaties/Documents/FATCA-Agreement-UK-9-12-2012.pdf (accessed 12 August 2015).

— (2012c) 'Agreement between the United States of America and Switzerland for co-operation to facilitate the implementation of FATCA': http://www.treasury.gov/resource-center/tax-policy/treaties/Documents/FATCA-Agreement-Switzerland-2-14-2013.pdf (accessed 12 August 2015).

— 2012d 'Joint statement from the United States, France, Germany, Italy, Spain and the United Kingdom regarding an intergovernmental approach to improving international tax compliance and implementing FATCA': http://www.treasury.gov/press-center/press-releases/Documents/020712%20Treasury%20IRS%20FATCA%20Joint%20Statement.pdf (accessed 12 August 2015).

— (2012e) 'Joint statement from the US and Switzerland regarding a framework for co-operation to facilitate the implementation of FATCA'. http://www.treasury.gov/resource-center/tax-policy/treaties/Documents/FATCA-Joint-Statement-US-Switzerland-06-21-2012.pdf (accessed 12 August 2015).

— (2014a) 'Foreign Account Tax Compliance Act (FATCA)': http://www.treasury.gov/resource-center/tax-policy/treaties/Pages/FATCA.aspx (accessed 12 August 2015).

— (2014b) 'General explanations of the Administration's fiscal year 2015 revenue proposals': http://www.treasury.gov/resource-center/tax-policy/Documents/General-Explanations-FY2015.pdf (accessed 12 August 2015).

Valda, A. (2012) 'Ganz-neue-Töne: Bekenntnis zum Datenaustausch', *Tages-Anzeiger*, December: http://www.tagesanzeiger.ch/schweiz/standard/Ganz-neue-Toene-Bekenntnis-zum-Datenaustausch/story/2314058 (accessed 12 August 2015).

Vasagar, J. and Houlder, V. (2014) 'Governments sign deal against tax evasion', *Financial Times*, October 29. http://www.ft.com/intl/cms/s/0/5ec1d4e0-5f99-11e4-8c27-00144feabdc0.html#axzz3LU6ZM7Tq (accessed 12 August 2015).

Woodward, R. (2016) 'A strange revolution: mock compliance and the failure of the OECD's international tax transparency regime', in Dietsch, P. and Rixen, T. (eds) *Global Tax Governance: What is wrong with it and how to fix it*, Colchester: ECPR Press.

World Bank (2013) 'Market capitalization of listed companies (current US$)': http://data.worldbank.org/indicator/CM.MKT.LCAP.CD (accessed 12 August 2015).

Zucman, G. (2014) *Steueroasen: Wo der Wohlstand der Nationen versteckt wird*, transl. Ulrike Bischoff, Berlin: Suhrkamp Verlag.

Chapter Seven

Does FATCA Teach Broader Lessons about International Tax Multilateralism?

Itai Grinberg

1. Introduction

Approximately $8.5 trillion, representing more than 6 per cent of all global wealth, is managed through offshore accounts. Until recently, the major developed economies had failed for decades in their efforts to achieve comprehensive administrative co-operation to address offshore tax evasion. Historically, much of both the investment earnings and the principal held in offshore accounts went untaxed.

Recent well publicised cross-border tax-evasion scandals have focused political attention on offshore tax evasion in the world's major economies. The details read like a thriller, with bankers smuggling toothpaste tubes full of diamonds across borders and governments buying stolen data files and handing new identities to the informants. Politicians became interested in these offshore tax-evasion scandals as a result of the budgetary pressures brought on by the financial crisis. Presidents and finance ministers began insisting on some form of improved transparency to combat offshore tax abuses, but the form such co-operation would take was unclear.

Projects proposing various approaches to enhance cross-border tax co-operation were launched by the United States, the OECD, the European Union and even, in a rearguard action, Switzerland. Eventually, the G20 endorsed a multilateral automatic information-exchange (AEI) system to address offshore tax evasion; they asked the OECD to produce a proposal for a new multilateral reporting standard for AEI, which the OECD released in February 2014. The G20's decision to task the OECD in this way, and incorporate AEI into its 'international financial law' architecture, is proving efficacious.[1] The resulting 'Common Reporting System,' is currently emerging as a widely adopted international standard that addresses offshore tax evasion in a manner that provides benefits to a wide range

---

1. International financial law encompasses a dizzying array of international agreements aimed at strengthening the prudential oversight and supervision of market participants; these agreements generally enjoy the political legitimacy bestowed by G20 convocation and endorsement but do not take the form of formal, legally binding treaties. *See* Section 3, 'The international financial-law architecture and offshore tax evasion', for more about what I refer to as 'international financial law' (Brummer 2011).

of sovereigns.[2] That development represents a significant evolutionary moment for the international tax system.

By far the most influential event in the shift toward AEI as a tool for combating offshore tax evasion was the enactment by the United States of the legislation known as 'FATCA' (Foreign Account Tax Compliance Act) (Grinberg 2012). What distinguished FATCA was that it used US market power in a coercive manner in order to force foreign financial institutions to comply with an extensive regime for identifying accounts of US taxpayers. Negotiations between the United States and other countries around the parameters of compliance with FATCA's requirements are broadly credited with substantially accelerating global discussions about multilateral automatic information-exchange. FATCA and the negotiations catalysed by its enactment put AEI on the multilateral agenda and eventually resulted in agreements at a political level at the G20 and at a technical level in the body of the common reporting system at the OECD.

The FATCA story raises two interesting questions of broader interest to both international tax specialists and others interested in international economic governance. First, how did the mechanisms for achieving international co-ordination in the area of offshore tax evasion operate, and why were they effective? Second, is this mechanism transposable to other areas of international tax relations among sovereigns? These questions are timely in light of more recent developments in international tax, especially the emergence of the Base Erosion and Profit Shifting (BEPS) project at the OECD, which represents a new multilateral international tax effort, this time focused on cross-border tax avoidance by multinational corporations rather than offshore tax evasion by individuals.

This chapter begins by describing the path from offshore tax evasion scandals in the midst of the financial crisis, to the enactment by the United States of FATCA, to agreement internationally on a 'Common Reporting Standard' for offshore accounts that has been endorsed by more than eighty countries and appears to be headed towards broad multilateral implementation. I explain how both tax information-exchange upon request and the FATCA-style model for automatic information-exchange became part of the G20's international financial-law architecture, and why that architecture has helped spur global change in this area. With that understanding in place, I then ask whether the FATCA model for global co-ordination spurred by unilateral action is likely to be replicated in other areas of international tax relations. I conclude that although the FATCA success story is remarkable, the combination of unilateral US coercive pressure and multilateral co-ordination towards a global standard for information-exchange succeeded because the underlying issue was an enforcement measure in which interests among major economic powers were generally aligned and the benefits

2. Unlike FATCA, the CRS does not have a withholding-tax mechanism in place to enforce compliance. Therefore it will rely on domestic law in the country of the financial institution to ensure that information is received by the country of residence of the taxpayer. In most cases, such laws have yet to be enacted, although dozens of countries have committed to doing so.

from agreement were non-rival. Furthermore, threats to make US market access conditional on compliance were both credible and particularly powerful in the financial-sector context. As a result, the FATCA/Common Reporting System story, while itself fascinating, is not a straightforward model for achieving global tax co-operation in areas affecting the tax burden imposed on taxpayers under substantive tax law and the division of the tax base and distribution of tax revenue among the major economies.

2. Offshore tax evasion and the path from unilateral action to a global standard

In 2008, the issue of offshore tax evasion featured prominently on the global political agenda, largely as a result of highly publicised tax-evasion scandals involving LGT bank in Lichtenstein and UBS in Switzerland. The latter scandal led the United States to act against UBS for conspiring to defraud the United States by helping US customers conceal their ownership of, or beneficial interest in, income and assets held through offshore accounts in Switzerland and other jurisdictions (*Tax Notes Today* 2009). Recognising that LGT and UBS were merely exemplars of a much broader problem, at the April 2009 G20 London Summit world leaders stated that they 'stand ready to take agreed action against those jurisdictions that do not meet international standards for tax transparency' (G20 2009a). The G20 called attention to a document the OECD published on the same day that listed countries that had not committed to or substantially implemented international standards for tax transparency. Importantly, that OECD list included the bank-secrecy countries that were OECD members.

Within a few years of being threatened with sanctions by the G20, those jurisdictions previously unwilling to exchange information upon request in accordance with OECD standards changed their position and began to comply with this new global norm. Shortly afterward, actions by legislatures, tax administrations and prosecutors of the world's major developed economies demonstrated their belief that information-exchange upon request was inadequate to fight offshore tax evasion. For instance, various G7 governments purchased account data stolen by insiders from banks; shared stolen information among themselves; used it to prosecute tax-evaders; and linked enhanced penalties for offshore tax evasion by their citizens to the tax transparency of the territory in which the income or gain arises.

The United States Congress took a more aggressive approach by enacting sections 1471 to 1474 of the Internal Revenue Code (FATCA),[3] which requires foreign financial institutions to report information on financial accounts of US persons and foreign entities with significant US ownership (each a 'US account')

3. Sections 1471 to 1474 of the Internal Revenue Code ('Code') were enacted in the Foreign Account Tax Compliance title (Title V) of the Hiring Incentives to Restore Employment Act of 2010 (HIRE Act) (United States Public Law No. 111–147, §§ 501–35).

directly to the Internal Revenue Service (IRS) beginning in 2015.[4] Foreign financial institutions must report the account balance or value of each such US account and the amount of dividends, interest, other income and gross proceeds from the sale of property credited to the account (United States Treasury Regulations 2013: §1.1471–4(a)–(d)(3)–(4)). The rules are intended to provide reporting both on accounts held directly by individuals and on interests in accounts held by shell entities owned by US individuals.

In order to 'force foreign financial institutions to disclose their US accountholders or pay a steep penalty for nondisclosure' (Levin 2010), FATCA imposed a withholding 'tax'[5] on specified payments from US sources and the proceeds from disposing of certain US investments ('withholdable payments') on foreign financial institutions that do not comply and become a participating foreign financial institution, or FFI (Internal Revenue Code §1473(1)(A)); Thus, if foreign financial institutions do not agree to report to the United States on income earned by US individuals, FATCA requires the withholding of a wide range of payments from the United States to those same financial institutions, regardless of whether the payments benefit US persons, non-US customers of the institution or the institution itself.

FATCA as enacted also required that participating foreign financial institutions withhold payments to non-participating foreign financial institutions in cases where the funding for those payments could be attributed to withholdable payments ('passthru payments') (Internal Revenue Code §1471(b)(1)(D)(i)). These 'passthru' payment rules, although hard to implement, were intended (1) to induce foreign financial institutions that were investing in or through participating financial institutions, but not investing in the United States, to participate in FATCA by creating concern that they might not be able to avoid its reach; and (2) to make participating foreign financial institutions consider whether they would stop doing business with non-participating financial institutions after FATCA was implemented, because business between participating and non-participating financial institutions would, at least in theory, require withholding under US law. FATCA's intent was to use the combined weight of US financial markets and financial institutions that must, as a practical matter, do business in the US markets as leverage with other foreign financial institutions to ensure near-comprehensive compliance with FATCA reporting.

Compliance with FATCA in the manner provided for in the legislation required foreign financial institutions in many jurisdictions to violate contractual relationships as well as the data-protection, bank secrecy and other laws of the jurisdiction in which they are located (Polayes 2011). As a result, it was clear at least to some participants even before enactment that the United States would find

---

4. The statutory effective date is 1 January 2013 but regulatory guidance delayed implementation (United States Department of Treasury 2012d).

5. FATCA is not a conventional withholding tax. It is better understood as a penalty regime intended to force foreign financial institutions to disclose information to the IRS.

it challenging to mandate comprehensive financial-institution participation with FATCA unilaterally.[6]

Nevertheless, non-US financial institutions felt trapped between a rock and a hard place. It dawned on them that they might have to choose between violating the law of the country in which they were based and US rules that could punish them quite severely if they did not comply with FATCA (Rojas 2012). The result was that many financial institutions proceeded down two separate paths: they urged the repeal of FATCA while also urging governments outside the United States to help them find a way to comply with FATCA without violating local law. In the two-year period between enactment of FATCA and the public launch of the intergovernmental FATCA process, there was substantial discussion of FATCA repeal or collapse. But public commentary by private-sector representatives arguing that the regime envisaged by FATCA was entirely implausible (Michel and Rosenbloom 2011) was accompanied by intensive private lobbying of foreign sovereigns to find a solution in intergovernmental discussions with the United States.

Then, in February 2012, the United States Treasury and the finance ministries of five large European governments (France, Germany, Italy, Spain and the United Kingdom, hereafter the 'G5') issued a joint statement announcing that they had reached an intergovernmental agreement for implementing FATCA (the 'Joint Statement') (United States Treasury 2012b). The Joint Statement benefited substantially from financial institutions lobbying governments outside the United States to find a way to make FATCA compliance possible. In the Joint Statement, the United States and the five largest EU governments committed to work together to achieve common reporting and due-diligence standards for financial institutions, in order to support a move to a more global system to combat offshore tax evasion. The framework adopted in the joint statement was based on reporting by financial institutions to the tax authority of the country in which they are located, followed by reciprocal automatic information-exchange between governments. That routing mechanism, in contrast to FATCA's statutory direct, one-way reporting to the IRS, resolved the conflict-of-law issues. The United States also committed, along with its partners, to work toward a common model for automatic information-exchange based on full reciprocity. The new routing mechanism and political commitment created the outlines of a potentially replicable model for a multilateral system. By July 2012, the US Treasury and the G5 had turned the Joint Statement into a detailed model intergovernmental agreement (IGA) to improve tax-compliance, based on reciprocal automatic information-exchange (United States Treasury 2012a).

After the G5 completed negotiations with the US, they relatively quickly agreed among themselves to adapt the FATCA rules into a proposal for a multilateral FATCA-style pilot project. Then the G20, largely spurred on by these same

6. Pre-enactment, commentators noted the conflict of law issues FATCA would raise in submissions to the US Congress and the US Treasury (Australian Bankers' Association 2009).

European members, moved towards a commitment to support automatic exchange of information as a new, global standard for cross-border tax-enforcement with respect to offshore accounts. That G20 commitment became a commitment to develop an international standard for automatic information-exchange, which eventually resulted in the OECD developing the Common Reporting Standard (CRS), which is rapidly becoming a global norm. As of July 2015, ninety-four countries had agreed to implement this new standard by 2018 (OECD 2015). Thus, by enacting FATCA unilaterally rather than negotiating from the outset for a multilateral solution, the United States catalysed a multilateral discussion about addressing offshore tax evasion that otherwise would likely have made only limited progress.[7]

The conflicts of law created by FATCA ensured that the regime initially enacted by the US Congress effectively could not be implemented. Meanwhile, the US domestic political imperatives that motivated FATCA, combined with the limited regulatory authority Congress gave the US Treasury to shape the legislation, ensured that one regime or another would, in fact, come into force. The key point here is that the US Treasury had some scope to modify the operation of FATCA but could not simply decline to enforce FATCA. As a result, FATCA was a 'ticking time bomb'. By imposing that structure, the US Congress changed the calculus of costs and benefits of co-operation for other states and also set off a global search for something better than FATCA to replace it while still addressing the relevant policy concerns. However, effective global co-ordination of such a solution required a multilateral outlet. Eventually, that outlet was found in the body of the G20's international financial-law architecture.

3. The international financial-law architecture and offshore tax evasion

The G20's power to convene standard-setting and monitoring processes would prove critical to developing a global solution that effectively addressed offshore tax evasion and achieved the objective of FATCA, both for the rest of the world and for the United States. The G20 describes itself as 'the premier forum for international co-operation on the most important aspects of the international economic and financial agenda' (G20 2015). At least since the financial crisis, the G20 has acted as the primary agenda-setter for international financial governance, defining broad strategic objectives for international financial regulation and giving them political momentum. In general, once international financial standards are developed in a standard-setting body, a monitoring body determines whether countries are meeting that standard, thereby imposing discipline. Enforcement mechanisms, often established by the G20 and tied to the monitoring body's judgments, provide further assurance that standards will be met. Finally, technical-assistance providers ensure that jurisdictions have the capacity to meet the

7. It is not clear whether the United States Congress anticipated this outcome, although some US Treasury officials were aware before FATCA was enacted that FATCA could create conflicts of law that might require multilateral negotiations to resolve.

standards. Taken together, the G20 and its associated standard-setters, monitoring bodies, enforcement mechanisms and enablers have created a soft-law framework for international financial law (Brummer 2011).

Organisations that drive standard-setting agendas at the international level operate across a wide array of subfields of international financial regulation. Although they are constituted by – and issue – agreements and declarations with no formal sense of international obligation, these organisations successfully function to regulate complex cross-border financial matters. They typically possess highly developed institutional structures, with membership and decision-making rules and processes. The Basel Committee, the Financial Action Task Force (FATF), the Financial Stability Board (FSB) and the International Organization of Securities Commissions (IOSCO) provide just a few examples[8] (Brummer 2012: 63–9); The effectiveness of these standard-setters is highly dependent on their enmeshed relationship with the G20 and its perceived authority to demand international co-ordination and convene monitoring bodies, enforcement vehicles and technical-assistance providers ('enablers').

When the cross-border tax-evasion scandals of 2008 led presidents and finance ministers from G20 countries to insist on improved transparency to combat offshore tax evasion, they turned to the international financial-law architecture for a solution. As a result, a section on 'Tax havens and non-cooperative jurisdictions,' was included in the 2009 G20 Leaders' Declaration on Strengthening the Financial System (G20 2009a). In that document, G20 leaders emphasised that they had agreed on a toolbox of counter-measures for countries to consider in addressing jurisdictions that did not meet international standards regarding tax transparency, much as they had done in earlier years in the context of addressing money-laundering and terrorism financing through the financial system. Simultaneously, the G20 asked the OECD to transform an existing body known as the Global Forum on Transparency and Administrative Co-operation in Tax Matters ('Global Forum') into an effective standard-setting and peer-review body.

Over a four-year period beginning in 2009, the Global Forum on Administrative Co-operation in Tax Matters developed terms of reference describing in detail international standards for information-exchange upon request in tax matters and created a 'methodology' for conducting peer-reviews to determine whether countries are meeting global standards regarding tax-information-exchange upon request. In other words, at the direction of the G20, the Global Forum took on both a standard-setting and a monitoring role. In addition, in order to successfully

8. The Financial Stability Board is focused on standards for macro-prudential regulation; the Basel Committee on Banking Supervision is best-known for its standards of capital adequacy at the individual institutional level; the International Organization of Securities Commissions is known for setting standards for international securities regulation; and the Financial Action Task Force focuses on combating money-laundering and the financing of terrorism. None of these organisations has any formal legal basis, in the sense of traditional international law, but each has deep influence on international regulatory co-ordination, in member- and non-member-states alike.

promulgate the new information-exchange-upon-request standards worldwide, the Global Forum searched for enablers to help implement the standard.

The reformed Global Forum was created with many features that were especially inspired by international financial regulatory efforts undertaken via the Financial Action Task Force (FATF). Indeed, the G20 mandate to reform the Global Forum in 2009 was part of an agreed 'peer-review trifecta', based on the FATF model, that also strengthened peer-review mechanisms used by the Financial Standards Forum (now the FSB). Thereafter, Global Forum reports to the G20 came to be treated as part of a broader international financial-law agenda. G20 communiqués addressed international administrative co-operation on tax in the same area as other parts of international financial law; and they discussed the Global Forum's peer-review mechanisms as one piece of a broader financial-law peer-review package. In that regard, the Global Forum proved relatively quickly that it was able to effectively evaluate whether standards were being complied with as a technical matter. Moreover, G20 countries clarified that when it came to tax administrative co-operation, they were prepared to take coercive action against other states in order to encourage progress. In the process, the subfield of international tax matters involving tax-information-exchange upon request came to incorporate internationally agreed-upon standards as well as a compliance monitor, enabling bodies and enforcement mechanisms: in other words, a governance structure that includes features that are highly similar to those of modern international financial law.

However, information-exchange upon request on its own is inadequate to combat offshore tax evasion. The ability to request information regardless of bank secrecy does have some chilling effect on tax evasion, because evaders cannot rely on bank secrecy to conceal their activities. At the same time, in order to receive information upon request, a tax administration is generally required to name the taxpayer, know which jurisdiction to ask for information, know at which financial institution a taxpayer holds her account and have a credible suspicion of tax evasion occurring. Otherwise, the request may be denied. The requirement that a requesting tax administration have such specific and detailed information severely limits the effectiveness of information-exchange upon request as a means for systematically combating offshore tax evasion (Grinberg 2012: 316).[9] As a result, the Global Forum as initially established represented a seriously incomplete response to offshore tax evasion.

The enactment of FATCA and subsequent negotiation of intergovernmental agreements to implement FATCA made a more robust Global Forum standard-setting and monitoring process possible. In April 2013, a little more than a year after the United States began concluding intergovernmental agreements on a reciprocal means to implement FATCA, the G20 finance ministers endorsed automatic information-exchange as an expected new international standard. They furthermore reached the conclusion that Global Forum peer-reviews, which

9. See also OECD 2008 (defining what constitutes a 'fishing expedition' in the context of information-exchange upon request).

had been ongoing for four years, could be deepened and expanded to examine jurisdictions' legal regimes and their practices surrounding automatic information-exchange (G20 2013a). The G20 tasked the OECD with developing the technical details of the CRS. Negotiations at the OECD eventually resulted in agreement on a set of standards and protocols for automatic information-exchange that were very similar to the IGA agreed between the United States and the G5. Simultaneously, the Global Forum created an automatic-information-exchange study group tasked with creating a mechanism for monitoring and reviewing the implementation of the new standard. Beginning at that point, the meta-architecture of standard-setting, monitoring bodies, enablers and enforcement threats – the meta-architecture of both international financial law and the Global Forum – were imported into a broader effort to address international standards for automatic information-exchange that was being developed under the auspices of the OECD's Common Reporting Standard. Today, all of tax-information-exchange appears set to incorporate governance processes analogous to the international financial-law architecture.

The final step for bringing automatic information-exchange within the international financial-law architecture is likely to involve the establishment of a credible enforcement threat. For information-exchange-upon-request, achieving universal compliance with international standards required global leaders to demonstrate willingness to take agreed action against jurisdictions that did not meet international standards for tax transparency; and to list noncooperative countries and suggest specific sanctions to be imposed (G20 2009b). Within a few years of being threatened with sanctions by the G20, those jurisdictions previously unwilling to exchange information in accordance with OECD standards, including some OECD member-states, changed their position and began to comply with what was now a global norm.

G20 leaders were prepared to agree on specific sanctions to enforce information-exchange upon request because those threats represented a collective response to a shared problem for which a solution would be non-rival. Offshore wealth represents 6.3 per cent of the more than $120 trillion of global wealth[10] (BCG 2011: 3). Indeed, the United States, although the first mover in addressing offshore tax evasion, is probably least affected by the problem. The best estimates suggest that less than 2 per cent of North-American wealth is held offshore. In contrast, about 5 per cent of Asian wealth, 8 per cent of European wealth, 25 per cent of all Latin-American household wealth and almost 33 per cent of all Middle-Eastern and African wealth is held offshore (BCG 2011: 3). The bulk of this offshore wealth is owned by residents of the large G20 economies. Information made available to any one of these jurisdictions about the offshore income or assets of a resident taxpayer does not limit the ability to provide information to another jurisdiction about the income or assets of its taxpayers; in

10. For this purpose, offshore wealth is defined as 'assets under management booked in a country where the investor has no legal residence or tax domicile' (BCG 2011: 13).

general, two jurisdictions do not assert overlapping taxing rights over the same income of the same taxpayer.

In the aftermath of the G20 finance ministers' April 2013 communiqué, and the subsequent endorsement of automatic information-exchange by eighty-nine jurisdictions in the Global Forum in October 2014, it is possible to imagine eventual use of coercive pressure against financial centres that are not prepared to participate in automatic information-exchange. Indeed, in multilateralising the US response to offshore tax evasion, G20 countries agreed to take more comprehensive action on a problem that is in their collective interest to solve, and which does not present distributive problems among themselves – even as the initiative almost certainly creates costs that outweighs benefits for some non-G20 financial centres. A coercive mechanism imposed by multiple sovereigns will, however, likely still need to be established to ensure compliance with – as opposed to nominal commitment to – a multilateral automatic information-exchange system that provides benefits to multiple sovereigns. Otherwise, noncooperative jurisdictions and institutions benefit from defecting from the emerging regime, because they can become repositories of choice for tax evaders' assets without paying a significant price for making that business decision. As long as the United States is the only country exercising coercive authority to ensure compliance, defection from the emerging regime remains a possibility. Like FATCA, the FATF and some of the other standards promoted by the Financial Stability Board threaten capital-market sanctions as the ultimate tool for ensuring compliance with their respective international regulatory architectures; but, unlike FATCA, in the case of the FATF and the FSB, the coercive pressures come explicitly or implicitly from multiple countries.

4. Are the lessons of the offshore tax evasion story applicable to efforts to encourage co-operation in other areas of international tax?

Is the FATCA information-exchange saga a relevant precedent that might inform both analysts' and policy-makers' consideration of whether other efforts at co-ordination of international tax rules might succeed? The question is timely because, in the last few years, corporate tax-planning for cross-border trade and investment has come under tremendous public scrutiny. Individual companies' tax-planning strategies have been highlighted in legislative hearings and government reports around the world, largely in light of pressure arising from studies by non-governmental organisations, academics and the press. The legislative inquiries contributed to a public perception that multinational corporations are not paying their 'fair share'.

In response to the political attention now given to corporate international tax matters, the G20 further broadened its interest in international tax affairs. In 2012, it identified base-erosion and profit-shifting by multinational enterprises as a priority issue for the G20's own public treasuries (G20 2012: para. 48). G20 communiqués then suggested, as part of efforts to 'reform the financial sector', that base-erosion and profit-shifting ('BEPS') practices by multinational enterprise, 'if left unchecked', would 'undermine the fairness and integrity of our tax systems', and therefore 'we must move forward in fighting BEPS practices so that we ensure a fair contribution of all productive sectors to the financing of public spending in our countries' (G20 2013). The G20 thus requested an 'action plan' from the OECD to address the newly-labelled 'BEPS' phenomenon[11] (OECD 2013a). Both the rhetoric used and the character of the actions taken by the G20 to expand its regulatory reach in international tax matters to encompass substantive rules for taxing the cross-border activities of multinational enterprises resemble the architecture used to address offshore tax evasion, as well as other areas of international financial law.

When one moves from offshore tax-evasion enforcement to considering broader questions of substantive international tax-law co-ordination that may have distributive consequences among major global powers, however, the prospects for using the international financial-law architecture to achieve global tax co-ordination become uncertain. Generalising across a broad swath of international economic law, one prominent line of analysis concludes that 'when faced with a collective action problem that requires co-operation ... national regulators take positions that reflect the interests of domestic constituencies. As a result, the adoption of common standards will require solving distributive problems where the interests of these constituencies diverge' (Verdier 2013: 1450). For this reason, soft international economic law – like the Common Reporting Standard – is much more likely to be both agreed and implemented where preferences are aligned and distributive problems are largely absent among the major economies (*see* Dietsch 2016, Chapter Eleven in this volume).

Unilateral coercive pressure of the type exercised by the United States in the FATCA story can succeed when the mechanisms credibly available to the acting state can impose sufficient coercive pressure to change the distributive calculus for other states. In the financial sector, the US market is sufficiently important to global financial institutions' business model, and the damage to the US public from excluding some foreign financial institutions sufficiently manageable, to make the withholding threat used by FATCA plausible. However, if attempted with respect to multinational enterprise in general, similar market-access pressures exerted by any one country likely would not be effective or sustainable in obtaining changes to law in other jurisdictions: no country is as indispensible a place to do business in general as the United States is as a place to engage in finance. Even more importantly, World Trade Organization rules and other international agreements limit countries' ability to use market access as a coercive tool in most sectors of the economy. As a consequence, the distribution of power in connection with international tax rules facing multinational enterprises is substantially less asymmetric than the distribution of power with respect to tax-compliance measures implemented by asset-managers.

11. The resulting OECD document, published in July 2013, called for fifteen specific actions to be taken to 'address the weaknesses in the current rules' (OECD 2013a: 13, 14–24).

There are certainly examples from international financial law where multilateral co-operation has been agreed without action by any single state that changes the cost/benefit calculus for other states. However, international regulatory bodies that adopt the 'international financial law' model tend to have hard-law effects only when international standards are incorporated in domestic legislative and regulatory mandates. A wide range of disciplinary sources – beginning with reputational consequences and explicit institutional shaming and ending with the application of actual sanctions – appear to effect substantial compliance-pull in some areas of international financial law. Indeed, in some instances, merely the promise of reciprocity from large states can be sufficient to engender state-level compliance from jurisdictions. But in other cases, 'outcasting' mechanisms and threats of sanctions are needed to enforce new international norms (Hathaway and Shapiro 2011). In particular, outcasting and threats of sanctions are often needed when issues with clear distributive consequences are at stake.

Agreements at the international level can occur where distributive issues exist among the major economies; and the major economies can also impose coercive pressures that change these conditions. However, a significant body of scholarship on previous agreements in international financial law (outside taxation) suggests that those agreements generally require either (1) technocratic regulatory consensus in an area where there is relatively little political attention; or (2) the exercise of coercion by a sufficiently powerful subset of leading political economies, entered into either out of a sense of economic necessity, or due to political imperatives, or both; or (3) economic dynamics that allow a small group of states to impose a standard simply by being first-movers, without affirmatively coercing other states to change their law.[12]

To provide just a few examples, some of the standards for financial-market infrastructure included in the Financial Stability Board's compendium of key international financial standards (such as the standards related to settlement, central securities depositories and exchange-of-value settlement systems) have been reached over decades in a low-salience process characterised by regulatory consensus (Ahdieh 2011: 546–50). These standards have been agreed even though, in principle, distributive consequences can be associated with these standards, because the gain in systemic stability associated with, for example, strongly encouraging the use of central counter-parties or clearing-houses may come at the expense of flexibility that can benefit innovating firms based in particular markets (Kroszner 2008). The Basel I Accord of the 1980s is an example of agreement under coercion. That Accord was preceded by a bilateral agreement between the United States and the United Kingdom regarding minimum capital-adequacy standards, followed by an implicit threat of market-closure by both countries against non-complying states (Singer 2004: 546). The international financial reporting standard (IFRS) benefits from market-based pressures to reduce the regulatory costs of cross-border finance, through convergence on

12. See, generally, Drezner 2007; Singer 2007; Helleiner and Pagliari 2012 and 2011; Verdier 2009; Bradford 2012.

a single set of rules that allow preparers, users, auditors and analysts to make comparisons across financial reports of companies listed in different jurisdictions (Verdier 2013: 1443). Similarly, the insurance core-principles articulated by the International Association of Insurance Supervisors (IAIS) benefit from market-based pressures for global insurers to face supervision under a well respected regulatory architecture, as well as pressure from global insurers themselves for governments to move to global convergence (KPMG 2013). Importantly, the continuing efficacy of these and other financial-law agreements often depends on the ease with which compliance can be evaluated and the extent to which enforcement mechanisms work (Walter 2008).

In the context of the BEPS initiative and other substantive international tax projects, significant distributive issues among major states arise. In various cases, source, residence and intermediary jurisdictions' interests do not align: different proposed solutions encourage the allocation of revenue, business activity or both between states in different ways. Distributive consequences of proposed changes to domestic law or international norms can often be mapped on to divides between lower-tax and higher-tax states, smaller, more open economies and larger, less open economies, or both. In this context, simple promises of reciprocity from large states are unlikely to engender state-level agreement or compliance from various jurisdictions, including influential states that seek to act as principal regional centres for multinational enterprise, potentially attracting income and employment to their jurisdiction in the process. Furthermore, as the BEPS issue is politically and economically salient to a range of powerful constituencies in multiple major economies, technocratic agreement by regulators insulated from political pressures seems unlikely. Finally, the economic dynamics of substantive co-ordination regarding the taxation of cross-border activities of multinational enterprises, which ultimately involves dividing a potentially contestable revenue base, are unlikely to create market pressure towards uniform compliance. Exceptions may exist: for instance, some scholars have argued persuasively that unilateral action by one or more high-rate countries to adopt a group-wide interest-expense allocation rules would act as an incentive to multinationals to locate borrowing elsewhere, and thereby encourage those jurisdictions to adopt similarly group-wide interest-expense allocation rules (Graetz 2008).[13] More generally, however, compliance even with agreed approaches to addressing cross-border taxation of MNEs consistently would likely require either self-implementing systems anchored in hard law (such as tax treaties) or co-ordinated measures with coercive effect that change the calculus for states and encourage compliance and implementation.

13. Some authors believe that unilateral moves by a few large market economies to formulary apportionment based on sales might, similarly, create economic forces that encourage other jurisdictions to adopt sales-based formulary apportionment (Clausing and Avi-Yonah 2007: 18). However, sales-based formulary apportionment is easily manipulated by structuring sales of intermediary goods to zero-tax jurisdictions and using independent distributors for final sales.

Careful analysis of the BEPS project's prospects thus requires delving below the surface of the project, rather than thinking of it as a single cohesive whole. In particular, a complete analysis would treat the various technical issues raised within the BEPS action plan separately. National interest and a focus on logics of consequences, rather than logics of appropriateness, is likely to shape most states' negotiating positions in each issue area and, perhaps more importantly, their choices with respect to implementation. The political pressures and distributive dynamics that apply in one area of the project will not necessarily apply in others. Agreement in some areas but not others may therefore be a plausible outcome. Moreover, independent of the areas in which agreement in principle may be reached, a complete analysis requires attention to the question of whether compliance pressures would be effective.

5. Conclusion

FATCA's enactment by the US Congress catalysed an evolutionary moment in cross-border administrative assistance for tax purposes. Broadly multilateral automatic information-exchange on offshore accounts appears set to profoundly change the capacity for enforcement of individual tax obligations with respect to offshore accounts. This success story in global tax co-operation was effectuated through the combination of unilateral action by the United States and the use of the G20's international financial-law architecture to convene standard-setting and monitoring bodies that could reimagine US legal developments and reshape them into a global regime with benefits for many sovereigns. The G20's push for automatic information-exchange to address tax evasion was followed in short order by a shift towards attention to tax avoidance by multinational enterprises. This raises the question of whether the FATCA success story provides a model for global co-ordination that is relevant to the G20's efforts in the BEPS project. However, the coercive authority that one state could credibly bring to bear, and the lack of distributional consequences among major economies, were distinct factors that provided a foundation for successful co-ordination in the area of offshore tax evasion. The BEPS project presents a more symmetric balance of power and more complicated distributional dynamics. These differences do not conclusively tell us anything about the BEPS project's future or the likelihood that agreements reached in that project will be implemented. They do, however, suggest that one should not look to FATCA and the CRS as a straightforward procedural precedent for a means to achieve substantive global co-operation in areas of international tax law that involve the division of the tax base and distribution of tax revenue among the major economies, as well as the tax burden legally imposed on taxpayers.

References

Ahdieh, R. (2011) 'Imperfect alternatives: networks, salience, and institutional design in financial crises', *University of Cincinnati Law Review* 79(2): 527–51.

Australian Banker's Association (2009) Letter to Charles Rangel, Chairman House Committee on Ways and Means and Richard Neal, Chairman, Subcommittee on Select Revenue Measures, pp. 144–50: http://www.gpo.gov/fdsys/pkg/CHRG-111hhrg63014/pdf/CHRG-111hhrg63014.pdf (accessed 6 August 2015).

Barr, M. (2014) 'Who's in charge of global finance?', *Georgetown Journal of International Law* 45(4): 971–1027.

Bates, R. and Lien, D. (1985) 'A note on taxation, development, and representative government', *Policy & Society* 14(1): 53–70.

Bennett, M. (2013) Letter to Achim Pross, Head of Division, International Co-operation and Tax Administration Division, Organization for International Co-operation and Development, and Philip Kerfs, Advisor, International Co-operation and Tax Administration Division, Organisation for International Co-operation and Development: http://www.theagc.com/2013-07-26%20AGC%20letter%20to%20OECD%20on%20TRACE.pdf (accessed 6 August 2015).

Bird, R. and Zolt, E. (2005) 'Redistribution via taxation: the limited role of the personal income tax in developing countries', *UCLA Law Review* 52: 1627–96.

Boston Consulting Group (2011) 'Global wealth 2011: shaping a new tomorrow': http://piketty.pse.ens.fr/files/BCG2011.pdf (accessed 6 August 2015).

Bradford, A. (2012) 'The Brussels Effect', *Northwestern Law Review* 107(1): 1–67.

Brummer, C. (2011) 'How international financial law works (and how it doesn't)', *Georgetown Law Journal* 99(2): 257–327.

— (2012) *Soft Law and the Global Financial System: Rule making in the 21st century*, Cambridge: Cambridge University Press.

Cavanaugh, M. (2003) 'Democracy, equality, and taxes', *Alabama Law Review* 54(2): 416–81.

Clausing, K. and Avi-Yonah, R. (2007) 'Reforming corporate taxation in a global economy: a proposal to adopt formulary apportionment', Brookings Institute, Discussion Paper 2007-08: http://www.brookings.edu/~/media/research/files/papers/2007/6/corporatetaxes-clausing/200706clausing_aviyonah.pdf (accessed 6 August 2015).

Dietsch, P. (2016) 'Whose tax base? The ethics of global tax governance', in Dietsch, P. and Rixen, T. (eds) *Global Tax Governance: What is wrong with it and how to fix it*, Colchester: ECPR Press.

Drezner, D. (2007) *All Politics is Global: Explaining international regulatory regimes*, Princeton, New Jersey: Princeton University Press.

Eccleston, R. (2012) *The Dynamics of Global Economic Governance: The financial crisis, the OECD and the politics of international tax co-operation*, Cheltenham: Edward Elgar.

Ferguson, N. (2002) *The Cash Nexus: Money and power in the modern world, 1700–2000*, New York: Basic Books Publishing.

Financial Accounting Standards Board (2015) 'Comparability in international accounting standards—a brief history': http://www.fasb.org/jsp/FASB/Page/SectionPage&cid=1176156304264 (accessed 6 August 2015).

G20 Finance Ministers (2013) 'Communiqué, meeting of finance ministers and central bank governors, Washington, DC, April 16–18': https://www.mof.go.jp/english/international_policy/convention/g20/20130419.pdf (accessed 6 August 2015).

G20 Leaders (2009a) 'Declaration on Strengthening the Financial System': http://www.treasury.gov/resource-center/international/g7-g20/Documents/London%20April%202009%20Fin_Deps_Fin_Reg_Annex_020409_-_1615_final.pdf (accessed 6 August 2015).

— (2009b) 'London Summit – Leaders' Statement': http://www.ilo.org/wcmsp5/groups/public/---dgreports/---dcomm/documents/statement/wcms_178769.pdf (accessed 6 August 2015).

— (2012) 'G20 Leaders Declaration': http://www.g20.utoronto.ca/2012/2012-0619-loscabos.html (accessed 6 August 2015).

— (2013) 'Tax Annex to the Saint Petersburg G20 Leaders Declaration': http://www.g20.utoronto.ca/2013/2013-0905-tax.html (accessed 6 August 2015).

Gratez, M. (2008) 'A multilateral solution to the income tax treatment of interest expenses', *Bulletin for International Taxation* 62: 486–93.

Gravelle, J. (2013) 'Tax havens: international tax avoidance and evasion', Washington, DC: Congressional Research Service: http://www.globaltaxjustice.org/wp-content/uploads/2014/11/Tax-Havens-Jane-Gravelle.pdf (accessed 6 August 2015).

Grinberg, I. (2012) 'The battle over taxing offshore accounts', *UCLA Law Review* 60: 304–83.

— (2016) 'The New International Tax Diplomacy', forthcoming *Georgetown Law Journal*.

Hathaway, O. and Shapiro, S. (2011) 'Outcasting: enforcement in domestic and international law', *Yale Law Journal* 121(2): 252–349.

Helleiner, E. and Pagliari, S. (2011) 'The end of an era in financial regulation? A postcrisis research agenda', *International Organization* 65: 169–200.

— (2012) 'Between the storms: patterns in global financial governance, 2001–2007', in G. Underhill, J. Blom and D. Mügge (eds.) *Global Financial Integration Thirty Years On: From reform to crisis*, Cambridge: Cambridge University Press, pp. 42–57.

Hinton, D. and Hancock, B. (2000) 'Outlook on LGT Bank in Liechtenstein A.G. revised to negative; ratings unchanged', *Standard & Poor's Global Credit Portal, RatingsDirect 155755*.

Kehone, R. and Nye, J. (2011) *Power & Interdependence*, Upper Saddle River, New Jersey: Pearson.

KPMG (2013) 'Evolving insurance regulation: a new dawn': http://www.kpmg.com/CN/en/IssuesAndInsights/ArticlesPublications/Documents/evolving-insurance-regulation-O-201303.pdf (accessed 6 August 2015).

Krasner, S. (1999) *Sovereignty: Organized hypocrisy*, Princeton, New Jersey: Princeton University Press.

Kroszner, R. (2008) 'Assessing the potential for instability in financial markets', address before the Risk Minds Conference, International Center for Business Information, Geneva, 8 December: http://www.federalreserve.gov/newsevents/speech/kroszner20081208a.htm (accessed 6 August 2015).

Lawson, K. (2013) Letter to Robert Stack, Deputy Assistant Secretary (International Tax Affairs), and Danielle Rolfes, International Tax Counsel, United States Department of the Treasury: https://www.iciglobal.org/pdf/27379.pdf (accessed 6 August 2015).

Levin, C. (2010) United States Congressional Record, March 18, 2010 daily edition, Washington, DC: United States Government Printing Office: https://www.congress.gov/congressional-record/2010/3/18/daily-digest (accessed 6 August 2015).

Meinzer, M. (2013) 'Towards multilateral automatic information-exchange: current practice of AIE in selected countries', Tax Justice Network: http://www.taxjustice.net/cms/upload/pdf/AIE2012-TJN-Briefing.pdf (accessed 6 August 2015).

Michel, S. and Rosenbloom, D. (2011) 'FATCA and foreign bank accounts – has the United States overreached?', *Tax Notes International* 62: 709–13.

Moore, M. (2007). 'How does taxation affect the quality of governance?', Institute of Development Studies, Working Paper No 280: http://www2.ids.ac.uk/futurestate/pdfs/Wp280.pdf (accessed 6 August 2015).

Moscovici, P., Schäuble, W., Grilli, V., Romero, C. and Osborne, C. (2013) Letter to Algirdas Šemeta, Commissioner for Taxation and Customs Union, Audit and Anti-Fraud, European Commission: https://www.gov.uk/government/uploads/system/uploads/attachment_data/file/208068/g5_letter_to_european_commission_090413.pdf (accessed 6 August 2015).

OECD (Organization for Economic Co-operation and Development, 2008) 'Articles of the Model Convention with Respect to Taxes on Income and Capital': http://www.oecd.org/tax/treaties/42219418.pdf (accessed 6 August 2015).

— (2011) 'Tax and Development Programme: Work Plan 2011/12': http://www.oecd.org/ctp/tax-global/48438767.pdf (accessed 6 August 2015).

— (2012) 'Tackling offshore tax evasion': http://www.s4tp.org/wp-content/uploads/2012/07/Tackling-Offshore-Tax evasion-OECD-publication-Jun-2012.pdf (accessed 6 August 2015).

— (2013a) 'Action plan on base erosion and profit shifting': http://www.oecd.org/ctp/BEPSActionPlan.pdf (accessed 6 August 2015).

— (2013b) 'Addressing base erosion and profit shifting': http://www.loyensloeff.com/nl-NL/Documents/OECD.pdf (accessed 6 August 2015).

— (2015) 'AEOI, status of commitments', Global Forum on Transparency and Exchange of Information for Tax Purposes: http://www.oecd.org/tax/transparency/AEOI-commitments.pdf (accessed 20 August 2015).

Polayes, F. (2011) Letter to Manal Corwin, International Tax Counsel, United States Department of the Treasury: http://www.cticompliance.com/assets/pdf/FATCA_HSBC.pdf (accessed 6 August 2015).

Prichard, W. (2010) 'Taxation and state building: towards a governance focused tax reform agenda', *Institute of Development Studies Working Papers* 341: 1–55.

Rojas, J. (2012) Letter to Manal Corwin, *et al.*, US Department of Treasury: http://www.bsmlegal.com/PDFs/FATCA_MexicanComments.pdf (accessed 6 August 2015).

Scheve, K. and Slaughter, M. (2007) 'A New Deal for globalization', *Foreign Affairs* 86: 34–47.

Sherman, H. (2010) 'The war on offshore tax evasion', *STEP Journal*: http://www.step.org/war-offshore-tax evasion (accessed 6 August 2015).

Singer, D. A. (2004) 'Capital rules: the domestic politics of international regulatory harmonization', *International Organization* 58(3): 531–65.

— (2007) *Regulating Capital – Setting standards for the international financial system*, Ithaca, New York: Cornell University Press.

Sullivan, M. (2012) 'An automatic brake on profit shifting in a territorial system', *Tax Notes*, 30 July.

Tax Notes Today (2009) 'DOJ announces deferred prosecution agreement with UBS', *Tax Notes Today*, 19 February.

US Department of Treasury (2012a) 'Joint communiqué by France, Germany, Italy, Spain, the United Kingdom and the United States on the occasion of the publication of the "Model Intergovernmental Agreement to Improve Tax Compliance and implement FATCA"': http://www.treasury.gov/press-center/press-releases/Documents/joint communique.pdf (accessed 6 August 2015).

— (2012b) 'Joint statement from the United States, France, Germany, Italy, Spain and the United Kingdom regarding an intergovernmental approach to improving international tax compliance and implementing FATCA': http://www.treasury.gov/press-center/press-releases/Documents/020712 Treasury IRS FATCA Joint Statement.pdf (accessed 6 August 2015).

— (2012c) 'Model intergovernmental agreement to improve tax compliance and to implement FATCA': http://www.treasury.gov/press-center/press-releases/Documents/reciprocal.pdf (accessed 6 August 2015).

— (2012d) 'Timelines for due diligence and other requirements under FATCA': http://www.irs.gov/pub/irs-drop/A-12-42.pdf (accessed 6 August 2015).

Verdier, P.-H. (2013) 'The political economy of international financial regulation', *Indiana Law Review* 88(4): 1405–74.

— (2009), 'Transnational regulatory networks and their limits', *Yale Journal of International Law* 34: 113–72

Walter, A. (2008) *Governing Finance: East Asia's adoption of international standards*, Ithaca, New York: Cornell University Press.

Chapter Eight

The G20, BEPS and the Future of International Tax Governance

Richard Eccleston and Helen Smith

1. Introduction

This volume highlights the challenges of international tax governance and the normative, political and institutional barriers to the effective regulation of international tax competition. Despite periodic attempts at co-ordinated reform, international tax co-operation has been notoriously difficult to achieve. States have been extremely reluctant to cede the sovereign right to make and administer domestic taxation law because of the profound impact these policies have on economic interests and competitiveness. Indeed, the most significant impediment to the creation of formal structures to enhance international tax co-operation is the perceived threat they pose to state sovereignty and established principles of international public law.

The need for greater international tax co-operation is now well understood but the international tax regime is highly path-dependent and constrained by the large number of bilateral treaties between states – which are only 'loosely coordinated by agreed standards' (Eccleston 2012: 69). Furthermore, and despite the projected benefits that tax co-operation would yield for the collective good, there remain powerful financial incentives for individual countries to defect from taxation agreements. Reducing tax rates or offering concessions and secrecy attracts mobile capital investment; and the incentives to defect from regimes aimed at countering these practices only increase with the number of states participating in the regime (Eccleston 2012: 74). The nature of the international tax system necessitates the complicity, or support at the very least, of powerful states in international tax governance, which, as will be demonstrated, is far from guaranteed. The incentives to defect also mean that governance regimes must be especially attentive with regard to compliance, arguably the Achilles heel of tax regulation (Drezner 2007). Given such challenges, reforming the international tax regime is a critical test of both international leadership and the G20's capacity to provide effective global governance.

Despite the historical absence of an effective multilateral regime to promote international tax co-operation there is growing optimism, especially among political leaders, that the financial crisis (FC) of 2008–9 and its aftermath has fostered renewed determination to establish more robust and effective international tax regulation. A wide range of FC-induced international tax initiatives have been implemented since 2008, as increasingly indebted governments seek to improve the integrity of their tax systems in an attempt to rein in budget deficits. Arguably the most significant post-crisis innovation in global governance has been the creation of the G20 Leaders' Forum, which, despite a broad and ambitious remit, has played a key role in endorsing various international tax initiatives since 2009 (Eccleston *et al.* 2013: 3). This chapter will provide an overview of the G20's role in post-crisis international tax governance, including an assessment of whether there is capacity for an effective and sustainable regime for regulating tax competition to be promoted through the G20.

The challenges of establishing multilateral regimes to promote international economic co-operation are well documented. Even when international agreement can be reached, intergovernmental bodies such as the G20 are still faced with the critical challenge of ensuring that these groups are not simply 'toothless talkshops' (Rachman 2010; Wolverson 2010), and that the commitments made by member states are honoured. As one of the most important international forums, whose membership includes the key players in international tax policy, these challenges mean that the G20's engagement with international tax issues and the impact of this engagement on global governance is of profound political and economic significance. Having endorsed the OECD's international tax agenda since 2009, the G20's credibility as a key actor in post-FC governance is dependent on its ability to promote effective compliance among its members. Yet while there is evidence that the G20's endorsement of the initiatives designed to promote tax-information-exchange has been successful, both in terms of encouraging states to commit to international standards and in ensuring subsequent compliance (Eccleston *et al.* 2013), it is less clear that the G20 has the capacity to foster agreement in relation to measures designed to limit international tax avoidance.

Reflecting these issues, this chapter seeks to assess the G20's role in global tax governance, with a particular emphasis on the politics of compliance. After providing a summary of the G20's role in promoting international tax transparency, the chapter assesses the G20's critical role in the OECD's new and more ambitious Base Erosion and Profit Shifting (BEPS) initiative. We argue that although it remains too early to tell whether BEPS will provide an effective framework for regulating international tax avoidance, given differing interests and incentives among the G20 member-states it appears increasingly likely that BEPS will not succeed in its ambition of curbing the increasingly aggressive tax-planning practices of multinational corporations (MNCs). In order to appreciate the governance challenges associated with international taxation, it is necessary to outline the conceptual differences (and political implications) between promoting international tax transparency on the one hand and regulating the international tax competition that makes avoidance possible on the other.

2. Two dimensions of the international tax agenda

As the chapters in this volume make clear, the governance of international taxation has two related dimensions, which, in turn, yield distinctive political considerations and normative debates. The first and less controversial issue is the extent to which governments should collect and exchange comprehensive tax and financial data to enable other jurisdictions to enforce their extra-territorial tax claims. As is outlined briefly below, this has been the focus of international initiatives since the 1990s. The second and more contentious issue has been the attempts to actively regulate international tax competition, either through the imposition of measures to promote tax harmonisation or, more recently, through the OECD's BEPS initiative, with its objective of ensuring that tax obligations occur in the jurisdiction where economic activity takes place. As we explain below, this measure is much more controversial because it limits the ability of international businesses to engage in the hitherto legal practice of profit-shifting. Furthermore, according to the critics of the proposed reforms, it amounts to an unprecedented threat to a state's sovereign right to tax as it sees fit. It is necessary to consider these distinctions between tax-information-exchange initiatives and tax-competition initiatives in order to fully appreciate the challenges the BEPS agenda poses to G20 solidarity in relation to international tax reform.

Sovereignty-preserving tax-information-exchange

The international tax regime is built on the principle of preserving sovereignty. The fundamental governance problem concerns which state has the right to tax the profits or income derived from international business and investment (Graetz and O'Hear 1997). In technical terms, the governance challenge is to develop a fair and efficient way to allocate the international tax base between sovereign states. One aspect of this challenge is that when governments attempt to tax the offshore investments of their residents, as Rixen (2008: 61) notes,

> very often tax authorities have to rely on the reports of taxpayers themselves, who have an economic incentive to under-report their true income. As a result the enforcement of resident taxation relies on the intense exchange of information between tax authorities.

This gives rise to the potential for significant international tax evasion if resident investors fail to declare their offshore investment income to tax authorities.

The international tax-transparency agenda of recent years has sought to tackle tax evasion through non-disclosure by implementing an international tax-information-exchange regime that requires participating governments to collect information on all funds invested in their jurisdiction and report it to the tax authority in which investors are resident. Although such a regime may not limit the sovereign right of governments to set tax policies as they see fit, information-exchange is controversial, nonetheless, and has prompted fierce resistance from jurisdictions that have used tax and financial secrecy to attract foreign investment (Picciotto 2011: 13). Yet, as is outlined below, the FC and its political and financial legacies have resulted in an unprecedented international commitment to establish an effective regime for promoting tax-information-exchange that should limit, if not eliminate, international tax evasion through non-disclosure.

Despite this progress, few would argue that implementing an effective information-exchange regime resolves all of the challenges associated with international tax avoidance and competition. Nevertheless, many concur that this represents a significant step in a wider war launched in 2013 – the struggle to reverse the erosion of the corporate tax base. The following section highlights some of the conceptual differences between this new front line of the international tax debate and previous transparency measures before the chapter moves to assessing the G20's capacity to promote and implement the ambitious BEPS agenda.

Sovereignty-threatening base-erosion provisions

World leaders have lauded the OECD's BEPS initiative as the next phase in the campaign against tax havens and international tax avoidance. It is true that there is an element of continuity, to the extent that the BEPS agenda builds on the significant progress which has been achieved in terms of enhancing international tax transparency and information-exchange. However, it is also important to recognise that the BEPS initiative is more politically contentious and ambitious than earlier reform efforts and will test international solidarity on tax issues.

The BEPS agenda (described below) is both ambitious and multi-dimensional. Insofar as our analysis is concerned, it can be distinguished from the transparency-related reforms endorsed and promoted by the G20 since 2009 in two important ways. First, it can credibly be argued that elements of the BEPS programme, including 'treaty abuse' and 'country-by-country reporting' provisions, represent a greater threat to state sovereignty than information-exchange. This is significant because, while there is a reasonably broad-based consensus concerning the desirability of increased international tax transparency, there has been fierce and effective resistance to tax-policy proposals that have the potential to limit state sovereignty in relation to tax matters and, potentially, to curtail various states' tax competitiveness (Sharman 2006; Ring 2009: 186–90; Eccleston 2012: 72). These pressures are particularly hard-felt in the US and UK, given their strong normative commitment to market liberalisation and competition, and by international organisations such as the IMF and OECD, which are founded on promoting these values.

Secondly, at a more tangible level, the BEPS programme is specifically designed to counter the increasingly aggressive internal tax-planning strategies used by MNCs to minimise or eliminate their global tax liabilities. This focus is understandable and appropriate, given increased evidence that large and powerful global firms from Starbucks to Apple have been systematically and significantly reducing their tax payments through exploitation of tax loopholes not available to domestic firms (Bowers 2014). However, it must be noted that the way in which BEPS targets MNCs is unprecedented. Indeed, the tax-transparency reforms introduced in the immediate aftermath of the FC were designed to target high-wealth individuals engaged in illegal tax evasion, rather than the aggressive tax avoidance practices of international business. Consequently, the BEPS agenda is likely to encounter resistance both directly – from the corporate sector – and indirectly – from G20 member-states as they consider the impact of the reform proposals on their domestic economies and associated political interests, a consequence of the prisoner's dilemma characteristic of international tax governance (Rixen 2011). It is on these dynamics that we focus in the second half of the chapter.

3. The G20 and tax transparency

The success of the BEPS agenda is critically dependant on the G20's capacity to promote and sustain political support for the initiative among member-states. The G20's transition from a forum primarily for finance ministers to a regular forum for dialogue and agenda-setting between the most powerful national leaders exacerbates the need to obtain G20 support, given its position as, arguably, the most influential multilateral political body. The G20's recently enhanced clout exacerbates the political imperative to obtain G20 support for the BEPS initiative that arises from the G20's track record of being a decisive player in the progression of international tax governance. To this end, the G20 possesses what has been termed an 'endorsement function', whereby the G20 Leaders' Forum lends credible and influential support to the work of specialist international agencies and organisations (Baker and Carey 2013). Furthermore, G20 endorsement could serve to enhance compliance because, though the G20 does not directly impose sanctions, preliminary evidence indicates that G20 member-states who have committed to a particular technical or regulatory standard through the Leaders' Forum will be more likely to 'honour their commitment and potentially enforce it unilaterally' (Eccleston *et al.* 2013: 6). The impact of this on international tax governance was illustrated when, for example, both France and the UK imposed withholding taxes and other penalties on jurisdictions that failed to comply with the tax-information-exchange standard that the Leaders' Forum had endorsed (Eccleston 2012: 151–2).

Indeed, the impact of G20 endorsement on OECD tax initiatives is evidenced by the revival of the tax-transparency agenda after 2008. The G20 Leaders' Forum endorsed the programme in November 2008 at the Washington Summit (G20 2008: 4), before strengthening its commitment at the London and Pittsburgh Summits in 2009 (G20 2009a; G20 2009b: 10). Arguably, the G20 Leaders' Forum's endorsement made a significant contribution to the rapid and widespread acquiescence to the OECD's tax-information-exchange efforts: only eleven bilateral OECD Tax Information-Exchange Agreements had been signed by 2006 but, by late 2014, this number had increased to some 1,600 (OECD 2014a). Furthermore, the range of tax-evasion-combating initiatives that emerged in the wake of the G20's 2009 endorsement, including non-OECD developments such as the Financial Stability Board's Legal Entity Identifier, suggests that the G20 endorsement signified 'a new phase in robust multilateral efforts to combat tax abuse backed by concerted political commitment' (Palan and Wigan 2014: 5). The OECD estimates that new information-exchange agreements have generated approximately $53 billion in revenue in roughly twenty OECD/G20 countries, through the increase in voluntary disclosures from taxpayers (Khadem 2014). These developments were more relevant to tax evasion than tax avoidance; it is the latter that is the subject of this chapter. All told, however, the evidence of G20 involvement in international tax governance suggests that G20 endorsement and member-state support would, at the very least, be extraordinarily beneficial to the OECD's agenda and, in all probability, vital to its success.

The G20 and BEPS

The Action Plan on Base Erosion and Profit Shifting (OECD 2013a) is an OECD initiative endorsed by the G20. The impetus for the initiative came from increasing evidence of the failure of international tax standards to reflect contemporary international business practices, especially in relation to intangible assets and the digital economy (OECD 2013b). Because the international taxation system was largely developed before MNCs became as dominant as they are now, the OECD has argued that the regime and national treasuries have both been weakened by exploitable gaps in the interactions between the tax rules of domestic jurisdictions and multi-jurisdictional treaties, exacerbated by the rise of e-commerce (OECD 2013a). The BEPS plan aims to rectify these problems by implementing a series of fifteen different Actions by the end of 2015. The critical point to note for our purposes is that this represents a shift beyond inter-jurisdictional information-exchange towards minimising tax competition itself.

The ambitious agenda aims to prevent double non-taxation, which occurs when MNCs are able to shift their profits away from the jurisdiction in which genuine economic activity takes place to low- or no-tax jurisdictions (OECD 2013a). The OECD argues that this practice undermines both the fairness and integrity of the international tax system, especially given the increasing tax burden on citizens and smaller private enterprises as governments repair their budgets in the aftermath of the FC (OECD 2013a).

The issue of large-scale corporate tax avoidance became a mainstream political issue that world leaders could no longer ignore in the aftermath of high-profile Congressional and Parliamentary Inquiries in the United States and United Kingdom in early 2013. The political imperative to combat tax avoidance was exacerbated by a spate of revelations about the behaviour of some of the most high-profile MNCs, including Apple and Starbucks, who were able to dramatically reduce their tax payments by shifting profits between jurisdictions (Christians 2013).

The BEPS agenda aims to circumvent these abuses by examining the policies used by tax havens that encourage tax avoidance, including 'diverging legal provisions, secrecy, opacity and inadequate information-exchange agreements' (Palan and Wigan 2013: 2). The goal is the introduction of a multilateral instrument to facilitate the rapid amendment of bilateral tax treaties, so that these bilateral treaties are reflective of the BEPS recommendations The BEPS initiative thus aims to combat profit-shifting activity by requiring companies to pay tax in the jurisdiction in which the economic activity actually occurs, so that 'domestic and international instruments … will better align rights to tax with economic activity' (OECD 2013a: 11).

The G20's official position is that it initiated the BEPS agenda. However, the push to broaden the international tax agenda to include profit-shifting came from within the OECD, and has been championed by Pascal Saint-Amans, the Director of the OECD's Centre for Tax Policy and Administration. The BEPS Action Plan subsequently devised by the OECD was fully endorsed by the G20 finance ministers and central bank governors at their Moscow meeting in July 2013 and by the G20 heads of state at their St Petersburg meeting in September 2013 (OECD 2014b; G20 2013a: 12), as part of the broader commitment to addressing tax avoidance through ongoing work on transparency and information-sharing between jurisdictions (G20 2013a: 13). Support for the initiative was reaffirmed at the May 2014 G20 Tax Symposium in Tokyo (G20 2014b), and the OECD recommendations were again 'welcomed' at the recent G20 summit in Brisbane (Khadem 2014). Moreover, the G20 also appears to be going beyond rhetorical support for the initiative and taking substantive action to achieve the BEPS goals. As of February 2014, the G20 countries had been playing an 'active and leading role' in the development of the BEPS policies, leading the OECD Secretary-General to state that he was, on balance, 'impressed' with the G20's commitment to the initiative (OECD 2014c: 4).

Yet there are some signs that, beneath the diplomatic rhetoric, the BEPS agenda is more politicised and contested than the earlier information-exchange project. The OECD Secretary-General's February 2014 report acknowledged that there were 'divergences' between participating states, and that more effort would be needed to achieve compromise between the differing state and political interests (OECD 2014c: 4). More controversial recommendations, such as those on 'patent boxes'[1] in particular, are likely to prove problematic (Michel 2014). Moreover, as will be discussed later in this chapter, there are conflicting economic interests and political messages within several of the critical G20 member-states, potentially undermining the ostensible unity of the G20's approach to the BEPS agenda.

4. The G20 and the political challenge and risk associated with BEPS

Before examining the specific tensions amongst G20 member-states, it is worth noting that the BEPS initiative faces two sets of political challenges. The first relates to the tangible impacts the agenda will have on specific businesses; while the second concerns the normative debate about fiscal sovereignty and tax competition.

First, the BEPS initiative has serious implications for the ways in which the world's most powerful corporations conduct their business operations, prompting a mixed response from the business sector. The OECD's Business and Industry

1. 'Patent boxes' are favourable tax conditions for intellectual property.

Advisory Committee (BIAC) concedes that base-erosion and profit-shifting is occurring (BIAC 2013a).

Nevertheless, other business groups have been increasingly critical of the OECD agenda and its impact on current business practice. For example, as a result of the rapid legislative changes that several countries have subsequently enacted, a recent survey found that a large majority of tax and finance executives felt their companies were experiencing more tax risk and uncertainty (Ernst & Young 2014a: 3), and anticipated more instances of double taxation as a result of the changes (Ernst & Young 2014a: 8). Moreover, US tax executives have reported concern about the impact of the initiative on 'long-standing international tax norms' (KPMG 2014). The OECD has also received criticism from powerful US and Russian companies (including Diageo and Gazprom), who see the plan as detrimental to investment; further public criticism has been put forward by peak industry bodies from a range of jurisdictions, including the US National Foreign Trade Council, Britain's Confederation of Business Industry and the French employers' group Medef (Chessell 2014).

Business' criticisms of the BEPS initiative have coalesced around three issues in particular. First, the transfer-pricing problem addressed in Actions 8–10 has been listed as the top concern of US tax executives (KPMG 2014). This is unsurprising, given that, if successful, these Actions will severely limit the capacity of the most powerful MNCs to engage in a range of currently permissible activities, including the over-capitalisation of low-taxed intra-group subsidiaries and the allocation of financial risk to low-tax environments (OECD 2013a: 20).

Second, businesses oppose the possibility of country-by-country reporting suggested by Action 13 (Picciotto 2014: 5; Ernst & Young 2014a: 8). There is some evidence that the CEOs of powerful corporations agree with the notion that MNCs should be required to report the revenues, profits and taxes accrued in each of the countries in which they do business (PricewaterhouseCoopers 2014a). However, others argue that country-by-country reporting would impose unreasonable administrative and compliance burdens on business (Ernst & Young 2014a: 8); and groups such as the Confederation of British Industry and the United States Council for International Business have asserted that the requirements would make it difficult to conceal confidential commercial information from competitors (Bergin 2013).

The third major criticism of the BEPS agenda from the business sector is that the timeframe for finalising and implementing the initiative is too ambitious. Many businesses consider the schedule to be too short to permit careful consideration of the impact of the recommendations (Ernst & Young 2014a: 7). Indeed, it has been argued that the timeline is more reflective of OECD member-states' political interests than a realistic period in which to implement sound policy solutions suitable for the diverse array of interests and capacities of the affected parties (PricewaterhouseCoopers 2013: 6).

Business may be concerned that the BEPS agenda is being driven by the political whims of OECD states, yet many states are concerned that the initiative will severely undermine their sovereignty. In attempting to address these concerns, the OECD has itself acknowledged that 'tax policy is at the core of countries' sovereignty' and that 'each country has the right to design its tax system in the way it considers most appropriate' (OECD 2013a: 9). Reflecting this, the G20 St Petersburg Declaration endorsing the BEPS initiative emphasised that the changes must be made 'while still respecting the sovereignty of each country to design its own rules' (G20 2013b: 4). At first glance, some of the proposed Actions may actually shore up state sovereignty. For example, Action 13 aims to develop rules that enhance the transparency of MNCs' financial structures for the purpose of tax administration. If the Action is fully implemented, MNCs are likely to be required to disclose information on income, economic activity and taxes paid across countries. Theoretically, this information should benefit domestic governments of all political persuasions, as they would be in a better position to make informed fiscal policy decisions and have more accurate information about the state of their economy and investment environment. Furthermore, the OECD argues that the development of a comprehensive set of common rules would prove beneficial rather than detrimental to state sovereignty, given that the current system has the potential to encourage a race to the bottom in tax rates – regardless of the fiscal interests or policy wishes of states (OECD 2013a: 17).

Although this assessment may be correct in some cases, it overlooks the fact that the strongest opposition to BEPS will likely come from those countries whose interests do lie in lower taxation and limited transparency. Furthermore, although many of the Actions are aimed at the behaviour of corporations, other Actions shift the onus of responsibility on to states. For example, Action 6, which is targeted at preventing treaty abuse, may be particularly detrimental to state autonomy. The Action is directed at identifying 'the tax policy considerations that, in general, countries should consider before deciding to enter into a tax treaty with another country'; and it also makes recommendations for the design of domestic taxation rules (OECD 2013a: 19). Although the recommendations are for the purpose of preventing double non-taxation, state parties to BEPS would still be required to allow the OECD recommendations to supersede their own, possibly diverging, views of optimal tax rules – or risk being blacklisted. These concerns are not merely academic. Previous multilateral taxation-regulation efforts have proven highly contentious for reasons of sovereignty. Indeed, the US – whose backing is critical to the success of BEPS – did not support previous OECD tax agendas under the Bush Administration, partly because of the agenda's 'potential to limit states' sovereign right to manage their own tax systems' (Sharman 2006: 61; Palan *et al.* 2010).

5. BEPS as a significant and critical test of international co-operation on tax and of the G20

Given these considerations, and despite the rhetoric surrounding international tax co-operation, the extent to which compliance with the emerging standards occurs in practice will be a critical test of the G20's capacities in relation to international taxation (and global governance more broadly). This is particularly so given that the BEPS agenda itself is substantively more ambitious than previous international tax reforms designed to promote transparency. In hindsight, the relative success of information-exchange initiatives was likely facilitated by their compatibility with the prevailing neo-liberal norms in global governance, in that they served to mitigate information asymmetry and improve efficiency (Sharman 2006: 81–2). They also coincided with the shock of the FC and the need for world leaders to be seen to be 'doing something'. This congruence of interests and timing meant that the objections of secrecy jurisdictions lacked credibility; this made it easier for the regime to accrue the support of critical players. In contrast, the OECD's Harmful Tax Competition (HTC) initiative of the late 1990s, which, in its early form, had strong parallels with the BEPS agenda, failed in part because of the threat it posed to state sovereignty and the highly differentiated impact it would have on participating OECD states – the initiative would have had a harsher effect on Switzerland, for example, than for member states not engaging in tax competition to such a significant degree (Eccleston 2012: 69). These and other considerations have led to the conclusion that international tax reform is contingent upon four conditions: 'the support of great powers, a robust compliance regime, prevailing norms, and the demands of domestic political circumstances' (Eccleston 2012: 76). Unless there has been a demonstrable shift in the normative consensus and economic interests surrounding tax competition, it is far from certain that the BEPS agenda can succeed where the HTC initiative failed.

More broadly, the effectiveness of the G20 in pushing the BEPS agenda should serve as a useful case study on the efficacy of post-crisis global governance more generally, given that it is generally accepted that the G20 was one of the more effective of the multilateral institutions in responding to the FC, if not the most effective (Kirton 2013). As the sense of urgency associated with the acute phase of the crisis wanes, it remains to be seen whether the G20's collective endorsement of the BEPS regime will be sufficient to override the incentives for individual countries to defect. Indeed, this uncertainty is reflected in much of the scholarship on the G20. Some of the more optimistic views see the G20 as replacing the G8 at the apex of a broader and more representative system of global governance that more accurately reflects the interests of emerging economies (Kirton 2013: 10; Kelly 2009; 10; Wang 2009). Others see the G20 as simply serving as a 'valuable reinforcement' for the work of the G8, as the latter also operates well in conjunction with the international financial institutions in pursuit of financial stability and economic growth (Kirton 2013; Alexandroff and Kirton 2010; Cooper 2010; Kharas and Lombardi 2012). However, critics see the G20 as becoming increasingly redundant and ineffective in the aftermath of the FC. These commentators regard more established organisations as being preferable, either for their effectiveness in that they do not need to accommodate the interests of a broad range of disparate states (in the case of the G7/8) or because they have greater legitimacy (Kirton 2013: 6; Aslund 2009). Other 'rejectionist' scholars have diagnosed a potential free-rider problem in the G20 in relation to international financial co-operation, because of the public-good nature of regulation and the fact that G8 members derive fewer individual benefits from G20 agreements (Kirton 2013: 7; Masson and Pattison 2010). Given the divergence of opinion on the utility and efficacy of the G20, its ability to shape a positive outcome for the BEPS agenda should serve as a useful litmus test of the institution's long-term utility as a vehicle for tax governance.

6. The prospects for G20 co-operation on BEPS

The prospects for achieving effective G20 co-operation on the BEPS agenda are uncertain. On the one hand, several of the factors that led to the failure of the similarly contentious and ambitious HTC initiative aren't present. For example, a key contributor to the failure of the HTC initiative was that it 'sought to regulate the activities of jurisdictions which were excluded from its deliberations' (Eccleston *et al.* 2013: 12). In contrast, non-OECD G20 members have been invited to participate in the BEPS process and developing countries have been asked to share their perspectives – although critics argue that such consultation is no more than a token (Quantrill *et al.* 2014).

However, the potential for tensions and disagreements is, arguably, greater than the likelihood of co-operation. Examination of the historical inter-state divisions that have plagued international tax regulation shows that the G20 members come to the table with widely differing interests and perspectives; an analysis of the contemporary differences between jurisdictions suggests the divisions may be too difficult to overcome for a regime as comprehensive as BEPS.

7. Historical tax cleavages

The G20 member-states have a mixed record regarding co-operation on tax competition and avoidance. In some instances, interests have coincided: for example, in the mid-1990s both France and Germany were concerned with reducing tax competition; Germany, in particular, faced large revenue losses because of undeclared savings held in Switzerland, Austria and Liechtenstein (Sharman 2006: 29). At the same time, the US was seeking to improve the transparency of Caribbean finance centres. This intersection of interests prompted the G7 to criticise tax competition in their 1996 communiqué, due to its detrimental effect on trade and investment and 'the erosion of national tax bases' (G7 1996).

Conversely, there have been frequent disagreements on international tax matters, especially concerning proposals to limit competition. Prior to the London 2009 G20 summit, for example, the US' policy priority was the promotion of economic growth whilst the continental EU countries, particularly France and Germany, were more concerned with regulating finance, including through strong measures against tax havens (Kirton 2013: 275). This discrepancy was reflective of the traditional stances of the major G20 players. The US has at various times (especially under conservative administrations and particularly under President George W. Bush) been hostile to international tax co-operation, and has tended to adhere to the view that international bureaucracies have no moral authority to interfere with national tax laws (Mitchell 2000). Although the US has increased its efforts to prosecute individual and corporate tax evasion, whilst implementing voluntary-disclosure schemes and the comprehensive US Foreign Accounts Tax Compliance Act (FATCA) (Eccleston 2012: 103), it has still been reluctant to cede its sovereignty to international governance regimes. The UK has, at least until recently, also been reluctant to pursue anti-evasion measures or regulate anti-secrecy jurisdictions for less ideological and more pragmatic reasons, chiefly, the City of London's dependence on Britain's offshore territories (Shaxon 2011: 689). Reflecting this commitment to liberalisation and market competition, Britain has traditionally sided with the US in opposing measures against jurisdictions that treat foreign corporations favourably. This opposition has been justified on the basis that such measures would threaten the 'sovereign right' of governments to adjust their budgets 'according to domestic political imperatives' (Eccleston 2012: 66; Weschler 2001). In contrast to the US and British stance, the European welfare states have shown considerably more enthusiasm in combating tax evasion. The EU has implemented policies such as the EU Code of Conduct on Business Taxation and the EU Savings Tax Directive and Common Consolidated Corporate Tax Base, and actively supported the OECD's information-exchange initiatives (Eccleston 2012: 102). France, in particular, has typically opposed Preferential Tax Regimes (PTRs) for foreign corporations, such as that created by Ireland (*Economist* 2011). As noted below, the political challenges associated with these historical cleavages are potentially compounded by the fact that G20 deliberation also needs to incorporate the diverse interests of key emerging economies.

Emerging tension within the G20

In combination, the broad and ambitious nature of the BEPS agenda and the diverse interests of G20 member-states on international tax matters represent a fundamental test of post-crisis global economic governance. Specifically, there is clear potential for conflict among G20 members in relation to the BEPS agenda between states rich in both capital and intellectual property and poorer jurisdictions. Indeed, preventing BEPS is more likely to benefit wealthy capital- and intellectual-property-exporting states; but G20 member-states including India, South Africa, Brazil and China would gain more from the formulary-apportionment approach supported by tax-justice NGOs such as the Tax Justice Network and Oxfam (Tax Justice Network 2014; Oxfam 2014: 17). If the OECD succeeds in moving towards a more source-based taxation model, the US, China and India will likely gain additional revenue while the UK and Switzerland will lose (PricewaterhouseCoopers 2013: 4). This suggests that conflict within the G20 and OECD will be more nuanced than a developed *versus* emerging economies dichotomy.

Furthermore, although the G20's initial endorsement of the BEPS initiative is undoubtedly significant, the regime's effectiveness is critically dependent on sustained and sincere commitment across the wide range of G20 member-states. The risk is that as the sense of international solidarity associated with the acute phase of the FC wanes, differences of opinion between G20 members will become more apparent. Potentially, member-states may choose to avoid their obligations through partial implementation and non-compliance: there is a long history in global economic governance of states failing to implement their international commitments when they run contrary to domestic political interests (Drezner 2007; Walter 2008).

Beyond potential implementation and compliance gaps, a second threat to the co-ordinated and effective adoption of the BEPS recommendations is the emerging shift towards unilateral policies to combat tax evasion – leading some commentators to argue that the true 'centre of gravity' in the struggle against tax avoidance actually lies in individual state efforts rather than multilateral agreements (Palan and Wigan 2014: 1). Despite rhetorical support for the OECD, the Obama Administration's international tax policy has focused on FATCA and the EU has also, as noted, been implementing its own policies. Moreover, Britain has recently announced its own 'Diverted Profits Tax' (Aston and Khadem 2014). Indications from Australia that it wants to introduce a similar tax have raised concerns that such unilateral Actions could undermine the BEPS agenda by increasing the likelihood of double taxation – and, indeed, Pascal Saint-Amans himself has expressed concerns about the possibility of unilateral Actions (Aston and Khadem 2014).

It may be too early to make a definitive assessment of whether the BEPS agenda will be implemented coherently and comprehensively enough by a sufficient number of countries to have a significant impact on corporate tax avoidance. However, we can already highlight both the challenges facing the initiative and preliminary evidence concerning dissent in relation to some of its key provisions. To this extent it is important to examine some of the emerging concerns held by key G20 member-states outside continental Europe in relation to BEPS.

The United States

The success of BEPS is critically dependent on US support, not only because 'the broad contours of international tax co-operation have been defined by changing US policy preferences' (Eccleston 2012: 125), but also because the OECD is significantly dependent on US funding (Carroll and Kellow 2011). This means that 'the absence of support from Washington can seriously undermine any attempt to regulate international taxation' (Eccleston *et al.* 2013: 10). There are positive indications the US will follow through with BEPS – support is more likely to be forthcoming under President Obama than the previous administration, although any measures which require legislative action will be vulnerable to an increasingly hostile and grid-locked Congress. Furthermore, the FC served as a catalyst for raising public awareness about the problem of tax evasion, mobilising electoral support for stronger anti-evasion legislation as part of the pushback against the banks and financial institutions. The US also has a strong economic incentive to comply, as recent reports estimate that there is roughly a US$550 billion shortfall in corporate tax revenue from the Fortune 500 companies in the US, due to offshore holdings by companies such as General Electric and Johnson & Johnson (Citizens for Tax Justice 2014).

This 'tax gap' is a consequence of US businesses having become particularly adept at navigating the loopholes and jumping the regulatory hurdles of US tax administration, evidenced by the recent increase in corporations 'inverting' to low-tax European jurisdictions such as the Netherlands and Ireland; just one of these inversions cut US tax liability by an estimated US$150 million *per annum*

(Gelles 2013). The temptation to invert also comes from much closer to home: the Canadian Harper government lowered the federal corporate tax rate from 28 per cent to 15 per cent in 2012, creating conditions that have already prompted inversions to Canada, notably from the famously American Burger King company (Hartley 2014). Indeed, the recent proliferation of corporate inversions has prompted President Obama to criticise these groups as 'corporate deserters', and pass legislation rendering it impossible for US corporations to take over smaller foreign companies for tax-avoidance purposes (Becker 2014). Given the ongoing budget deficit, concerns about the impact of such practices on Treasury revenues are unlikely to abate – at least among Democrats.

However, the risk that political support for more robust international tax governance will wane is exacerbated by the success of the Republican Party in the 2014 Congressional elections, as a hostile Congress is a complicating factor in any further domestic Action to mitigate tax avoidance or pass legislation in line with the BEPS agenda. Although the BEPS Action Plan is scheduled to be implemented by 2015, if the ambitious timetable isn't met a new conservative administration may prove less amenable to BEPS – particularly given the Republican Party's scepticism towards FATCA (it recently passed a resolution urging its repeal) (Rubenfeld 2014) and its general preference for lowering corporate tax rates. Indeed, the comparatively high corporate tax rate in the US has been the impetus for several high-profile companies moving to low-tax jurisdictions: Pfizer praised the low British corporate tax rate (soon to be 20 per cent, compared to the US rate of 35 per cent) (Neate and Farrell 2014); Fiat Chrysler is moving its global headquarters to London, citing tax issues as a key factor in the decision (Buss 2014); and Medtronic is moving to Ireland to access its offshore funds for similar reasons (Mider 2014). This suggests it may be in the US' interest to cut corporate tax rates and retain funds onshore, rather than attempt to enforce the current high rates unsuccessfully.

Furthermore, the US has a potential conflict of interest with the BEPS policies directed at the digital economy. Despite the US co-chairing the digital economy working group, many of the most notorious tax-avoiding MNCs are US companies trading in the digital economy – including Google, Amazon, Facebook and Apple. NGOs such as Oxfam have criticised the US position in the working group because of its vested interest in protecting these companies (Oxfam 2014: 11–12), and French officials are reported as having concerns that the US will not support BEPS because of the initiative's focus on American companies (Chessell 2014). These considerations raise the possibility that US support for the BEPS agenda will be contingent on domestic political vagaries and could be susceptible to ongoing business pressure.

The United Kingdom

The UK has publicly supported the BEPS initiative (Neate 2013) and used its chairmanship of the G8 Summit to keep tax evasion on the agenda (Prime Minister's Office 2013). The UK has also supported a form of country-by-country reporting – part of the BEPS initiative – and its position on beneficial-ownership transparency has shifted. Furthermore, the UK has committed to creating a public register of company beneficial ownership and encouraged other G8 members and its own Overseas Territories and Crown Dependencies to increase transparency (Christian Aid 2013: 57).

Despite these steps, the current government has been sending mixed political and policy signals. The Conservative government has publicly endorsed the BEPS initiatives on the G20 stage and made its own efforts to crack down on domestic tax evasion, through the criminal code (UK Government 2014a); recently, it announced a crackdown on tax avoidance through the planned 25 per cent 'Diverted Profits Tax' on MNCs that artificially shift profits generated from UK economic activity (*The Age* 2014). However, the government reduced the corporate tax rate to 20 per cent in April 2015 – making it the lowest in the G7 and joint-lowest in the G20 (UK Government 2014b). Chancellor of the Exchequer George Osborne has also been introducing a range of corporation-friendly tax policies, including a low-tax regime for patent-owning businesses and new approaches to offshore-finance subsidiaries (*Guardian* 2013). These policy developments suggest the UK's efforts are directed more at tax evasion than at the tax competition and avoidance that is at the heart of the BEPS agenda.

This is perhaps unsurprising, given that Britain faces fewer financial and revenue incentives than the US and other EU states to reduce tax competition. In fact, the most recent edition of the Tax Justice Network's Financial Secrecy Index shows that if Britain were joined with its Crown Dependencies and offshore territories, it would displace Switzerland at the top of the list; Britain and its island territories account for between one-third and one-half of the entire global market for offshore financial and corporate services; and a substantial portion of the funds involved moves through the City of London (*Economist* 2013). Given the importance of the City to the UK's economy, the government is no doubt reluctant to reduce incentives for foreign investment.

Britain's position can be contrasted with that of other key G20/EU member-states. France, for example, is estimated to lose between €30 and €36 billion annually through tax avoidance (Christian Aid 2013: 26), whilst the Italian government has recently estimated that almost €200 billion of Italian capital is currently held in other jurisdictions for tax-avoidance purposes (with the bulk of it being in Switzerland) (Christian Aid 2013: 36). This shows that there are even intra-EU discrepancies in the incentives for G20 members to follow through in a substantive way.

The BRIC response

More promisingly, the BRIC countries (Brazil, Russia, India and China) are notionally supportive of the BEPS agenda. The OECD wisely opted to accept the non-OECD G20 members (including all the BRIC nations) as full members of the BEPS working parties, which has permitted inclusion of the BRIC's concerns in the negotiation process and, most likely, forestalled criticisms of BEPS as being a reflection of purely Western interests.

Furthermore, the BEPS agenda dovetails – to a degree – with the domestic tax interests of the BRICs. Brazil passed legislation that more effectively taxes its MNCs' profits (whether repatriated or not) in May 2014, which, much like the OECD initiative, was catalysed by declining treasury revenues relative to expenditure (UK Government 2014c). This legislation closely mirrors aspects of the BEPS recommendations and, in defending the legislation, the Brazilian government argued that the change was on-trend with the international G20/ OECD approach (UK Government 2014c). Similarly, Russia has been pursuing its own 'de-offshoring of the economy' strategy since the end of 2013, through domestic legislative change: the proposals are expected to take effect in 2015 and curb tax avoidance through new corporate-residence and controlled-foreign-company rules, reflecting several of the BEPS Actions (Deloitte 2014). These substantive changes to the Russian tax regime suggest that Moscow is reasonably likely to follow through with the political support it has already given to the initiative.

However, India and China may prove slightly more reluctant to implement the full suite of recommendations. India has remained relatively silent on the issue and, though it has had quite a strong focus on transfer-pricing over the last decade, its concern for developing its economy may see it adopt a unilateral approach to several of the recommendations even as it supports the project as a whole (Transfer Pricing Associates 2014). China, in turn, has formally supported the Action Plan (Transfer Pricing Associates 2013) but has shown itself not to be above using tax competition in order to attract financial investment, by offering artificially lower corporate tax rates in some of its jurisdictions (Gough 2014). Furthermore, China may be resistant to what it perceives as a Western initiative; and has previously not shied away from protecting its own economic interests from the OECD tax agenda – as when it insisted that Macau and Hong Kong be removed from the OECD's list of tax havens (Eccleston *et al.* 2013: 13). Overall, the BRICs appear to be tentatively supportive, but there is cause for caution in assuming unqualified backing for the more controversial or sovereignty-threatening OECD recommendations.

8. The compliance challenge

The extent to which overt commitments made in support of the BEPS agenda at the G20 translate to actual implementation will depend in large measure on the effectiveness of the OECD's compliance mechanisms. This may be problematic, in that there do not seem to be any especially strong compliance mechanisms outlined in the Action Plan. Although some Actions will see changes in the OECD Model Tax Convention, the OECD itself notes that the Convention is 'not directly effective without amendments to bilateral tax treaties' (OECD 2013a: 24). Furthermore, most of the Actions consist of developing recommendations for countries to implement – their enactment remains highly contingent on the willingness of member-states to adopt the guidelines themselves. This is especially problematic given that the success of the initiative depends on holistic, multilateral implementation to avoid ongoing tax loopholes. There are no compliance mechanisms analogous to those used in the more successful tax initiatives of recent decades, such as the US' FATCA legislation and the OECD's own Global Forum on Tax Transparency and Information-Exchange.

Rather, the OECD appears to be primarily relying on achieving compliance through a consensus-based approach. The Action Plan is at pains to emphasise the 'inclusive and effective process' by which relevant stakeholder countries are included in the fulfilment of the fifteen Actions (OECD 2013a: 25). The OECD has taken several steps to this end, including conferring 'Associate' status on interested non-OECD G20 member countries (OECD 2013a: 25); holding a series of regional BEPS consultations in early 2014 (in Korea, Colombia, South Africa, and France) (OECD 2014d); making some effort to note the concerns of developing countries (through forums such as the UN and the Task Force on Tax and Development) (OECD 2014e); and pledging to maintain ongoing consultations with non-governmental stakeholders in business (represented through the BIAC and the Trade Union Advisory Committee) and civil society (OECD 2014e). Whether this approach proves to be sufficient to overcome the lack of formal compliance measures remains to be seen.

9. Conclusion

The G20 has played a pivotal role in terms of elevating international tax issues on to the global policy agenda by ensuring that member states made significant commitments to promoting tax-information-exchange and, most recently, addressing tax-base erosion and profit-shifting. We have argued that G20 endorsement of international tax-reform measures has been significant in both highlighting the consequences of international tax evasion and through increasing the political pressure on member-states to act accordingly. To this extent, the G20 has enhanced the political authority of technically orientated organisations such as the OECD, which initially developed many of the reform initiatives that have been implemented since 2009.

Despite these developments, we are less sanguine about the prospects for the proposed BEPS agenda. Our concerns in this regard are two-fold. First, we have noted that the BEPS Action Plan, with its focus on corporate tax avoidance, is more contentious than earlier reforms promoting tax transparency. The growing corporate campaign against BEPS and the subtle concerns being raised by G20 member-states are testimony to this. Compounding the challenge is the increasingly dominant view that the authority of the G20 itself is waning with time, as member-states increasingly go about pursuing their disparate interests. One result may be that while G20 meetings may continue to discuss and promote the BEPS agenda, scarce attention will be paid to implementation and compliance issues, effectively allowing states – particularly the great powers – to adhere to BEPS provisions only as they see fit.

It is too early to predict the success or otherwise of BEPS. What is clear is that the stakes are high, both in terms of the international community's capacity to tax MNCs and in terms of the G20's ability to make a meaningful contribution to post-crisis global economic governance.

References

Alexandroff, S. and Kirton, J. (2010)' "The great recession" and the emergence of the G20 leaders' summit', in Alexandroff, A. and Cooper, A. (eds) *Rising States, Rising Institutions: Challenges for global governance*, Washington, DC: Brookings Institution Press, pp. 178–95.

Aslund, A. (2009) 'The Group of 20 must be stopped', *Financial Times*, 26 November: http://www.ft.com/cms/s/0/37deaeb4-dad0-11de-933d-00144feabdc0.html#axzz3MbewrMXn (accessed 22 December 2014).

Aston, H. and Khadem, N. (2014) 'Joe Hockey eyes Britain's 'Google Tax' to boost tax take', *The Age*, 4 December: http://www.theage.com.au/federal-politics/political-news/joe-hockey-eyes-britains-google-tax-to-boost-tax-take-20141204-1201wy.html (accessed 23 December 2014).

Baker, A. and Carey, B. (2013) 'Flexible "G Groups" and network governance in an era of uncertainty and experimentation', in Payne, T. and Phillips, N. (eds), *Handbook of International Political Economy of Governance*, Cheltenham: Edward Elgar Publishing.

Becker, B. (2014) 'Obama hits "corporate deserters" ', Washington, DC: The Hill: http://thehill.com/policy/finance/213271-obama-to-call-for-action-on-offshore-tax-deals (accessed 14 August 2014).

Bergin, T. (2013) 'Big companies push back against G20 tax avoidance plan', Reuters: http://uk.reuters.com/article/2013/10/23/oecd-taxavoidance-companies-idUKL5N0ID3A420131023 (accessed 14 August 2014).

BIAC (Business Industry Advisory Committee to the OECD, 2013a) 'BIAC Holds International Business Dialogue on BEPS with OECD': http://biac.org/wp-content/uploads/2014/05/130328_BIAC_BEPS_Press_Release.pdf (accessed 5 August 2015).

— (2013b) 'BIAC business dialogue with the OECD on Base Erosion and Profit Shifting (BEPS)': http://www.biac.org/members/tax/BEPS/24_October_2013_BIAC_Letter_to_OECD_on_BEPS.pdf (accessed 14 August 2013).

Bowers, S. (2014) 'Apple, Starbucks and Fiat's tax affairs examined by European commission', *Guardian*, 11 June: http://www.theguardian.com/business/2014/jun/11/apple-starbucks-fiat-tax-affairs-european-commission (accessed 14 August 2014).

Buss, D. (2014) 'Marchionne may get tax pushback in locating Fiat Chrysler HQ in London', Forbes: http://www.forbes.com/sites/dalebuss/2014/05/09/marchionne-may-get-tax-pushback-in-locating-fiat-chrysler-hq-in-london%20/ (accessed 14 August 2014).

Carroll, P. and Kellow, A. (2011) *The OECD: A study of organisational adaptation*, Cheltenham: Edward Elgar Publishing.

Chessell, J. (2014) 'Close tax loopholes, urges OECD', *Sydney Morning Herald*: http://www.smh.com.au/business/world-business/close-tax-loopholes-urges-oecd-20140314-34qwn.html (accessed 14 August 2014).

Christian Aid (2013) 'Giving with one hand and taking with the other: Europe's role in tax-related capital flight from developing countries': http://www.christianaid.org.uk/images/Campaigns-tax-capital-flight-report-Dec-2013.pdf (accessed 14 August 2014).

Christians, A. (2013) 'How Starbucks lost its social licence – and paid £20 million to get it back', *Tax Notes International* 71(7): 637–40.

Citizens for Tax Justice (2014) 'Dozens of companies admit using tax havens': http://ctj.org/ctjreports/2014/05/dozens_of_companies_admit_using_tax_havens.php#.U-wZnflxWSr (accessed 14 August 2014).

Cooper, A. (2010) 'The G8–G20 partnership' in Kirton, J. and Koch, M. (eds) *G8 & G20: The 2010 Canadian Summits*, London: Newsdesk, pp. 306–7.

Deloitte (2014) 'World Tax Advisor – 25 April 2014': http://www.deloittetax.at/wp-content/dtt_tax_worldtaxadvisor_140425.pdf (accessed 14 August 2014).

Drezner, D. (2007) *All Politics is Global: Explaining international regulatory regimes*, Princeton, New Jersey: Princeton University Press.

Eccleston, R. (2012) *The Dynamics of Global Economic Governance: The financial crisis, the OECD and the politics of international tax co-operation*, Cheltenham: Edward Elgar.

Eccleston R. *et al.* (2013) 'G20 endorsement in post crisis global governance: more than a toothless talking shop?', *British Journal of Politics and International Relations* 17(2): 298–317.

Economist (2011) 'Tax torment', 17 March: http://www.economist.com/node/18396230 (accessed 14 August 2014).

— (2013) 'Lifting the veil', 6 November: www.economist.com/blogs/schumpeter/2013/11/index-financial-secrecy (accessed 14 August 2014).

Ernst & Young (2014a) 'Bridging the divide: highlights from the 2014 Tax Risk and Controversy Survey', Ernst & Young: http://www.ey.com/Publications/vwLUAssets/EY-2014-tax-risk-and-controversy-survey-highlights/$File/EY-2014-tax-risk-and-controversy-survey-highlights.pdf (accessed 14 August 2014).

G7 (1996) 'Economic communiqué: making a success of globalization for the benefit of all', G8 Information Centre: http://www.g8.utoronto.ca/summit/1996lyon/communique.html (accessed 14 August 2014).

G20 (2008) 'Declaration: summit on financial markets and the world economy – November 15, 2008', Washington, DC: G20: https://www.g20.org/sites/default/files/g20_resources/library/Washington_Declaration_0.pdf (accessed 13 August 2014).

— (2009a) 'London Summit – Leaders' Statement, 2 April 2009': https://www.g20.org/sites/default/files/g20_resources/library/London_Declaration.pdf (accessed 13 August 2014).

— (2009b) 'Leaders' Statement: The Pittsburgh Summit – September 24–25 2009': https://www.g20.org/sites/default/files/g20_resources/library/Pittsburgh_Declaration_0.pdf (accessed 13 August 2014).

— (2013a) 'G20 Leaders' Declaration – September 2013', St. Petersburg: http://www.g20.org/about_g20/past_summits/2013_st_petersburg (accessed 14 August 2014).

— (2013b) 'Tax Annex to the St. Petersburg G20 Leaders' Declaration: September, 2013': https://www.g20.org/sites/default/files/g20_resources/library/Saint%20Petersburg%20G20%20Leaders%20Declaration%20-%20Tax%20Annex_0.pdf (accessed 14 August 2014).

— (2014) 'G20 International Tax Symposium, May 9 and 10, Final Report': https://g20.org/wpcontent/uploads/2014/12/G20%20International%20Tax%20Symposium%20Report.pdf (accessed 14 August 2014).

Gelles, D. (2013) 'New corporate tax shelter: a merger abroad', *New York Times*, 8 October: http://dealbook.nytimes.com/2013/10/08/to-cut-corporate-taxes-a-merger-abroad-and-a-new-home/ (accessed 14 August 2014).

Gough, N. (2014) 'A muddy tract now, but by 2020, China's answer to Wall St', *New York Times*, 2 April: http://dealbook.nytimes.com/2014/04/02/a-financial-center-is-envisioned-on-a-muddy-tract-in-southern-china/?_php=true&_type=blogs&_r=0 (accessed 14 August 2014).

Graetz, M. and O'Hear, M. (1997) 'The "original intent" of U.S. international taxation', *Faculty Scholarship Series*, Paper 1620: http://digitalcommons.law.yale.edu/fss_papers/1620 (accessed 3 September 2015).

Guardian (2013) 'Watch the Coalition lead the battle against tax havens … such as Britain', 8 September: http://www.theguardian.com/business/2013/sep/08/coalition-battle-low-tax-jurisdictions-britain (accessed 14 August 2014).

Hartley, J. (2014) 'Burger King's tax inversion and Canada's favourable corporate tax rates', *Forbes*, 25 August: http://www.forbes.com/sites/jonhartley/2014/08/25/burger-kings-tax-inversion-and-canadas-favorable-corporate-tax-rates/ (accessed 16 December 2014).

Kelly, P. (2009) 'Shift to G20 was matter of time', *Australian*, 27 September.

Khadem, N. (2014) 'G20 nations to share tax information on multinationals to beat the cheats', *The Age,* 17 November: http://www.theage.com.au/business/g20-nations-to-share-tax-information-on-multinationals-to-beat-the-cheats-20141116-11nszo.html (accessed 23 December 2014).

Kharas, H. and Lombardi, D. (2012) 'The Group of Twenty: origins, prospects, and challenges for global governance', Washington, DC: Brookings Institution: http://www.brookings.edu/~/media/research/files/papers/2012/8/g20%20global%20governance%20kharas%20lombardi/g20%20global%20governance%20kharas%20lombardi.pdf (accessed 22 December 2014).

Kirton, J. (2013) *G20 Governance for a Globalised World*, Surrey: Ashgate Publishing.

KPMG (2014) 'KPMG survey: corporate tax leaders skeptical that OECD will meet goals of "BEPS" action plan by deadline': http://www.kpmg.com/us/en/issuesandinsights/articlespublications/press-releases/pages/kpmg-survey-corporate-tax-leaders-skeptical-that-oecd-will-meet-goals-of-beps-action-plan-by-deadline.aspx (accessed 14 August 2014).

Masson, P. and Pattison, J. (2010) 'Financial regulatory reform: using models of co-operation to evaluate current prospects for international agreement', Toronto: University of Toronto: www.g8.utoronto.ca/g20/biblio/G20reforms.pdf (accessed 22 December 2014).

Michel, A. (2014) 'OECD tax chief: corporate tax avoidance while taxpayers suffer "simply not acceptable"', International Consortium of Investigative Journalists: http://www.icij.org/project/luxembourg-leaks/oecd-tax-chief-corporate-tax avoidance-while-taxpayers-suffer-simply-not (accessed 22 December 2014).

Mider, Z. (2014) 'Medtronic is biggest yet to renounce U.S. tax citizenship', *Bloomberg*, 16 June: http://www.bloomberg.com/news/2014-06-16/medtronic-is-biggest-firm-yet-to-renounce-u-s-tax-status.html (accessed 14 August 2014).

Mitchell, D. (2000) 'An OECD proposal to eliminate tax competition would mean higher taxes and less privacy' *Economic Policy Series Research Paper.* Washington DC: Heritage Foundation.

Neate, R. (2013) 'Lords say Amazon-style tax avoidance schemes must end', *Guardian*, 31 July: http://www.theguardian.com/business/2013/jul/31/tax avoidance-schemes-crackdown-lords (accessed 14 August 2014).

Neate, R. and Farrell, S. (2014) 'Pfizer reiterates its commitment to fostering research – and praises UK's low corporate tax', *Guardian*, 12 May: http://www.theguardian.com/business/2014/may/12/pfizer-defends-research-record-takeover-astrazeneca (accessed 14 August 2014).

OECD (2013a) 'Action Plan on Base Erosion and Profit Shifting': Paris: OECD: http://www.oecd.org/ctp/BEPSActionPlan.pdf (accessed 13 August 2014).

— (2013b) 'Declaration on Base Erosion and Profit Shifting – Adopted on 29 May 2013', Paris: OECD: http://www.oecd.org/tax/C-MIN(2013)22-FINAL-ENG.pdf (accessed 13 August 2014).

— (2014a) 'Tax Transparency 2014 Report on Progress', Paris: OECD: http://www.oecd.org/tax/transparency/GFannualreport2014.pdf (accessed 18 December 2014).

— (2014b) 'About BEPS', Paris: OECD: http://www.oecd.org/tax/beps-about.htm (accessed 14 August 2014).

— (2014c) 'OECD Secretary-General Report to the G20 Finance Ministers and Central Bank Governors', Sydney: OECD: https://www.g20.org/sites/default/files/g20_resources/library/OECD%20Tax%20report%20to%20G20%20Finance%20Ministers.pdf (accessed 14 August 2014).

— (2014d) 'OECD holds regional consultations on BEPS in Asia and Latin America', Paris: OECD: http://www.oecd.org/ctp/beps-regional-consultations-asia-latin-america.htm (accessed 14 August 2014).

— (2014e) 'BEPS – frequently asked questions', OECD: Paris: http://www.oecd.org/ctp/beps-frequentlyaskedquestions.htm (accessed 14 August 2014).

Oxfam (2014) 'Business among friends: why corporate tax dodgers are not yet losing sleep over global tax reform': http://www.oxfamnovib.nl/Redactie/Downloads/Rapporten/Business%20Among%20Friends.pdf (accessed 14 August 2014).

Palan R. and Wigan, D. (2014) 'Herding cats and taming tax havens: the US strategy of "not in my backyard" ', *Global Policy* 5(2): 1–10.

Palan, R. *et al.* (2010) *Tax Havens: How globalisation really works*, Ithaca, New York: Cornell University Press.

Picciotto, S. (2011) *Regulating Global Corporate Capitalism,* Cambridge: Cambridge University Press.

Picciotto S. (2014) 'Briefing on base erosion and profit-shifting (BEPS): implications for developing countries, February 2014', Tax Justice Network: http://www.taxjustice.net/wp-content/uploads/2013/04/TJN-Briefing-BEPS-for-Developing-Countries-Feb-2014-v2.pdf (accessed 14 August 2014).

PricewaterhouseCoopers (2013) 'Tax policy bulletin: OECD initiative on base erosion and profit shifting (BEPS)': http://www.pwc.com/en_GX/gx/tax/newsletters/tax-policy-bulletin/assets/pwc-oecd-base-erosion-profit-shifting.pdf (accessed 14 August 2014).

— (2014) 'CEOs confidence rises for 2014', Davos: PricewaterhouseCoopers: http://www.pwc.com/jp/en/japan-news/2014/ceo-survey2014.jhtml (accessed 14 August 2014).

Prime Minister's Office (2013) 'G8 Lough Erne Declaration', London: UK Government: https://www.gov.uk/government/publications/g8-lough-erne-declaration/g8-lough-erne-declaration-html-version (accessed 14 August 2014).

Quantrill, T. *et al.* (2014) 'Letter to the OECD Committee on Fiscal Affairs', Tax Justice Network: http://www.taxjustice.net/wp-content/uploads/2013/04/Civil-Society-concerns-on-OECD-BEPS-process-June-2014.pdf (accessed 22 December 2014.)

Rachman, G. (2010) 'Seven pillars of friction', *Financial Times*, 8 November.

Ring, D. (2009) 'What's at stake in the sovereignty debate? International tax and the nation-state', *Virginia Journal of International Law* 49(1): 154–233.

Rixen, T. (2008) *The Political Economy of International Tax Governance: Transformations of the state,* New York: Palgrave Macmillan.

— (2011) 'From double tax avoidance to tax competition: explaining the institutional trajectory of international tax governance', *Review of International Political Economy* 18(2): 197–227.

Rubenfeld, S. (2014) 'Republican Party backs FATCA repeal resolution', *Wall Street Journal*, 24 January: http://blogs.wsj.com/riskandcompliance/2014/01/24/republican-party-backs-fatca-repeal-resolution/ (accessed 14 August 2014).

Sharman, J. (2006) *Havens in the Storm*, Ithaca, New York: Cornell University Press.

Shaxon, N. (2011) *Treasure Islands: Uncovering the damage of offshore banking and tax havens*, New York: Palgrave Macmillan.

Tax Justice Network (2014) 'Transfer pricing': http://www.taxjustice.net/topics/corporate-tax/transfer-pricing/ (accessed 14 August 2014).

Transfer Pricing Associates (2013) 'OECD increased efforts with Brazil': http://tpa-global.com/newsitem247823/ (accessed 14 August 2014).

— (2014) 'BEPS project updates – Pacific Asia developments': http://www.tpa-global.com/news/2014/06/26/beps-project-update-ndash-pacific-asia-developments (accessed 14 August 2014).

UK Government (2014a) 'Government to introduce new criminal offence for tax evaders': https://www.gov.uk/government/news/government-to-introduce-new-criminal-offence-for-tax-evaders (accessed 14 August 2014).

— (2014b) 'Budget 2014: key announcements': https://www.gov.uk/government/news/budget-2014-key-announcements (accessed 14 August 2014).

— (2014c) 'Brazil: radical BEPS measure cuts incentives for investing abroad': https://www.gov.uk/government/publications/brazil-radical-beps-measure-cuts-incentives-for-investing-abroad/brazil-radical-beps-measure-cuts-incentives-for-investing-abroad (accessed 14 August 2014).

Walter, A. (2008) *Governing Finance: East Asia's adoption of international standards*, Ithaca, New York: Cornell University Press.

Wang, G. (2009) 'Financial crisis: its impacts on international economic system and geopolitics', *Global Review* 3: 24–38.

Weschler, W. (2001) 'Follow the money', *Foreign Affairs* 90(4): 40–57.

Wolverson, R. (2010) 'G20's tepid economic reform', Council on Foreign Relations analysis brief: http://www.cfr.org/world/g20s-tepid-economic-reform/p23218 (accessed 14 August 2015).

PART THREE

NORMATIVE PRINCIPLES FOR GLOBAL TAX GOVERNANCE

Chapter Nine

Tax Competition: A Problem of Global or Domestic Justice?

*Miriam Ronzoni**

1. Introduction: tax competition, global justice, and global institutional design

High capital mobility enabled by contemporary globalisation puts significant pressure on the capacity of states, and their citizens, to tax as they see fit. As a result, fiscal policy choices become increasingly responsive, not only to domestic needs and democratic inputs, but also to the external pressure exercised by global markets or threats of capital outflow. Indeed, some would argue, they have become *more* responsive to the latter than to the former. This, intuitively, strikes most observers as being normatively problematic. Where exactly does the problem lie, however?

In this chapter, I shall attempt to recast that question along the classical terms of the global justice debate: does tax competition harm (if harm results at all) the internal functioning of self-determining *polities* or patterns of distributive justice among *individuals* across the globe? In other words, should we worry about tax competition regardless of which conception of global justice we hold? I shall answer this question with a qualified yes. Tax competition, I shall argue, has problematic features both for cosmopolitans – who believe that the scope of demanding principles of distributive justice is global – and for their critics – who believe that robust obligations of justice only hold within polities and that obligations of justice are both weaker and structurally different. However, it is a problem of a different kind for the two camps. Whereas cosmopolitans have reason to worry about tax competition insofar, and as long, as it exacerbates global inequalities between people, non-cosmopolitans ought to be concerned about its threat to the problem-solving capacity of what they regard as the justice-provider *par excellence* in their view – namely, the state. Thus, *both* perspectives on global justice provide reasons to think that tax competition makes a significant difference to the nature and content of our obligations of justice beyond borders – but on different

* I am grateful to Peter Dietsch, Thomas Rixen, Laurens Van Appeldoorn and Gabriel Wollner for their extremely helpful comments.

grounds.[1] In both cases, our obligations change and become more demanding, but in different ways; and such a difference, in turn, has crucial implications for global institutional design. The difference between the two perspectives matters for the precise contours of such new and strengthened obligations – and for what we should do to discharge them. In this chapter, I am going to focus on a specific non-cosmopolitan outlook: internationalism (Rawls 1999; Sangiovanni 2007). For internationalists, unlike other, more radical, non-cosmopolitans,[2] duties of justice beyond borders *do* exist, but are either 1) principles that hold between individuals, but are much less demanding in content (they do not, for instance, set *egalitarian* standards); or 2) obligations that *states*, rather than individuals, have towards one another. For the purpose of this paper I am going to focus on (2) and, in particular, on reciprocal obligations, jointly held by states, not to hinder one another's capacity to be adequate providers of domestic justice. The business of international justice, on this reading, is the 'justice of societies'– or, to put it more precisely, the realisation of the international preconditions that *enable* societies to be just[3] – rather than 'the wellbeing of individuals' (Rawls 1999: 119).

Some scholars have argued recently that the content and significance of such duties is deeper than one might think (Ronzoni 2009; Dietsch 2011b). In particular, under certain empirical conditions, securing the conditions that enable all states to be functioning and self-determining polities might entail regulating some of the socio-economic dynamics triggered by globalisation – tax competition arguably being one of them. Yet, to the extent that unregulated tax competition is unjust from an internationalist perspective, this is due to how it affects political self-determination (and, arguably, domestic justice), not global inequality. Accordingly, the institutional responses to tax competition that internationalists ought to support differ significantly (if not entirely) from those which cosmopolitans would advocate. The aim of such institutional responses would be to rescue fiscal self-determination, rather than to reduce the global inter-individual inequalities caused by global tax competition. A reduction of inequalities (between as well as within states) would be likely to follow – for fighting the negative impact of tax competition on fiscal self-determination would probably lead to the resurgence of more progressive fiscal systems, as well as making the accumulation of wealth through the exploitation of fiscal loopholes and tax havens harder to achieve. Yet this would not be the direct aim of an internationalist system of global tax

1. A more detailed defence of this view is offered in Ronzoni 2014. Congenial approaches are also developed in Dietsch 2011b, Rixen 2011, and Dietsch and Rixen 2014a. On the underappreciated demandingness of internationalist accounts of global justice in general (i.e., over and above tax governance in particular), see also Ronzoni 2009 and 2012 and Laborde and Ronzoni forthcoming.
2. See, for instance, Nagel 2005.
3. This chapter will remain silent on the issue of obligations towards societies which are capable of being just but fail to be, for domestic reasons. This issue is open to wide disagreement on 1) whether any such obligations exist at all; 2) their scope and content (what are we obliged to do and in which cases?); and 3) their status (are they obligations of justice or humanity?).

governance. Thus, the contribution that this chapter aspires to make is twofold: I shall argue that tax competition puts pressure on internationalists to a) have a more demanding account of inter-state obligations, yet b) in a way that still remains faithful to their fundamental non-cosmopolitan commitments.

What then, if anything, is unjust about tax competition? From a cosmopolitan perspective, international tax competition is a problem because (and to the extent that) it increases inter-individual inequalities, both between and within countries.[4] It is, in other words, a cause of *global distributive injustice*. The natural institutional response to such a normative diagnosis is, at least *prima facie*, to move the power to tax – and redistribute – beyond the nation-state. Depending on the precise empirical diagnosis of the phenomenon of tax competition, this might turn out not to be feasible.[5] However, from a perspective of global justice, there is no *principled* normative reason to resist a supranationalisation of the power to tax.

From an internationalist perspective, instead, inter-individual inequalities, *qua* inequalities, are only a problem within the shared institutions of a polity. What we owe to one another beyond borders is, instead, to respect our equal right to establish and maintain a polity that is genuinely self-determining and a robust provider of domestic justice.[6] We all have a right to be members of a polity that is worth the name, namely, one that can steer its own fate and over which citizens can exercise genuine control. Yet, societies cannot be autonomous, let alone just, if they do not enjoy sufficiently favourable structural conditions at the global level – and tax competition is one dynamic which might make such conditions excessively hard to maintain. Therefore, I suggest, even internationalists must recognise that tax competition poses a systemic threat to one crucial component of the capacity of a society to be independent (and just) – namely, its fiscal self-determination. To restore the capacity of national institutions to tax 'as they see fit' (or, better still, as their citizens see fit), significant global institutional reforms are required. Yet, if this is the guiding normative rationale, the demand for a stronger institutional regulation of tax competition need not be interpreted as a demand for the supranationalisation of the *power to tax* itself. My broad suggestion in this chapter is, therefore, that the issue of institutional design might well be more complex and multi-faceted for internationalists than it is for cosmopolitans. Tackling tax competition globally in order to restore the fiscal self-determination

4. I am not claiming here that this is the only concern that cosmopolitans would have but rather that it is their most distinctive concern.

5. For one such analysis, see Dietsch and Rixen 2014b.

6. However, internationalists can (and many of them do) endorse more modest, sufficientarian theories of inter-individual distributive justice at the global level, according to which inequalities *per se* are not the problem but nobody should ever fall beyond a certain baseline of resources, opportunities, capabilities or well-being (Blake 2001; Sangiovanni 2007). Moreover, some global inequalities do matter to internationalists to the extent that they threaten the equality of polities – societies that are internally too unequal in socio-economic terms tend to have poorer institutions due to generalised unrest and violence as well as widespread lack of social cohesion; and societies that are too poor cannot be equal citizens of the international community.

of states might well require acting simultaneously from more than one angle, rather than simply transferring the power to tax to a supranational authority.

The chapter unfolds as follows. Section 2 provides a brief overview of the phenomenon of tax competition and of the variety of ways in which it can be a problem from the point of view of justice. Section 3 further explores the point introduced in the present section, namely that both cosmopolitans and internationalists have reasons to worry about certain aspects of tax competition and respond to it through institutional design – yet not in the same way. Section 4 argues that an internationalist institutional response to tax competition requires a tripartite strategy, which entails: 1) moving *some* fiscal powers to the supranational level (yet with extreme caution and with a rationale different from that of cosmopolitans); 2) harmonising certain fiscal areas; and 3) empowering supranational institutions to sanction specific kinds of behaviour.

2. The phenomenon of international tax competition

Tax competition has recently attracted a great deal of attention in normative political philosophy, and within global justice debates in particular.[7] In order to understand the general contours of the phenomenon, let me start with a definition:

> *Tax competition* is defined as independent governments adopting their tax policies strategically. They design their tax systems to attract new investment and tax bases of other countries. Governmental tax strategies can involve every aspect of a national tax system. International tax differentials may thus be reflected in tax rates, tax bases, and the enforcement of tax laws. The expectation is that countries will attempt to undercut one another in tax burdens (Rixen 2011: 449).

Tax competition sheds light on one way in which untamed globalisation empowers powerful private actors, such as transnational corporations, over public ones. States ostensibly choose to compete in order to attract capital, but capital and business are able to pressure states into competing by a 'threat to leave'. According to classical rational-choice theory, tax competition naturally leads to a race to the bottom in taxation rates;[8] as a result, the rich become richer and the poor become poorer everywhere, and public provision of certain goods (such as roads, military defence and health care) becomes extremely difficult. If tax competition were to unfold in this way, its normative significance would be unambiguous for cosmopolitans and internationalists alike. Cosmopolitans would be concerned about the rise in global inequality among individuals, whereas internationalists would worry about the deepening of domestic social injustices in each and every

7. To mention but some of the pioneering works in this respect, *see* Dietsch 2011a and Brock 2008. For a different diagnosis, upon which the present chapter draws, *see* Ronzoni 2014.

8. For non-technical presentations of this stronger thesis, *see*, for instance, Scharpf 1997; Avi-Yonah 2000; Wilson and Wildasin 2004.

society – inequalities would rise not only across but also within countries, and states would lose their primary instrument of redistribution, namely, fiscal policy (Dietsch 2011a: 95). In short, they would both have reasons to argue that justice demands a regulation of the phenomenon.

However, no such clear-cut race to the bottom seems to be occurring. Whereas empirical data on tax competition are deeply contested, it seems reasonably clear that its effects are more multi-faceted than rational-choice theory would have it. First of all, tax competition impacts different countries differently (Steinmo 2002; Swank and Steinmo 2002; Genschel and Schwarz 2011). Second of all, some scholars go as far as to argue that domestic institutions have their own means to offset, or indeed even erase, race-to-the-bottom dynamics (Basinger and Hallerberg 2004). Third of all, only countries with specific features (most notably, small countries) have a genuine, strong incentive to become *universal* tax havens (rather than in one fiscal sector only); and service-oriented economies like the UK have a stronger incentive to become tax havens than countries with a strong productive sector (such as Germany). To the extent that it is happening, tax competition does not generate a race to the bottom that harms all countries, but tends instead to have winners and losers (*see* Genschel and Seelkopf 2016, Chapter Three in this volume). Finally, real states are not uncooperative utility maximisers, and therefore tend to respond to tax competition through a good deal of cooperative co-ordination and harmonisation, thus often preventing escalation (Genschel 2002).

Claiming that no clear-cut race to the bottom is occurring does not, however, mean that tax competition has no problematic implications. The fact that no uniform race to the bottom is occurring does not mean that tax competition is not undermining the capacity of the state to deliver social justice in other ways. As Dietsch and Rixen argue (2014a: 4), fiscal self-determination has two aspects: a) the capacity of the state to maintain the overall desired size of the budget (in terms of overall revenues and expenditures); and b) its capacity to maintain the desired extent of redistribution. Even if no uniform race to the bottom takes place, hardly any country is capable of preserving both (a) and (b) intact under conditions of unregulated tax competition. OECD countries, generally speaking, remain capable of preserving the desired size of the budget, but they do so by broadening and changing the tax-base; most notably, the tax burden is shifted from capital to labour, and from income to consumption taxes. Thus, the preservation of the size of the budget is secured at the cost of the second aspect of fiscal sovereignty: changes in the tax-base make the nature of national tax systems less progressive and therefore undermine the extent of overall redistribution (Loretz 2008; Dietsch and Rixen 2014a: 6). Developing countries, instead, have difficulties in preserving both sides of their fiscal self-determination, because changing and increasing the size of the budget requires more institutional capacity and effective public power than they actually have (Keen and Simone 2004; Dietsch and Rixen 2014a: 7).

Moreover, although harmonisation and co-ordination efforts are laudable attempts to prevent a race to the bottom from undermining state capacity altogether, harmonisation itself has its problematic effects on the fiscal autonomy of states, for it deprives them of fiscal flexibility. Harmonisation can prevent states from reacting to the specific circumstances of their domestic scenarios in a sufficiently swift and context-sensitive manner; it can, for instance, prevent 'governments from raising taxes in response to rising spending requirements and from detaxing labor in response to growing unemployment' (Genschel 2002: 245). In sum, there is a third aspect of fiscal self-determination, 3) flexibility over time, which practices of harmonisation often undermine, even when they do succeed in letting states maintain intact both the desired size of the budget and the desired extent of redistribution at the time of harmonisation (something that hardly ever happens anyway). In best-case scenarios, where the relevant jurisdictions have the same fiscal preferences at the time of the harmonisation (and such cases are plausibly fairly rare), harmonisation enables a state to keep (a) and (b) at the desired level at the time of the harmonisation, but only at the cost of forfeiting (c) in the long run. When countries harmonise, they forfeit their capacity to react flexibly – that is to say, with a sufficient degree of speed and discretion – to changed domestic circumstances.

In sum, although the simple hypothesis of standard economic theory, according to which tax competition leads to a uniform race to the bottom, seems to be disproved, this does not mean that tax competition thereby automatically receives an acquittal from the point of view of global justice. Tax havens do exist and do contribute to tax-evasion. Tax competition does lead to changing the tax-base towards more regressive forms of taxation. And downward pressures on fiscal rates do exist; developing countries, in particular, experience difficulties in raising revenues and providing services that are financed by taxes. Finally, even when states manage to resist uncooperative tendencies by harmonising (intentionally or reluctantly) their fiscal structure, they thereby lose flexibility and the capacity to react to their domestic circumstances in a context-sensitive way. Thus, most countries do suffer losses in their fiscal self-determination, with respect to either a) the size of the budget; b) the extent of redistribution; or c) flexibility – and some countries in more than one or even all of the above. Moreover, the fact that no simple race to the bottom occurs means, as we have seen, that tax competition does not affect all countries equally; and this unequal impact may well be a reason for normative concern (a source of unfairness, as it were) in and of itself. If we care about the equal self-determination of polities, we should care about how tax competition affects the self-determination of different societies in unequal ways. Tax competition may well be less harmful for some than for others. It may even not be harmful at all for some, especially small countries (and small democracies in particular). However, the fact that it disadvantages some countries disproportionately, rather than constituting an equal catastrophe for all, may well be a problem in and of itself.

So far, I have simply claimed that tax competition, however we assess its empirical effects, has 'problematic' implications from a normative point of view. It is now time to make our normative diagnosis more precise.

3. Who is afraid of tax competition? And why?

For the limited aims of this chapter, I distinguish between two approaches within the global justice debate: cosmopolitanism and internationalism.[9] Cosmopolitan approaches regard *individuals* to be the units of moral concern in all questions of justice, regardless of whether these occur within or across borders (Pogge 2002: 169–70) and argue, on these grounds, that at least most (if not necessarily all) obligations of justice are global in scope and roughly equal in content.[10] For cosmopolitans, therefore, global inter-individual inequalities are always *prima facie* problems from the point of view of justice – even if, for some and in some cases, they can be justified all things considered. For cosmopolitans, the harmful effects of tax competition are clearly problems of justice, at least *prima facie* – for, in one way or another, they increase inequalities (in resources or opportunities) among individuals (even if not necessarily in a race-to-the-bottom fashion).

Internationalists, instead, a) consider justice to be fundamentally restricted in scope, content and subjects according to different and specific areas (justice between the members of a family, citizens of a state, states within the international community and so on); and b) do not consider individuals to be the relevant units of concern in all areas of justice. Justice is always justice of a specific domain; this requires that we specify both the nature of the domain and who the relevant subjects within it are – which, in turn, will heavily influence what the content of demands of justice within in it is (for example, whether the demands are or are not egalitarian, or even whether they are of a distributive nature at all). Domestic social justice, for instance, is inter-individual and distributive in nature: we care about individuals and we care about the relative inequalities between them. Internationalists offer a range of different reasons as to why distributive equality is a demand of justice within state boundaries, ranging from the national ties which (ideally) exist between fellow citizens (Miller 1995); the coercive nature of state institutions which demands distributive equality to be justified (Blake 2001); or to the special form of social co-operation aimed at the production of essential collective goods in which citizens engage, and which calls for an egalitarian distribution of its burdens and benefits (Sangiovanni 2007). Beyond borders, however, things change. The special and morally relevant relations that exist between fellow citizens do not hold, and demands for equality are not, therefore, justified. Obligations of justice do exist, but are very different in kind and content. The existence of obligations of justice between individuals is commonly accepted by internationalists, but such obligations are deemed to be sufficientarian, rather than egalitarian, in content: what we owe foreigners is that they enjoy, no matter

9. The characterisation of the global justice debate as being split into cosmopolitan and internationalist approaches is a gross simplification. For instance, a number of intermediate approaches have been put forward in the literature in recent years (Cohen and Sabel 2006 and Valentini 2011 are but two particularly insightful examples). For an account of why a simple and stark dichotomy between cosmopolitans and anti-cosmopolitans within the global justice debate is both factually inaccurate and normatively counterproductive, see, for instance, Ronzoni 2013.

10. For a distinction between weak and strong cosmopolitanism, see Scheffler 2001: 114.

what, the sufficient means to live a decent or autonomous life (for the latter, *see*, in particular, Blake 2001). What is more, most internationalists envisage the existence of international obligations between states; such obligations, however, do not have a distributive nature but concern instead just conduct among peoples – the constraints they must honour in order to respect one another's freedom and equality as independent polities (Rawls 1999).

Now, internationalist obligations among states can be interpreted in more or less demanding ways. More often than not, minimal accounts are put forward: what states owe to one another is the duty to refrain from interfering in one another's internal affairs, to honour agreements, and perhaps to assist one another in case of dire need – when some polities are so badly off, in terms of either resources or institutional failure, that they lack 'the essentials of political autonomy' (Rawls 1999: 118). However, at closer inspection, minimalist accounts do not appear defensible. The 'essentials of political autonomy' might be threatened by systemic factors and require systemic answers, rather than one-off acts of assistance. When transnational corporations are so strong as to keep weak states under their thumb, what is needed is a structured response to this excessive power. Similarly, the so called 'resource curse' – the phenomenon according to which states that are rich in resources but with poor institutional infrastructure are particularly likely to be exposed to civil conflicts, coups and dictatorial regimes – requires an institutional response so as to remove the incentive that political groups and élites in such countries have to appropriate such resources to secure and perpetuate their power by selling them to the international community (Pogge 2002: 153–66; Wenar 2008). Tax competition, if the analysis provided in the previous section is correct, is yet another example of how internal self-determination might be hindered by systemic global factors.

This suggests that, for states to be able to behave justly towards one another and, in particular, to treat one another as free and equal actors, the *background conditions* for their freedom and equality must obtain (Ronzoni 2009). When states are too unequal, their bargaining power becomes disproportionate and some states can dominate others – if states are exposed to domination, they can neither regard themselves nor act as free and equal members of the international community. The same holds when certain global and international dynamics are such that some states no longer enjoy sufficient internal problem-solving capacity to regard themselves as genuine sovereigns: what happens within their borders is more influenced by forces that they do not control than by domestic public policy. They cannot be genuinely self-determining polities. This problem is even more acute when it affects some states much more gravely than others. Therefore, the minimalist account seems implausible: in order to truly respect one another's status as free and equal sovereigns, states must not only exercise self-restraint, honour agreements and assist one another in one-off cases of dire need – they must also jointly *secure* the background conditions for their genuine freedom and equality. They must make sure that all states enjoy external favourable conditions to be truly sovereign polities, capable of determining their own fate. States and their citizens, then, have the responsibility to make good on such conditions – and if they do not, this is a problem of domestic, rather than international, justice. But guaranteeing such conditions is fully within the scope of an internationalist theory of global justice.

Protecting one another against the consequences of tax competition that the previous section has unpacked falls, I submit, within the scope of the internationalist obligations of justice that states have towards one another. Tax competition, even if does not cause a uniform race to the bottom, undermines the background conditions for the freedom and equality of states as sovereign and self-determining actors within the international community. Tax havens prevent other states from collecting revenues in an adequate manner. The broadening of the tax-base or the pressure to harmonise fiscal systems often deprives states of crucial aspects of their fiscal sovereignty. Moreover, tax competition exacerbates inequalities between states by affecting OECD and developing countries differently. Now, the fact that this increases economic inequalities between states and their members need not be a problem *per se* from an internationalist perspective, which does not regard distributive issues beyond borders as being automatically a concern of justice. Yet, both inequality and deprivation have important indirect effects on self-determination which internationalists have reason to worry about, for 1) inequalities can become so high as to undermine the equal status of sovereign states in the international community; and, 2) it surely *is* a problem of inter-state fairness, from an internationalist perspective, if the self-determination of some countries is (due to absolute deprivation and/or disproportionate international inequality) more endangered than that of others in a structural and systematic manner. Therefore, I submit, internationalists must acknowledge that states have a mutual obligations to tackle tax competition in order to secure the background conditions for their freedom and equality *qua* sovereign states – and that doing so requires establishing robust supranational mechanisms.

However, an internationalist case for global tax governance remains different from a cosmopolitan case – and, in particular, it is not necessarily a case for global *fiscal* institutions. For cosmopolitans, the problem with harmful tax competition is (mainly) that it exacerbates inter-individual inequalities. Therefore, the *prima facie* normative case for creating global institutions – capable of collecting taxes in an efficient way without suffering from the shortfalls of tax competition – seems fairly straightforward. Of course, there could be reasons other than reasons of distributive justice for resisting such a reform: for instance, the despotic dangers of a global fiscal authority. Cosmopolitans might also reject global fiscal institutions on a series of empirical grounds, ranging from feasibility to efficiency. But as such, the cosmopolitan approach to global justice has no *principled* reason against the argument that global tax governance must be a system of global fiscal authority.

Internationalists, instead, worry about tax competition because they are concerned about the systemic threats it poses to fiscal sovereignty and self-determination, understood as an essential component of sovereignty and self-determination more generally. For obvious reasons, simply transferring the power to tax elsewhere cannot be a good way of securing fiscal sovereignty and self-determination – it would be a way of *destroying* them. Internationalists should favour, instead, stronger global institutions to regulate tax competition in such a way as to give fiscal powers *back* to states as much as possible. This aim, I shall argue in the next section, is best achieved through a more complex, tripartite strategy.

4. How can internationalists regulate tax competition?

In this section, I shall provide a brief sketch of the strategy that internationalists might adopt to regulate tax competition *for fiscal self-determination's sake*. The basic idea underlying such a strategy is the following. Internationalists are committed to opposing tax competition because of the damaging effects it has on fiscal self-determination. Tackling such damaging effects through global institutional responses cannot, however, boil down to globalising the power to tax *simpliciter* – for that would replace, rather than protect, the power of different polities to tax as they see fit. On the other hand, global tax governance, if it is to be effective, cannot avoid constraining domestic policy, and domestic fiscal policy in particular, at least to some extent. As we have seen, tax competition may well be an indicator of the increasing power of private actors to escape public regulation in our globalised world; global tax governance is one attempt to change that balance. Its aim, from an internationalist perspective, is to empower states and their regulatory systems; but in the process of doing so, we cannot but interfere with them, at least up to a point. If competition is to be made less harmful, competing actors must also be constrained in some fashion. We need to strike a very delicate balance: regulate enough so that effective counter-measures are in place, whilst at the same time leaving as much room as possible for domestic fiscal discretion. My suggestion is that the strategy that is most likely to accomplish this goal is a complex one – and one within which global taxation should play a role, but a suitably limited one. The three elements of such a strategy are: 1) moving *some* fiscal powers to the supranational level (yet with extreme caution and with a distinctively internationalist rationale); 2) harmonising up to a certain level for the sake of enabling variation beyond that level; and 3) empowering supranational institutions to punish specific kinds of behaviour effectively. In the remainder of this section, and by way of a conclusion to this chapter, I shall briefly describe these three elements in turn.

Moving some fiscal powers

Internationalists have reasons to be cautious about global taxation but need not oppose it in all its forms. Indeed, some global taxes might turn out to be the best, or indeed even the only, way to tackle some of the harmful effects of tax competition on effective statehood. Yet since internationalists endorse global taxation on grounds different from cosmopolitans, this should lead them to support only some forms of global taxation, and with very specific aims. The point, for internationalists, is not to collect revenues globally in order to provide services to individuals across the globe, or to redistribute global wealth. However, there are two other important cases where internationalists might find some forms of global taxation appropriate.

First, in a globalised economy, only a global authority might be able to tax certain global actors with a sufficient degree of certainty and regularity. This is the case, for instance, for transnational financial transactions and for some transnational corporations: it might simply prove too difficult for a territorial authority to hold them accountable from a fiscal point of view. If this is the case, internationalists might have reason to support global taxation in these self-contained areas. Of course, internationalists have reason to pursue other avenues before reaching this conclusion; but it might well turn out to be the case that, at least for the time being (that is, before a more robust system of global regulation is in place), allowing a global authority to tax certain agents proves more feasible than taxing each relevant actor in the jurisdiction in which its economic or financial activity takes place.[11] Closing loopholes so as to allow states to tax as much as possible by themselves is always the favoured route for internationalists; however, they too must concede that, in certain cases, global taxation is better than no taxation at all.

Second, and perhaps even more relevantly from an empirical point of view, internationalists have reason to favour those forms of global taxation that create effective *incentives* against harmful competitive dynamics. This could speak in favour of both a tax on financial transactions to slow down international financial speculation and, conversely, a centrally organised system of tax benefits for companies that decide to invest locally. Whether both avenues should be pursued (that is, whether a successful internationalist battle against harmful tax competition cannot do without them) is a question that cannot be addressed here; what matters for our present discussion is that these form of global taxation/fiscal easing are worth discussing even from a non-cosmopolitan perspective. These forms of taxation are grounded on the political goal of incentivising or disincentivising certain kinds of behaviour (by promoting global public goods and discouraging the production of global public bads, so to speak), rather than on that of collecting revenues in order to redistribute wealth or provide certain services. Significant chunks of domestic taxation also have such incentivising and disincentivising purposes. The issue of what to do with revenues collected in this way is then a separate issue, and one on which a genuinely open debate could take place.

Limited harmonisation

As we have seen, harmonisation can succeed in blocking uncooperative dynamics and thereby reduce or even stop the competitive downward spiral. Yet, in doing so, it can force countries to adopt uniform and rigid fiscal policies, preventing them from adapting to their different circumstances. Nevertheless, some forms of harmonisation can bypass this danger. The introduction of a universal *minimum* rate for either income or corporate tax (or both) constitutes an example. On the one hand, a minimum rate can offer a good protection against threats to the capacity of a state to maintain the extent of redistribution. On the other, if taxation never falls below a certain minimum (that is to say, if certain extreme cases of tax competition are ruled out) this can, under the right circumstances, slow down competition even above the baseline. Especially in the case of corporate tax, tax advantages might

11. Whether this is the case is an empirical issue that cannot be settled here.

not be enough to offset the loss in know-how, human capital, good infrastructure and so on. If this takes place, the pressure to retain capital and business by offering attractive fiscal packages reduces and it becomes easier for different jurisdictions to implement different fiscal systems over and above the baseline, without fearing the (fiscal) competitive dynamic too much. This, in turn, allows states to retain the third aspect of fiscal sovereignty, as well – namely flexibility and context-sensitivity. This kind of harmonisation works as a *constraint*, rather than as a convergence on fiscal policy *objectives*: one gives up some flexibility in fiscal policy through it, but in order to regain flexibility within the boundaries set by it. A proposal along these lines, restricted to the eurozone, has been put forward recently by Thomas Piketty and others in 'Our manifesto for Europe' (Piketty *et al.* 2014). The proposal envisages eurozone countries sharing a minimum corporate income tax (CIT) rate of 20 per cent, with each country setting their own CIT rate over and above this common base.

Empowering supranational institutions

Finally, and perhaps most importantly, internationalists have reason to transfer coercive sovereign powers *other* than the power to tax from the national to the supranational level. In particular, they might favour transferring the power to punish certain kinds of harmful behaviour. Plausibly, a duty that states have from an internationalist perspective is to agree to outlaw certain kinds of fiscal behaviour.[12] Such an agreement would also be an agreement on establishing a global authority with the power to enforce such a prohibition. This sanctioning power need not be associated with the power to levy taxes. Similarly, as noted above, agreeing on a global minimal tax rate could be a good way to contain harmful tax competition. Now, such a minimal tax rate need not be collected at a global level – states can perfectly well take care of it. For such a remedy to be effective, however, global institutions must be in place and they must enjoy the power to enforce such agreements – and enacting sanctions against non-compliers in a reliable, regular way that is sufficiently certain and costly to the offender would be part and parcel of such a power.

Exactly how the three strategies should be combined and balanced against each other is a question that depends on a series of empirical variables. In this chapter, my aim has been to provide a sufficiently complete list of 'ingredients' – a well balanced recipe for combining them is a task for another day. Nevertheless, I submit that such a tripartite strategy can be a useful blueprint for institutional design in global fiscal matters.

12. For a discussion of this, based on the morally relevant distinction between luring and poaching behaviour in tax competition, see the proposals put forward by Dietsch and Rixen (2014a), which also envisage a global deliberative forum and a dispute-settlement mechanism *à la* WTO to generate and arbitrate on global fiscal policy.

References

Avi-Yonah, R. (2000) 'Globalization, tax competition, and the fiscal crisis of the welfare state', *Harvard Law Review* 113(7): 1573–1676.

Basinger, S. and Hallerberg, M. (2004) 'Remodeling the competition for capital: how domestic politics erases the race to the bottom', *American Political Science Review* 98(2): 261–76.

Blake, M. (2001) 'Distributive justice, state coercion, and autonomy', *Philosophy and Public Affairs*, 30(3): 257–96.

Brock, G. (2008) 'Taxation and global justice: closing the gap between theory and practice', *Journal of Social Philosophy* 39(2): 161–84.

Cohen, J. and Sabel, C. (2006) 'Extra rempublicam nulla justitia?', *Philosophy and Public Affairs* 34(2): 147–75.

Dietsch, P. (2011a) 'Tax competition and its effects on domestic and global justice', in Banai, A. *et al.* (eds) *Social Justice, Global Dynamics: Theoretical and empirical perspectives*, London: Routledge, pp. 95–113.

— (2011b) 'Rethinking sovereignty in international fiscal policy', *Review of International Studies* 37(5): 2107–2120.

Dietsch, P. and Rixen, T. (2014a) 'Tax competition and global background justice', *Journal of Political Philosophy* 22(2): 150–77.

— (2014b) 'Redistribution, globalisation, and multi-level governance', *Moral Philosophy and Politics* 1(1): 61–82.

Gardiner S. *et al.* (eds) (2010) *Climate Ethics: Essential readings*, Oxford: Oxford University Press.

Genschel, P. (2002) 'Globalization, tax competition, and the welfare state', *Politics & Society* 30(2): 245–75.

Genschel, P. and Schwarz, P. (2011) 'Tax competition: a literature review', *Socio-Economic Review* 9(2): 339–70.

Genschel, P. and Seelkopf, L. (2016) 'Winners and losers of tax competition', in Dietsch, P. and Rixen, T. (eds) *Global Tax Governance: What is wrong with it and how to fix it*, Colchester: ECPR Press.

Keen, M. and Simone, A. (2004) 'Is tax competition harming developing countries more than developed?', *Tax Notes International* 34 (Special Supplement): 1317–25.

Laborde, C. and Ronzoni, M. (forthcoming) 'What is a free state? Republican internationalism and globalisation', *Political Studies*, available on Early View at http://onlinelibrary.wiley.com/doi/10.1111/1467-9248.12190/abstract (accessed 26 January 2016).

Loretz, S. (2008) 'Corporate taxation in the OECD in a wider context', *Oxford Review of Economic Policy* 24(4): 639–60.

Miller, D. (1995) *On Nationality*, Oxford: Oxford University Press.

Nagel, T. (2005) 'The problem of global justice', *Philosophy & Public Affairs* 33(2): 113–47.

Piketty, T. *et al.* (2014) 'Our manifesto for Europe', *Guardian*, 2 May: http://www.theguardian.com/commentisfree/2014/may/02/manifesto-europe-radical-financial-democratic (accessed 26 January 2016).

Pogge, T. (2002) *World Poverty and Human Rights*, Cambridge: Polity Press.

Rawls, J. (1999) *The Law of Peoples*, Cambridge, Massachusetts: Harvard University Press.

Rixen, T. (2011) 'Tax competition and inequality: the case for global tax governance', *Global Governance: A review of multilateralism and international institutions* 17(4): 447–67.

Ronzoni, M. (2009) 'The global order: a case of background injustice? A practice-dependent account', *Philosophy and Public Affairs* 37(3): 229–56.

— (2012) 'Two conceptions of state sovereignty and their implications for global institutional design', *Critical Review of International Social and Political Philosophy* 15(5): 573–91.

— (2013) 'For (some) political and institutional cosmopolitanism, (even if) against moral cosmopolitanism', in Brock, G. (ed.): *Cosmopolitanism versus Non-Cosmopolitanism: Critiques, defenses, Reconceptualizations,* Oxford: Oxford University Press, pp. 156–74.

— (2014) 'Global tax governance: the bullets internationalists must bite – and those they must not', *Moral Philosophy and Politics* 1(1): 37–59.

Sangiovanni, A. (2007) 'Global justice, reciprocity, and the state', *Philosophy and Public Affairs* 35(1): 3–39.

Scharpf, F. (1997) 'Introduction: the problem solving capacity of multilevel governance', *Journal of European Public Policy* 4: 520–38.

Scheffler, S. (2001) *Boundaries and Allegiances: Problems of justice and responsibility in liberal thought*, Oxford: Oxford University Press.

Steinmo, S. (2002) 'Globalization and taxation: challenges to the Swedish welfare state', *Comparative Political Studies* 35(7): 839–62.

Swank, D. and Steinmo, S. (2002) 'The new political economy of taxation in advanced capitalist democracies', *American Journal of Political Science* 46(3): 642–55.

Valentini, L. (2011) *Justice in a Globalized World: A normative framework*, Oxford: Oxford University Press.

Wenar, L. (2008) 'Property rights and the resource curse', *Philosophy and Public Affairs* 36(1): 2–32.

Wilson, J. and Wildasin, D. (2004) 'Capital tax competition: bane or boon?', *Journal of Public Economics* 88(6): 1065–91.

Chapter Ten

International Taxation and the Erosion of Sovereignty

*Laurens van Apeldoorn**

The current international taxation regime may, by and large, seem designed to protect the fiscal sovereignty of states. It is true that states are subject to many bilateral taxation treaties; but these treaties have the aim of establishing the jurisdictional boundaries of the respective sovereign states. The basic problem with the international movement of capital is that both the source and the destination country may lay a claim to tax. This opens up the possibility of double taxation, which the treaties aim to prevent by means of the 'territorial disentanglement' of the tax systems. Once jurisdiction is established, countries are free to devise fiscal policies as they see fit, including rules determining the tax base and tax rates. (Rixen 2008: 64; Rixen 2010: 10) There is no co-ordination of tax policies and nor is there, strictly speaking, any superseding international law of taxation; and it has therefore been said that the current system is 'sovereignty-preserving' (Rixen 2008: 64).

Nevertheless, there are significant concerns about the possible erosion of state sovereignty as a result of the current regime. One such concern is much discussed. A central feature of the resulting arrangement is competition between the various sovereign jurisdictions. This is possible because of two further aspects of the system. Global economic integration – as well as a number of regulatory changes such as the reduction of capital controls – have enormously increased the cross-border mobility of capital. Furthermore, states are fiscally interdependent, which is to say that the policy choices of individual governments influence the allocation of the overall tax base. By lowering tax rates, or by otherwise developing an attractive investment climate, states can attract taxable mobile capital, in the form of private wealth, the profits of multinationals and foreign direct investment. The resulting competition limits the effective freedom of states to pursue their desired fiscal policies. After all, they may lose their tax base if they price themselves out of the market.

* Versions of this paper have been presented at the conference Political Legitimacy and the Paradox of Regulation, University of Leiden, 2013; the ECPR Joint Sessions, University of Mainz, 2013; Leuven University (2013), and Utrecht University (2014). I should like to thank the participants of these events for their very helpful comments on drafts of this paper as well as Johan Olsthoorn, Gabriel Wollner, an anonymous reviewer for the ECPR Press. A special thanks is due to the editors of this book for their support and encouragement. I completed this paper while visiting the Centre de recherche en éthique, Université de Montréal, whose financial assistance I gratefully acknowledge.

Commentators conceive this reduction of policy discretion or effectiveness as an erosion of sovereignty. This is sometimes described in terms of a conflict between 'Westphalian' and 'domestic' forms of sovereignty. By signing up to tax treaties that accomplish territorial disentanglement while preserving states' right to determine their own tax base and tax rates, states assert their right to non-interference in internal affairs and, specifically, in their fiscal policy (Dietsch 2011b: 2110; Rixen 2011a). But as a result, their domestic sovereignty, understood as policy discretion or effectiveness, is undermined. It is 'because countries struggle to preserve their Westphalian sovereignty that arbitrage becomes possible and the erosion of domestic sovereignty results' (Dietsch 2011b: 2110).

Other commentators have described this as a conflict between *de jure* and *de facto* sovereignty (Dietsch and Rixen 2014: 153; Rixen 2008: 27). States protect their *de jure* sovereignty, their right to rule, but the resulting tax competition limits their discretionary space to pursue the fiscal policies they want. 'Mobile factors of production have the opportunity to "shop around" to minimize their tax burden. This interdependence of national tax regimes generates external effects that undermine the *de facto* sovereignty of states.' (Dietsch and Rixen 2014: 151). States lose 'the ability to effectively achieve the desired goals of tax policy' (Rixen 2008: 27). Ronzoni (2012) makes this claim in terms of a contrast between 'negative' and 'positive' sovereignty.

In this paper, I aim to provide an alternative account of the erosion of sovereignty in the context of international taxation. While I agree that tax competition undermines sovereignty, I disagree with the arguments that are presented in the literature to arrive at this conclusion. I provide in Sections 1 and 2 an analysis of the concepts of Westphalian and domestic sovereignty as they have been used in the literature. In Section 3, I show that these conceptions of sovereignty cannot be used to support the claim that tax competition undermines sovereignty. In Section 4 I give an account of 'sovereignty as responsibility' (building on Dietsch 2011) and show how this concept can be used show that the decreasing effective fiscal-policy discretion of states in the face of tax competition can be considered an erosion of sovereignty. Finally, in Section 5, I develop an alternative interpretation of the claim that states ought to have effective or positive sovereignty. In the literature, the focus in this context has been exclusively on guaranteeing the *external* conditions that allow states to effectively secure their desired tax-policy goals. I maintain that in the context of international taxation, it is also important to look at the *internal* conditions of effective or positive sovereignty. I do so by emphasising that the authority, and thereby sovereignty, of a state depends on enabling conditions, including specifically democratic decision-making. This enabling condition is not always satisfied in the case of international tax legislation. The predicament of many contemporary states with regard to their fiscal sovereignty is therefore more complex and precarious than has generally been thought. This conclusion leads me to suggest that institutional reforms to increase effective or positive sovereignty in the context of international taxation should focus not only on reshaping the external environment within which states develop their fiscal policies but also on strengthening the democratic character of collective will-formation.

1. Westphalian sovereignty

The concept of what has variously been called 'external', 'negative', or 'Westphalian sovereignty' has at its core the value of non-interference. It is codified in international law and associated with the formally equal status that is bestowed on recognised states in international relations. As a normative concept, it can best be conceptualised as an effective claim-right to non-interference by external actors. I will call such a claim-right to non-interference an 'immunity' (not to be confused with Hohfeldian immunities) or a 'negative right'.[1] This means that for every such right, external actors have a corresponding duty of non-interference. The right to non-interference can be further specified as follows. First, Westphalian sovereignty entails what is called 'territorial integrity', a right to the absence of the occupation or conquest of one's territory. Secondly, it entails a 'right to non-interference in internal affairs' (Buchanan 2007: 263), including the organisation of one's political, social and economic affairs.[2] To say that sovereignty requires the claim-right to non-interference in order to be 'effective' is to say that it is a necessary condition for sovereignty that the corresponding obligations are observed.

In sum, a state has Westphalian sovereignty if and only if it has a claim-right to non-interference by external actors and those external actors observe the corresponding obligations. This is consistent with, for example, Krasner (1999: 20), who defines Westphalian sovereignty as 'territoriality and the exclusion of external actors from domestic authority structures'. 'Rulers', he writes, 'may be constrained, sometimes severely, by the external environment, but they are still free to choose the institutions and policies they regard as optimal. Westphalian sovereignty is violated when external actors influence or determine domestic authority structures.' Similarly, Dietsch (2011b: 2109) maintains that the 'basic rule of Westphalian sovereignty is non-intervention in the internal affairs of other states', which guarantees 'the autonomy of the domestic political authorities over a state's territory'.

In order to emphasise the resulting autonomy of domestic political structures, one might further argue that Westphalian sovereignty includes the right, in Buchanan's terms, 'to promulgate, adjudicate, and enforce legal rules within its territory' (Buchanan 2007: 263). If one does so, however, one should make clear that this right is an immunity. It is a right to the *absence of interference* in promulgating, adjudicating and enforcing legal rules. External actors have an obligation not to interfere in domestic authority structures and, in particular, in the promulgation, adjudication and enforcement of legal rules. By contrast, external

1. Here I follow Ronzoni (2012: 577). A Hohfeldian immunity is an immunity against having one's rights, privileges, claims or powers altered by another. In my terminology, an immunity is a claim-right to non-interference.
2. The UN Charter, Article 2(4) captures both conditions: 'All Members shall refrain in their international relations from the threat or use of force against the territorial integrity or political independence of any state.'

actors do not have an obligation to refrain from altering the environment within which states exercise their authority, short of violating their territorial integrity.

This shows why this form of sovereignty may also be appropriately called 'external' (as in, for example, Philpott 1995: 357). Westphalian sovereignty is only concerned with the distribution of rights and obligations with regard to actors external to the state. It is implausible that sovereign states can only claim immunities with regard to citizens and other internal actors. Rather, it seems more likely that citizens have duties to actively support these activities, including a duty to obey the law. Westphalian sovereignty thus captures only *some* of the rights that the state might be said to enjoy.

Because these rights are immunities, or negative rights, it is also appropriate to call Westphalian sovereignty 'negative sovereignty' (Ronzoni 2012: 577). Ronzoni argues on this basis that this form of sovereignty is 'purely formal' and usually 'impossible to take advantage of' (582). This is so, she maintains, because negative sovereignty has no 'substantive and empirical dimension' (577). States with merely negative sovereignty 'have a formal equal status with other states, but are often forced to accept deals and agreements that they are not, objectively, in a position to refuse' (581). Since these claims are supposed to apply to Westphalian sovereignty, Ronzoni seems to conflate two distinct issues.[3] On the one hand, one may distinguish, as I have done, between negative and positive rights. Westphalian sovereignty can indeed be termed negative because it is based on the attribution of rights to non-interference. On the other hand, one may also distinguish between the formal, negative dimension of having a right and the substantive, positive dimension of having a right respected. With regard to this second distinction, Westphalian sovereignty has a positive dimension, since it requires both that a state has a right to non-interference *and* that the corresponding obligations are, in fact, observed. It therefore provides a real and substantive constraint on the behaviour of states in their international relations, even if this constraint applies to a narrow set of actions. Westphalian sovereignty might not be undermined if a weaker state is forced to accept a deal it would not have accepted had it been more powerful. But Westphalian sovereignty *is* undermined when outsiders arm a militia, overthrow the government and install an autocrat who is more favourable to their interests.[4]

It is worth emphasising that the concept of Westphalian sovereignty does not entail an anarchic system of states operating in a moral vacuum. Dietsch (2011: 2109) maintains that Westphalian sovereignty 'provides the foundation' for that

3. See, for example, Ronzoni 2012: 578 for the definition of Westphalian sovereignty in terms of an 'immunity of non-intervention' and the equation of Westphalian sovereignty with negative sovereignty.

4. One may further note that, morally speaking, the threat-advantage of powerful states is also strictly limited by their obligations to non-interference. A state cannot credibly threaten, say, to start a ground war, since it is not permitted to start a ground war. This is also reflected in UN Charter, Article 2(4), which prohibits the 'threat or use of force'.

latter view,[5] while Krasner (1997: 658) writes that Westphalian sovereignty 'is a basic ontological assumption' of the view that 'states are free of external authority'. But the association of a right to non-intervention with an untrammelled right to self-help is incoherent. If we define Westphalian sovereignty as an effective claim-right to non-interference, as both these authors seemingly do, then the sovereignty of others is at least limited by the duty to respect that right. Henry Shue (2004: 15) eloquently puts it as follows: 'if sovereignty is a right, sovereignty is limited. Sovereignty is limited because the duties that are constitutive of the right, and without which there can be no right, constrain the activity of every sovereign belonging to international society.' What Dietsch and Krasner might have better said is that the two views *share* an ontological assumption, namely, the view that there exist territorially bound, independent states with internally complex political organisations that allow them to operate as agents in an international arena. Or they could have maintained, alternatively, that the rights associated with sovereignty are limited to internal actors while external actors are left free from moral constraints. (This is a possibility that Shue seems to disregard.) But in that latter case we are no longer speaking of Westphalian sovereignty, based on a principle of non-interference, but of what I term domestic sovereignty.

2. Domestic sovereignty

Domestic sovereignty is concerned with the internal composition and, specifically, the political institutions, of the state. Since this conception of sovereignty is contrasted with Westphalian sovereignty (which concerns the obligations of outsiders) domestic sovereignty is sometimes called 'internal' sovereignty, clarifying that this conception of sovereignty (only) concerns the obligations of internal actors.[6] Some authors associate this form of sovereignty exclusively with (absolute and final) political authority.[7] They maintain that sovereignty requires the right to rule, which can be further specified in terms of the right to promulgate, adjudicate and enforce legal rules. Others equate domestic sovereignty with *effective* authority. These authors maintain that sovereignty requires not only the right to rule but also the effective capacity to do so. For example, in one influential

5. He furthermore contrasts 'Westphalian sovereignty that is centred on the notion of non-intervention' with a view of 'sovereignty that assigns duties as well as rights to states' (2011: 2108). My point is that Westphalian sovereignty also assigns rights and duties to states, albeit minimal ones.

6. As Philpott (1995: 357) maintains, 'internal' sovereignty consists of 'supremacy over the land's inhabitants', whereas 'external' sovereignty is concerned with the obligations of outsiders, namely, 'independence from unwanted intervention by an outside authority'. See also Dietsch 2011: 2109: 'Whereas the focus of domestic sovereignty lies on the internal affairs of the state, *Westphalian sovereignty* is a principle meant to govern relations between states.'

7. For instance, F. H. Hinsley (1986: 25–6): 'At the beginning, the idea of sovereignty was the idea that there is a final and absolute political authority in the political community … and no final and absolute authority exists elsewhere.'

account, Krasner (1999: 4) defines domestic sovereignty as involving 'both authority and control, both the specification of legitimate authority within a polity and the extent to which the authority can be effectively exercised'. I follow Krasner and assume that authority and control are both necessary, and jointly sufficient, conditions for domestic sovereignty (and below give an argument for why this assumption is plausible).[8] Authority is the right to rule, the right to promulgate, adjudicate and enforce legal rules within a territory.[9] Citizens (and others present within the territory) have obligations to facilitate and support the exercise of these competences by the state. If one assumes that all government functions are mediated by an effective legal system then it suffices to demand that they obey the law. If the legal system is not functioning properly, or if political institutions are otherwise defective, citizens may have additional obligations to improve these institutions. Since authority is developed in terms of various obligations of citizens to facilitate and support the state in its activities, one may also call this a 'positive' account of sovereignty (in contra-distinction to the 'negative' account of Westphalian sovereignty that requires only non-intervention).[10] Control is to have these rights effectuated, that is to say, to have citizens act on their obligations, in particular on the obligation to obey the law. A state has control if and only if citizens act in accordance with their obligations that are correlated with the right to rule.

In the literature, another account of control is often proposed. Instead of maintaining that control consists of citizens discharging their obligations, as I have done, authors take control to consist simply in the ability of the state to get its way. Krasner (1999: 12), for instance, suggests that control depends on whether a state is able to 'maintain order, collect taxes, regulate pornography, repress drug use, prevent abortion, minimize corruption, or control crime'. The better a state is able to accomplish these goals (provided that it aims to accomplish these goals), the more it is in control and, therefore, the more sovereign it is. This account of the control component of sovereignty as consisting of policy-effectiveness is, ostensibly, shared by Dietsch and Ronzoni. Dietsch, for instance, maintains that domestic sovereignty in the fiscal context depends on the state's ability to effectively determine the 'size of the state as well as the level of the redistribution of income and wealth' (Dietsch 2011b: 2109). Similarly, Ronzoni maintains that a state has 'positive' sovereignty when

8. But I conceive of control differently from Krasner, for reasons I explain in Section 3.

9. Some authors deny that modern nation-states have such authority. For instance, Simmons (1979) and Morris (2002: 213) maintain that authority (and the corresponding obligation to obey) requires explicit consent. Associating sovereignty with authority accordingly has the consequence of denying that modern nation-states are generally sovereign. This is a bullet that Morris is willing to bite. He writes that '[o]ur world in fact turns out to be one of states without sovereignty. In this world, social order is maintained, sometimes only precariously, by power, interest, justice, convention, compromise, benevolence, religious sentiments, ties of kin and nation, and the like.' (Morris 2002: 217).

10. See Ronzoni 2012.

it 'possesses the internal resources to decide which *kind of polity* it wants to become and acts on it successfully' (Ronzoni 2012: 577).

This account of control does not sit well with a rights-based conception of sovereignty. It is far from obvious that a sovereign state has a *right* to be successful in maintaining order, collecting taxes, determining the level of redistribution and so forth. A state may have the right to try to accomplish all those things, in so far as it has the right to rule, and citizens may have corresponding obligations to facilitate and support the state in aiming to accomplish these goals. However, once citizens have discharged these obligations, there is nothing else a sovereign-state can demand as a matter of sovereign-right. This is generally recognised in areas where the lack of control is not due to the failure of actors to discharge their obligations associated with the state's right to rule. Thus we would not generally say that state's sovereignty is undermined as the result of floods or earthquakes, or the limitations of the laws of physics.[11]

Perhaps I should emphasise that this should not lead us to conclude that sovereignty has no control component at all. Shue notes, as I have done, that limited policy effectiveness by itself is no reason to deny a state's sovereignty:

> that the actual control over their economic fortunes that can be successfully exercised by modern states is, in fact, limited is, of course, not at all the same thing as their sovereignty over economic matters being limited, since sovereignty is a matter of the proper authority to try to exert power even where the exertions may turn out to be futile. Domestic criminal law is regularly broken, but until the violations approach the point of general disorder, only the power, not the authority, of the state is put in question by the lawbreaking (1997: 348).

Shue thus seems to think sovereignty is best accounted for in terms of authority alone. Only when authority is undermined, for instance because of the state's inability to guarantee individual safety and public order, can we say that sovereignty is eroded. But this view is unable to account for situations in which large-scale law-breaking undermines the effectiveness of policies without, however, causing general disorder. An example is the attempt of the United States government in the 1920s to prohibit the manufacture and sale of alcoholic beverages. The policy was largely ineffective. Although alcohol consumption declined, large-scale home-brewing and bootlegging could not be prevented. This did not undermine the (presumed) authority of the state. However, individuals did not act on their (presumed) obligations to support the state in its endeavour to rule, as the result of which the policy-effectiveness of the state was undermined. The policy of prohibition would have been effective had citizens obeyed the law and

11. This claim should be qualified, since the authority of the state may be dependent on guaranteeing certain minimal conditions, such as relative stability and public order, which could be upset by natural disasters. However, in such a case it is the authority component of domestic sovereignty, not the control component, that is undermined.

thereby discharged their obligations associated with the authority of the state. It thus seems appropriate to say that, in such cases, in which the state is unable to effectuate its policy goals due to a failure of citizens to discharge their obligations, the domestic sovereignty of the state is eroded.

3. International taxation: Westphalian and domestic sovereignty

It seems that the current international-taxation regime is both sovereignty-preserving – since it disentangles the territoriality of tax systems and thereby protects the authority of states to determine fiscal policy – and sovereignty-undermining – since the resulting tax competition decreases states' fiscal policy discretion. As noted, this paradox is sometimes expressed in terms of a conflict between Westphalian and domestic sovereignty (for example, Dietsch 2011: 2110).

Although the claim that tax competition is sovereignty-undermining is a version of a common view about the effect of processes of globalisation on state sovereignty,[12] it cannot be defended on the basis of the account of Westphalian and domestic sovereignty just outlined. In accordance with the definition provided above, domestically sovereign states have a right to promulgate, adjudicate and enforce legal rules, which translates into associated obligations of citizens to support the policies of the state. Domestic sovereignty is eroded when the state is unable to effectuate its policy goals due to a failure of citizens to discharge their obligations. However, the decreased ability of states to effectively pursue desired fiscal policies is not due to internal actors neglecting to discharge their obligations, such as, for instance, their obligation to pay tax. One may, of course, maintain that the decline in effective fiscal policy control, as the result of tax competition, is regrettable, since it exacerbates inequalities within and between states (Dietsch and Rixen 2014: 151; Dietsch 2011a). However, there are many things that states cannot do that might lead to a more just and equitable world. In order to show that the states' inability to pursue them is an erosion of sovereignty, it must be shown that these effects are the result of non-compliance with the obligations correlated with the authority of the state. The same may be said with regard to the concepts of *de facto* sovereignty employed by Dietsch and Rixen (2014) and positive sovereignty employed by Ronzoni (2012). It cannot be enough simply to point out that either the effectiveness of policies or the range of realistic policy options has decreased. In order to show that the control component of sovereignty is eroded, one must show that the state is unable to reach its desired policy goals *because relevant parties do not discharge their obligations to support the state in its effort to rule*. For this reason, I maintain that the authors discussed in this section fail to show that tax competition leads to an erosion of sovereignty.

---

12. Krasner, for instance, maintains that in a globalised world, states still have authority, that is, the right to legislate and adjudicate and implement law, but that they are increasingly limited in their capacity to reach their policy goals (Krasner 1999: 12).

4. Sovereignty as responsibility

Westphalian and domestic sovereignty, as outlined above, can consistently be attributed simultaneously to one state. It is conceptually coherent to maintain that states have positive rights to be supported in their activities by internal actors, while they only have negative rights to non-interference with regard to external actors. It is, however, an open question whether this best captures the rights that states have. In particular, the principle of non-interference may not best capture the obligations that states have with regard to other states. May it rather be the case that outsiders, too, have positive obligations to support a state in its endeavour to rule?

It is this kind of question that has led commentators to develop the concept of 'sovereignty as responsibility'.[13] To be a sovereign state, the argument goes, does not only entail having certain rights but also entails a number of responsibilities. A state loses its authority, its right to rule, and thereby its sovereignty, if it fails to discharge these responsibilities. This, by itself, is compatible with the concept of domestic sovereignty. Even Thomas Hobbes, who gave us one of the classic accounts of domestic sovereignty, maintains that the capacity to ensure the safety of individuals and the presence of order is a necessary condition for authority.[14] One can further argue that the authority of a sovereign state is dependent on discharging the responsibility to protect the human rights of its citizens, to promote their well-being, or to secure a reasonably just society, without going beyond the concept of domestic sovereignty. Those who defend the concept of 'sovereignty as responsibility', however, argue that these responsibilities of states are not limited to their citizens but that states also have obligations to take into account the effects of their policies on outsiders, in ways that go over and above the Westphalian obligation of non-intervention (see Dietsch 2011b: 2115; Shue 2004).

Dietsch (2011b) utilises this argument to show that tax co-operation does not necessarily conflict with sovereignty. Tax co-operation seems to erode sovereignty since it requires surrendering certain juridical prerogatives with regard to determining fiscal policy. However, Dietsch observes that

> under the paradigm of sovereignty as responsibility, it seems that sovereignty so understood is much less likely to conflict with tax co-operation in the first place. After all, the goal of tax co-operation is precisely to create an institutional framework under which the efforts of states to promote the fundamental interests of their citizens are not undermined by other states (2011b: 2115).

The sovereign state is limited by a set of obligations but 'these constraints are not to be viewed as constraints *on* sovereignty, but as constraints *of* sovereignty.' (2011b: 2116).

13. For an early argument, see, for example, Deng *et al.* 1996.

14. Some would even make the case that it is a sufficient condition, since he claims that there exists a 'mutuall Relation between Protection and Obedience' (Hobbes 1991: 491).

In what follows I want to suggest that the concept of sovereignty as responsibility also allows us to argue for the converse claim, namely, that sovereignty *is* eroded as the result of tax competition. The argument starts by following Dietsch (2011b) in maintaining that states have, by virtue of their sovereignty (as responsibility), obligations to promote the fundamental interests of individuals external to the state, over and above non-interference. These obligations can be characterised as obligations that correlate to the right of other states to rule. This claim rests on the view that states have authority – the right to promulgate, adjudicate and enforce laws – because this is more likely to promote the fundamental interests of individuals than other arrangements.[15] The authority of the state is thus grounded in the instrumental relationship it has to promoting the fundamental interests of individuals (which could be expected if one takes the pursuit of those fundamental interests to be an enabling condition of authority). This means that state A can best discharge its obligations to citizens of state B by supporting state B's ability to rule. Conversely, the correlating obligations to the right of state B to rule are shared by the citizens of state B and by (the citizens of) state A. In other words, for the same reason that state A has the right to rule because it is the best way to promote the fundamental interests of citizens of state A, state A has the obligation to support state B in ruling because that is the best way to promote the fundamental interests of citizens of state B.

This has implications for the conceptualisation of the control component of sovereignty. Above, I maintained that (domestic) sovereignty consists of both authority and control, and that the control component of sovereignty should be understood in terms of having *effective* authority, which is to require that all those who have obligations correlating to the right to rule discharge their obligations. The conclusion now follows that the control of states, and thereby their sovereignty, may be eroded if other states fail to act on their obligations to support the state to rule. The effective authority of a state may be undermined if citizens fail to discharge their obligations to obey the law; but it may also be undermined if other states fail to act on their obligations to support the state in pursuing its policy objectives.

Dietsch (2011a) has shown that, arguably, tax competition leads to greater inequality within and between countries and therefore may be thought to exacerbate domestic and global distributive injustice. Take the former. I argued above that this phenomenon is not plausibly the result of citizens failing to discharge their obligations with regard to the authority of the state and therefore that it could not be conceived as an erosion of sovereignty. But now it could be argued that the

15. Following Dietsch and Rixen (2014: 173–4), one can provide at least two arguments for this position. First, with Caney (2006), one may argue that a cosmopolitan concern for each individual as ultimate unit of moral concern requires a certain amount of state autonomy if there exists pluralism about conceptions of justice. If people disagree about what justice requires, then state authority could ensure that we do not impose a conception of justice on individuals who might not share it. Secondly, with Goodin (1988), one may maintain that state authority might be the best way to promote the interests of individuals worldwide, since states are better able to identify and cater to the interests of individuals than, for example, a world government.

reduced fiscal policy effectiveness is due to other states failing to discharge their obligations correlated to the authority of the state. Dietsch (2011b) has shown that tax co-operation may be required to satisfy the enabling conditions of authority – since it may be a way to ameliorate the harmful effects of tax competition and so would increase domestic distributive justice – or at least for states adequately to 'take into account the effects of their policies on the citizens of other states' (2115). If this is true, then we can also conclude that tax competition leads to an erosion of sovereignty. Tax competition results from states refraining from discharging obligations (which they have by virtue of their sovereignty-as-responsibility) that are correlated with the right other states have to rule. The reduced fiscal-policy effectiveness that is due to continuing tax competition therefore constitutes an erosion of control and thereby an erosion of sovereignty.[16]

5. Sovereignty and collective will-formation

This emphasis on the enabling conditions of authority also points towards a second relevant form of sovereignty-erosion. In the previous section, I argued that sovereignty may be eroded if the state lacks *control*, understood as effective authority. I will now argue that sovereignty can also be eroded if the enabling conditions of the *authority* of the state are not satisfied. Plausibly, one such enabling condition is a process of what one might call collective will-formation. This was recognised by Hobbes. The Hobbesian sovereign speaks for all subjects because they have all submitted their will to his will. It is from this unity of the will of all individuals, Hobbes claims, that sovereignty is born (Hobbes 1991: 120). Other accounts of collective will-formation are, of course, possible. I assume that democratic decision-making is an enabling condition for authority. That is to say, that the state can act with authority if its legislation and enforcement is democratically legitimated. I further assume that the justification for requiring democratic decision-making in this way is partly instrumental and partly intrinsic. There is an intrinsic value to democracy because of the importance of political participation and conferring equal political rights. There is an instrumental value to democracy because democratic decision-making is apt to increase the justness of the decisions, since the interests of all affected are taken into account.

The importance of democratic decision-making for sovereignty in the context of fiscal policy is not always fully recognised. Ronzoni (2012), who conceives of 'positive sovereignty' as analogous to positive freedom, a form

16. Note that this argument renders claims about (the erosion of) sovereignty dependent on a prior account of what justice requires. This means that it is not possible, as Ronzoni (2012) apparently does, to argue that an arrangement is unjust *because* it leads to erosions of sovereignty. Ronzoni argues that 'the global order might be politically unjust in that it creates unjustifiable systemic obstacles to positive sovereignty' (583). I have argued that her account of positive sovereignty as policy effectiveness fails to make explicit what rights-claims support that demand for policy effectiveness. The conclusion I draw here is that these rights-claims must be based on a theory of justice.

of 'self-mastery' (577), nevertheless only focuses on the external conditions that allow states to do what they will. However, self-mastery presumably also includes an appropriate process of collective will-formation and thus a specific form of internal organisation.[17] Dietsch and Rixen (2014) and Dietsch (2011b) do not mention democratic legitimation as an enabling condition for the authority of the state. Indeed, Dietsch and Rixen make 'the simplifying assumption that governments perfectly track their citizens' preferences' (2014: 153), thereby presupposing the existence of a democratic process of collective will-formation. By relaxing this assumption, it becomes possible to conceptualise a second form of sovereignty-erosion, namely, erosion due to a lack of *authority* as opposed to a lack of *control*. That may happen if a state lacks effective political institutions that guarantee democratic collective will-formation. I provide two examples. These examples come from a literature that is critical of the way in which legislation is written and enacted in states that most aggressively pursue policies of tax competition, namely, so-called tax havens. Tax havens are countries that aim to attract 'international trade-oriented activities by minimization of taxes and the reduction or elimination of other restrictions on business operations' (Johns 1983: 20). They are the 'crowbars' of tax competition.

The first example is the introduction of the Financial Center Development Act of 1981 in Delaware, a small state in the north-east of the USA. Among other things, the law eliminated caps on consumer interest rates, also called 'usury' restrictions, and applied a regressive corporate tax structure to the income generated by the banks within Delaware. At the time, the *New York Times* noted that the legislation was drafted 'in private', by 'lawyers for two large New York banks, the Chase Manhattan Bank and J. P. Morgan & Company, without any written analysis by any Delaware official involved'. Other parties, including the press and the public were 'intentionally kept in the dark'. When the bill was passed, many of the legislators claimed they 'did not understand the complicated measure before voting on it' (Gerth 1981). Several further bills were developed and passed in the years that followed, including legislation that would allow foreign banks to benefit from the regressive tax structures; laws that, according to some, turned Delaware into a full-blown tax haven. They were largely written by lawyers representing 'Morgan, Chase, Citicorp, Bank of New York, and Bankers Trust' (Shaxson 2011: 174).

A similar pattern can be observed in the second example, the introduction of the 1996 Special Limited Liability Partnership Law in Jersey, a British Crown Dependency. The law allows companies, in particular, the big accountancy firms, to operate under limited liability while also benefiting from the perks that

17. This is noted by Isaiah Berlin, on whom Ronzoni draws to develop her analogy of sovereignty with freedom, when he writes in 'Two concepts of liberty' that ascribing to someone positive freedom requires identifying the individual with the 'real' or 'autonomous' self, 'which calculates and aims at what will satisfy it in the long run', as opposed to the 'heteronomous' self, driven by 'irrational impulse, uncontrolled desires' (Berlin 2002: 179).

come with being a partnership, such as less disclosure, lower taxes and weaker regulation. The bill was proposed and drafted by Ernst & Young and Price Waterhouse, 'fast-tracked', and implemented with no meaningful opposition from the legislature. Several commentators see the episode as indicative of the condition of political institutions in Jersey: 'As exemplified by the LLP legislation episode, major firms can draft their own laws and the Jersey government promises to simply nod them through with minimal scrutiny.' (Mitchell *et al.* 2002: 53). This was possible because, first, political power in Jersey is highly concentrated in the hands of a small group of people. One member of Jersey's parliament comments that '[f]or over a century Jersey's ruling elite has had an unchallenged monopoly of power … With no clear division between the legislature, judiciary and executive there is an absence of checks and balances.' (Mitchell *et al.* 2002: 35). A second reason was that many of the members of the parliament had hardly any experience or knowledge of the complexities of international finance: 'They can argue at enormous length about the budget for the local pony club … but a new limited liability law or a new trust law will go unchallenged. It's the captured state.' (Shaxson 2011: 181).

Much of the recent literature, discussed above, maintains that tax competition is the result of the structural features of the current international financial system. Assuming that states perfectly track their citizens' preferences and interests, they respond to competitive pressures by lowering their tax rates and otherwise aiming to provide an attractive investment climate. States have limited fiscal policy discretion but they do what is best for their citizens given the circumstances. These examples, however, tell a different story. In these cases, the legislation is not simply the result of limited fiscal policy discretion. Rather, it is the result of a political process that fails to pass the test of democratic legitimacy. This is how we can understand the worry of several commentators that these tax havens have their 'legislature for hire' and their 'sovereignty for sale' (*see*, for example, Palan 2002b; Christensen and Hampton 1999. See also Palan *et al.* 2010: 187). In these cases, the authority-component of sovereignty is eroded. This raises the question whether these laws do, in fact, further the interests of the citizens of the state in question. An answer to this question is difficult to give, because it would involve providing an account of the counter-factual, in which the democratic process did function properly. It is clear enough, though, that in so far we value democratic government for intrinsic reasons, it is not in the interest of the citizens of Jersey or Delaware to have laws passed without proper consultation and oversight. And since very specific interest-groups shaped the content of these laws, it would be coincidental, at best, if they did, in fact, further the interests of citizens.

6. Conclusion

In the preceding sections, I have pursued two objectives. First, I have discussed recent literature on the concept of sovereignty in the context of international taxation. I have attempted to show that these recent accounts are unsuccessful in their attempts to show that tax competition undermines or erodes the sovereignty of states. This is because it is assumed that it is enough to show that fiscal policy discretion or effectiveness has decreased as the result of such competition. I have argued that this conclusion requires instead showing that the decreasing policy effectiveness is due to actors failing to discharge their obligations correlated with the authority of the state. I have provided such an argument. Secondly, I have shown that the recent literature has insufficiently emphasised the importance of the authority component of sovereignty. It is the authority component that comes under pressure when states allow the financial sector to determine legislation in ways that evade democratic control. The sovereignty of states may thus be eroded in two distinct ways. A state may lack *control* because it is unable to effectively implement and enforce policies it legislates (or wants to legislate), due to the failure of individuals or other states to discharge their obligations to support the state in its efforts to rule. But it may also lack *authority* because the process of collective will-formation is defective.

Dietsch and Rixen (2014) have proposed an institutional scheme that could limit the strategic behaviour that states are allowed to engage in in order to attract foreign capital, and so would curb tax competition. Although this proposal would require sovereign states to accept certain limitations on their authority to write fiscal legislation, these limitations would restore the control component of sovereignty. It would provide countries greater freedom to determine the size of the public budget and the extent of redistribution, and so allow them to better pursue the fundamental interests of their citizens. However, since, as I have argued, sovereignty also requires democratic decision-making, such institutional reforms to curb tax competition as proposed by Dietsch and Rixen must be pursued in tandem with reforms to increase democratic control over fiscal policy legislation, where such control is shown to be defective. Policies to improve the quality of democratic decision-making, which could include institutional capacity-building, more robust consultation procedures or transparency initiatives, may not be easy, given the highly technical nature of much international tax legislation. However, only if legislation tracks the preferences of citizens can we be assured that states utilise the greater control they are afforded to the benefit of their citizens.

Bibliography

Berlin, I. (2002) *Liberty: Incorporating Four Essays on Liberty*, edited by Hardy, H. and with an essay by Harris, I., Oxford: Oxford University Press.

Buchanan, A. (2007) *Justice, Legitimacy and Self-Determination*, Oxford: Oxford University Press.

Caney, S. (2006) 'Cosmopolitan justice and institutional design: an egalitarian liberal conception of global governance', *Social Theory & Practice* 34(4): 725–56.

Christensen, J. and Hampton, M. P. (1999) 'A legislature for hire: the capture of the state in Jersey's Offshore Finance Centre', in Hampton, M. P. and Abbott, J. (eds) *Offshore Finance Centers and Tax Havens: The rise of global capital*, West Lafayette, Indiana: Purdue University Press.

Deng, F. *et al*., (1996) *Sovereignty as Responsibility: Conflict management in Africa*, Washington, DC: Brookings Institution Press.

Dietsch, P. (2011a) 'Tax competition and its effects on domestic and global justice', in Banai, A., Ronzoni, M. and Schemmel, C. (eds.) *Social Justice, Global Dynamics: Theoretical and empirical perspectives*, London: Routledge.

— (2011b) 'Rethinking sovereignty in international fiscal policy', *Review of International Studies* 37(5): 2107–20.

Dietsch, P. and Rixen, T. (2014) 'Tax competition and global background justice', *Journal of Political Philosophy* 22(2): 150–77.

Gerth, J. (1981) 'New York banks urged Delaware to lure bankers', *New York Times*, 17 March.

Goodin, R. (1988) 'What is so special about our fellow countrymen?', *Ethics* 98(4): 663–86.

Hinsley, F. H. (1986) *Sovereignty*, Cambridge: Cambridge University Press.

Hobbes, T. (1991) *Leviathan* [Revised Student's Edition], Cambridge: Cambridge University Press.

Johns, R. A. (1983) *Tax Havens and Offshore Finance*, New York: St Martin's Press.

Krasner, S. (1997) 'Pervasive not perverse: semi-sovereigns as the global norm', *Cornell International Law Review*, 30(3): 651–80.

— (1999) *Sovereignty: Organized hypocrisy*, Princeton, New Jersey: Princeton University Press.

Mitchell, A. *et al*. (2002) *No Accounting for Tax Havens*, Basildon, Essex: Association for Accountancy & Business Affairs.

Morris, C. (2002) *An Essay on the Modern State*, Cambridge: Cambridge University Press.

Palan, R. (2002a) 'Trying to have your cake and eating it: how and why the state system has created offshore', *International Studies Quarterly* 42(4): 625–43.

— (2002b) 'Tax havens and the commercialization of state sovereignty', *International Organization* 56(1): 151–76.

Palan, R. *et al.* (2010) *Tax Havens: How globalization really works*, Ithaca, New York: Cornell University Press.

Philpott, D. (1995) 'Sovereignty: an introduction and brief history', *Journal of International Affairs* 48(2): 353–68.

Rixen, T. (2008) *The Political Economy of International Tax Governance*, Basingstoke: Palgrave Macmillan.

— (2010) 'From double tax avoidance to tax competition: explaining the institutional trajectory of international tax governance', *Review of International Political Economy* 18(2): 197–227.

— (2011) 'Tax competition and inequality – the case for global tax governance', *Global Governance: A Review of Multilateralism and International Institutions* 17(4): 447–67.

Ronzoni, M. (2012) 'Two conceptions of state sovereignty and their implications for global institutional design', *Critical Review of International Social and Political Philosophy* 15(5): 573–91.

Shaxson, N. (2011) *Treasure Islands*, London: Bodley Head.

Shue, H. (1997) 'Eroding sovereignty: the advance of principle', in McKim, R. and McMahan, J. (eds) *The Morality of Nationalism*, Oxford: Oxford University Press.

— (2004) 'Limiting sovereignty', in Welsh, J. M. (ed.) *Humanitarian Intervention in International Relations*, Oxford and New York: Oxford University Press.

Simmons, A. J. (1979) *Moral Principles and Political Obligations*, Princeton, New Jersey: Princeton University Press.

Wilson, J. D. and Wildasin, D. E. (2004) 'Capital tax competition: bane or boon?', *Journal of Public Economics* 88(6): 1065–91.

Chapter Eleven

Whose Tax Base? The Ethics of Global Tax Governance

*Peter Dietsch**

The debate on the social implications of tax competition has come a long way in recent years. Catalysed initially by the OECD study on 'harmful tax competition' in 1998, the practices by which individuals and multinational corporations are able to either evade or avoid paying taxes in an environment of tax competition have increasingly come under scrutiny. Global estimates of private wealth being stashed away illegally in offshore bank accounts, or of the billions of dollars that governments are thought to lose to profit-shifting by multinational enterprises (MNEs) every year,[1] underline the significance of the question; and the coming to light of particular cases[2] contributes just as much – if not more – to public outrage.

Public awareness of and disgust with the *status quo* of global tax governance have pushed open a window of opportunity for reform. Multilateral measures by both the EU and the OECD to increase transparency and to curtail the possibilities for profit-shifting are starting to bite; and even some unilateral reforms – like the Foreign Account Tax Compliance Act (FATCA) passed by the US in 2010 – are producing encouraging results (*see* Hakelberg 2016, Chapter Six; and Grinberg 2016, Chapter Seven in this volume). Yet, while real progress is no doubt being made, I think it is fair to characterise the regulatory response to the phenomenon of tax competition thus far as *ad hoc*. Granted, the fact that coordinated, multilateral reform is happening represents a step in the right direction; but not enough thought is given to the *principles* that should guide this reform. Today's policy is driven by the need for cash-strapped governments to find ways to increase their tax take as well as by a motivation to target specific practices that have stoked public anger, rather than by a coherent, well-thought-out vision of what would constitute a just system of global tax governance.

---

* I thank Lyne Latulippe, Thomas Rixen, and Miriam Ronzoni for their very helpful comments.

1. Given the opaqueness of tax evasion and avoidance, estimates are hard to come by. Figures for the global undeclared wealth held offshore range from $5.1 trillion (Zucman 2013) to $21–31 trillion (Henry 2012). As to the profit-shifting practices of MNEs, consider the following statistic from a recent report (McIntyre *et al.* 2014). Out of 288 Fortune 500 companies that were profitable in every single year between 2008 and 2012, 111 of them (39 per cent) paid zero or less (i.e., they got a refund) corporate tax in the US in at least one of the five years.
2. At the individual level, think of the French minister Jérôme Cahuzac, who had to resign following a tax-evasion scandal; *see* Laurent 2013. At the corporate level, recent examples include the preferential treatment Apple received in Ireland and Amazon in Luxembourg. See Bradshaw *et al.* 2014 and Houlder *et al.* 2014b.

The objective of this chapter is to provide an overview of some candidate principles that could sustain such a vision. It is based on the premise that we should take seriously the value of fiscal autonomy of states, where fiscal autonomy refers to the *effective* capacity of polities to set their fiscal policy.[3] I do not mean to play down either the value of reform efforts to date or the challenge of overcoming collective-action problems and vested interests when pursuing reform. However, setting out the fundamental normative choices we have to make for such reform is not merely necessary but will, in fact, make the case for reform stronger.

The chapter starts by distinguishing *virtual* from *real* tax competition. In short, virtual tax competition refers to what the OECD has called the 'poaching' of tax base from another country (OECD 1998: 16). While the tax base, that is, the individual wealth or the corporate profits, shifts, the owner of the capital or the economic activity in question stays put. Real tax competition, on the other hand, involves individuals changing their residence or corporations moving their economic activity to another jurisdiction. (*See* Section 1 for a more detailed analysis of these two types of tax competition.) When asking in what sense either of these practices might be problematic from an ethical standpoint, we need to establish what value or principle, if any, they violate.

I argue that the normative questions raised by virtual tax competition are relatively straightforward to deal with. More specifically, Section 2 argues that some form of an economic-nexus principle is hard to dismiss and that such a principle will call for an outright ban on poaching. In addition, I explain where such a ban differs from existing initiatives against tax evasion and, in particular, against tax avoidance. Incidentally, this establishes a direct link to Part Two of this volume concerning the shortcomings of the current regulatory framework and of various reform initiatives that are being proposed in response. The case of real tax competition, by contrast, proves to be considerably more controversial from an ethical perspective. The final section of the paper lays out a number of positions one might defend on this issue.[4] Depending on the normative weight these positions assign to the value of fiscal autonomy, and on how they interpret this concept, they end up being more or less tolerant towards real tax competition.

1. Two kinds of tax competition: virtual versus real

The expression 'tax competition' refers to interactive tax-setting by independent governments in a non-cooperative, strategic way. In a system with capital

3. What I call fiscal autonomy is coextensive with Rixen's (2016, Chapter Fifteen in this volume) term of *de facto* sovereignty. Ronzoni (2016, Chapter Nine in this volume) uses fiscal autonomy and fiscal sovereignty interchangeably, as do I. Van Apeldoorn (2016, Chapter Ten in this volume) makes a distinction between sovereignty, which he uses for interstate relations and in a weaker sense compared to my notion, and autonomy, which he uses when referring to domestic political structures.

4. Together with Thomas Rixen, I have taken a more definitive stance on this issue elsewhere: see Dietsch and Rixen 2014a. In the present chapter our position in this previous work is merely considered as *one possible* normative response to real tax competition.

mobility, jurisdictions use both their tax rates and other aspects of the regulatory fiscal environment to attract capital from abroad.[5] Two basic scenarios have to be distinguished here.

Virtual tax competition

In the first scenario, the favourable tax environment in country A leads individual residents of country B or MNEs that are engaged in economic activity in B to shift their wealth or paper profits to country A. Note that in these cases, the residence of the individual taxpayer and the location of the economic activity of the MNE are not affected. This is crucial, since the residence principle (for individuals) and the source principle (for the active business income of MNEs) are generally accepted principles for the allocation of tax base. Both the residence and the economic activity remain in country B in this first scenario; it is only the individual or corporate *capital* that shifts to country A. Therefore, we can call this kind of tax competition *virtual* tax competition – there is no actual change in fiscal status but the mere appearance of it. That said, the distributive effects of virtual tax competition are very real.

This way of presenting what is going on also explains why the OECD has qualified these forms of tax competition as instances of *poaching*. Country A is straying into what, according to the residence and source principles, should really be part of the tax base of country B.

To make our analysis more tangible, consider two different cases. First, in the case of individuals, those who hide part of their income from the tax authorities of their country of tax residence – in this case mostly capital gains generated by wealth held offshore – are breaking the law. It is only because they can hide their wealth behind the veil of bank secrecy or the privacy protection of trust law that they are able to get away with it. As the estimates cited in the introduction show, and despite recent efforts to curtail tax evasion, people seem to be quite successful at getting away with it.

Second, with respect to the corporate shifting of profits from active business income, consider the by now infamous 'Double Irish' tax structure, which is used by Google and a host of other MNEs. With this and other structures, MNEs exploit differences between the tax codes of two countries. For instance, they create two subsidiaries in Ireland, one of them being controlled and managed in Ireland and the other formed in Ireland but controlled and managed in a low-tax jurisdiction, say, Bermuda. Skipping some of the technical details of this arrangement (*cf.* Darby III 2007), the Bermuda-controlled subsidiary will then license intellectual property to the Ireland-controlled subsidiary. For US tax purposes, the two subsidiaries will be treated as one Irish entity, making the intra-firm licence agreement fiscally irrelevant. For Irish tax purposes, on the other hand, the licence fees received by the Bermuda-controlled subsidiary will not be taxable either. The difference between

5. While this chapter focuses on tax competition between *states*, other levels of government, such as provinces or municipalities, also engage in tax competition.

the two tax regimes that allows MNEs to get away with double non-taxation is that the US determines the tax base with reference to the jurisdiction of incorporation, whereas in Ireland it matters where the corporation is managed and controlled. The Double Irish allows a number of MNEs to reduce their tax burden significantly. To get an idea of the sums at stake, Google funnelled €9bn of royalty payments to Bermuda in 2012 alone (Houlder 2013).

Even though Ireland has recently given in to international pressure and vowed to close the Double Irish loophole (Boland 2014), victory in this one battle against corporate tax avoidance does not imply that governments are winning the war. The Double Irish is just one item on a long menu of tax-avoidance strategies that MNEs employ. Other prominent examples that also involve one state poaching parts of the tax base of another include transfer-pricing (using over- or under-invoicing to transfer profits to low-tax jurisdictions); booking e-commerce transactions in low-tax jurisdictions; and earnings-stripping (taking out loans from foreign subsidiaries with the interest payments becoming tax-deductible). In contrast to individual tax evasion, most of these strategies of corporate tax-avoidance respect the letter of the law,[6] even though they clearly violate its spirit. A revealing statistic in this context is the fact that 60 per cent of international trade is intra-firm (OECD 2002). Given the ample opportunities to minimise taxes that international intra-firm trade offers, it is plausible to think that a significant proportion of it is fiscally motivated.

In sum, both individual tax-evasion and corporate profit-shifting constitute virtual tax competition because neither individual residence nor the location of economic activity change. The government that engages in virtual tax competition is poaching the tax base of other states.

Real tax competition

By contrast, real tax competition triggers a change of residence or a relocation of economic activity respectively. From the perspective of the government that engages in real tax competition, the tax base in question is *lured* to become a legitimate part of the competing government's tax base, even if this does not imply that any tax will actually be levied (Dietsch and Rixen 2014a: 161*ff.*).

Consider the following illustrations. When the French actor Gérard Depardieu moves to Russia, or when a whole battery of sports stars set up their residence in Monaco or a low-tax Swiss canton, they take their tax base with them.[7] While this kind of case regularly captures the attention of the media, it is not clear how important a phenomenon this represents in practice. After all, individuals are socially attached to their residence – it is not a mere residence, it is home – and

6. Though this is not true for all of them. Transfer mispricing, for example, regularly violates OECD and WTO regulation on the issue.

7. The rule of thumb to determine residence for tax purposes is whether one has spent more than 182 days in a given country. Incidentally, this has led to the phenomenon of the permanent tourist – a small number of very wealthy people who are regularly on the move in order to not be liable to pay taxes anywhere.

so the fiscal incentive to move has to be substantial to have any bite. Of course, the question of how widespread such moves are is a separate issue from their acceptability.

The situation is different for MNEs. Foreign direct investment (FDI) decisions are, in part, based on fiscal considerations, and some countries make a concerted effort to lure FDI. While FDI obviously depends on a number of factors, including the quality of infrastructure and of human capital, empirical studies confirm that fiscal policy plays an important role. In practice, multinationals frequently 'shop around' for a favourable tax arrangement among a number of potential locations (Palan 2002). They will identify a number of locations that equally satisfy their general business needs and then play the different jurisdictions off against each other to negotiate the best deal.[8] Empirical studies confirm that FDI is sensitive to tax rates but they also find that the strength of the correlation is very much affected by the method of measurement and the kinds of taxes investigated (de Mooij and Ederveen 2008).

In addition to the luring of FDI, we need to mention another practice, which can be characterised as a cross between luring and poaching.[9] While the active business income of MNEs is generally taxed according to the source principle, the same is not true for passive income. Here, the right to tax, by and large, lies with the country of residence. However, when the country of residence decides to exempt foreign-source income, or at least to tax it less heavily, it thereby creates an incentive for MNEs to relocate their headquarters or residence to its territory. These headquarters havens do not lure the economic activity that underlies the active business income of MNEs; but they do lure in the administrative tasks that determine residence, thus creating significant tax-avoidance potential regarding passive income. Exploiting this potential is one important motivation behind the recent wave of 'corporate inversions' (Houlder *et al.* 2014a). Since shifting a head office is a relocation of real economic activity, these cases represent a type of luring; at the same time, since the active income-generating activity stays put, they are forms of poaching.

To complete this overview of poaching and luring practices, let me add two observations that will be relevant to whether we should consider them ethical or not. First, note that there is a potentially very significant substitutive relationship between poaching and luring. As long as MNEs are able to reduce their effective tax rate through profit-shifting, their opportunity-costs of doing business in a nominally high-tax environment are relatively low (Keen 2001; Dharmapala 2008: 671–76). However, a crackdown on poaching would clearly increase the

8. See Story 2012 for an insightful survey of this phenomenon in the US. For an extreme but not unique case of tax-break or subsidy-shopping, consider the move by Nokia from Bochum in Germany in 2008 – after it had received €60m in subsidies the year before with the understanding that its factory would operate for eleven years – first to Romania – where the Romanian state contributed another €37m– and then to China in 2011. See *Financial Times* 2008 as well as Thorpe 2011.

9. I thank Lyne Latulippe for encouraging me to treat separately the phenomenon described in this paragraph.

incentives for MNEs to actually relocate. This is an important parameter for any reform agenda for global tax governance.

Second, the dynamics of both poaching and luring favour small states. Whereas for large states, the loss of revenue resulting from lowering a particular tax rate is likely to outweigh the revenue gain, due to capital inflows, the reverse is true for small countries.[10] While this is not to say that large states do not engage in tax competition, they are at a structural disadvantage compared to small ones.

Based on this description of how the two basic forms of tax competition work in practice, what should we say about poaching and luring from an ethical perspective? The next two sections of the paper discuss the normative criteria we might employ to answer this question.

2. The case for a ban on poaching tax base

When asking in what sense, if any, poaching is ethically troublesome, we need to establish what value or principle poaching might constitute a violation of. What is the normative principle that underpins the allocation of tax base to various states? As pointed out above, current practice relies on the residence principle for individuals and the source principle for active MNE income. What is the justification for adopting these principles?

The traditional answer given to this question in the literature on international tax law and public finance is this.[11] One has a duty to contribute to the public goods and to fiscal redistribution wherever one is part of the economic nexus, that is, where one conducts one's economic activities such as work, production, consumption and so on. Why? Both individuals and MNEs are part of a cooperative venture. In order to make this venture possible, some public goods and infrastructure are necessary. If you are part of the economic nexus, you benefit from these and, thereby, incur an obligation to contribute to financing them. This idea is by no means new. For example, it informed the League of Nations' appeal to economic allegiance as the principle that should ground our obligation to pay tax (Rixen 2008: 89). Dietsch and Rixen (2014a) have cashed out this idea of the economic nexus by formulating what they call the 'membership principle'. Two important features of the membership principle are that membership can come in degrees and that it does not presuppose the benefit principle; one's tax payments might well be based on the ability to pay instead. Defining the precise contours of membership is subject to technical difficulties, but I bracket these here. The residence and source principles do not track membership perfectly but they are, arguably, close enough proxies for practical purposes.

The economic-nexus argument raises the further question of where to draw the line between one economic nexus and another. This is arbitrary to some

10. For a detailed discussion of the tax-rate effect and the tax-base effect, see Dehejia and Genschel 1999: 408 as well as Rixen 2008: 43.

11. For an insightful discussion of the contours of this debate, see Musgrave and Musgrave 1972, especially 64–6, and Li 2003.

extent. While the argument for sub-unit autonomy appeals to the idea that people should have a say over the (fiscal) decisions that affect them (Follesdal 1998), current state boundaries are just one possible way among infinitely many to carve up the world into fiscal entities. What matters in our context is that we have normative reasons – namely the value of self-determination – to carve the world up into sub-units.[12] These sub-units then constitute the contingent, but nonetheless normatively salient economic nexus that underpin our practical tax principles.

Against this background, it is hard to see how poaching could be viewed as an acceptable practice. If one accepts the relatively weak premises of fiscal autonomy for states, on the one hand, and of this autonomy being delineated by the concept of economic nexus, on the other hand, then it follows that poaching should be viewed as a violation of fiscal autonomy.

To see why these two premises are indeed weak, consider what rejecting them entails. First, as far as I can see, the only conceptual alternatives to a model of global governance that contains a dose of state autonomy are either anarchy or some form of global government. It is not clear that either of these is desirable, let alone feasible. Yet, once you grant a right to state autonomy of some sort, then violating this autonomy is, by definition, problematic. Poaching constitutes such a violation. A sceptic will object that it is not clear why accepting some sort of state autonomy would entail the economic-nexus principle.

This leads us to examine the second premise. Again, let us ask what the conceptual alternatives are to an appeal to economic nexus. Taxes are levied on economic activities or financial transactions of some sort. What justification could there possibly be for giving the power to tax to a jurisdiction *other* than the one where the activity or transaction actually takes place? Why tax a sale in state A when the buyer lives in state B? Why tax a profit in state C when it has been generated in state D? I am not claiming that developing a justification for such arrangements constitutes a logical impossibility, but I am claiming that no plausible justification of this kind has ever been developed regarding active business income.[13] The most serious, albeit indirect attempt to do so is perhaps to argue that allowing tax competition is economically efficient. However, I have shown elsewhere that this argument fails (*see* Dietsch 2016, Chapter 3). The lack of a plausible alternative leads me to conclude that accepting a principle of economic nexus or allegiance is relatively uncontroversial.[14]

---

12. For a discussion of how this argument can be extended to non-democratic states, see Dietsch 2015, section 4.5.

13. *See* footnote 11. Note that this is consistent with the practice of some countries that tax the income of their resident multinationals on a worldwide basis, because this right to tax based on residence is secondary to the right to tax of the source country.

14. Note that I am not saying that the membership principle defended by Dietsch and Rixen (2014a) is *as* uncontroversial. There are several ways to cash out the idea of economic nexus (Musgrave 1991) and the membership principle is merely one of those. However, all of the potential principles one might develop for this purpose will regard poaching as an unacceptable form of free-riding.

What I have said so far is not quite enough to justify an outright ban on poaching. Why? Someone might argue that while poaching represents a violation of the principle of economic allegiance, there are circumstances in which tolerating poaching is acceptable because it promotes other, independent moral values. In particular, a strong case could be made for tolerating poaching by developing countries in order to compensate for structural injustices in other policy areas or, more generally, as a means to redistribute income towards their development goals.

In such a case, the defender of poaching as a fiscal practice would concede that its violation of the principle of economic allegiance gives us a *pro tanto* reason to condemn it but would argue that, due to its redistributive effects, we should accept it *all things considered.*[15]

Two scenarios should be distinguished here. First, counterfactually, suppose the background institutions of the international economy were just. In other words, while inequalities in income and wealth between countries exist under this scenario, we stipulate that international trade (James 2012) as well as monetary arrangements (Reddy 2003) are just, that some form of economic allegiance principle effectively governs global taxation, and so on. In such a hypothetical world, allowing poor countries to poach tax base from rich ones would disrupt the sound institutional structure in place and should therefore be avoided. On top of the economic convergence that would plausibly happen on its own in such a world, any additional redistribution should instead happen through direct development aid from rich countries.

The second and more practically relevant scenario corresponds to our world, in which just international background institutions are lacking. In our world, not only are developing countries structurally disadvantaged by the international order – one need look no further than the weight they receive in the voting of many international organisations such as the World Bank or the IMF – but the fiscal policy of low corporate taxation, including practices that involve poaching, has in fact been recommended to them and even, in some cases, forced upon them, through loan-conditionality and other policies, by these very same institutions. In this case, tolerating poaching by low-income countries seems to represent a form of reverse imperialism that should not only be permitted but is, arguably, morally required.

Thus, *in principle*, there will be situations in which, all things considered, poaching by low-income countries should be allowed. However, let me mention three caveats that suggest that *in practice*, such situations will be few and far between. First, as pointed out in Section 1, for large states, poaching through tax competition is unlikely to be worthwhile, since the loss of domestic tax revenue is likely to outstrip the revenue gain from capital inflows. Second, given that tolerating poaching for reasons of redistribution involves correcting one injustice (structural disadvantage) with another (poaching as a form of free-riding), presumably the weight of the redistributive concern diminishes with the level of

15. The following analysis of this argument is a synopsis of a more detailed treatment in Dietsch 2015: section 5.2.

income of the developing country. One might think, for example, that a country such as Panama, whose gross national income (GNI) per head for 2012 lies $3000 above the world average, should not be allowed to resort to poaching.[16] Third, and finally, whether or not the small country with a below-average GNI should be allowed to use poaching might plausibly depend on what the country will do with the poached tax revenue. Will it be used to combat poverty, for instance, or for purposes alien to considerations of social justice? After all, it would be absurd to tolerate poaching for reasons of social justice without demanding that the resulting revenues be used to promote this goal. I merely sketch these arguments here.[17] They might not be conclusive but they do warrant the claim that situations in which poaching should be tolerated are rarer than one might think *prima facie*.

In sum, the considerations in this section warrant a qualified ban on poaching. I have shown, first, that if one accepts the relatively weak premises of fiscal autonomy for states and of using economic allegiance to define the boundaries of this fiscal autonomy, then one is bound to see poaching as an unacceptable form of free-riding. Second, I have argued that while there might, in principle, be situations in which the moral bad of free-riding is overridden by other considerations, notably ones of distributive justice, such situations are likely to be rare in practice. Except for these exceptional cases, the case for banning poaching is strong.

It is worth highlighting what a ban on poaching would entail, and where it differs from existing initiatives against tax evasion and avoidance. As one can see from consulting the various forms of poaching listed in Section 1, on top of better enforcement of anti-evasion measures, it requires putting an end to the abuse of transfer-pricing rules, earnings-stripping, booking e-commerce transactions in jurisdictions alien to the sale, headquarters inversions and other practices in violation of the principle of economic allegiance.

While the current OECD initiative on base erosion and profit shifting (BEPS) certainly represents a step in the right direction, it remains to be seen whether it can get us all the way there in its current form. While I like to be optimistic, I see two substantive reasons to be doubtful on this front.[18] As to the first of these, consider a basic choice of international tax governance with respect to the taxation of multinationals. *Either one treats the subsidiaries of MNEs as if they were independent entities.* In this case, transactions between them are governed by the 'arm's-length' principle, which demands that they should be conducted at market prices. Respecting the arm's-length principle rules out transfer-mispricing, but it does not rule out profit-shifting as such. Experience shows that MNEs are very creative when it comes to finding alternative ways to shift their profits. *Or, and this is the second possibility, one treats the various subsidiaries of an MNE as one single corporation.* In this case, one needs a way to assign the right to tax

16. In contrast to the more widely used measure of GDP, GNI does not include income to foreigners, which makes it a more precise measure of the wealth of a country.
17. For a more thorough defence, see Dietsch 2015: section 5.2.
18. Eccleston and Smith 2016, Chapter Eight in this volume, come to a similar conclusion.

the profits of this corporation to the various states in which it operates. Unitary tax and formulary apportionment (UT+FA) provides such a way, with the most popular formula assigning equal weight to assets, sales and payroll of MNEs.[19] In contrast to a system based on the arm's-length principle, UT+FA writes the idea of economic allegiance directly into the ground-rules of global tax governance, thus drastically reducing opportunities for profit-shifting. Tax avoidance will not be eliminated under UT+FA but it will certainly be more costly.

The recommendations formulated by the OECD thus far give us reasons to believe that the organisation aims to close the loopholes of the arm's-length world rather than to propel us into a world of UT+FA.[20] This strategy is futile. The tax-avoidance industry is likely to always be one step ahead of regulators in a world governed by the arm's-length principle. There is thus a real possibility that despite a more aggressive discourse against tax avoidance and, very likely, a number of concrete measures that will be adopted by the G20 on the recommendation of the OECD, these reforms will not make much of a difference.

Second, a more general worry about a crackdown on profit-shifting that is centred around closing loopholes in the present system rather than fundamental reform is that it opens the door to what Richard Woodward (2016) in Chapter Five of this volume calls 'mock compliance'. Mock compliance occurs when someone fulfils the formal requirements of a standard, for instance by ratifying a treaty, but fails to deliver on its substance, for instance by dragging his feet on enforcement. As Woodward states,

> ... mock compliance is most likely to come about in situations where states recognise that there would be serious repercussions of outright defiance but where full compliance would impose significant costs on powerful domestic groups and actors (such as the financial services industry) and where it is difficult for third parties to ascertain and expose non-compliance (Woodward 2016, Chapter Five of this volume).

These conditions seem to be met in the present context, given the complex nature of the interactions between the various subsidiaries of an MNE. Therefore, it seems fair to say that enforcing compliance from tax havens is a tall order under the arm's-length paradigm, compared to a world of UT+FA. This is a serious drawback.

---

19. For a defence of a UT+FA approach as opposed to the arm's-length standard (ALS), *see* Avi-Yonah 2016, Chapter Thirteen in this volume. Incidentally, I agree with Avi-Yonah that intangibles – which underlie numerous tax-avoidance strategies such as the Double Irish mentioned *above* – should not be included in formulary apportionment because '(a) their value results from physical and human capital and from the market and those elements are included, and (b) you cannot allocate their value and trying to include them invites manipulation' (Avi-Yonah 2016, Chapter Thirteen in this volume).
20. Pascal Saint-Amans, the OECD's top tax official, explicitly said as much in April, when he 'insisted the BEPS action plan involved "no hidden agenda" that would usher in formulary apportionment. He said the goal was "to save the arm's length principle" by fixing its flaws.' (Houlder 2014).

3. The more controversial case of *luring*

While poaching is clearly on the radar of regulators today, this is not the case for luring.[21] Take the example of Ireland. The debate is centred on instances of poaching like the Double Irish loophole, but neither the OECD nor the EU have insisted on the question of whether the low Irish corporate tax rate of 12.5 per cent is problematic in itself. This is both surprising and, I shall argue, a mistake. It is surprising because taxes and subsidies are merely two sides of the same coin. Since subsidies are, in all but some exceptional circumstances, condemned by the World Trade Organisation (WTO) as introducing an unfair bias into commercial relations, it would only be coherent to advance a parallel argument in the case of taxation. One way to describe Ireland's low corporate tax rate is as a general subsidy to Irish businesses, including the Irish subsidiaries of MNEs. It is generally accepted that this was a crucial ingredient for the pre-financial-crisis economic success of the 'Celtic tiger'. Of course, the mere requirement of coherence does not yet tell us whether we should condemn both low taxation and subsidies or, on the contrary, accept them both. This is why the present section will delve into the normative justifications we might provide for either accepting or condemning luring practices, that is, instances of *real* as opposed to *virtual* tax competition.

Independently of the ethical stance we take on this issue, it would be a mistake to ignore the question. This is so especially due to the substitutive relationship between poaching and luring, mentioned above. If we respect the conclusion of the previous section and ban poaching altogether, the incentive for corporations to actually relocate their activities will increase significantly. One would expect the inflows of productive capital into low-tax jurisdictions like Ireland to go up. What, if anything, is wrong with that from an ethical perspective?

This question gives a new meaning to the question of 'whose tax base?' in the title of this chapter. Whereas in the case of poaching the problem is that one state appropriates a part of the tax base that legitimately belongs to another state, no such violation of fiscal autonomy occurs in the case of luring. After all, when an MNE moves its production facility from state A to state B, it ceases to belong to the economic nexus of A – at least as far as this particular production facility is concerned. The question here becomes the following: are there any situations in which we can say that a country enjoys more than its just share of the global tax base? If so, what are the arguments that sustain this sort of claim?

This is a very broad question and, as a first step, it will be useful to give it a sharper focus. To do so, I will borrow a distinction that Aaron James employs to deal with a similar issue in the context of international trade (James 2012: 144*ff.*). On the one hand, one might think that a country enjoys more or less than its just share of the global tax base *for external reasons*. These are reasons that do not appeal to features of global tax governance as such but to independent reasons we might put forward. On the other hand, one might think that a country enjoys more

21. I focus exclusively on the case of luring *corporate* capital in this section, bracketing the case of how individuals react to lower taxes elsewhere.

or less than its just share of the global tax base *for internal reasons*. These are reasons that appeal to characteristics of the institutions of global tax governance as they exist today. If these institutions were different, the same reasons would not hold, or at least they would not operate in the same way.

This chapter will, by and large, focus on internal reasons.[22] But let me briefly say a few words on external reasons, to illustrate what falls into this category. One can develop a variety of arguments to claim that the global tax base is distributed unjustly. For instance, a utilitarian might argue that a more equal dispersion of economic activity, and thus of the global tax base, would be utility-maximising. Alternatively, suppose we consider the tax base to be a primary good to which individuals – through their respective states – should have access, and whose distribution should be governed by a global difference principle (for example, Beitz 1999). Again, this would call for a different global basic structure, presumably with low-income countries getting a larger share of the global tax base. Finally, and this list is by no means exhaustive, one might claim that giving certain countries privileged access to the global tax base is an adequate way to compensate them for either past or present structural injustices in global economic institutions (for example, Pogge 2002). In all these cases, it is particularly tempting to look for redistribution through the differential allocation of tax base globally since, at the domestic level, fiscal policy already represents the primary tool for redistribution.

I certainly do not mean to claim that arguments based on external reasons are less important than those based on internal reasons. But until recently, the latter have been somewhat neglected in the global justice literature. This neglect could be counterproductive, in that socio-economic institutions of global governance that suffer from internal injustices will require a more and more important correction for external reasons. Think of an analogy: market outcomes have grown more unequal in terms of the distribution of income in recent decades, thus calling for a more and more progressive tax-and-transfer scheme if one's goal is to preserve a certain level of economic inequalities. And while we might be indifferent between promoting justice through internal reform or through external correction in terms of their normative desirability, putting all one's eggs into the basket of external reasons, arguably, fares worse in terms of feasibility.[23]

Hence my focus, by and large, on internal reasons. What internal reasons, if any, do we have to think that the distribution of global tax base between states should respect certain parameters? I shall stipulate in this section that the value that informs our response to this question is fiscal autonomy – just as in the case of poaching discussed in the previous section. This stipulation in

22. For an assessment of tax competition focusing on external reasons, see Brock 2008.

23. For a development of this argument with respect to global tax governance, see Dietsch and Rixen 2014b. The financial transactions tax (FTT) discussed by Wollner (2016) in Chapter Fourteen of this volume is an interesting case in this context. While originally defended for internal reasons (the stability of the global financial system) the FTT has more recently also been advocated for external reasons (e.g., to fund efforts to reduce poverty).

itself might be challenged but I shall not provide a defence of it here.[24] Instead, I will provide a menu of different ways in which fiscal autonomy might be interpreted, to then spell out the ramifications of these interpretations for global tax governance.

As a preliminary to this discussion, consider the following analogy between fiscal autonomy and individual liberty. The protection of individual liberty, in order to be effective, requires constraining individual liberty in a way that makes it compatible with guaranteeing the same kind of individual liberty for other members of society. These constraints include prohibitions such as hitting someone else over the head or stealing their possessions. The liberties of different individuals are in tension with one another. Society has to find a way to balance them and make a decision about where to draw the line around the core of individual liberty it will protect.

Similarly, under capital mobility, there will be tensions between the fiscal autonomy of different states. When state A lowers its tax rate on corporate profits below the level in effect in state B, there will be a capital outflow from B to A. The question that arises is whether this is problematic and, if so, how the international community should protect the fiscal autonomy of state B. In other words, what should, and what should not, be considered part of the fiscal autonomy of states? Consider the following responses to this question.

First, let us try to unpack the normative assumptions implicit in the *status quo*. Ireland exercises its fiscal autonomy by choosing a corporate tax rate that, at 12.5 per cent, is considerably below the average rate of other countries. Even though this might have repercussions on other countries, in the form of reducing their tax base, it does not undermine these other countries' choices to set *their* corporate tax rate as they see fit.

In the fiscal realm, state autonomy is usually taken to encompass two basic democratic choices, namely, one concerning the size of the state – usually measured by the ratio of government expenditures over GDP – and one concerning the level of redistribution – reflected in the progressivity of the fiscal system (see for example Avi-Yonah 2000). Ireland's tax policy does not infringe upon the formal right of other countries to make either of these two choices.

The interpretation of fiscal autonomy in this picture is congruent with the idea of Westphalian sovereignty.[25] 'The basic rule of Westphalian sovereignty is non-intervention in the internal affairs of other states' (Krasner 2007: 656), where the internal affairs of the state are territorially defined. Thus, when Ireland sets a low tax rate and attracts corporations from Sweden, say, Swedish fiscal autonomy is unimpaired, because the relocated economic activity is no longer happening in Sweden. I shall come back to this later.

---

24. For such a defence, see Dietsch forthcoming.
25. I understand Westphalian sovereignty as governing inter-state relations and distinguish it from domestic sovereignty (concerning the legitimacy and effectiveness of the authority structure within the state) and from international legal sovereignty (defining the status of states in the international community). *See also* Dietsch 2016, Chapter Four.

We now turn to a critique of this Westphalian interpretation. Real tax competition, while preserving formal or *de jure* sovereignty over the two fiscal choices above, undermines effective or *de facto* control over them (Rixen 2010). The formal liberty of choosing your tax rate becomes meaningless if choosing a high rate will result in capital outflows that seriously dent revenues. In a world of capital mobility, Westphalian sovereignty is, arguably, no longer the appropriate notion of sovereignty. Instead, a modern notion of sovereignty should be sensitive to the effectiveness of the fiscal choices political communities make. Drawing an analogy with liberty, one might liken the critique of Westphalian sovereignty here to the internal critique put forward by left-libertarians (Vallentyne 2001). Just like the latter argue that a formal concept of liberty limited to the notion of self-ownership is meaningless without addressing the question of property rights over the resources one needs to exercise one's liberty, I am arguing here that the formal right to set one's tax rate is meaningless if it does not include some level of control over revenues, too. From this perspective, fiscal autonomy, like liberty or any other right, comes not only with privileges but also with obligations.[26] In particular, it comes with the obligation to respect the fiscal choices of other states, even if they differ from ours. What does an interpretation of fiscal autonomy look like that would allow us to do this?

Dietsch and Rixen (2014a: section 2.B) have put forward a principle of global tax justice capable of playing this role. What we call the *fiscal policy constraint* states that the question of whether a particular fiscal policy by country A respects the fiscal autonomy of other states depends both on its effects and its intentions. More specifically, a fiscal policy is unacceptable if it is *both* strategically motivated *and* has a negative impact on the aggregate level of effective self-determination of other states, that is, if it leads to a net capital outflow from other states.[27] To illustrate, think again of Ireland. Given the huge inflows of FDI into Ireland over the years, this suggests that the consequentialist criterion is easily met; to the extent that the capital outflows in question result from Ireland's tax policy, the effective level of fiscal self-determination of other states will, in the aggregate, suffer. But how to assess the intentions of fiscal policy? We propose a counterfactual criterion that asks whether Ireland would have pursued the same corporate tax policy in the absence of the resulting capital inflows. If the answer is yes, then its tax policy might be in tension with that of other states, but it respects them. If the answer is no, then Ireland's low-corporate-tax policy should be considered unethical, in the sense that it does not respect the fiscal autonomy of other states.

Why should intentions be relevant to our ethical assessment of tax policy in this way? Because we want to respect the variance in political preferences of different political communities when it comes to choosing the size of the state and the level

26. *Cf.* the idea of 'sovereignty as responsibility' developed in Dietsch 2011.

27. The two-pronged criterion ensures that two kinds of legitimate fiscal policies are not ruled out. On the one hand, the consequentialist component ensures that potentially beneficial kinds of competition, such as investments in education or infrastructure, are permitted; on the other hand, the intentions-based component ensures that the fiscal autonomy of polities is respected.

of redistribution. Suppose for a moment that countries do not act strategically in setting tax policy at all but that the Swedes prefer a bigger state and more redistribution than the English. If we imposed constraints on English tax policy in this scenario in order to limit capital outflows from Sweden, this would amount to preferential treatment in favour of Sweden's fiscal choices. However, once we admit strategic tax-setting to the picture, the verdict changes. Suppose England's tax policy was exclusively motivated by strategic reasons, while Swedish tax policy was exclusively motivated by 'pure' political preferences and thus non-strategic considerations. In this case, protecting the fiscal autonomy of Swedes seems not only permissible but also ethically required.[28]

Dietsch and Rixen's interpretation of fiscal autonomy just outlined can, in turn, be criticised in at least three ways. First, someone might take issue with our position that the protection of fiscal autonomy should include a degree of policy effectiveness. This, I take it, is the position that Laurens van Apeldoorn (2016) defends in Chapter Nine of this volume. He questions our position that fiscal interdependence warrants a kind of normative interdependence and that it imposes constraints on the fiscal policies a state should be allowed to adopt. When Ireland chooses to set its corporate tax rate at a low level, rather than violating the fiscal autonomy of other states, van Apeldoorn will say that this merely changes the parameters under which these other states make their own fiscal choices. The point here is not to criticise this position – given what I have said about Westphalian sovereignty on which this criticism relies, it will be obvious that I disagree – but to include it on the menu of possible interpretations of fiscal autonomy.

Moreover, the appeal to intentions set out in the discussion above on the two-pronged criterion has repeatedly come under fire. A second criticism states that making the intentionality of luring a necessary condition for condemning instances of tax competition is too narrow a criterion.[29] Extending the analogy between individual liberty and state self-determination, this argument objects that sometimes even actions whose consequences were unintended should be punished.

The third criticism of Dietsch and Rixen's interpretation of fiscal autonomy is that assessing the intentions of states in policy-making is simply not feasible. Setting aside the counter-arguments to this criticism,[30] taking this consideration as a hard feasibility constraint could lead to the following, pragmatic modification of Dietsch and Rixen's position. Someone who agrees with the desirability of limiting luring due to its impact on *de facto* sovereignty but is reluctant to invoke intentions as a criterion might want to impose a cap on tax-rate differentials between states.[31] Stopping short of rate harmonisation, such a policy would have the effect of

28. For a more detailed defence of the arguments in the last two paragraphs, see Dietsch and Rixen 2014a.

29. I thank Miriam Ronzoni for this formulation of the objection.

30. While conceding that assessing intentions is difficult, Dietsch and Rixen point to other policy areas in which this is already done, to illustrate that it is indeed possible (2014a: 168–9).

31. Or, alternatively, a minimum tax rate across states, as discussed by Ronzoni (2016) in Chapter Nine of this volume.

containing luring at a certain level. For example, the permitted differential could be capped at 15 percentage points. In the case of Ireland and the US, for instance, this would mean that Ireland would have to raise its corporate tax rate to 20 per cent if we take the statutory rate of 35 per cent in the US as benchmark. In sum, this sort of approach is informed by the same normative assessment of fiscal autonomy – and thus of luring – as Dietsch and Rixen, but it arrives at different policy recommendations, based on considerations of feasibility.

The last interpretation of fiscal autonomy I will discuss differs, in that it appeals to both internal and external reasons. I include this mixed account here given the weight and urgency of some of the external reasons we have to give low-income countries a larger share of the global tax base.

Independently of the interpretation of fiscal autonomy one might endorse, admitting autonomy as the sole normative value to assess luring will invite what Simon Caney (2006: 732) has called the 'wrong priorities objection'. People cannot ignore what is going on beyond the borders of their state. The literature on theories of global justice shows that the precise way in which they should take this into account is controversial. However, there is a consensus among most theories of global justice that humanitarian disasters generate moral obligations for rich countries. The normative weight of this minimal threshold of justice – which I shall not attempt to define with any precision here – trumps considerations of autonomy. We might call this an account of self-determination with a sufficientarian constraint of global justice.[32]

There are several political implications from such a position. First, it means that global humanitarian causes take priority over political measures, including instances of luring, that are designed to promote the interests of citizens. Second, if it is in their interest, states experiencing humanitarian disasters are not subject to any constraints on luring. Third, where questions of the attribution of global tax base to individual states arise – as for instance under UT+FA – states experiencing humanitarian disasters should receive preferential treatment.[33]

4. Conclusion

More work is needed on the question of which aspects of fiscal autonomy of states should be protected. And yet, I have argued that we can already draw a number of useful conclusions. First, if one accepts the idea that we should rely on the idea of an economic nexus to establish the contours of a state's fiscal autonomy, then a strong case can be made for an outright ban on the poaching of foreign tax base. This in itself calls for a radical reform of global tax governance. In particular, it is hard to see how this goal could be achieved under the current arm's-length

32. Several so-called statist theories of global justice can be interpreted in this way. See, for example, Rawls 1999; Nagel 2005; or Sangiovanni 2007. I develop an account of global tax justice that can be interpreted along statist lines in Dietsch forthcoming.

33. Musgrave and Musgrave's (1972) proposal of a staggered rate-schedule for corporation taxes in capital-exporting *versus* capital-importing countries goes in a similar direction.

standard. Second, the evaluation of luring practices from an ethical perspective is bound to be more controversial. For example, should strategic intent and negative consequences for other states be considered jointly necessary for condemning a given practice of luring, or is it more plausible to consider some kinds of negative consequences as sufficient to draw this conclusion? Does the fiscal autonomy of states include some guarantee for the effectiveness of tax policies or is this too thick an understanding of autonomy? While I have provided tentative answers to these kinds of questions, Section 3 has shown that the normative landscape is much less well defined in the case of luring. More work on this issue is urgently needed, especially given the fact that poaching and luring are in a substitutive relationship. If poaching is stopped, more luring will occur.

This chapter is based on the assumption that the only value that informs our *internal* reasons for designing global tax governance is fiscal autonomy. One avenue for future research might be to relax this assumption. Are there considerations outside those of fiscal autonomy that we might appeal to in order to assess poaching and luring practices from an ethical perspective? This is just one of the intriguing questions that normative work on global tax governance has yet to answer.

References

Avi-Yonah, R. (2000) 'Globalization, tax competition, and the fiscal crisis of the welfare state', *Harvard Law Review* 113(7): 1573–1676.

— (2016) 'A proposal for unitary taxation and formulary apportionment (UT+FA) to tax multinational enterprises', in Dietsch, P. and Rixen, T. (eds) *Global Tax Governance: What is wrong with it and how to fix it*, Colchester: ECPR Press.

Beitz, C. (1999) *Political Theory and International Relations*, Princeton, New Jersey: Princeton University Press, revised edition.

Boland, V. (2014) 'Dublin ditches "Double Irish" to save low tax regime', *Financial Times*, 15 October: http://www.ft.com/cms/s/2/1f740b46-539b-11e4-929b-00144feab7de.html#axzz3izX001jj (accessed 16 August 2015).

Bradshaw, T. *et al.* (2014) 'Apple hit by Brussels findings over Irish backroom tax deals', *Financial Times*, 29 September: http://www.ft.com/cms/s/0/ae979ad0-4708-11e4-8c50-00144feab7de.html#axzz3izX001jj (accessed 16 August 2015).

Brock, G. (2008) 'Taxation and global justice: closing the gap between theory and practice', *Journal of Social Philosophy* 39(2): 161–84.

Caney, S. (2006) 'Cosmopolitan justice and institutional design: an egalitarian liberal conception of global governance', *Social Theory & Practice* 32(4): 725–56.

Darby III, J. B. (2007) 'Double Irish more than doubles the tax saving: hybrid structure reduces Irish, U.S. and worldwide taxation', *Practical US/International Tax Strategies* 11(9): 2–16.

Dehejia, V. H. and Genschel, P. (1999) 'Tax competition in the European Union', *Politics & Society* 27: 403–30.

de Mooij, R. A. and Ederveen, S. (2008) 'Corporate tax elasticities: a reader's guide to empirical findings', *Oxford Review of Economic Policy* 24(4): 680–97.

Dharmapala, D. (2008) 'What problems and opportunities are created by tax havens?', *Oxford Review of Economic Policy* 24: 661–79.

Dietsch, P. (2011) 'Rethinking sovereignty in international fiscal policy', *Review of International Studies* 37: 2107–20.

— (2015) *Catching Capital – The ethics of tax competition*, New York: Oxford University Press.

— (forthcoming) 'The state and tax competition – a normative perspective', in O'Neill, M. and Orr, S. (eds) *Political Philosophy and Taxation*, Oxford: Oxford University Press.

Dietsch, P. and Rixen, T. (2014a) 'Tax competition and global background justice', *Journal of Political Philosophy* 22(2): 150–77.

— (2014b) 'Redistribution, globalisation, and multi-level governance', *Moral Philosophy & Politics* 1(1): 61–82.

Eccleston, R. and Smith, H. (2016) 'The G20, BEPS, and the future of international tax governance', in Dietsch, P. and Rixen, T. (eds) *Global Tax Governance: What is wrong with it and how to fix it*, Colchester: ECPR Press.

Financial Times (2008) 'German protests grow over Nokia relocation', 19 January: http://www.ft.com/cms/s/0/d2a85cf6-c632-11dc-8378-0000779fd2ac.html#axzz3i94dwq5t. (accessed 15 August 2015).

Follesdal, A. (1998) 'Survey article: subsidiarity', *Journal of Political Philosophy* 6(2): 190–218.

Grinberg, I. (2016) 'Does FATCA teach broader lessons about international tax multilateralism?', in Dietsch, P. and Rixen, T. (eds) *Global Tax Governance: What is wrong with it and how to fix it*, Colchester: ECPR Press.

Hakelberg, L. (2016) 'Redistributive tax co-operation: automatic exchange of information, US power and the absence of joint gains', in Dietsch, P. and Rixen, T. (eds) *Global Tax Governance: What is wrong with it and how to fix it*, Colchester: ECPR Press.

Henry, J. S. (2012) *The Price of Offshore Revisited: New estimates for 'missing' global private wealth, income, inequality, and lost taxes*, report for the Tax Justice Network: http://www.taxjustice.net/cms/upload/pdf/Price_of_Offshore_Revisited_120722.pdf (accessed 19 September 2014).

Houlder, V. (2013) '"Dutch sandwich" grows as Google shifts Euros 9bn to Bermuda', *Financial Times*, 11 October: http://www.ft.com/cms/s/0/89acc832-31cc-11e3-a16d-00144feab7de.html#axzz3i94dwq5t (accessed 15 August 2015).

— (2014) 'OECD denies new rules are biased against low-tax countries', *Financial Times*, 3 April: http://www.ft.com/cms/s/0/5f06a9f8-ba80-11e3-a905-00144feabdc0.html#axzz3i94dwq5t (accessed 13 August 2015).

Houlder, V., *et al.* (2014a) 'Tax avoidance: the Irish inversion', *Financial Times*, 30 April: http://www.ft.com/cms/s/2/d9b4fd34-ca3f-11e3-8a31-00144feabdc0.html (accessed 13 August 2015).

— (2014b) 'EU's Amazon probe steps up pressure over tax deals', *Financial Times*, 8 October: http://www.ft.com/cms/s/0/44fbcf44-4e36-11e4-adfe-00144feab7de.html#axzz3i94dwq5t (accessed 13 August 2015).

James, A. (2012) *Fairness in Practice*, New York: Oxford University Press.

Keen, M. (2001) 'Preferential regimes can make tax competition less harmful', *National Tax Journal* 54: 757–62.

Krasner, S. D. (2007) 'Pervasive not perverse: semi-sovereigns as the global norm', *Cornell International Law Journal* 30: 651–80.

Laurent, S. (2013) 'Si vous n'avez rien suivi de l'affaire Cahuzac', *Le Monde*, 30 August: http://www.lemonde.fr/politique/article/2012/12/10/si-vous-n-avez-rien-suivi-de-l-affaire-cahuzac_1804062_823448.html (accessed 11 March 2015).

Li, J. (2003) *International Taxation in the Age of Electronic Commerce*, Toronto: Canadian Tax Foundation.

McIntyre, R. S. *et al.* (2014), *The Sorry State of Corporate Taxes. What Fortune 500 firms pay (or don't pay) in the USA and what they pay abroad – 2008 to 2012*, report by Citizens for Tax Justice and the Institute on Taxation and Public Policy, Washington: http://www.ctj.org/corporatetaxdodgers/sorrystateofcorptaxes.pdf (accessed 22 October 2014).

Musgrave, P. (1991) 'Fiscal coordination and competition in an international setting', in Eden, L. (ed.), *Retrospectives on Public Finance*, Durham, North Carolina: Duke University Press, pp. 276–305.

Musgrave, R. A. and Musgrave, P. (1972) 'Inter-nation equity', in Bird, R. M. and Head, J. G. (eds) *Modern Fiscal Issues: Essays in honor of Carl S. Shoup*, Toronto: University of Toronto Press, pp. 63–85.

Nagel, T. (2005) 'The problem of global justice', *Philosophy & Public Affairs* 33(2): 113–47.

OECD (Organization for Economic Co-operation and Development, 1998) *Harmful Tax Competition – An Emerging Global Issue*, Paris: OECD Publications: http://www.oecd.org/tax/transparency/44430243.pdf (accessed 22 October 2014).

— (2002) *Intra-industry and intra-firm trade and the internationalisation of production*, special chapter of the *OECD Economic Outlook* 71, June: http://www.oecd.org/economy/outlook/2752923.pdf (accessed 22 October 2014).

Palan, R. (2002) 'Tax havens and the commercialization of state sovereignty', *International Organization* 56(1): 151–76.

Pogge, T. (2002) *World Poverty and Human Rights*, Cambridge: Polity Press.

Rawls, J. (1999) *The Law of Peoples*, Cambridge, Massachusetts: Harvard University Press.

Reddy, S. (2003) 'Developing just monetary arrangements', *Ethics & International Affairs* 17(1): 81–93.

Rixen, T. (2008) *The Political Economy of International Tax Governance*, Basingstoke: Palgrave Macmillan.

— (2010) 'From double tax avoidance to tax competition: explaining the institutional trajectory of international tax governance', *Review of International Political Economy* 18(2): 197–227.

— (2016) 'Institutional reform of global tax governance: a proposal', in Dietsch, P. and Rixen, T. (eds) *Global Tax Governance: What is wrong with it and how to fix it*, Colchester: ECPR Press.

Ronzoni, M. (2009) 'The global order: a case of background injustice? A practice-dependent account', *Philosophy & Public Affairs* 37(3): 229–56.

— (2016) 'Tax competition: a problem of global or domestic justice?', in Dietsch, P. and Rixen, T. (eds) *Global Tax Governance: What is wrong with it and how to fix it*, Colchester: ECPR Press.

Sangiovanni, A. (2007) 'Global justice, reciprocity, and the state', *Philosophy & Public Affairs* 35(1): 3–39.

Story, L. (2012) 'As companies seek tax deals, governments pay high price', *New York Times*, 1 December: http://www.nytimes.com/2012/12/02/us/how-local-taxpayers-bankroll-corporations.html?pagewanted=all&_r=0 (accessed 13 August 2015).

Thorpe, N. (2011) 'Romania's 'Nokia City' hopes dashed', *BBC*, 22 December. http://www.bbc.co.uk/news/world-europe-16290078 (accessed 22 October 2014).

Vallentyne, P. (2001) 'Introduction: left-libertarianism – a primer', in Vallentyne, P. and Steiner, H. (eds) *Left-Libertarianism and Its Critics: The contemporary debate*, New York: St Martin's Press, pp. 1–20.

van Apeldoorn, L. (2016), 'International taxation and the erosion of sovereignty', in Dietsch, P. and Rixen, T. (eds) *Global Tax Governance: What is wrong with it and how to fix it*, Colchester: ECPR Press.

Woodward, R. (2016) 'A strange revolution: mock compliance and the failure of the OECD's international tax transparency regime', in Dietsch, P. and Rixen, T. (eds) *Global Tax Governance: What is wrong with it and how to fix it*, Colchester: ECPR Press.

Zucman, G. (2013) *La Richesse cachée des nations – Enquête sur les paradis fiscaux*, Paris: Seuil.

PART FOUR

FROM THEORY TO PRACTICE: JUST INSTITUTIONS FOR INTERNATIONAL TAX GOVERNANCE

Chapter Twelve

Towards an International Yardstick for Identifying Tax Havens and Facilitating Reform

Markus Meinzer

1. Introduction

No jurisdiction likes to be labelled a tax haven. In 2013, after a US-Senate investigation of Apple's corporate tax structure dubbed Ireland a tax haven alongside Bermuda and Cayman Islands, the *Financial Times* reported that 'Ireland will deploy ministers to counter "tax haven" claims' (United States Senate 2013: 154; Smyth 2013). This is one among many similar denials, when disputes about naming (and shaming) a particular country as a 'tax haven' have erupted publicly.[1] Yet, the recurrent quarrelling about this term suggests a deeper conflict that deserves more systematic exploration and analysis.

The first prominent multilateral effort to demand reforms of tax havens dates back more than fifteen years and resulted in a list of thirty-five tax havens drawn up by the OECD in 2000 (OECD 2000). Revived by the G20 in the context of the financial crisis at the April 2009 summit, this initiative compelled tax havens to sign at least twelve bilateral information-exchange treaties to escape counter-measures. While many hundreds of such treaties have subsequently been signed, econometric analysis by Johannesen and Zucman (2014: 89) shows that the treaties left 'roughly unchanged the total amount of wealth managed offshore'. By the same token, the authors found no evidence that offshore wealth-holders are now showing higher rates of tax compliance. In line with the findings of Woodward 2016 (*see* Chapter Five in this volume) about 'mock compliance', only a relocation of a small fraction of wealth held offshore to jurisdictions with fewer treaties could be identified as resulting from the wave of tax information-exchange agreements (TIEAs) signed since 2009. With worldwide private wealth accumulated offshore under conditions of secrecy in the order of between US$21 and 32 trillion in 2010 (Henry 2012), tax havenry appears to have survived relatively unscathed by the high-level political declarations of the G20, OECD and various other organisations. Similarly, rather than being contained, corporate tax avoidance has generated ever more headlines over the last five years, prompting the OECD to

1. For a cursory compilation, see http://taxjustice.blogspot.ch/2008/09/we-are-not-tax-haven.html (accessed 12 June 2014).

initiate its Base Erosion and Profit Shifting (BEPS) project (*see* Eccleston and Smith 2016, Chapter Eight in this volume).

This chapter considers why attempts to rein in tax havens have largely failed in the past twenty years. By comparing and analysing various national and international tax-haven listings, it argues that the principal reason for this failure lies with the unsuitable terminologies focused on tax, such as 'tax haven', which escape consistent definition and identification. As an alternative, the term 'secrecy jurisdiction' is introduced and operationalised through the Financial Secrecy Index (FSI). By shifting the focus away from tax aspects on to secrecy, and by using transparent and verifiable criteria and data sources, it overcomes a sharp – but largely artificial and arbitrary – binary distinction between 'tax havens' and others (Wójcik 2012: 7). The FSI assesses the degree to which a jurisdiction's legal and regulatory system contributes to global financial secrecy and thus facilitates corrupt practices, including those stemming from tax abuse. It can help to shape reforms in three main ways. First, the high ranking of major OECD powers underlines their need to lead through example, by enacting domestic policy reform before imposing it on others. These reforms must ensure that their domestic laws and regulations do not enable people or entities to escape or undermine the laws, rules and regulations of other jurisdictions. Second, once these reforms are implemented, a broad menu of finely graduated counter-measures can be adopted, targeting specific aspects of the financial secrecy of all jurisdictions. Third, by focusing on transparency as an intermediate step to achieving fair international tax rules, more sustained public support for reform efforts against the resistance of vested interests is likely to emerge.

Section Two of this chapter will discuss existing approaches for dealing with tax havens and point out their flaws before introducing 'secrecy jurisdiction' as a preferable alternative term. The third section will describe the FSI, while Section 4 will discuss its implications for the design of counter-measures in the light of current debates around the reform and justice of international tax policies. Section 5 concludes.

2. 'Tax haven' listings

Conceptual context of 'tax havens'

The conventional academic wisdom usually embeds the term 'tax haven' in an analytical framework referred to as 'tax competition' or 'tax wars' (Shaxson and Christensen forthcoming). While there is disagreement about who benefits from 'tax competition' (*see* Genschel and Seelkopf 2016, Chapter Three in this volume; Shaxson and Christensen 2013), it is not disputed that many jurisdictions commonly known as tax havens engage in poaching the tax bases of other nations (Slemrod and Wilson 2006; Dietsch and Rixen 2012, 2014). This poaching activity can take the form of specific laws and regulations designed to attract (mobile) capital offering reduced tax and regulation.

This base-poaching is mostly conceptualised as a zero-sum game, in which tax havens grab a greater slice of the pie at the expense of larger and higher-tax countries (Slemrod and Wilson 2006; Genschel and Schwarz 2011: 341–2, 354). A minority, however, holds that the net effects of tax havenry on other countries is economically beneficial. For instance, Desai *et al.* (2006) argue that a multinational company's presence in low-tax jurisdictions spurs economic growth in nearby 'high-tax' countries. Hines and Rice (1994) claim that a multinational firm's benefiting from reduced tax rates could lead to higher tax revenue in the country of residence of the ultimate parent holding-company of a multinational firm. However, these minority views have recently been criticised by IMF officials, who have argued that the aforementioned paper by Desai *et al.* (2006) is 'essentially uninformed by empirical knowledge' (IMF 2014: 23).

As a response to the success of the 'parasitic' state strategy of tax-base poaching (Abbott *et al.* 1999: 166–84), victims first resorted to unilateral counter-measures, which led to a 'proliferation spiral' of a domestic arsenal of increasingly complex counter-measures, followed by more sophisticated avoidance and evasion strategies (Rixen 2008: 144). As a second response, the parasitic state strategy was partially copied by victims, in an attempt to become poachers themselves (Shaxson 2011: 124–46).

More recently, international standards have been created to contain and prevent the most egregious misalignments and abuses. However, those standards can, arguably, be framed as 'club' or 'sham' standards imposed by a relatively small group of countries on a larger set of jurisdictions. According to Drezner (2005), the process of international standard-setting in any policy field is subject to interest-configurations among and across norm-creators and norm-takers and can, among others, result in 'club standards' or 'sham standards'. 'Club standards' are imposed by a relatively small group of powerful countries with homogeneous interests in a particular field of policy on a larger set of jurisdictions with a set of diverging preferences. Club standards ensure asymmetric benefits for the club members *vis-à-vis* non-members, while 'sham standards' are largely ineffective, being the result of diverse interests not only between norm-creators and norm-takers, but also among the norm-creators themselves[2] (Drezner 2005).

Reacting to the pressure to comply with standards imposed from outside, jurisdictions may adapt by choosing less direct means of poaching, ticking the box of imposed law reform but engaging in only 'mock compliance' (*see* Woodward 2016, Chapter Five in this volume) with those standards. Some even run the risk of directly, but secretly, violating supranational or even domestic law through dubious administrative practice (European Commission 2014). Such mock compliance

2. While Drezner (2005) evaluates the standards and initiatives in the policy field of anti-money laundering by FATF and FSF up until roughly 2003 as being club standards 'successfully' imposed on, among others, offshore financial centres, it could be argued that, since then, the nature of the standards has become 'sham', as divergences among FATF-members have grown in importance. For instance, in the process towards the overhaul of the 40 recommendations of the FATF and the related peer-review methodology in 2012, a divide about the role of public registries for company beneficial ownership as well as for trusts ran through the FATF membership, a conflict that has become particularly visible in the negotiations around EU's fourth anti-money-laundering directive during 2013–15.

is a response by conflicted administrations and governments to the conflicting demands of external actors and the domestic financial-services industry; and is at the centre of current debates about tax havens.

Problems in defining 'tax havens'

In 2014, the IMF stated that the term 'tax haven' was 'unhelpful and ill-defined' (IMF 2014: 17, footnote 30). This follows many years of wide and recurrent use of the term, both in academia and policy-making, at national and international levels. Moreover, not only has the term been widely used and defined for decades but the practice of using or creating listings of havens and similar places has invariably accompanied the proliferation of this or other tax-focused terminology.[3] While implications for research (Cobham *et al.* 2015) and definitional problems have been explored in greater detail elsewhere (*ibid.*; Murphy 2008), this section briefly reviews debates around the definition of tax havens and other tax-focused concepts in a policy-making context.

There are various examples of international organisations or influential authors testifying to the inadequacy of the term tax haven. Probably the first comprehensive study into tax havens was written by Gordon (1981) in a report to the US Treasury. He summarised definitions of tax havens

> to include any country having a low or zero rate of tax on all or certain categories of income, and offering a certain level of banking or commercial secrecy. Applied literally, however, this definition would sweep in many industrialized countries not generally considered tax havens, including the United States (Gordon 1981: 14).

A few years later, the OECD (1987: 21) agreed the futility of trying to define tax havens by stating that: '[a]ttempts to provide a single definition of a "tax haven" are bound to be unsuccessful. ... It can be argued that the "tax haven" concept is such a relative one that it would serve no useful purpose to make further attempts to define it' (OECD 1987: 21). Picciotto agreed that 'virtually any country might be a "haven" in relation to another' (2013[1992]: 132) if a tax haven encompasses facilitating a reduction of tax liability in another country. Two of the best examples of the subjectivity and circular logic inherent in attempts to define tax havens can be found in the Gordon report, which suggested a '"smell" or reputation test' (Gordon 1981: 14) to identify tax havens. The second example is US Senator Chuck Grassley, ex-Chairman of the Finance Committee of the US Senate, who compared a tax shelter to pornography, stating: 'You can't define it, but you know it when you see it' (United States Senate, Committee on Finance 2002).

Despite the term's apparent inappropriateness, it has been widely used in international policy-making. Probably the most prominent of recent uses was in

3. See, for instance, Hines and Rice 1994; Desai *et al.* 2006; Johannesen and Zucman 2014; Genschel and Seelkopf 2016, Chapter Three in this volume.

the context of the Harmful Tax Competition project, when, in the late 1990s, the OECD (1998, 2000) heavily invested in the term 'tax haven', culminating in a listing of thirty-five tax havens published in the year 2000. By failing, however, to deliver a consistent and objective definition and identification of tax havens, the initiative was vulnerable to accusations of illegitimacy and political bias, ultimately contributing to the project's failure (Sharman 2006).

Since the financial crisis of 2008 and the OECD's (2009) publication of its white-, grey-, and black-lists under G20 mandate in April 2009, the language of an 'internationally agreed tax standard' has become the widely shared reference point for various national listing approaches. The notion of a 'tax haven' lost ground against a jurisdiction's commitment to abide by the transparency and co-operation standard the OECD and associated jurisdictions have shaped since their Harmful Tax Competition project. While this is a welcome departure from mainly tax-focused, one-dimensional and non-transparent listings and mitigates some of its deficiencies, including by reducing the scope for arbitrariness and political bias, using the international standard for tax co-operation or related listings remains problematic for the purpose of policy-design and that of research. The standard has been analysed as being an ineffective sham, favouring OECD member-state interests (Meinzer 2012a; Sheppard 2009). In addition, political demands by non-OECD G20 member-states and others to go beyond the agreed standard (Pandey 2011) have evidenced the need for a more ambitious approach in tackling tax-base poaching than relying on the 'internationally agreed tax standard'.

As an illustration of the 'sham' quality of the standard it is helpful to consider the definition of the term 'beneficial owner' of a company. Because tax evasion by wealthy individuals and tax avoidance by corporations, as well as high-level bribery, usually depend on intermediate or shell companies for financial transactions, the unambiguous identification of the natural persons ultimately owning or controlling a company is an important backbone of any international standard seeking to address the issues of tax evasion and avoidance. In accordance with this conventional wisdom, the anti-money-laundering agency FATF has long defined beneficial owners as the 'natural person(s) who ultimately owns or controls a customer and/or the natural person on whose behalf a transaction is being conducted. It also includes those persons who exercise ultimate effective control over a legal person or arrangement' (FATF 2012: 110).

In accordance with this, in a report published in 2001, the OECD explicitly uses the notion of a beneficial owner being a natural person (OECD 2001: 14). Contrary to this, the influential model tax convention of the OECD has allowed a legal entity to be considered as the beneficial owner (OECD 2008: 12). This notion influenced the entire work of OECDs Global Forum on Transparency and Exchange of Information for Tax Purposes (henceforth, 'Global Forum') which created and still reviews compliance with the international tax standard. In the backbone of this standard, the model Tax Information-Exchange Agreement (TIEA) of 2002, the term 'beneficial owner' is not defined but refers to discrete national definitions (OECD 2002: para. 51 of Commentary). Notwithstanding this lack of definition, the term is used in OECD's and Global Forum's joint annual Tax Co-Operation Reports 2006–10. However, while the term 'legal owner' is clearly defined, the definition of a 'beneficial owner' lacks fundamental intellectual rigour by relying on circular logic:

> Legal ownership refers to the registered owner of the share, which may be an individual, but also a nominee, a trust or a company, etc. Beneficial ownership reporting requirements refers to a range of reporting requirements that require further information when the legal owner is not also the beneficial owner (OECD 2006: 148).

This unclear language testifies to a sham standard that leaves the door wide open for tax abuses, since it creates and perpetuates uncertainty that can be easily exploited by lawyers and other advisers. Furthermore, the conflation of definitions of legal and beneficial ownership facilitates the main avoidance strategy of 'triangulation' presented in Table 12.1.

Review of national 'tax haven' listings

Long before international organisations started to use tax-haven listings, national governments had been compiling and using such listings, informing various policy measures to prevent shifting of the tax base (OECD 1987: 29–36). Most measures prominently feature controlled foreign company rules that, under certain conditions, would treat for tax purposes some income of a foreign legal entity that is controlled by domestic shareholders as if this income was earned domestically. These and similar rules date back to the 1930s: the USA introduced foreign personal holding company legislation in 1937; and, from 1938, Belgium shifted the burden of proof on to taxpayers for certain transactions with low-tax jurisdictions if they wanted to enjoy advantageous tax treatment (OECD 1987: 32–3). Later on, for implementing this kind of law, countries issued implicit illustrative lists of jurisdictions (for example, Germany), or more explicit legally binding lists of jurisdictions (Italy, Spain, Argentina; Sharman and Rawlings 2006). Other countries (such as the UK, Australia and New Zealand) use the opposite approach, where a 'white-list' names those jurisdictions which would be exempt from special CFC-tax rules (Gurney 2005; HMRC 2011). In some cases, the defining criterion for which legal entities would fall under CFC-rules relies on the tax rate payable by the legal entity in its jurisdiction of incorporation (in German law, the threshold is 25 per cent corporate tax rate; in US law, 31.5 per cent[4]).

Because the term 'tax haven' is seldom used explicitly in national legislation or regulation, other terminologies with specific national legal implications

4. The corporate tax threshold of US.CFC rules is arrived at as follows: subpart F legislation in the US exempts from the scope of US CFC rules income which has been taxed with a rate exceeding more than 90% of the highest US corporate tax rate (Rienstra 2014). By taking 35% tax rate in the US as a basis, the threshold for exempting foreign income from CFC rules is 31.5%. For Germany, see Perdelwitz (2014).

Figure 12.1: Jurisdictions' incidence on national tax-haven listings

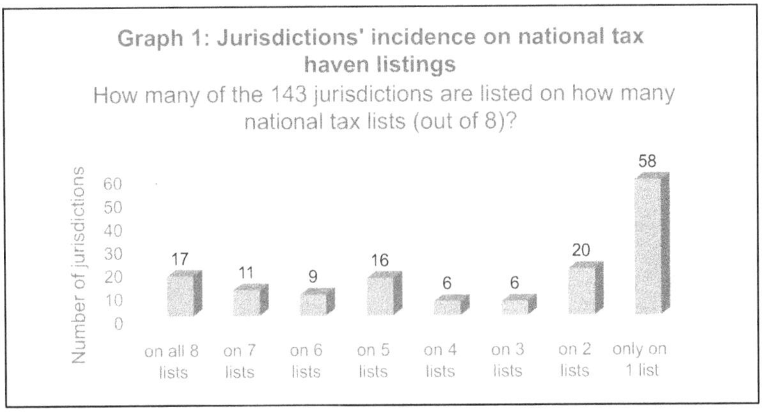

Source: see footnote 7.

are defined instead.[5] Depending on the purpose, some countries are applying more than one term and listing (for example, 'low-tax jurisdiction' or 'uncooperative states and jurisdictions' in German and French law; 'tax shelter' in US law[6]). However, all the different terms share some characteristics and problems.

The following Graph 12.1 shows the incidence of jurisdictions on various national tax-related listings. These listings were either used for illustrative purposes or explicitly for the purpose of implementing controlled foreign company legislation or similar measures to counter corporate tax avoidance. Other listings which relate to aspects such as compliance with international standards have been ignored in order to increase comparability. The countries covered are Argentina (2000), Brazil (2002), Italy (2003), France (1975), Germany (2004), Russia (2007), Spain (2003), and USA (1994).[7] Most of the listings refer back ten years or more since there has been an observable shift in the use of blacklists in recent years. While there is a trend in CFC rules to replace explicit and published listings with generalised rules that are applicable to all jurisdictions (Japan, France), the use of blacklists appears to increase within the context of compliance with international standards (France, Argentina).[8]

5. For the sake of readability, throughout this article the term tax haven is used synonymously with those alternative terminologies.
6. Author's own translations from laws or regulations of each country.
7. These lists were compiled partly based on Sharman/Rawlings 2005: 19, 28, 31, 33 and personal communication with authors of that paper in June 2014. In addition, the following sources were used: Germany BMF 2004; Italian Ministry of Economy and Finance 2001; France: Email Christian Chavagneux on 4 July 2014 (General Tax Code Article 238A, instruction du 26 juin 1975, Bulletin Officiel 4C.8.75); Russia: Zakharov 2008.
8. The source for these three country examples is Deloitte 2014: 2; communication with Christian Chavagneux, Krishen Mehta and Vincent Drezet in July 2014.

Of the total of 143 jurisdictions listed on the eight reviewed lists, 17 are named on all eight lists but fifty-eight are only on one list. There are various reasons for this curious dispersal. A lack of expertise or care in creating the listings is a first important explanation. As Sharman (2010) has shown, there are errors in some listings, for instance, including non-existent territories due to misspelling; referring to places that lack tax sovereignty or which in international law ceased to exist long ago; or denoting unclear geographic regions rather than legally defined jurisdictions (*ibid*: 17–19). Worse, some of the consistency observable in the listings appears not to be grounded in a consensus about especially harmful tax havens. Rather, in instances of 'dysfunctional policy transfer', idiosyncratic errors of listings have been copy-pasted from lists of other countries abroad, in one instance even leading to a situation of a country blacklisting itself (*ibid*: 6, 20). Sharman concluded that errors by 'over-committed' policy-makers have contributed to an 'often arbitrary and inaccurate nature of such lists' (*ibid*: 5).[9]

Leaving aside the problems of inconsistency and variation, national blacklists in most cases lack the leverage to induce legal reforms in the blacklisted jurisdictions because of relatively small reputational risks. Instead, they usually serve as a basis for a broad range of measures intended to counter the specific harmful effects associated with them. Table 12.1 provides an overview of the counter-measures contemplated under the eight reviewed national listings and others, as well as an indication of how those counter-measures could be avoided.

The most important weakness of national tax-listing approaches, however, is the ease of their avoidance through 'triangulation'. Even if a country succeeded in creating an accurate, tailored and highly idiosyncratic list of tax havens that are harmful to its economy, and even if it was successful in updating the list every year or even monthly, it would remain easy to circumvent any counter-measures based on that listing. Under the current configuration of the world economy and the international 'club' and 'sham' tax rules, the trick would simply require the interposition of another legal structure in a jurisdiction that is not blacklisted but through which the dubious transactions could ultimately reach their destination in a blacklisted jurisdiction (triangulation). The conflation of beneficial and legal ownership (discussed previously) is the bedrock of this triangulation strategy.

An example of this problematic is the restricted applicability of the controlled-foreign-company rules against any company located in another EU member-state after the European Court of Justice's Cadbury-Schweppes ruling of 2006. The Court effectively reduced the application of CFC-rules within the EU to 'wholly artificial tax arrangements', without defining what those entail (ECJ 2006; Ford *et al.* 2013; Perdelwitz 2014; Picciotto 2013). Because EU members such

9. In order to correct for the bias, this dysfunctional transfer of listings would have implied for our review, only one of the lists by those four countries for which erroneous copy-pasting has been identified has been included in the review. These four countries were Mexico, Argentina, Portugal and Venezuela (Sharman 2010: 18).

Table 12.1: Overview of counter-measures against listed jurisdictions ('LJ')[10]

National list	Counter-measure	Avoidance strategy
Argentina	All transactions with persons in LJ assumed to be between related parties; all of their income treated and taxed as if distributed.	Triangulation
Brazil	25% withholding tax on payments to residents of LJ and transactions treated as between related parties; no simplified transfer-pricing calculation.	Triangulation
Italy	Dividend exemption cancelled and limits on deduction of expenses unless proven real business activity.	Triangulation; fake 'real business activity'
France	None [illustrative list[11]]; profits of subsidiaries in certain territories will be taxed as if earned by French parent.	Triangulation
Germany	None [illustrative list]; passive income of subsidiaries in certain territories is not exempt and taxed as if earned by German shareholder.	Triangulation, transform passive into active income
Russia	9% tax on dividends received from entities in LJ.	Triangulation
Spain	Assumption of passive income and of minimum taxable income in Spain.	Triangulation
USA	None [illustrative list] – under certain conditions, income of CFCs will be taxed as if earned by U.S. shareholder.	Triangulation; deferral
Other lists	**Counter-measure**	**Avoidance strategy**
G20 toolbox 2009	Increased disclosure requirements for transactions; withholding taxes; denial of deductions of expense payments; reviewing tax treaty and 'public investment' policies.	Triangulation

Source: Sharman and Rawlings 2005: 19–33; Lesage 2010: 3–4; Deloitte 2014: 20–3, 64–5; Zakharov 2008. Author's own research and analysis.

as Cyprus, Ireland or Luxembourg do not have CFC-rules of their own (Deloitte 2014: 71) and are known to require very lenient transfer-pricing documentation (CMS 2013), any European multinational seeking to shift profits out of any EU member-state can achieve this by creating a controlled subsidiary in any of those countries and routing investments and/or transactions through those subsidiaries.

10. This table is not a comprehensive summary of the entire spectrum of counter-measures. One listing may trigger various different sets of counter-measures. Instead, this table focuses on those measures linked to controlled-foreign-company rules or similar provisions countering corporate tax-avoidance.

11. Meaning that the list of countries does not serve for legally enabling counter-measures; the list is presented as being purely 'illustrative'; everybody understands that the tax administration will apply this list in practice, nonetheless.

Because it is nigh-on impossible for a tax administration to prove in court that an arrangement in an EU member-state is 'wholly artificial', companies can easily avoid CFC rules.

Another telling example is the case of France, which blacklisted Jersey and Bermuda in its 2013 list of uncooperative jurisdictions (among others). Under French law, hefty penalty taxes are due for transactions with related entities located in those listed jurisdictions. In practice, however, the listing had no tangible effects, since retaliation measures such as the penalty taxes have never been used for any transactions with those places, although French banks maintain subsidiaries in the Islands (Robert 2014). Instead of direct transactions, more indirect channels for routing of payments have apparently been used.

Review of international 'tax haven' listings

The tax-listings compiled by international organisations and academics share some of the problems with the national listings, but also have another set of specific problems of their own. Generally, they do not serve directly as a basis of 'hard law' national counter-measures, but inform and influence policy-making at both international and national levels through 'soft law' (Abbott *et al.* 2000), including through reputational threats.

Figure 12.2 shows the dispersion of jurisdictions listed on eight tax-related listings that have been created or used by international organisations or influential academics over the past thirty-five years.[12] The initial sample of listings has been taken from Murphy (2009), who reviewed eleven listings created by national or international organisations and academics, including listings focusing on 'offshore' jurisdictions from angles other than tax (that is, money-laundering, financial stability). The original sample was adjusted by removing those listings with no direct tax linkages, which resulted in a remaining total of six listings by IBFD (quoted in Irish 1982: see Irish 1982; Hines and Rice 1994; OECD 2000; TJN 2005 and the specialist website Lowtax.net 2008). Two additional recent listings have been included in the review.[13] The first is the listing used by the IF campaign (ActionAid 2013), a coalition of more than a hundred NGOs demanding tax and transparency reform at the G8 summit in the UK in 2013.[14] Finally, the listing used by Johannesen and Zucman (2014) has also been included.

12. To make the lists comparable to one another and over time, a few adjustments have been made. For example, the islands Sark and Alderney have been counted in original listing by TJN (2005) as separate jurisdictions, while they belong to the Bailiwick of Guernsey – they have thus been subsumed under Guernsey. Furthermore, the Netherlands Antilles was dissolved in 2010, and split in various parts. Among the new countries, Curaçao is and was the dominant player in offshore finance and therefore was treated as synonymous with Netherlands Antilles throughout the listings.

13. Inspired by Cobham *et al.* 2015. The grey- and blacklists of OECD (2009) were not used, since this listing explicitly referred to adherence to the international tax transparency and co-operation standard and thus differs from the other listings in a fundamental way.

14. This listing relied on an extended version of a 2008 listing published by the US Government Accountability Office (US GAO 2008). The extension consisted in adding Delaware (counted as US in our review) and the Netherlands.

Figure 12.2: Incidence of tax haven listings: on how many tax lists (out of eight maximum) are each of the eighty-four jurisdictions named?

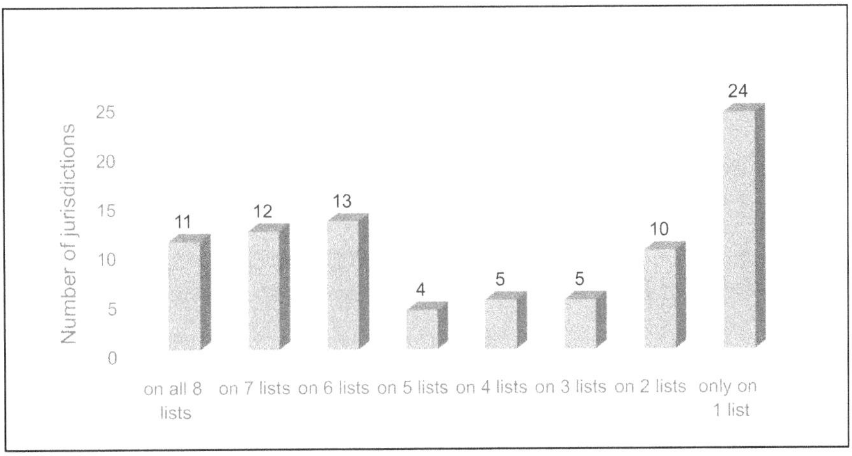

With twenty-four jurisdictions featuring on only one list, the graph illustrates that the range of jurisdictions seen from an international and academic tax perspective as 'tax havens' is considerable. The twenty-four jurisdictions that figure on only one list indicate the high degree of disagreement among international observers. Intuitive explanations for the level of 'expert [dis]agreement' (Haberly and Wójcik 2014: 6), such as the large span of time between the oldest and most recent of the eight reviewed listings, appear not to explain the principal reason(s) for the variation.

When comparing the number and incidence of jurisdictions in the national and international tax-haven listings, a notable difference emerges. In the eight analysed national tax listings, a total of 143 jurisdictions are named; whereas the total number of the international listings is eighty-four. Similarly, the ratio of incidence of one to all lists in the eight national lists is 3.4:1, considerably higher than the ratio in international listings, which is 2.2:1. While the results should be taken with some caution,[15] these differences could at least partially be explained by the specificity of each country's tax laws and terminology, which is expected to result in a specialised pattern of tax havens for each country, increasing the total number of jurisdictions potentially considered tax havens. At the international level, in contrast, which is concerned rather with soft law and reputational effects, these specificities would lose relevance. Also, more diverse political interests could further narrow the listed jurisdictions to the lowest common denominator.

15. There are various reasons to be cautious and not to place too heavy an emphasis on the listings. For instance, the status of the national tax-haven listings varies considerably. Whereas the administration in the USA claims to use some of the listings for statistical purposes, others use them as illustrative examples (Germany) and still others have given the listings the status of delegated legislation (e.g., Argentina, Russia).

The evident tendency and requirement to create consensus in international tax listings is one of their most important weaknesses, because they only allow for the lowest common political denominator. Club members of listing organisations often enjoy preferential treatment or even veto-rights against being blacklisted themselves. This effect is growing in proportion to the diplomatic status of the listing organisation. The OECD list (OECD 2000) was clearly more constrained by diplomatic straddling than, for instance, the listings by the tax-avoidance portal 'lowtax.net' or by the Tax Justice Network. The resulting 'club consensus' is rife with inconsistencies and bias, which fuel accusations of 'imperialism' by groupings targeted by the 'club consensus'. Trying to impose compliance with 'club' or 'sham' standards under those conditions results, at best, in mock compliance. An example is the demand by the OECD for all targeted jurisdictions to sign at least twelve TIEAs, resulting in many TIEAs being signed between small island 'tax havens' (Shaxson and Christensen 2011).

Overlapping issues of national and international blacklists

The most fundamental problems associated with listing approaches, however, are valid both for national and international blacklists. Figure 12.3 summarises the policy-oriented shortcomings and risks inherent in tax-related listing approaches.

An obvious problem with any tax-listing approach concerns the risk of serious time lags. Some authors argue that the listings are 'sticky', making it very difficult for jurisdictions to exit a listing, even if they have modified specific laws and regulations (Sharman and Rawlings 2006: 42–4). Similarly, time lags in detecting new relevant players may also result in problematic omissions from listings. More recently, as listings are increasingly linked to compliance with an international

Figure 12.3: Shortcomings of national and international (tax) blacklist approaches

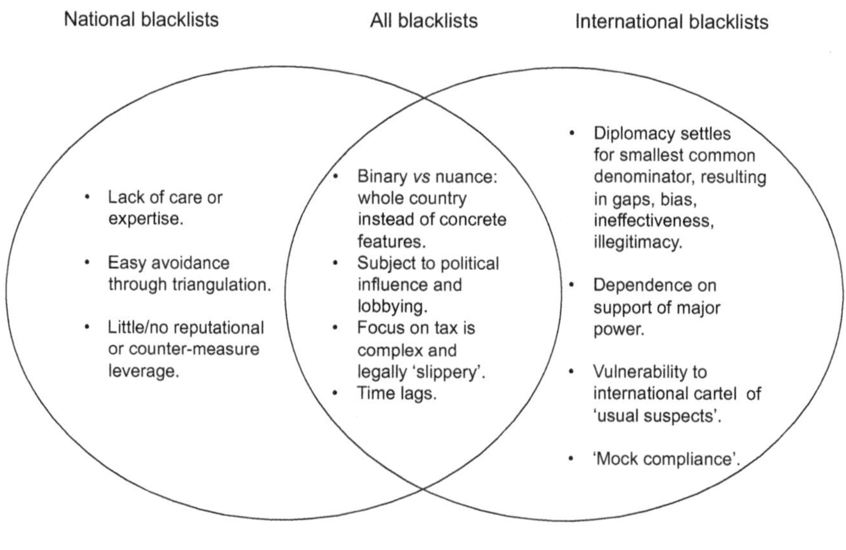

standard of co-operation and information-exchange, this problem appears less relevant than before. For instance, in many national contexts the signature of a treaty allowing for exchange of information upon request is nowadays enough to exit a national (tax) blacklist. For example, Argentina (Meloni 2014: 26) and France (Robert 2014) update their new lists every year.

The anecdote about tax havens signing near-useless TIEAs with one another illustrates a more fundamental problem with both national and international tax-haven listings. It is hard to insulate lists from political manipulation. A famous example of recent high-level tax diplomacy concerns the outcome of the G20 summit in London 2009, where the French and Chinese presidents wrestled over the inclusion of Hong Kong and Macao in the grey-list prepared by the OECD. After mediation by President Obama, the two special administrative regions of China were relegated to a footnote adjacent to mainland China, itself on the white-list. Furthermore, Chinese negotiators successfully ensured that the G20 merely 'took note' of the OECD listings instead of endorsing them (Lesage 2010: 4–5). Another example is the preferential treatment of OECD members in the subsequent Global Forum peer-review process (Meinzer 2012a: 10).

On the national level, blacklists of tax havens are vulnerable to the influence of economic lobby groups. Rixen (2009: 33) shows how US and German anti-tax-haven law proposals of 2009 were watered down during the legislative process.[16] As a result, in the German case the main counter-measures contemplated in the law have never been applied in practice because, to date, no jurisdiction has been named 'uncooperative' by the government.[17]

Another fundamental weakness of any blacklisting approach is the potential for indiscriminately listing an entire country. Forcing the tax systems of hundreds of jurisdictions into a dichotomous straitjacket lacks both objectivity and legitimacy. In most cases, a jurisdiction's economy will host legitimate business mixed with poaching activities. As a consequence, concerns rarely arise from jurisdictions and their entire populations but are generally focused on particular financial or legal measures and the agents abusing those measures.[18] Thus, 'tax havenry' is a matter of degree, not a binary variable (Wójcik 2012: 7). As Cobham (2014: 2) illustrates, illicit financial flows facilitating tax abuse and base-shifting are closely intertwined with world trade, and are not some alien aspect that can be defined and isolated away with a stroke of the pen. Without nuance to take account of these intricacies, attempts to list jurisdictions will remain fraught with difficulty.

16. See also http://steuergerechtigkeit.blogspot.de/2009/05/wirtschaftslobby-macht-mobil-gegen.html (accessed 30 June 2014).

17. See http://www.bundesfinanzministerium.de/Content/DE/Downloads/BMF_Schreiben/Internationales_Steuerrecht/Allgemeine_Informationen/001a.html?__act=renderPdf&__iDocId=178606; and http://www.bundesfinanzministerium.de/Content/DE/Downloads/BMF_Schreiben/Internationales_Steuerrecht/Allgemeine_Informationen/001_a.pdf?__blob=publicationFilev=3 (accessed 30 June 2014).

18. The German illustrative list is exceptionally specific in either targeting specific types of legal regimes in the listed jurisdiction (i.e. 'international finance and trading companies' or 'special economic zones') or in justifying the listing by reference to a particular feature (i.e. '17.5% rate tax on profits'; 'exemption of capital gains' [author's translation of BMF 2004]). However, because it was published in 2004, it is outdated in many respects.

Most fundamental of all problems with tax blacklists, however, is the complexity of tax law and practice. Tax appears to be too complex, too unstable and subject to legal dispute to serve as a useful basis for counter-measures. Any country in the world might be a tax haven for another one simply by accident, for example, by treating certain legal entities or income differently for tax purposes than another country ('hybrid mismatches'; BEPS Monitoring Group 2014). While double-tax treaties are supposed to address such mismatches across countries' tax systems, they are increasingly recognised as part of the problem rather than the solution (IMF 2014; Sheppard 2013; Rixen 2011). Anti-treaty-shopping provisions – aimed at preventing a taxpayer from routing his payments through jurisdictions with the most favourable tax treaties – and similar measures to prevent abuse of tax treaties exemplify the spiralling complexity of international tax law that decreases legal certainty and hence opens further room for abuse by economic actors.[19] Sharman and Rawlings identify this problem succinctly:

> There are hundreds of tax regimes maintained by sovereign states and other fiscally-autonomous territories. Even taken individually these codes are often monstrously complex and subject to frequent updates and revisions. Even if an accurate blacklist of jurisdictions were drawn up, it would need constant monitoring and revision to keep pace with the rate of change in tax codes. The prospect of working through each of these, to emerge with a dichotomous classification of each at the end is daunting in the extreme (Sharman and Rawlings 2006: 45).

3. The definition and operationalisation of a 'secrecy jurisdiction'

In response to these problems with the concept of a tax haven, which appear to bar it from robust and useful operationalisation, Murphy (2008) defined and explored the concept of secrecy jurisdictions as an alternative. By shifting the emphasis away from tax aspects of jurisdictions, and focusing instead on questions of transparency and secrecy, the definition of criteria and verification of compliance becomes easier. While this is only partially true for information whose access is restricted to competent authorities (such as bank-account information), it is relevant in terms of information that is placed on public record via the internet, allowing everyone to verify compliance and to report cases of non-compliance.

The following definition of a secrecy jurisdiction is used in this chapter: 'A jurisdiction which provides facilities that enable people or entities to escape or undermine the laws, rules and regulations of other jurisdictions elsewhere, using secrecy as a prime tool' (Meinzer 2012b: 1; TJN 2011: 5; inspired by Murphy 2008).

To operationalise this definition, the Financial Secrecy Index combines a measure of secrecy (secrecy score) with a quantitative Global Scale Weight (GSW).

19. This dynamic is well explored in Rixen 2008.

The secrecy score indicates the degree to which a country's legal and regulatory system (or absence thereof) provides the secrecy that enables illicit financial flows. The GSW indicates the size of each jurisdiction's share of the global market for financial services provided to non-resident clients. After adjusting both for their different range of values, they are multiplied with each other to arrive at one single value reflecting the potential global harm done by each jurisdiction.[20] The resulting ranking is the Financial Secrecy Index, which is updated bi-annually. The notion of a spectrum applicable to all countries echoes the recent reframing by the IMF of tax competition in terms of the 'tax spillover effects' one country's tax system can have on other nations (IMF 2014: 23). While the FSI only covered eighty-two jurisdictions in 2013, eventually global, or near-global coverage is envisaged.[21] The ranking of the FSI can be accessed at Cobham *et al.* 2015 and at TJN 2013: 78–80.

The secrecy score is based on fifteen explicit, detailed and verifiable indicators[22] (key financial secrecy indicators, KFSIs) and allows for comparisons of countries on an imagined continuum from highly secretive to perfectly transparent. This approach overcomes the false dichotomy between tax haven or not (or secrecy jurisdiction or not), but underpins and is consistent with the notion that a secrecy jurisdiction is a matter of degree and empirical enquiry. Rather than being set in stone, these KFSI can change over time, subject to refinement, data-availability or new insights. The guiding principle for data-collection was to always look for and assess the lowest standard (or denominator) of transparency available in each jurisdiction and for each KFSI. Taken together and weighted equally, these indicators result in one compound secrecy score allocated to each jurisdiction. The scores are normalised to a range zero to 100 and in practice vary between 32 (Sweden, relatively transparent) and 88 (Samoa, secretive) (TJN 2013: 91).

The 15 KFSIs can be grouped around four broad dimensions of secrecy: 1) knowledge of beneficial ownership of bank accounts, legal entities and agreements (three KFSIs); 2) public corporate transparency with respect to ownership, accounts and country-by-country reporting (three KFSIs); 3) efficiency of tax and financial regulation as regards the handling of tax information, unilateral rules for the avoidance of 'double' taxation as well as tolerance of harmful legal vehicles (four KFSIs); and 4) international standards and co-operation in tax information-exchange, anti-money-laundering, judicial co-operation and various international treaties (five KFSIs). A more detailed discussion about each indicator can be found elsewhere (TJN 2013; Cobham *et al.* 2015).

The FSI offers various advantages over existing listing approaches. First, because the secrecy score and the global scale weight are both based on publicly

20. For more details on the combination of both, please read Cobham *et al.* 2015 and TJN 2013: 70–2.

21. More information about the selection of the 82 countries can be found at TJN 2013: 5–6. The selection process for the initial 60 jurisdictions is explained in detail in Murphy 2009.

22. The dataset underlying the 15 KFSIs is available online for review here: www.financialsecrecyindex.com/database/menu.xml (accessed 7 July 2014).

available data sources, they allow for verification and replication of the data. Most importantly, to the extent to which the KFSIs measure online availability of information, the FSI mitigates the risks of 'mock compliance', since it makes the information accessible to a wide audience, with easy detection of fake compliance.[23] Second, in contrast to the OECD and Global Forum's assessment of 'upon request' information-exchange, the FSI applies stricter standards in terms of financial transparency and information-exchange, eschewing the notion of 'sham' standards, as well as in terms of global coverage and multilateralism, mitigating the risk of 'club' standards serving only the selected few. Third, and closely related to this, by weighting the secrecy offered by any jurisdiction by the size of its cross-border financial sector, the FSI mitigates against the risk of repeating the most blatant hypocrisies witnessed by past initiatives, which saw major political powers applying standards to the rest of the world without themselves abiding by those (Cobham *et al.* 2015). Nonetheless, when considering the FSI as a more legitimate and successful basis for devising counter-measures compared to listing approaches and the concept of tax havens or similar approaches, a number of considerations have to be taken into account.

4. Counter-measures and the Financial Secrecy Index

Discussions around counter-measures against tax-base poaching by jurisdictions raise profound questions about the boundaries of the self-determination of states and the (in)justice of the international economic order. Beginning with a notion of justice rooted in 'moral cosmopolitanism', which ascribes to all human beings an unalienable dignity, Dietsch and Rixen (2012) have explored some implications of tax competition. Today's unfettered tax competition would exacerbate unjust economic inequalities within and across states by impacting the size of state budgets (in developing countries) as well as the tax mix (in both developed and developing countries). By focusing on the 'rules of the game' of tax competition instead of direct (re)distributive policies and outcomes on a supranational level, national redistributive capacities could be strengthened and the political prospects for reform would improve (Dietsch and Rixen 2014).

The authors suggest two principles that delimit legitimate tax policies from illegitimate ones with respect to tax competition. The first principle is the membership principle, which suggests that 'Natural and legal persons should be liable to pay tax in the state of which they are a member' (Dietsch and Rixen 2012: 9). Under this principle, the poaching of tax bases both through a multinational company's paper-profit shifting (largely tax avoidance) and through an individual's portfolio investments (tax evasion) would be illegitimate. With respect to the attraction of real direct foreign investment, a fiscal policy constraint principle is suggested. According to this principle, luring of foreign investment

23. The online availability of information is checked by KFSIs 2, 4, 5 and 6. Indirectly, KFSI 10 also allows for easy verification, since it concerns the availability of certain legal vehicles which could be verified by anyone pretending an interest to create such a vehicle.

into the domestic economy is 'illegitimate when it both is strategically motivated and leads to a reduction in the aggregate level of fiscal self-determination of other states' (Dietsch and Rixen 2014: 73). The strategic motivation refers to a country's intention to lure foreign tax base through fiscal policies, while the level of fiscal self-determination refers to tax-base losses elsewhere. As a by-product of implementing those principles, international redistribution would be improved compared to today's situation.

For the enforcement of those principles, the authors suggest an International Tax Organisation (ITO), which would monitor and discipline a jurisdiction's fiscal policies. The authors assume that the data and information for determining strategic intention and tax-base losses 'are readily available' (Dietsch and Rixen 2012: 19). At the same time, they concede that complexities in determining causal relationships for challenging particular fiscal policies before the ITO may lead to 'controversies over the right interpretation' (*ibid.*). Furthermore, the authors state that monitoring of compliance would not pose a major problem 'since governments can be expected to launch a complaint if other governments violate' the principles, and enforcement of complaints is ensured through a binding dispute-settlement body (Dietsch and Rixen 2012: 20).

It is on these two points that the present article partly differs and to which it contributes, by suggesting that the likelihood of fiscal-policy reforms along the lines suggested by Dietsch and Rixen is low unless an intermediate step for increasing transparency is taken. The current rules on international accounting and (absence of) tax disclosure reduces the possibilities for determining the extent of compliance with both the fiscal constraint and membership principles. In the absence of firm-level tax and accounting data on a country-by-country basis, it is virtually impossible to reliably estimate tax-base losses, let alone to establish causal relationships (Murphy 2012a: 288–95). Today, even tax administrations can only look at a small snippet of the full picture of a modern multinational company's network of subsidiaries and controlled transactions (Murphy 2012b).

Even if a fuller picture about the extent of base-poaching and -luring was available to tax administrations and governments, however, it remains questionable whether this would lead to a virtuous cycle of mutual compliance. The assumption of a neutral dispute-settlement body adjudicating on internationally agreed fair rules seems oblivious to existing power configurations. Because the incentives for free-riding persist and many advanced economies are invested in international tax rules allowing for tax-base-poaching and -luring, collusion between governments to jointly reject the institution of fair rules and a supranational dispute settlement body with binding powers should be expected. Drawing parallels to the area of world trade, the historical record shows how biased in favour of rich countries' economic interests the world trade rules and the WTO have been (Stiglitz and Charlton 2005), possibly even exacerbating existing inequalities among countries.

Considering the current fundamentally different levels of consensus in the private sector and the general public around fair-tax rules today, compared to free-trade rules at the time of the creation of the WTO, governments are unlikely to agree on or submit to supranational fair-tax principles. However, to the extent that governments are democratically accountable, publicity and voter awareness around the scale and nature of tax-base poaching and luring could lead to a shifting of governments' positions over time, and reach a tipping point, paving the way for international reform. Therefore, instead of focusing on counter-measures based on specific tax policies, it is suggested that a more promising intermediate step would be to frame counter-measures around transparency, or the lack thereof. This might mobilise public opinion because transparency, by definition, is a catalyst for reliable information and thus compliance; it may be easier to reach political consensus about transparency and co-operation for law enforcement, compared to the more difficult task of agreeing on principles of legitimate rules of the game with direct and far-ranging distributive implications.

This is in line with what Stiglitz and Charlton suggested in 2005 for containing and countering the ruinous dynamics of tax and incentive competition in developing countries. The authors laid out three strategies to counter this harmful competition, each of which reflects another level of ambition in the objectives to be achieved:

> In ascending order these are: (1) transparency-enhancing obligations on firms and countries; (2) co-operation between jurisdictions; and (3) the putting in place of enforceable international rules (Stiglitz and Charlton 2005: 133).

While the authors only frame the stages in terms of ambition, it is argued ere that these stages are, to a significant degree, sequential. Based on the discussions above about the catalytic effects of transparency by raising public awareness and boosting compliance by allowing independent investigators to expose abuse, levels 2 and 3 appear to a large degree to be dependent upon previous achievement of level 1 obligations, which are transparency-enhancing. Furthermore, transparency on the degree of co-operation (level 2) is another indispensable step towards level 3.

In this light, in its two major assaults on 'harmful tax competition' (1998–2002) and 'uncooperative jurisdictions' (2009–12), the OECD appears to have been counterproductive. It committed political blunders twice by being overambitious in aiming for levels 2 and 3 without ensuring transparency of firms and jurisdictions first. The OECD's original foray in 1998 succeeded merely in creating a united front of opposition, which was accommodated by inviting tax havens to join the policy-formulation process. Hardly surprisingly, this resulted in a sham standard that once more paved the way for a distorted outcome. Worse, the 2009 black-, grey- and white-lists initiative provided the many tax havens who achieved a white listing on the basis of having a mere twelve TIEAs to jubilantly market themselves as having OECD white-list status.

In contrast to these failed initiatives, the Financial Secrecy Index helps chart a long-term course for reform and offers a point of departure for consideration of counter-measures around the lack of financial transparency and co-operation. First, by weighting the secrecy on offer by the scale of activity in its ranking, the onus for reform is placed on those potentially causing most harm. Avoiding yet another exercise in pointing fingers at the usual suspects of small players, a picture of shared responsibility between rather small, traditional 'tax havens' and major political powers emerges. The legitimacy of counter-measures depends on, and increases with, a country's ability and success at domestic reform. These reforms must ensure that domestic laws and regulations do not enable people or entities to escape or undermine the laws, rules and regulations of other jurisdictions by offering a veil of secrecy.

Second, once these reforms are in place, a broad menu of finely graduated counter-measures can be adopted to target specific aspects of financial secrecy. To satisfy the principles of specificity and commensurability, counter-measures should not be directed at entire jurisdictions but, instead, be targeted at specific practices or legal entities. In a first stage of counter-measures, the payments with targeted entities could be monitored publicly and/or taxed at source. In a second stage, ownership of any assets in the domestic jurisdiction by the targeted entities should be made illegal and ownership titles be disregarded. In the third stage, access to payment and clearing systems, including credit-card services and online payment services, should be cancelled. Stages one and two of any particular secrecy counter-measure should only be allowed if the country fully complies itself with the specific transparency requirement. Stage three should only be available after a jurisdiction has a completely compliant record in all transparency indicators itself and has, over a period of three years, enforced stages 1 and 2 of counter-measures against the targeted legal entities.

Not all KFSIs are equally suitable for devising counter-measures, because the nature of transparency required in the indicators differs substantially. Some KFSIs require information placed on public record online for everyone to verify (company accounts and ownership), whereas others only require unhindered access by the tax administration (bank secrecy, automatic information-exchange). Indicators that check whether specific data has been placed on public record are most reliable as a basis for counter-measures. An important corollary of the public data would be raising public awareness around the issues, which would help galvanise long-term political momentum for reform. Other indicators, however, make verification of compliance more difficult and may entail dependence on an international review procedure. Where this is the case, the review should not be carried out with the exclusive participation of government and private-sector delegates, in order to mitigate the risk of collusion among them; delegates from civil-society organisations as well as neutral academics should be included. Based on each KFSI, Table 12.2 presents an overview of suggested counter-measures and rules around the stages of intensity.

5. Conclusion

Decades of policies aimed at countering tax-base poaching and other harmful effects of tax havens have largely failed. At the core of this failure has been a lack of clarity and consistency in both the definitions and identification of tax havens. The lack of rigour in the terminology has, time and again, allowed national interests and the clash of ideologies to remain largely hidden from the public.

Table 12.2: Overview of KFSIs and potential counter-measures

KFSI	Verification of compliance	Counter-measure for non-compliance
1 Banking secrecy	Difficult, non-public	Public monitoring of payments to banking groups
2 Trusts and foundations register	Easy, public	Legal-entity-specific counter-measures*
3 Recorded company ownership	Difficult, non-public	Not sufficient as basis for counter-measures
4 Published company ownership	Easy, public	Legal-entity-specific counter-measures*
5 Published company accounts	Easy, public	Legal-entity-specific counter-measures*
6 Country-by-country reporting	Easy, public	Legal-entity-specific counter-measures*
7 Fit for information-exchange	Not suitable as basis for counter-measures	
8 Efficiency of tax administration	Not suitable as basis for counter-measures	
9 Avoids promoting tax evasion	Medium	Consider cancelling DTA and trigger CFC rules
10 Harmful legal vehicles	Easy, public	Legal-entity-specific counter-measures*
11 Anti-money-laundering	Not suitable as basis for counter-measures	
12 Automatic information-exchange	Medium	Financial institution specific counter-measures**
13 Bilateral treaties	Easy, public	Consider cancelling DTA and trigger CFC rules
14 International transparency commitments	Not suitable as basis for counter-measures	
15 International judicial co-operation	Not suitable as basis for counter-measures	

General legitimacy consideration: stages one and two of any counter-measure used only if specific KFSI is fully compliant in respective jurisdiction. Any stage 3 only if all KFSIs are domestically compliant.

*Legal-entity-specific counter-measures (LSC):
Stage 1: penalty withhold taxes for payments to non-compliant legal entities/agreements and disallow deductibility for payments to those entities.
Stage 2: prevent them from owning domestic assets.

Suggested cumulative rule for LSC: if neither KFSI 5 nor 6, then stage 2; if only one, stage 1; stage 3 only after at least three years of stages 1 or 2.

Suggested cumulative rule for FSC: if neither KFSI 12 (multilateral automatic information-exchange) nor 13 ('upon request'), then stage 2; if only one of both, stage 1; stage 3 only after at least three years of stages 1 or 2.

**Financial-institution-specific counter-measures (FSC):
Stage 1: Public statistics about which financial institutions (entire group principle) are not participating and public statistical monitoring of (bilateral) payments to them (including mutual funds, insurance companies and wealth-managers).
Stage 2: Penalty withholding taxes for all transfers to any account held by financial institutions in the jurisdiction and prevent them from owning domestic assets and financial-services delivery, including closure of related entities and branches in the domestic jurisdiction.
Stage 3: Disallow transactions with/access to domestic payment area and financial market for all financial institutions (including interbanking market).

Suggested cumulative rule for FSC: if neither KFSI 12 (multilateral automatic information-exchange) nor 13 ('upon request'), then stage 2; if only one of both, stage 1; stage 3 only after at least three years of stages 1 or 2.

As a consequence, the public could only have a vague idea about the issues and so easily fell prey to the fool's gold of symbolic politics.

The OECD's 1998 harmful tax competition project illustrates the ineffectiveness of this approach – to the point of its being counter-productive. By greatly enhancing the co-operation among the listed 'tax havens' in a coalition of interest against the OECD initiative and, subsequently, accommodating this coalition by offering a seat at the norm-setting table, the political influence of listed 'tax havens' has been greatly amplified. The intensive distributive conflict inherent in the process of international tax policy-making – both between norm-makers and norm-takers, as well as among norm-makers themselves – helps explain its outcome of asymmetrical and ineffective 'sham' standards (Drezner 2005).

The ensuing shift of emphasis towards adherence to 'international standards' of tax co-operation has hardly contained international tax avoidance and evasion. Instead, the problem has been shifted from arbitrary definitions and listings to a largely ineffectual international standard. The OECD's 2009 black-, grey- and white-listing achieved mixed results at best, with white-listed jurisdictions openly using their status to market their financial sectors.

It has been argued that those failures both in listing processes and standard-setting are inevitable when the focus is kept on a yardstick that works on the basis of tax criteria. Instead, transparency or secrecy is a more promising avenue for achieving policy change. Whereas tax-related policy reforms encounter classic problems of international enforcement, focusing on transparency as an intermediate step is, to some extent, self-enforcing and helps maintain the political momentum for deep policy reforms.

To create enforceable international tax rules before creating the transparency that facilitates monitoring of compliance with those rules is like putting the cart before the horse. Empirical and historical evidence suggests that policy-making and norm-setting cannot be assumed to be neutral and equitable. Instead, the creation of sustainable and equitable international institutions will require a high level of public awareness and corrective vigilance of investigators outside the inner power circles of governments and businesses to expose misconduct and conflicts of interest.

Conceptualised as a public good, financial transparency provides the basis for both increased public awareness and ease of investigation beyond and independent of government administrations. Financial transparency has the capacity to enhance market and governance integrity by changing the incentive structures towards compliance with the spirit of tax laws, where the economic substance is aligned with the legal form. It has the potential to become the springboard for moves towards more inclusive and balanced international tax rules, with or without a world tax organisation.

References

Abbott, J. *et al.* (1999) *State Strategies in the Global Political Economy*, London and New York: Pinter.

ActionAid (2013) 'FTSE 100 tax haven tracker: the new data': http://www.actionaid.org.uk/tax-justice/ftse-100-tax-haven-tracker-the-new-data#faq_7 (accessed 2 July 2014).

BEPS Monitoring Group (2014) 'Neutralising the effects of hybrid mismatch arrangements (submission to OECD discussion paper on hybrid mismatch arrangements)': http://bepsmonitoringgroup.files.wordpress.com/2014/05/bmg-hybrid-mismatches-submission.pdf (accessed 11 July 2014).

BMF (Bundesministerium der Finanzen, 2004): Grundsätze zur Anwendung des Außensteuergesetzes (Anwendungserlass BMF, BStBl 2004 I S. 3 Sondernummer 1), Berlin: http://treffer.nwb.de/completecontent/dms/content/000/132/Content/000132067.htm (accessed 14 July 2014).

Cobham, A. (2014) *The Impacts of Illicit Financial Flows on Peace and Security in Africa*, study for TANA High-Level Forum on Security in Africa 2014, London: http://www.tanaforum.org//illicit_financial_flows_conflict_and_security_in_africa_final.pdf (accessed 24 June 2014).

Cobham, A. *et al.* (2015) 'The financial secrecy index: shedding new light on the geography of secrecy', *Economic Geography* 91(3): 281–303.

CMS (2013) *Tax Connect. Transfer pricing: managing documentation requirements in 30 countries*: http://www.cmslegal.ru/Hubbard.FileSystem/files/Publication/2af5e803-8202-440d-b90a-811604bcede7/Presentation/PublicationAttachment/bda6809c-b1bd-44aa-92b9-8241df5dd99a/Tax_Connect_-_Transfer_Pricing_lo-res.pdf (accessed 9 July 2014).

Deloitte (2014) 'Guide to controlled foreign company regimes': http://www2.deloitte.com/content/dam/Deloitte/global/Documents/Tax/dttl-tax-guide-to-cfc-regimes-120314.pdf (accessed 9 July 2014).

Desai, M. *et al.* (2006) 'Do tax havens divert economic activity?', *Economic Letters* 90(2): 219–24.

Dietsch, P. and Rixen, T. (2012) 'Tax competition and global background justice', *Journal of Political Philosophy* 22(2): 150–77.

— (2014) 'Redistribution, globalisation, and multi-level governance', *Moral Philosophy and Politics* 1(1): 61–81.

Drezner, D. W. (2005) 'The power of clubs and the governance of global finance', paper given at the Globalization Seminar, Woodrow Wilson School of Public and International Affairs, Princeton University, 10 February: www.princeton.edu/~smeunier/Drezner.doc (accessed 3 February 2010).

Eccleston, R. and Smith, H. (2016) 'The G20, BEPS, and the future of international tax governance', in Dietsch, P. and Rixen, T. (eds) *Global Tax Governance: What is wrong with it and how to fix it*, Colchester: ECPR Press.

European Commission (2014) 'Alleged aid to Amazon by way of a tax ruling', http://ec.europa.eu/competition/state_aid/cases/254685/254685_1614265_70_2.pdf (accessed 1 April 2015).

ECJ (European Court of Justice, 2006) Judgment of the Court of Justice in Case C-196/04 - Cadbury Schweppes plc and Cadbury Schweppes Overseas Ltd v Commissioners of Inland Revenue: Press Release No 72/06 - J: http://curia.europa.eu/jcms/upload/docs/application/pdf/2009-02/cp060072en.pdf (accessed 14 July 2014).

FATF (Financial Action Task Force, 2012). *International Standards on Combating Money Laundering and the Financing of Terrorism and Proliferation: The FATF recommendations*, Paris: OECD/FATF: http://www.fatf-gafi.org/media/fatf/documents/recommendations/pdfs/FATF_Recommendations.pdf (accessed 6 June 2013).

Ford, J. *et al.* (2013) 'Cadbury: the great tax fudge', *Financial Times*, 20 June: http://www.ft.com/intl/cms/s/0/90b042b4-d4ff-11e2-b4d7-00144feab7de.html#axzz37SJlBYLl (accessed 14 July 2014).

Genschel, P. and Schwarz, P. (2011) 'Tax competition: a literature review', *Socio-Economic Review* 9(2): 339–70.

Genschel, P. and Seelkopf, L. (2016) 'Winners and losers of tax competition', in Dietsch, P. and Rixen, T. (eds) *Global Tax Governance: What is wrong with it and how to fix it*, Colchester: ECPR Press.

Gordon, R. (1981) *Tax Havens and Their Use By United States Taxpayers – An overview*, Washington, DC: Books for Business.

Gurney, P. B. (2005) 'Circumventing the controlled foreign company and foreign investment fund regimes in Australia and New Zealand', *New Zealand Postgraduate Law E-Journal* 1: https://cdn.auckland.ac.nz/assets/nzpglejournal/Subscribe/Documents/2005-1/6%20Philip%27s%20(final).pdf (accessed 24 August 2015).

Haberly, D. and Wójcik, D. (2014) 'Tax havens and the production of offshore FDI: an empirical analysis', *Journal of Economic Geography*: DOI:10.1093/jeg/lbu003.

Henry, J. S. (2012) 'The price of offshore revisited: new estimates for missing global private wealth, income, inequality and lost taxes', London: Tax Justice Network: www.taxjustice.net/cms/upload/pdf/Price_of_Offshore_Revisited_26072012.pdf (accessed 11 December 2012).

Hines Jr, J. R. and Rice, E. M. (1994) 'Fiscal paradise: foreign tax havens and American business', *Quarterly Journal of Economics* 109(1): 149–82.

Hines, J. R. (2007) 'Tax havens', WP 2007-3, Ann Arbor: Office of Tax Policy Research. http://www.bus.umich.edu/otpr/WP2007-3.pdf (accessed 12 June 2014).

HMRC (Her Majesty's Revenue and Customs, 2011) 'Controlled foreign companies: exemptions – excluded countries: List of excluded countries' (INTM203130): http://www.hmrc.gov.uk/manuals/intmanual/intm203130.htm (accessed 11 July 2014).

International Bureau of Fiscal Documentation (1977) quoted in Irish, C. R. (1982) 'Tax havens', *Vanderbilt Journal of Transnational Law* 15(3): 449–510.

IMF (International Monetary Fund, 2014) 'Spillovers in international corporate taxation', IMF Policy Paper, Washington, DC: IMF: http://www.imf.org/external/np/pp/eng/2014/050914.pdf (accessed 26 June 2014).

Irish, C. R. (1982) 'Tax havens', *Vanderbilt Journal of Transnational Law* 15(3): 449–510.

Italian Ministry of Economy and Finance (2001) Decreto ministeriale del 21 novembre 2001, 'Individuazione degli Stati o territori a regime fiscale privilegiato di cui all'art. 127-bis, comma 4, del testo unico delle imposte sui redditi (cd. "black list")', ['Identification of the states or territories with favourable tax regimes']: http://www.ilsole24ore.com/art/SoleOnLine4/Speciali/2006/documenti_lunedi/13febbraio2006/DM_21_11_2001_BLACK_LIST.pdf?cmd%3Dart (accessed 15 July 2014).

Johannesen, N. and Zucman, G. (2014) 'The end of bank secrecy? An evaluation of the G20 tax haven crackdown', *American Economic Journal: Economic Policy* 6(1): 65–91.

Lesage, D. (2010) 'The G20 and tax havens: maintaining the momentum?', paper given at the conference Governing the Global Economy: The Role of the G20, University of Toronto – Munk School of Global Affairs, 18 June: www.g8.utoronto.ca/g20/biblio/lesage-tax-havens.pdf (accessed 10 July 2014).

Lowtax.Net (2008) [website promoting tax havens/secrecy jurisdictions]: www.lowtax.net (accessed 22 January 2008).

Meinzer, M. (2012a) 'The creeping futility of the Global Forum's peer reviews' (Tax Justice Briefing): www.taxjustice.net/cms/upload/GlobalForum2012-TJN-Briefing.pdf (accessed 16 July 2012).

— (2012b) 'White Paper on the FSI 2011. Where to draw the line? Identifying secrecy jurisdictions for applied research': http://www.taxjustice.net/cms/upload/pdf/FSI_2012_Cut-Off-Point.pdf (accessed 26 July 2013).

Meloni, E. O. (2014) *Argentina – Corporate Taxation* (Country Surveys IBFD, accessed 25 June 2014), Amsterdam.

Murphy, R. (2008) 'Finding the secrecy world. Rethinking the language of "offshore"': http://www.taxresearch.org.uk/Blog/2008/08/27/finding-the-secrecy-world/ (accessed 8 September 2008).

— (2009) 'Where are the world's secrecy jurisdictions?': http://www.financialsecrecyindex.com/Archive2009/Notes%20and%20Reports/SJ_Mapping.pdf (accessed 18 July 2013).

— (2012a) 'Accounting for the missing billions', in Reuter, P. (ed.) *Draining Development? Controlling Flows of Illicit Funds from Developing Countries*, Washington, DC: World Bank, pp. 265–308.

— (2012b) *Country by Country Reporting. Accounting for globalisation locally*: http://www.taxresearch.org.uk/Documents/CBC2012.pdf (accessed 11 June 2012).

OECD (Organization for Economic Co-operation and Development, 1987) *International Tax Avoidance and Evasion. Four related studies*, (Issues in International Taxation), Paris: OECD.

— (1998) *Harmful Tax Competition. An emerging global issue*, Paris: OECD.

— (2000) 'Towards global tax co-operation: report to the 2000 Ministerial Council meeting and recommendations by the Committee on Fiscal Affairs: progress in identifying and eliminating harmful tax practices, Paris: OECD: http://www.oecd.org/dataoecd/9/61/2090192.pdf (accessed 7 December 2005).

— (2001) *Behind the Corporate Veil. Using corporate entities for illicit purposes*, Paris: OECD.

— (2002) 'Agreement on exchange of information on tax matters' (TIEA), Paris: OECD: http://www.oecd.org/ctp/exchange-of-tax-information/2082215.pdf (accessed 18 July 2014).

— (2006) *Tax Co-operation. Towards a level playing field*, Paris: OECD: http://www.oecd.org/tax/transparency/44430286.pdf.

— (2008) 'Model tax convention on income and on capital. Condensed version', Paris, OECD: http://www.oecd.org/dataoecd/14/32/41147804.pdf (accessed 18 May 2014).

— (2009) 'A progress report on the jurisdictions surveyed by the OECD Global Forum in implementing the internationally agreed tax standard', 2 April, Paris: http://www.oecd.org/dataoecd/38/14/42497950.pdf (accessed 4 June 2009).

Palan, R. (2002) 'Tax havens and the commercialization of state sovereignty', *International Organization* 56(1): 151–76.

Pandey, V. (2011) 'PM Manmohan Singh reminds G20 about pledge to end bank secrecy', *Economic Times*, 4 November: http://articles.economictimes.indiatimes.com/2011-11-04/news/30359509_1_tax-evasion-or-tax-exchange-of-tax-related-information-bank-secrecy (accessed 17 July 2014).

Perdelwitz, A. (2014) Germany – Corporate Taxation (Sec. 7, Country Surveys IBFD), Amsterdam: http://online2.ibfd.org/document/gtha_de_s_7 (accessed 14 July 2014)

Picciotto, S. (2013[1992]) *International Business Taxation. A study in the internationalization of business regulation*, Cambridge: Cambridge University Press and at: www.taxjustice.net/cms/upload/pdf/Picciotto%201992%20International%20Business%20Taxation.pdf (accessed 29 August 2015).

— (2013) 'Can the OECD mend the international tax system?', *Tax Notes International*: 1105–15: http://www.taxjustice.net/cms/upload/pdf/Picciotto_130916_Taxanalysts_beps.pdf (accessed 29 August 2015).

Rienstra, J. G. (2014) United States – Corporate Taxation (Sec. 7, Country Surveys IBFD), Amsterdam: http://online2.ibfd.org/document/gtha_us_s_7 (accessed 14 July 2014).

Rixen, T. (2008) *The Political Economy of International Tax Governance*, Basingstoke: Palgrave Macmillan.

— (2009) 'Paradiese in der Krise. Transparenz und neue Regeln für Steuer- und Regulierungsoasen', Berlin: Heinrich Böll Stiftung – Schriften zu Wirtschaft und Soziales – Band 4): http://www.boell.de/sites/default/files/091119_Studie_Steuerparadiese_Steueroasen.pdf (accessed 30 June 2014).

— (2011) 'From double tax avoidance to tax competition: explaining the institutional trajectory of international tax governance', *Review of International Political Economy* 18(2): 197–227.

Robert, A. (2014) 'Paris wants to remove Bermuda and Jersey from tax haven list', EurActiv.com: http://www.euractiv.com/euro-finance/paris-wants-remove-bermuda-jerse-news-532587 (accessed 11 July 2014).

Seelkopf, L. (2014) 'Tax competition and national welfare', in Ötsch, W. *et al.* (eds), *The Political Economy of Offshore Jurisdictions*, Marburg: Metropolis-Verlag, pp. 27–38.

Sharman, J. C. (2006) *Havens in a Storm: The struggle for global tax regulation*, Ithaca, New York: Cornell University Press.

— (2010) 'Dysfunctional policy transfer in national tax blacklists', *Governance* 23(4): 623–39.

Sharman, J. C. and Rawlings, G. (2005) 'Deconstructing national tax blacklists. Removing obstacles to cross-border trade in financial services (a report prepared for the Society of Trust and Estate Practitioners)': http://www.step.org/sites/default/files/Comms/DeconstructingNationalBlacklists.pdf (accessed 11 July 2014).

— (2006) 'National tax blacklists: A comparative analysis', *Journal of International Taxation* 17(9): 38–54.

Shaxson, N. (2011) *Treasure Islands: Tax havens and the men who stole the world*, London: Bodley Head.

Shaxson, N. and Christensen, J. (2011) 'Time to black-list the tax haven whitewash', *Financial Times*, 4 April: http://www.ft.com/cms/s/0/0f687dee-5eea-11e0-a2d7-00144feab49a.html?siteedition=intl#axzz1IcwBEiPA (accessed 11 July 2014).

— (2013) *The Finance Curse. How oversized financial centres attack democracy and corrupt economies*, London: Tax Justice Network: http://www.taxjustice.net/cms/upload/pdf/Finance_Curse_Final.pdf (accessed 12 June 2013).

— (forthcoming) 'Tax Wars' (working title), in Mehta, K. and Pogge, T. (eds), *Global Tax Justice* (working title), Oxford: Oxford University Press.

Sheppard, L. (2013) 'How can vulnerable countries cope with tax avoidance?', *Tax Analysts*: 410ff.

Slemrod, J. and Wilson, J. D. (2006) 'Tax competition with parasitic tax havens', NBER Working Paper No. 12225: http://www.nber.org/papers/w12225 (accessed 17 July 2014).

Smyth, J. (2013) 'Ireland will deploy ministers to counter "tax haven" claims', *Financial Times*, 27 May: http://www.ft.com/cms/s/0/70c74edc-c6ec-11e2-8a36-00144feab7de.html#axzz3hxKMBsug (accessed 26 January 2016).

Stiglitz, J. E. and Charlton, A. (2005) *Fair Trade For All: How trade can promote development*, Oxford and New York: Oxford University Press.

TJN (Tax Justice Network, 2005) 'Tax us if you can. The true story of a global failure': www.taxjustice.net/cms/upload/pdf/tuiyc_-_eng_-_web_file.pdf (accessed 5 May 2009).

— (2011) 'Introducing the 2011 Financial Secrecy Index': http://www.financialsecrecyindex.com/Archive2011/FSI-2011/FSI-Homepage.pdf (accessed 7 July 2014).

— (2013) *Financial Secrecy Index 2013 – Methodology*: http://www.financialsecrecyindex.com/PDF/FSI-Methodology.pdf (accessed 7 July 2014).

USGAO (United States Government Accountability Office, 2008) 'International taxation: large U.S. corporations and federal contractors with subsidiaries in jurisdictions listed as tax havens or financial privacy jurisdictions' (GAO-09-157), Washington, DC: http://www.gao.gov/assets/290/284522.pdf (accessed 23 July 2013).

United States Senate, Committee on Finance (2002) 'Grassley works to stop abusive tax shelters, corporate flight', 10 May, Washington, DC: http://www.finance.senate.gov/newsroom/ranking/release/?id=770c61f8-32ad-4ca9-b447-0c22ea0b7df7 (accessed 30 September 2013).

United States Senate (2013) 'Offshore profit shifting and the U.S. Tax Code–Part 2 (Apple Inc.)', Permanent Subcommittee on Investigations, 21 May, Washington, DC: http://www.gpo.gov/fdsys/pkg/CHRG-113shrg81657/pdf/CHRG-113shrg81657.pdf (accessed 12 June 2014).

Wójcik, D. (2012) 'Where governance fails: advanced business services and the offshore world', *Progress in Human Geography*: DOI 10.1177/0309132512460904.

Woodward, R. (2016) 'A strange revolution: mock compliance and the failure of the OECD's international tax transparency regime', in Dietsch, P. and Rixen, T. (eds) *Global Tax Governance: What is wrong with it and how to fix it*, Colchester: ECPR Press.

Zakharov, A. S. (2008) 'Russian list of the offshore jurisdictions for tax purposes (Translation of Russian Ministry of Finance Order No. 108n with List of the States and Territories providing preferential tax treatment and (or) not requiring disclosure and furnishing of the information upon conducting of financial transactions (offshore zones))': http://materialotzakharova.narod.ru/RUSSIAN_LIST_OF_OFFSHORE_JURISDICTIONS_FOR_TAX_PURPOSES.htm (accessed 9 July 2014).

Appendix: Table 12.3 Key financial secrecy indicators (KSFIs): qualitative index components of Financial Secrecy Index

KSFI	Description	Result	Component weighting
		KNOWLEDGE OF BENEFICIAL OWNERSHIP	
1 Bank secrecy	Does it have a statutory basis?	YN	20%
	To what extent are banks subject to stringent customer due diligence regulations (FATF-recommendation 5)?	1: compliant; 2: largely compliant; 3: partially compliant; 4: non-compliant	20%
	To what extent are banks required to maintain data records of its customers and transactions sufficient for law enforcement (FATF-recommendation 10)?	1: compliant; 2: largely compliant; 3: partially compliant; 4: non-compliant	20%
	Are banks and/or other covered entities required to report large transactions in currency or other monetary instruments to designated authorities?	YN	10%
	Are banks required to keep records, especially of large or unusual transactions, for a specified period of time, e.g. five years?	YN	10%
	Sufficient powers to obtain and provide banking information on request?	1: Yes without qualifications; 2: Yes, but some problems; 3: Yes, but major problems; 4=No, access is not possible, or only exceptionally	10% (only if answer is 1)
	No undue notification and appeal rights against bank information-exchange on request?	1: Yes without qualifications; 2: Yes, but some problems; 3: Yes, but major problems; 4=No, access and exchange hindered.	10% (only if answer is 1)
2 Trust and Foundations Register	Trusts available?	0: Foreign law trusts cannot be administered and no domestic trust law; 1: Foreign law trusts can be administered, but no domestic trust law; 2: Domestic trust law and administration of foreign law trusts.	Complex Assessment - see KFSI 2 for details; trusts maximum of 50% in KFSI 2

Table 12.3 (continued)

KSFI	Description	Result	Component weighting
	Convention of 1 July 1985 on the Law Applicable to Trusts and on their Recognition	YN	
	Trusts: is any formal registration required at all?	0: Foreign law trusts (and domestic law trusts if applicable) must be registered; 1: No registration requirement of foreign law trusts, but registration of domestic law trusts mandatory; 2: No registration requirement of domestic law trusts, but of foreign law trusts; 3: Neither foreign law trusts nor domestic law trusts (if applicable) require registration.	
	Trusts: is registration data publicly available ('on public record')?	0: No, neither for foreign law trusts nor domestic law trusts (if applicable); 1: Only for domestic law trusts, but not for foreign law trusts (if applicable); Yes, for both domestic and foreign law trusts (if applicable).	
	Foundations available (private)?	YN	Complex Assessment - see KFSI 2 for details; foundations maximum of 50% in KFSI 2
	Foundations: is any formal registration required at all?	YN	
	Is the settlor named?	YN	
	Are the members of the foundation council named?	YN	
	Are the beneficiaries named?	YN	
	Must the constitution / foundation documents be submitted, including changes and all bylaws / letters of wishes?	YN	
	Foundations: Is registration data publicly available ('on public record')?	0: No online disclosure for all private foundations; 1: Partial online disclosure for all private foundations; 2: Yes, full online disclosure of all private foundations.	

Table 12.3 (continued)

KSFI	Description	Result	Component weighting
3 Recorded company ownership	Companies: registration comprises owner's identity information?	0: no; 1: only legal; 2: BO always recorded	BO=100%; condition that update is not "no"
	Is the update of information on the identity of owners mandatory?	YN	
KEY ASPECTS OF CORPORATE TRANSPARENCY REGULATION			
4 Public company ownership	Companies: registration comprises owner's identity information?	0: no; 1: only legal; 2: BO always recorded	LO=20%; BO=100%; condition that update is not "no"
	Is the update of information on the identity of owners mandatory?	YN	
	Companies – online availability of information: on public record (up to 10 €/US$): owners' identities?	0: no; 1: only legal; 2: BO always recorded	
5 Public company accounts	Accounting data required?	YN	Only if all answered "Yes" = 100%
	Accounts submitted to public authority?	YN	
	online availability of information: on public record (up to 10 €/US$): accounts?	YN	

Table 12.3 (continued)

KSFI	Description	Result	Component weighting
6 Country-by-Country Reporting	Requirement to comply with country-by-country reporting standard for companies listed on the national stock exchange?	0:No; 1: No, except one-off EITI-style disclosure for new listed companies; 2: No, except for partial disclosure in either extractives or banking sector; 3: Yes, partial disclosure for both extractives and banking sector; 4: Yes, full country-by-country reporting for all sectors.	1: 10%; 2: 25%; 3: 50%; 4: 100%
Efficiency of tax and financial regulation			
7 Fit for Information-Exchange	Are all payers required to automatically report to the tax administration information on payments to all non-residents?	0: no, none; 1: yes div, no int; 2: no div, yes int; 3: yes, both	100% (div and interest each 50%)
8 Efficiency tax administration	Does the tax authority make use of taxpayer identifiers for information reporting and matching for information reported by financial institutions on interest payments and by companies on dividend payments?	0: no, none; 1: yes int, no div; 2: no int, yes div; 3: yes, both	80% (div and int each 40%)
	Does the tax authority have a dedicated unit for large taxpayers?	YN	20%
9 Avoids promoting tax evasion	Absent a bilateral treaty, does the jurisdiction apply a tax credit system for receiving interest income payments?	3: yes, all three types of resident recipients [i) legal person – independent party; ii) legal person – related party; iii) natural person]; 2: for 2; 1: for 1; 0 for none	0: 0%; 1: 10%; 2: 20%; 3: 50%
	Absent a bilateral treaty, does the jurisdiction apply a tax credit system for receiving dividend income payments?	3: yes, all three types of recipients; 2: for 2; 1: for 1; 0 for none	0: 0%; 1: 10%; 2: 20%; 3: 50%
10 Harmful legal vehicles	Companies - available types: cell companies?	YN	50%
	Trusts - Are trusts with flee clauses prohibited?	YN	50%

Table 12.3 (continued)

KSFI	Description	Result	Component weighting
	INTERNATIONAL STANDARDS AND CO-OPERATION		
11 Anti-money laundering	Money laundering: overall compliance score of FATF-standards in percentage (100% = all indicators rated compliant, 0%=all indicators rated non-compliant)	49 criteria (each given an equal weight); each criteria: 1: compliant; 2: largely compliant; 3: partially compliant; 4: non-compliant	scaled up to 100%
12 Automatic information-exchange	EUSTD participant (or equivalent)?	YN	100%
13 Bilateral treaties	Number of double tax agreements (DTA)	Number	Sum % of 46; or
	Number of tax information-exchange agreements (TIEA)	Number	
	1988 CoE/OECD convention/amending protocol	YN	Yes, then 100%
14 International transparency commitments	1988 CoE/OECD convention/amending protocol	YN	20%
	UN Convention Against Corruption	YN	20%
	UN Drug Convention 1988	YN	20%
	UN International Convention for the Suppression of the Financing of Terrorism	YN	20%
	UN Convention Against Transnational Organized Crime	YN	20%

Table 12.3 (continued)

KSFI	Description	Result	Component weighting
15 International judicial co-operation	Will mutual legal assistance be given for investigations, prosecutions, and proceedings (FATF-recommendation 36)?	1: compliant; 2: largely compliant; 3: partially compliant; 4: non-compliant	20%
	Is mutual legal assistance given without the requirement of dual criminality (FATF recommendation 37)?	1: compliant; 2: largely compliant; 3: partially compliant; 4: non-compliant	20%
	Is mutual legal assistance given concerning identification, freezing, seizure and confiscation of property (FATF recommendation 38)?	1: compliant; 2: largely compliant; 3: partially compliant; 4: non-compliant	20%
	Is money-laundering considered to be an extraditable offense (FATF recommendation 39)?	1: compliant; 2: largely compliant; 3: partially compliant; 4: non-compliant	20%
	Is the widest possible range of international co-operation granted to foreign counterparts beyond formal legal assistance on anti-money-laundering and predicate crimes (FATF recommendation 40)?	1: compliant; 2: largely compliant; 3: partially compliant; 4: non-compliant	20%

Chapter Thirteen

A Proposal for Unitary Taxation and Formulary Apportionment (UT+FA) to Tax Multinational Enterprises

Reuven S. Avi-Yonah

1. A historical introduction

In the last thirty years, a debate has been raging in international tax circles between advocates of the OECD transfer-pricing guidelines and the arm's-length standard (ALS) they embody and advocates of 'unitary taxation and formulary apportionment' (UT+FA) (Langbein 1986: 625). The ALS is a standard stating that each corporation in a group of companies under common control should be treated as a separate taxpayer; and that transaction between such companies should conform to hypothetical transactions entered into at arm's length. UT+FA treats the entire group as a single entity, ignores transactions among them and allocates their combined income based on a formula. This issue can be traced as far back as the 1930s, when the ALS was originally conceived and introduced into the first model treaties (Avi-Yonah 2006: 310). However, before the 1960s there was not much transfer-pricing enforcement and the ALS was rather indeterminate in the absence of concrete transfer-pricing methods. UT+FA, in the meantime, was applied by the US states but was not seriously considered as a method of resolving transfer-pricing at the international level.

In 1962, the US House of Representatives passed a bill that would, for the first time, have applied UT+FA to address transfer-pricing at the federal level. This was in the context of increasing transfer-pricing concerns evidenced by the *Dupont* case (which began in the 1950s, even though it was not decided until 1979) and the enactment of IRC 951-960 (also known as the US Controlled Foreign Corporation rules or subpart F), which, at least in part, responded to such concerns. However, Stanley Surrey, the new Assistant Secretary for Tax Policy and a great believer in the ALS, thought he had a better approach and in the end the legislation merely authorised the Treasury to write regulations under the Internal Revenue Code (IRC) 482 implementing the ALS.

The regulations Surrey authored were eventually finalised in 1968 and, for the first time, imbued the ALS with practical meaning, by formulating the three classical methods of 'comparable uncontrolled price' (CUP),[1] 'cost-plus' and 'resale price', all of which depended on finding comparable uncontrolled transactions to those engaged in by the related parties. These regulations were the basis for US transfer-pricing litigation in the 1970s and 1980s, as well as the basis for the original OECD transfer-pricing guidelines issued in 1977.

The problem that gradually became evident was that the traditional methods did not work in the majority of transfer-pricing cases. The General Accounting Office did a study in the early 1990s that indicated that in over 90 per cent of the cases, the three traditional methods could not be applied because comparable uncontrolled transactions could not be found (GAO 1992). Moreover, after winning *Dupont* in 1979, the IRS lost every single major transfer-pricing case it litigated between 1980 and 1995, including cases against all the US pharmaceutical companies and many other US multinationals. The major reason for these losses was that the courts refused to accept the comparables used by the IRS under the traditional methods; they either accepted bogus comparables manufactured by the taxpayers or, more frequently, simply made up a transfer-price that also favoured the taxpayer (Avi-Yonah 2006).

In the meantime, UT+FA became more prominent because the US Supreme Court twice (in 1984 and 1993) upheld California's use of the method to apportion the worldwide income of multinationals doing business in the state. The multinationals and their supporters argued that UT+FA was inconsistent with the internationally accepted ALS, and therefore that California's reliance on it was unconstitutional, but the Court rejected this argument, once for a US-based and again for a foreign-based multinational. As a result, the literature from the early 1990s is full of debates between advocates of ALS and UT+FA (Avi-Yonah 2006; Bucks and Mazerov 1993; Cofill and Wilson 1993; Wilkins and Gideon 1994).

Ultimately, the result was a compromise. In 1995, the US adopted new transfer-pricing regulations that incorporated two new methods, the 'comparable profit' method (CPM) and 'profit split', which relied much less on comparables (CPM uses comparability very loosely; in profit split, the residual is not allocated based on comparables). The OECD followed suit and amended the transfer-pricing guidelines to include the new methods, which it calls the 'transactional net margin' method (TNMM) and profit split; in deference to opponents of FA, though, it still rejected FA and emphasised that the traditional methods were to be preferred to the new ones (OECD 1995). It also changed the name CPM to TNMM, to emphasise that it does not involve a global profit-allocation but, rather, allocation for the particular transaction, since the former is closer to UT+FA.

Nevertheless, it is clear that by moving beyond traditional comparability, the OECD was moving closer to accepting UT+FA. Once you do not base the ALS

1. CUP is a method that depends on finding a transaction between *unrelated* parties that is strictly comparable to the transaction between the related parties. The cost plus and resale price methods also depend on finding comparables among unrelated parties. An extensive economics literature has demonstrated why finding such comparables is unlikely in theory and long experience has shown that it is very hard in practice.

on finding comparables, then it is not very meaningful to say that a particular method is or is not compatible with the ALS, because, if there are no comparables, you cannot prove that the result reached by that method was not what unrelated parties would have done at arm's length. That is why it is possible to argue that UT+FA is compatible with Article 7 of the OECD model treaty, which focuses on the results that unrelated parties would have reached and permits (in Art. 7(4)) the use of formulas, as long as the result is compatible with the ALS (Avi-Yonah and Clausing 2008a; LeGall 2006). And that is why a group of senior tax officials from OECD member-countries concluded, in 1993, that the distinction between the ALS and UT+FA was largely a matter of semantics, not substance (Arnold and McDonnell 1993).

The ALS/UT+FA debate died down somewhat after the adoption of the 1995 regulations and the new OECD guidelines because everyone was waiting to see whether the issue had been resolved. However, while a few cases have been decided, it is clear by now that the transfer-pricing problem is as bad as it ever was. That is why my co-authors Kimberly Clausing, Michael Durst and I have re-proposed adopting UT+FA (Avi-Yonah *et al.* 2009).

However, it is clear from the reactions we received that it is unlikely we will persuade advocates of the ALS, the OECD in particular, that UT+FA is the way forward (although this may change if the EU adopts the Common Consolidated Corporate Tax Base (CCCTB), which is the EU Commission's proposal to adopt UT+FA for the EU). Thus, I would like to propose a compromise: use UT+FA in the context of the ALS. Specifically, I would suggest using UT+FA to allocate the residual profit in the profit split method.

The rest of this chapter is devoted to (a) explaining the drawbacks of ALS as currently applied; (b) developing the above proposal; and (c) concluding with a plea for further discussion by both sides of the UT+FA/ALS debate.

2. The problems of the ALS

At the heart of the ALS system, with its reliance on estimated arm's-length prices, is the assumption that each affiliated company within the group transacts with the other members of the group in the same way that it would transact if the members were unrelated. That central assumption defies reality and it is not surprising that a system of arm's-length pricing cannot yield sensible results.

First, and most fundamentally, the ALS system ignores the fact that multinational groups of companies arise precisely in order to avoid the inefficiencies that arise when unrelated companies must transact with one another at arm's length. Multinational enterprises arise in large part due to their organisational and internalisation advantages relative to the efforts of unrelated, separate companies that seek to do business with one another. Such advantages mean that within multinational enterprises, profit is generated in part by internalising transactions within the firm. Thus, for firms that are truly integrated across borders, holding related entities within the commonly controlled group to an arms-length standard for the pricing of intra-company transactions does not make sense; nor does allocating income and expenses on a country-by-country basis. In fact, a very similar logic was behind the use of UT+FA for US state governments and among the Canadian provinces; in an integrated economy, it does not make sense to attribute profits and expenses to individual jurisdictions using separate-entity accounting (Avi-Yonah *et al.* 2009).

Second, the porosity of current transfer-pricing rules creates an artificial tax incentive to locate profits in low-tax countries, both by locating real economic activities in such countries and by shifting profits toward more lightly taxed locations. It is apparent that US multinational firms book disproportionate amounts of profit in low-tax locations. For example, Figure 13.1 shows the ten highest-profit locations for US multinational firms in 2005, based on the share of worldwide (non-US) profits earned in each location. While some of the countries are places with a large US presence in terms of economic activity (the United Kingdom, Canada, Germany, Japan), seven of the top-ten profit countries are locations with very low effective tax rates.

The literature has consistently found that multinational firms are sensitive to corporate-tax-rate differences across countries in their financial decisions (*see* Clausing 2016, Chapter Two in this volume). Estimates from the literature suggest that the tax base responds to changes in the corporate tax rate with an average semi-elasticity of about -2; thus, countries with high corporate tax rates are likely to gain revenue by lowering their tax rate (de Mooij 2005). One recent study suggests that corporate income tax revenues in the United States were approximately 35 per cent lower due to income-shifting in 2004 (Clausing 2008).

Figure 13.1: Where were the profits in 2005? (profits as % of worldwide total)

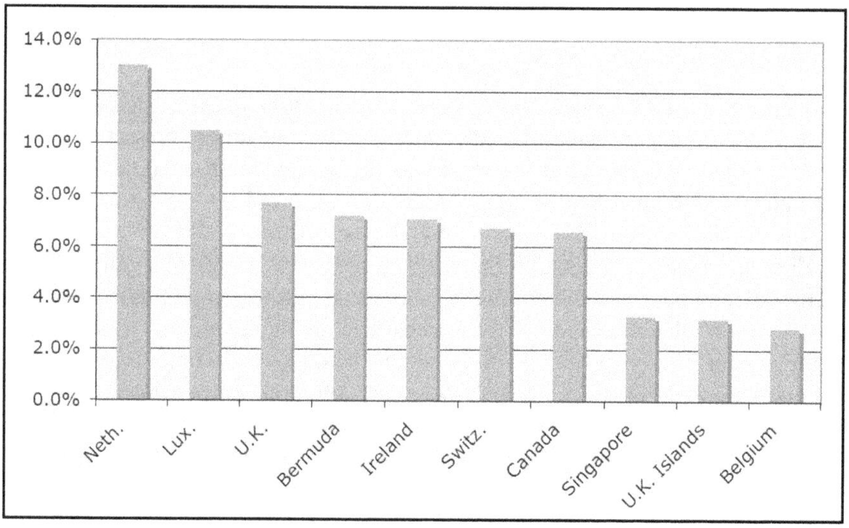

Source: BEA, 2005 and Avi-Yonah *et al.* 2009

This problem has worsened as US corporate rates have become increasingly out of line with those of other countries. In the past twenty years, most OECD countries have lowered their corporate income tax rates, whereas US rates have been relatively constant. This increasing discrepancy between US rates and foreign rates likely results in increasing amounts of lost revenue for the US government, due to strengthening income-shifting incentives.

Also, the literature suggests a substantial responsiveness of real economic activities to tax-rate differences among countries (de Mooij 2005). These findings imply both less activity in United States and less tax revenue for the US government. However, the tax responsiveness of real activity is less immediately apparent in the data. For example, Figure 13.2 shows the top-ten employment locations for US multinational firms in 2005, based on the share of worldwide (non-US) employment in each location. The high-employment countries are the usual suspects – large economies with close economic ties to the United States. As the accompanying table indicates, tax rates are not particularly low for this set of countries.

Third, the current system is absurdly complex. As Taylor notes, observers have described the system as 'a cumbersome creation of stupefying complexity' with 'rules that lack coherence and often work at cross purposes' (Taylor 2005). Altshuler and Ackerman note that observers testifying before the President's Advisory Panel on Federal Tax Reform found the system 'deeply, deeply flawed', noting that 'it is difficult to overstate the crisis in the administration of the international tax system of the United States' (Altshuler and Ackerman 2005). Current transfer-pricing rules have spawned a huge industry of lawyers, accountants and economists whose professional role is to assist multinational companies in their transfer-pricing planning and compliance.

Figure 13.2: Where were the jobs in 2005? (employment as % of worldwide total)

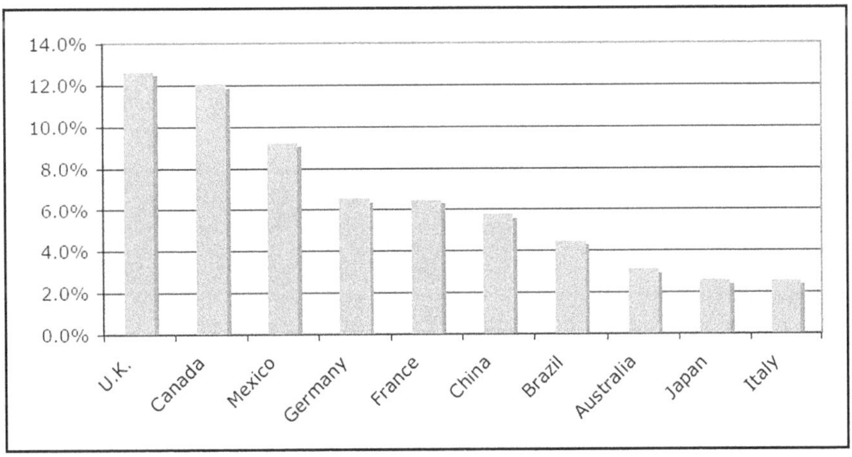

Source: BEA 2005

Fourth, particularly given the high US corporate statutory tax rates, the US corporate-tax system raises relatively little revenue. For most OECD countries, revenues have increased as a share of GDP even as corporate tax rates have declined; the average OECD country receives about 3.25 per cent of GDP from corporate tax revenue by the end of the sample. Most observers attribute this trend to a broadening of the tax base for many OECD countries during this time period. For the United States, revenues are lower; although they fluctuate with the cyclical position of the economy, they tend to be closer to 2.25 per cent of GDP. There are several plausible reasons for the lower amount of US revenue, including: the increasingly aggressive use of corporate tax shelters; a narrower corporate tax base; and stronger incentives for tax avoidance, which tend to strengthen as the US tax rate increases relative to other countries.

Finally, it is important to note that the problems with the current system derive not from rules at its periphery but, instead, from a fallacy that lies at the system's core: namely, the belief that transactions among unrelated parties can be found that are sufficiently comparable to transactions among members of multinational groups that they can be used as meaningful benchmarks for tax compliance and enforcement (Avi-Yonah 2006; Langbein 1986; Durst and Culbertson 2003). For example, if one wants to determine the arm's-length level of profitability of a US distribution subsidiary of a foreign manufacturer of automobiles, one identifies one or more independent US distributors of automobiles operating in economically similar circumstances and uses the income of the independent distributor or distributors to benchmark the income of the US subsidiary.

Such an approach might well have made sense eighty years ago, when the legislative language underlying today's arm's-length standard for income-tax purposes was first developed. At that time, although multinational groups existed, available transportation and communications technology did not permit close centralised management of geographically dispersed groups. Therefore, members of multinational groups functioned largely as independent entities: and so benchmarking their incomes or transactions based on uncontrolled comparables probably made good sense.

That situation changed, however, with the technological changes precipitated by the Second World War. Today, it is possible to exercise close managerial control over multinational groups; and these groups develop in all industries and geographic market segments in which the efficiencies of common control have significant economic advantages. Moreover, in those industries and markets where common control does result in advantages, typically, it is economically unfeasible to remain in the market using a non-commonly-controlled structure (for example, by maintaining distributors that are economically independent of manufacturers). Therefore, in those markets in which multinational groups operate – that is, in those markets in which transfer-pricing issues arise – it is unlikely that reasonably close 'uncontrolled comparables' can be found. For example, to my knowledge, there are no independently owned distributors of mass-market automobiles in the United States; all of the distributors are owned by their manufacturers (Durst and Culbertson 2003: 47–8)

The same is true of virtually every other industry that is conducted on multinational scale. In sum, no matter how assiduously one performs 'functional analyses' designed to identify uncontrolled comparables that are reasonably similar to members of multinational groups, one is rarely going to find them. Certainly, such comparables will not be – and have not been – found with sufficient regularity to serve as the basis for a workable transfer-pricing system. If the transfer-pricing rules are going to be made tolerably administrable, Congress will need to restate them on a basis other than that of reliance on uncontrolled comparables.

The results of the current system, which assumes the availability of useful comparables in an economic environment in which they are very unlikely to be found, are predictable:

I. Companies and the government spend extraordinary sums each year on efforts at compliance and enforcement, largely through the preparation of 'contemporaneous documentation' by taxpayers and attempts at comprehensive examinations by the IRS involving some of the Service's most experienced and skilled personnel.

II. Despite the expense of compliance and enforcement, companies and the IRS typically are dramatically far apart in their determinations of arm's-length pricing. Controversies routinely involve hundreds of millions of dollars and are resolved at amounts that resemble neither the government's nor the taxpayer's positions, thereby casting grave doubt on the conceptual soundness of the underlying rules (GAO 1992; Nutt 2007).

III. The inability to predict whether their positions will be sustained leaves companies and their investors with large areas of uncertainty in their financial statements.

IV. The absence of clear standards for compliance, coupled with the ability under the arm's-length standard to apportion income to low-tax countries through legal arrangements governing the siting of intangibles and (more recently) the bearing of risk, make it impossible for Congress to predict with reasonable accuracy the actual amount of federal revenue that will be raised as a result of any particular corporate tax rate that Congress believes it has enacted.

V. The fact that neither taxpayers nor enforcement authorities typically have clear standards for judging compliance means that issues involving very large amounts – billions of dollars – of federal revenue are resolved in examination, settled in Appeals, resolved in negotiations under tax treaties with foreign governments, negotiated through advance-pricing agreements, or settled by attorneys out of court after examination. In most cases, federal privacy laws require that this decision-making occur away from the public eye. In my experience, those involved in this process have carried out their roles with both integrity and skill. Nevertheless, the resolution of issues involving such large amounts of money, without the benefit of clearly discernible decision-making standards and public scrutiny, is not healthy for the tax system.

VI. A related problem is that the uncertain results under current transfer-pricing law degrade the quality of tax practice on the parts of both taxpayer and government representatives, regardless of the high standards of practice that both sides seek to maintain. Both sides are tempted to state, as 'starting points' for what is expected to be extended negotiation, positions that strain the limits of what most would consider reasonable. The resulting atmosphere contributes to a lessening of the publicly perceived credibility of both corporations and the government – a development that is seriously damaging to what will always remain a largely mixed economic system.

VII. The vulnerability of the current transfer-pricing system to the shifting of income based on intangibles ownership and risk-bearing makes necessary numerous additional complexities in the international tax system. If the current transfer-pricing regime were replaced by a more formulary approach such as that suggested below, Congress could eliminate from the Code many or all of the 'base company' provisions of subpart F, retaining only those portions of subpart F dealing with passive investment income. There would still be considerable complexity, of course, but much would be eliminated. Similarly, transfer-pricing vulnerabilities probably constitute the most pressing argument against adoption of a territorial tax system. Reforming transfer-pricing rules could tip the policy-making balance in favour of adopting a territorial system, thereby permitting elimination of the grossly complex foreign tax-credit system, except as it relates to US taxpayers' passive investment income (which would remain subject to US tax jurisdiction and for which credit rules would need to be retained) (Kleinbard 2007). The current transfer-pricing system can be seen as the tail that wags the dog of much unnecessary tax complexity, therefore.

3. The problems of formulary apportionment

As stated above, these problems of the ALS are well known. However, they do not persuade proponents to abandon the ALS in favour of UT+FA. Instead, the advocates of the ALS point to a list of alleged deficiencies of UT+FA, including:

1) UT+FA is inherently arbitrary;
2) UT+FA will produce double taxation because some countries will apply the ALS and others UT+FA, and the UT+FA countries will each have a different formula;
3) UT+FA requires an impossible to achieve uniformity of the tax base;
4) UT+FA violates tax treaties;
5) UT+FA will be impossible to enact because of the opposition of the multinationals and of countries that will lose from its implementation (Spenser, 2014).

I believe that there is an answer to each of these criticisms, as I will now explain.

1) Is UT+FA arbitrary?

Some would consider basing the corporate income tax liability on a formula to be arbitrary. Still, it is not clear that the current ALS regime is less arbitrary, given the incentive to shift profits to low-tax jurisdictions. Under the current regime, it is quite possible that a MNE will not pay taxes either in the location of production (because of tax competition and production tax havens) or in the location of distribution (because it can avoid having a permanent establishment or minimise the profits attributable to the distribution function), while any tax due to its residence jurisdiction is subject to deferral or exemption. Such a result is more arbitrary than consistently assigning profits to the market jurisdiction, especially if most countries adopt similar formulas.

It is true that any formula can produce arbitrary results in a given industry. For example, the oil industry has long argued that it is unfair to tax it based on payroll, assets or sales because most of its profits result from the oil reserves themselves, which are not reflected in the formula (since they are typically not assets of the company for any length of time). However, while some industries will lose under any proposed formula, others will win; and most taxpayers would gain from the increased simplicity and transparency of the UT+FA regime. If companies are willing to pay one level of tax and are only concerned about double taxation, they should be willing to accept the UT+FA option, which prevents not only double taxation but also double non-taxation.

2) The problem of double taxation

It would be ideal for most major countries to co-ordinate implementation of UT+FA and to come to a joint agreement on the definition of the formula for apportioning global income. Given that the European Union is already pursuing the possibility of UT+FA within Europe, a natural forum for reaching international consensus on these issues would be the OECD. With international co-operation, the possibility of double or non-taxation would be reduced and there would be less room for multinational firms to respond strategically to variations in country formulas.

Even without formal co-operation, however, unilateral adoption by the United States of a reformed system for taxing international income would create a powerful incentive for other countries using separate accounting to adopt similar new systems. In a world with both formulary and separate-accounting-system countries, formulary countries will immediately appear as tax havens from a separate-accounting-country perspective. For example, a multinational firm operating in both separate-accounting and formulary countries would have an incentive to book all their income in formulary countries, as the tax liability in such countries does not depend on the income booked there but rather on the fraction of a firm's activities in that location. Such responses would likely greatly reduce the tax revenues of remaining separate-accounting countries. Thus, separate-accounting countries will have a strong incentive to adopt formulary approaches, particularly if large economies adopt formulary approaches.

Still, if the United States adopts a formulary approach unilaterally and other countries do not follow suit (or follow suit much later), or if countries adopt different formulas, there is the potential for double or zero taxation. This is, arguably, the largest obstacle to unilateral adoption of a formulary system; but the significance of the obstacle should not be overstated. Although situations of double taxation or double non-taxation could arise, it is not clear that a formulary approach would produce more double or non-taxation than the current regime. The notorious absence of clear standards under the current separate-accounting system means that different countries routinely reach widely disparate divisions of income based on the same facts. It is hard to imagine that a reformed system, which at least provides clear quantitative benchmarks, would lead to as many double taxation, or double non-taxation, disputes as the current system already produces.

For example, the IRS recently settled a major transfer-pricing case with the British firm Glaxo for $3.4 billion. This additional revenue resulted from shifting to the US profits that Glaxo claimed belonged in the UK (*Daily Tax Report* 2006, 2007). However, the UK tax authorities refused to accept the result of this settlement: under the US–UK tax treaty, they are not required to do so. (Art. 9 of the treaty only states that a country must make a 'correlative adjustment' when profits are shifted by the other treaty partner if it agrees that the profit shift was justified.) The result was full double taxation. The dispute-resolution mechanism in most current tax treaties does not provide for binding arbitration and therefore does not necessarily lead to a resolution. As Justice Brennan observed in the *Container* case (approving California's application of worldwide UT+FA to US-based MNEs), it is not clear which method (UT+FA or ALS) produces more over- or under-taxation, even when some countries use UT+FA and the others use ALS, or when different formulas are used (*Container Corp. v. Franchise Tax Board*, 463 US 159 (1983)).

In summary, with respect to the potential problem of double taxation, it must be remembered that the current system, which typically provides only wide ranges of potential 'answers' to any given transfer-pricing issue, often results in very different positions being taken by different countries, even when both countries are ostensibly applying the same arm's-length principles. Therefore, as a starting point, it should not be thought that a revised transfer-pricing regime would move us from a system *without* substantial double taxation to a system *with* double taxation; in fact, it is not at all clear whether adoption of a statute like that below would lead to more or less danger of double taxation. Of course, to the extent other countries, particularly those within the European Union, develop formulary systems of their own, a formulary approach by the United States would fit well into an international system for avoiding double taxation (Durst and Culbertson 2003: 80–1; OECD Committee on Fiscal Affairs 2008)

In order to evaluate the question of double taxation during the period when a formulary system might be mixed with arm's-length systems in other countries, it should be recognised that those multinational groups that have, to date, adopted tax-minimisation structures involving transfer-pricing have typically sought to minimise their taxable incomes in all high-tax countries in which they operate, not only the

United States, and to shift income into low- or zero-tax countries. As a result, a unilateral move by the United States to a formulary system is not likely to increase disputes with other high-tax countries; rather, it is likely to increase disagreements with low-tax countries that have sought actively to attract income and business from the United States. It is not clear that avoidance of these kinds of tax disputes constitutes a valid reason to delay reform of the US transfer-pricing rules.

It nevertheless needs to be recognised that a unilateral move to a formula-based approach is likely to result in political controversy with the low-tax countries and, because the interests of those countries will coincide with those of companies that seek to retain the subsidies implicit in the current system, those governments may find themselves in political alliance with multinational companies themselves. How to resolve the resulting controversy is a question that will need to be decided by Congress – but the controversy should be recognised as primarily political in nature. Overall, it would not appear that concerns about double taxation, significant though they may be, should be sufficient to deter Congress from taking action that could substantially improve the efficiency and apparent fairness of the US international tax system.

3) Defining the tax base

It would, of course, be desirable for a move to a formulary system to be accompanied by international co-ordination of the tax base. A common definition of the tax base (as opposed to harmonised tax rates, which are unlikely as well as undesirable) could, plausibly, be achieved because MNEs already use uniform accounting for world-wide financial-reporting purposes. Thus, it is quite possible to use financial reporting as the starting point for calculating the global profit of the MNE, to be allocated to jurisdictions based on the UT+FA formula. While there are still differences in accounting among countries, those are diminishing due to the spread of the International Financial Reporting Standards (IFRS, the new international accounting standards), which have been adopted in the EU and Japan. Further, the US Securities and Exchange Commission announced in August 2008 that it would allow some large US multinational firms to begin using international accounting standards as early as next year, and eventually require all American companies to do so. Alternatively, it may be possible to let each MNE use its home-country's accounting methods for calculating the global tax base (as suggested by the EU Commission for inter-EU purposes) (Commission of the European Union 2001: 13.1). Such changes would also have the advantage of more closely aligning book income and tax income. This could act as damper on both the under-reporting of income for tax purposes as well as the overstatement of income for the purpose of signalling profitability to financial markets.

However, if co-ordination of the tax base with accounting-based measures were unachievable or undesirable, the proposed formulary approach could also be implemented unilaterally by the US, using its own definition of taxable income and applying it to the entire MNE. US-based MNEs already have to calculate the earnings and profits of CFCs for purposes of subpart F and the foreign tax credit, so the additional information required for unilateral adoption would not be overly burdensome. For non-US based MNEs, the US system could use financial reporting to shareholders (already required by the SEC or by home-country regulators) as the base for calculating worldwide income. While this would create a disparity between US- and non-US-based MNEs, the disparity would probably be no more significant than it is under current transfer-pricing regimes around the world, which often must operate from measures of income as determined under local accounting systems.

Concern is sometimes expressed that a transfer-pricing system depending on application of an apportionment formula to global income will require the IRS to gain access to information on both US and foreign multinational groups' operations outside the United States. Current transfer-pricing law, however, already requires access to such information, both in the application of the profit-split method and in the course of examinations. Indeed, current law requires both US and foreign companies to retain and provide on request to the IRS voluminous information on non-US operations. There is no way to avoid offering national tax administrations access to information on activities in other jurisdictions.

4) Interaction with tax treaties

Some have argued that tax treaties will need modification with adoption of formulary apportionment. However, it is not clear that existing US tax treaties will have to be renegotiated, at least in the short term.

Transfer-pricing is currently governed by Article 9 of the treaties, which seems to assume the ALS method because it addresses the commercial or financial relations between associated enterprises. In addition, Article 7 of the treaties provides generally for the application of ALS principles in apportioning income among branches of single corporations – a technically complex topic not directly addressed in this article, although it raises issues similar to those raised when dealing with apportionment among separate affiliates.

There can be no question that, historically, both Article 7 and Article 9 have been interpreted as incorporating arm's-length concepts such as resorting to supposed 'comparables' and the other accoutrements of attempted transfer-pricing administration under the ALS regime. There is no reason, however, why the United States and its treaty partners could not agree, under the 'competent-authority' process contained in each treaty and discussed above, to interpret their treaties to accept the reformed apportionment approach as the closest feasible, and administrable, approximation to the arm's-length results envisaged in Articles 9 and 7. Except for low-tax, tax-haven countries, one would expect many if not most US tax-treaty partners to accept such an approach eagerly, since these treaty partners face the same difficulties in enforcement and administration of transfer-pricing rules that the United States faces.

There may, to be sure, be some countries that will insist on retaining the current ALS-based analysis in their treaty dealings with the United States. In such instances, case-by-case negotiation will be necessary in order to avoid double taxation – but such negotiations are required to an unacceptably large extent even under the current system, the vagueness of which leads to numerous conflicts among tax jurisdictions over particular cases. The legislation I propose includes provisions designed to ensure that US negotiators have authority to interpret US tax treaties as authorising the proposed reformed transfer-pricing methodology in double-taxation negotiations with treaty partners.

One can expect low-tax countries, as well as those multinational businesses that are favoured under the current transfer-pricing regime, to assert vigorously that the new regime is in violation of income-tax treaties. Such assertions will, however, reflect disagreement with the reformed system on policy grounds, rather than any highlighting serious impediment in the tax-treaty system to the adoption of the new system. Political opposition to the reform from low-tax countries and from businesses that will pay relatively larger shares of the corporate tax burden must be respected and dealt with – but such political opposition should be recognised for what it is.

5) Negative effects on some corporate stakeholders

Analysts have noted that adoption of UT+FA would negatively affect some industries and firms disproportionately. For example, Shackelford and Slemrod (1998) find that UT+FA raises tax liabilities for some industries and firms, lowering burdens for others. They estimate that the oil and gas industry would see an increase in tax liabilities of 81 per cent under UT+FA, compared with 29 per cent for all other firms in their study. (The mean oil and gas company in their study reports 68 per cent of assets in the United States, 70 per cent of sales in the United States and 78 per cent of total compensation paid to US employees; but such companies book 42 per cent of pre-tax earnings in the United States.) The authors also estimate that some firms will experience a tax decrease, including Boeing and Procter & Gamble. The update of Clausing and Lahav (2011) suggests a similar pattern, with tax increases for oil companies (such as Exxon, BP and Mobil) and tax decreases for Boeing, Procter & Gamble and Intel.

Also, negative impacts may be muted by several considerations. First, firms will benefit from reductions in complexity and compliance burdens. Small and medium-size businesses should be particularly appreciative of such benefits. Second, accompanying the adoption of a more formulary system with a reduction in the corporate income tax rate would increase the number of firms benefiting from the adoption. A rate reduction would also appeal to those concerned that the US is losing competitiveness because of the current rate disparity.

4. Adopting formulas in the context of the ALS

As noted above, I believe there is a good answer to each of the problems raised by opponents of UT+FA (Avi-Yonah *et al.* 2009; Avi-Yonah and Clausing 2008b). However, I also realise that my answers are unlikely to persuade UT+FA opponents. Thus, I want to use this article to propose a more modest step forward: adopting UT+FA only in the context of ALS (rather than replacing the ALS with UT+FA).

The basic problem arises in situations where there are no good comparables. If good comparables exist, the traditional methods (CUP, cost-plus and resale price) can be used, and that would end the story. But as the OECD guidelines acknowledge, in many cases, good comparables are hard to find.

The next alternative under the OECD guidelines is TNMM. However, TNMM requires a tougher comparability test than the US CPM, which is good because CPM has proven to be the most manipulable of the current methods: an informed economist working for a major accounting firm has told me he can achieve any result the client wants using CPM. CPM is also a huge source of transactional complexity, a boon to the large accounting firms and a problem for those who cannot afford their services. But the tougher OECD TNMM comparability standard means that TNMM cannot be applied in many cases in which CPM is used in the US.

This leaves the profit split method. Under profit split, comparables are used to allocate the return on routine functions. But that usually leaves a residual in place, which arises precisely because multinationals exist to earn a return that cannot be achieved in an arm's-length relationship. That, as explained above, is why good comparables are hard to find.

Thus, the key issue in current transfer-pricing is how to allocate the residual under the profit split method. The US regulations assume that the residual is the result of high-profit intangibles and allocate it to where such intangibles were developed. However, this method is not helpful because (a) the OECD and the rest of the world rejects it; (b) it penalises multinationals for conducting R&D in the US; and (c) it encourages multinationals to enter into cost-sharing agreements that artificially shift profits to low-tax jurisdictions. In addition, as the court stated in *Bausch & Lomb*,[2] if the value of the intangible results from the fact that two parties are related, that added value is distinct from where it was developed.

If the US approach is rejected, the question is how to allocate the residual. The OECD guidelines are silent on this issue. This presents an opportunity: perhaps in this context, it would be possible to adopt a formula to allocate the residual?

One needs to realise that if there are no comparables (by definition) and the residual results from the relationship between the parties and would disappear if they were unrelated, then the ALS is meaningless and any allocation is arbitrary. Under these circumstances the key is to adopt the formula that is most likely to achieve consensus.

2. Bausch & Lomb *v.* Commissioner, 92 TC 525 (1989), aff'd, 933 F2d 1084 (2nd cir. 1991). In that case, B&L had an unpatented intangible (knowhow) that enabled it to manufacture contact lenses at a much lower cost that any competitor. If B&L (US) did not control B&L (Ireland) where the intangible was located, the added profit that resulted would disappear because competitors would have access to the knowhow.

In the unilateral US context, I supported a sales-based formula similar to the destination-base formula for VAT. This choice of formula favours exports and therefore is likely to be politically popular and it favours the US because of its trade deficit (Avi-Yonah and Clausing 2008b). In the OECD context, I would prefer a more balanced formula with three components: payroll, tangible assets and sales.

These three components are, of course, the traditional formula used by US states for FA. This formula has proven to be remarkably successful since, in addition to the US states, it is also the basis for the global dealing regulations in the US and OECD; and it is a leading candidate for the CCCTB formula. I believe it makes sense because each of its elements is objective (payroll and sales are transactions with outside parties and, while tangible assets depend on valuations, there is a lot of experience with asset-based formulas, such as the US interest-allocation formula). Intangibles are excluded but, in my opinion, that is appropriate because (a) their value results from physical and human capital and from the market, and those elements are included; and (b) you cannot allocate their value and trying to include them invites manipulation.

Thus, I would propose that in hard transfer-pricing cases, in which no comparables can be found beyond the return on routine functions, the OECD endorse using the traditional three-factor state formula to allocate the residual under the profit split method.

I believe this proposal addresses the problems with FA outlined above.

1. While the formula is arbitrary it relates to economic reality – and any allocation is arbitrary in the absence of comparables. The current OECD Guidelines are also arbitrary in not allocating residuals.
2. It is unlikely that this outcome would lead to more double taxation than what already occurs for residuals under the ALS. If the US allocates residuals based on location of research and development (R&D) and other countries disagree, double taxation is already a threat. Disputes can be resolved using the new arbitration provision under the OECD model.
3. If the OECD accepts the residual formula under ALS, it does not violate treaties and it can be handled in the context of Article 9.
4. Since it is only a residual formula, the base has already been defined under ALS.
5. A balanced formula is less likely to produce consistent losers.

5. Conclusion

The OECD's base-erosion and profit-shifting (BEPS) project calls for a reform of transfer-pricing. However, the OECD has made it clear that it is not willing to consider a full-fledged move to UT+FA in the BEPS context.

This debate is unlikely to be resolved in the near future. However, there is little dispute that the current transfer-pricing methods do not work well and result in massive profit-shifting to low-tax jurisdictions. It is also clear that a large part of the problem results from lack of consensus on how to deal with residual profits left over after comparables have been exhausted. This paper is an attempt to contribute to a solution of this issue within the bounds of the ALS. In the longer term, I believe that a general move to UT+FA and abandonment of the ALS is more congruent with how modern MNEs operate; and it would enable countries to adopt purely territorial systems that ignore the largely artificial residence of corporate parents. But we are not there yet and, in the meantime, progress needs to be made on preventing BEPS.

References

Arnold, B. J. and McDonnell, T. E. (1993) 'Report on the invitational conference on transfer-pricing: the allocation of income and expenses among countries', *Tax Notes*, 13 December: 1377–81.

Altshuler, R. and Ackerman, J. (2005)'International aspects of recommendations from the President's Advisory Panel on Federal Tax Reform', paper presented at the International Tax Policy Forum, December 2: www.itpf.org/action/document/download?document_id=70 (accessed 1 September 2015).

Avi-Yonah, R. (2006) 'The rise and fall of arm's length: a study in the evolution of US international taxation', *Finance and Tax Law Review* 9: 310 (updated version of *Virginia Tax Review* (1995) 15: 89–).

Avi-Yonah, R. and Clausing, K. (2008a) 'Business profits (Article 7 OECD Model Convention)', in M. Lang *et al.* (eds) *Source versus Residence: Problems arising from the allocation of taxing rights in tax treaty law and possible alternatives*, The Hague: Kluwer Law International, pp. 9–20.

— (2008b) 'Reforming corporate taxation in a global economy: a proposal to adopt formulary apportionment', in Furman, J. and Bordoff, J. (eds) *Path to Prosperity: Hamilton Project ideas on income security, education, and taxes*, Washington, DC: Brookings Institution Press, pp. 319–44.

Avi-Yonah, R. *et al.* (2009) 'Allocating business profits for tax purposes: a proposal to adopt a formulary profit split', *Florida Tax Review* 9(5) and: http://taxblog.com/rsaviyonah/allocating-business-profits-for-tax-purposes-a-proposal-to-adopt-a-formulary-profit-split/ (accessed 29 August 2015).

BEA (Bureau of Economic Analysis, 2005) *Operations of US Parent Companies and Their Foreign Affiliates*, Washington, DC: US Department of Commerce, Business and Statistics Administration, Bureau of Economic Analysis.

Bucks, D. R. and Mazerov, M. (1993) 'The state solution to the federal government's international transfer-pricing problem', *National Tax Journal* 46(3): 385–92.

Clausing, K. (2008) 'Multinational firm tax avoidance and US government revenue', *National Tax Journal* LXII(4): 703–25: http://www.ntanet.org/NTJ/62/4/ntj-v62n04p703-25-multinational-firm-tax-avoidance.html (accessed 12 August 2015).

— (2016) 'The nature and practice of tax competition', in Dietsch, P. and Rixen, T. (eds) *Global Tax Governance: What is wrong with it and how to fix it*, Colchester: ECPR Press.

Clausing, K. A. and Lahav, Y. (2011) 'Corporate tax payments under formulary apportionment', *Journal of International Accounting, Auditing and Taxation* 20(2): 97–105: http://www.sciencedirect.com/science/article/pii/S1061951811000188 (accessed 12 August 2015).

Cofill, E. J. and Wilson Jr., P. (1993) 'Federal formulary apportionment as an alternative to arm's length pricing: from the frying pan to the fire?', *Tax Notes* 15 May.

Container Corp. v. *Franchise Tax Board*, 463 US 159 (1983).

Daily Tax Report (2006) 'GlaxoSmithKline to pay $3.4 billion to settle largest dispute in IRS history', 12 September at GG-1.

Daily Tax Report (2007) 'Glaxo preparing to litigate transfer-pricing "heritage product"', 7 March at I-3.

de Mooij, R. A. (2005) 'Will corporate income taxation survive?', *De Economist* 153: 277–301.

Durst, M. C. and Culbertson, R. E. (2003) 'Clearing away the sand: retrospective methods and prospective documentation in transfer-pricing today', *Tax Law Review* 57: 37–84.

Commission of the European Union (2001) 'Company taxation in the internal market', Commission Staff Working Paper, COM (2001) 582 Final 13.1: http://ec.europa.eu/taxation_customs/resources/documents/company_tax_study_en.pdf (accessed 1 September 2015).

GAO (General Accounting Office, 1992) 'International taxation problems persist in determining tax effects of intercompany prices', GAO/GGD 92-89: http://www.gao.gov/assets/160/151994.pdf.

Kleinbard, E. D. (2007) 'Throw territorial taxation from the train', *Tax Notes Today*, 5 February: 547–64: http://www.taxanalysts.com/www/features.nsf/Articles/5A846114FF6AC58F852579CD0064DE32?OpenDocument (accessed 1 September 2015).

Langbein, S. I. (1986) 'The unitary method and the myth of arm's length', *Tax Notes* 30: 625.

LeGall, J. F. (2006) 'When is a subsidiary a permanent establishment of its parent?' Tillinghast Lecture, New York University (forthcoming in *Tax Law Review*).

Nutt, A. (2007) 'News analysis: another transfer-pricing dispute in the litigation pipeline', *Tax Notes Today*, 23 January.

OECD (Organization for Economic Co-operation and Development) Committee on Fiscal Affairs (1995) *Transfer-pricing Guidelines for Multinational Enterprises and Tax Administrations*, Paris: OECD.

— (2008) *Transfer-pricing Aspects of Business Restructuring: Discussion draft for public comment*: http://www.oecd.org/tax/transfer-pricing/41346644.pdf (accessed 1 September 2015).

Shackelford, D. and Slemrod, J. (1998) 'The revenue tax consequences of using formulary apportionment', *International Tax and Public Finance* 5: 41–59.

Spencer, D. (2014) 'Formulary apportionment is not a panacea', *Journal of International Taxation* 35(May).

Taylor, W. (2005) Testimony before the President's Advisory Panel on Federal Tax Reform, 31 March 2005, *Tax Notes* April 4, Doc 2005-6654.

Wilkins, W. J. and Gideon, K. W. (1994) 'Memorandum to Congress: you wouldn't like worldwide formulary apportionment', *Tax Notes* 69: 1259–.

Chapter Fourteen

International Financial Transaction Taxation, Public Goods and Justice

*Gabriel Wollner**

An international financial transaction tax (IFTT) is a tax levied globally on transactions involving particular assets, for example, stocks, bonds, currencies or derivatives; the proposed tax rate is usually low: depending on the type of asset, somewhere between 0.01 per cent and 1 per cent of the value of the transaction; and imposition of the tax may be subject to a number of conditions, for example, that the transaction takes place across borders or that the seller is reselling the asset only a short time after having purchased it.[1] This paper offers two sets of arguments in defence of levying an international financial transaction tax.[2] The first set of arguments turns on the role that an IFTT would play in providing a stable international financial system: an IFTT would help to internalise the externalities that come with interacting on financial markets and ensure that those who benefit from the existence of an international financial system contribute to the costs of its provision and maintenance. The second set of arguments turns on the promise of an IFTT as an instrument for realising independent requirements of justice: an IFTT could play an important role in realising requirements of both domestic and global justice.[3]

My argument proceeds in four steps.[4] First, I shall identify four related dynamics or features that characterise the international financial system in its current form. These dynamics establish the background for my normative argument. Second, I shall put forward the first set of arguments in defence of an IFTT: the imposition of an IFTT would ensure that those transacting on financial markets bear the costs that their activities create for others and offer a fair way of sharing the burden of providing the public good of a stable and well functioning financial system. Third, I shall put forward the second set of arguments: an international financial

* I am very grateful to Peter Dietsch, Itai Grinberg and Miriam Ronzoni for very helpful comments on earlier drafts of the paper.

1. For the original proposal of a financial transaction tax, see Keynes 1965 and Tobin 1978.
2. For a more comprehensive defence of international financial transaction taxation as an instrument for achieving justice in finance, see Wollner 2014.
3. Both sets of arguments are about justice: the first one turns on the idea that an IFTT would help to ensure fairness or justice within the practice of finance.
4. The structure of my argument mirrors Daniel Halliday's distinction between three different functions a tax may fulfil, i.e., taxation's role in 'solving certain sorts of collective action problems', 'securing a just distribution of tax burdens' and 'suppressing harmful behaviour' (Halliday 2013: 1).

transaction tax is a promising instrument for achieving justice because of its direct effect on distributions of income and wealth and because of its impact on the ability of political institutions to practically realise the requirements of distributive justice. This reasoning holds for both domestic and global justice. Finally, I shall briefly discuss some alternative proposals for reforming the international financial system. I argue that while an IFTT has some distinct advantages over these alternatives, there is no reason to view these different reform proposals as mutually exclusive.

1. Four features of the international financial system

There are four features of the international financial system that should matter to those who think about reforming it: capital mobility; financialisation; financial instability; and the crisis of the fiscal state. These features, which are closely interrelated, matter because they distinguish the contemporary version of the international financial system from previous versions and because they account for the ethical challenge to which the international financial system as we know it today gives rise. As I shall argue in the next section, the moral deficits of the international financial system that an IFTT would address are closely linked to these four characteristics.

Almost perfect capital mobility and deep financial integration account for the first defining feature of the current international financial system. Until at least the 1970s, financial markets were, as a consequence of capital controls and the absence of current-account and capital-account convertibility, largely nationally self-contained.[5] But with the demise of the Bretton Woods system and the abandonment of capital controls, financial markets became increasingly integrated. Financial assets can now easily be traded across borders at low transaction cost and international financial flows have increased to many times their 1970s levels. Take the example of foreign-exchange markets: in April 2007, the average value of currency transactions on foreign-exchange markets was $3.2 trillion per day, according to Dani Rodrik (2012: 107) 'orders of magnitude larger than the volume of trade'; in 2010 the volume had risen to $4.0 trillion; and in April 2013 it averaged $5.3 trillion (BIS 2013a).

A second important aspect of the international financial system is its absolute and relative size. Finance has become increasingly important and many economies have undergone a process of financialisation. There are at least two dimensions to the phenomenon of financialisation.[6] First, there is a growing number and variety of financial instruments. Financial innovation over the past 20 years has led to the development of previously unknown financial instruments, many of which became notorious during the 2007 crisis. Second, there is an increase in the volume and value of financial instruments. Today the financial sector accounts for a much larger share of economic activity than twenty years ago and for every real or

5. For a description of the Bretton Woods system, see, for example, Eichengreen 2009, chapter 4.
6. For a fuller discussion of the phenomenon, see Palley 2007.

tangible asset there is a larger number of financial assets, for example, in the form of derivatives: in 1995, annual turnover on spot and derivative markets amounted to approximately 25 times world GDP; in 2007, it amounted to 70 times global output (von Weizsäcker and Darvas 2010: 5). The global amount of outstanding over-the-counter-derivatives increased from less than $100 trillion in 1998 to more than $600 trillion in 2013 (BIS 2013b).

A third defining feature of the contemporary international financial system is its instability and vulnerability to financial crises. After the demise of the Bretton Woods institutions in the 1970s, the frequency of banking and sovereign-debt crises has greatly increased. In the current international financial system, banking crises occur more often than in the past and they affect rich and poor countries alike. According to Reinhart and Rogoff, the proportion of countries suffering from banking and external-debt crises increased beginning in the early 1980s (2009: 73 ff.) Associated with banking crises, there is a decline in tax revenues due to lower profits which, in combination with a crisis-induced increase in public spending and other factors, contributes to a second type of crisis: public-debt crises.

These public-debt crises are indicative of the final feature that I would like to consider: the crisis of the fiscal state. States suffer from a lack of financial resources and find it increasingly difficult to muster the funds needed to provide important public goods, engage in redistribution and offer the welfare-state services of the past. In part, the fiscal crisis of the state is a function of the other features. For example: because capital can leave at little or no cost and assets can be moved with great ease – a function of both the absence of capital controls and the availability of relevant financial instruments – there is pressure on national governments to lower rates on capital and corporate income. As a consequence, tax revenues go down, corporations avoid and evade taxes and the tax burden or composition of the revenue shifts.[7] The result is a transformation of the tax-state into a debt-state: instead of tax income, the state relies on debt to fund its activities. According to Wolfgang Streeck, the increase in public indebtedness in a number of OECD countries, including Germany, France and the US, coincides with a decrease in tax revenues, both in terms of GDP and relative to public spending (Streeck 2014: chapter 2).[8]

2. The first set of arguments: externalities and public goods

The first two arguments in defence of an IFTT rest on minimalist assumptions and build on an important insight: well functioning financial markets are important to allocating capital to its most productive use and thus enhance overall economic well-being. An IFTT is a promising idea because the tax would contribute to the maintenance of well functioning and morally justifiable international financial

7. For a discussion of this phenomenon, *see* Clausing 2016, Chapter Two in this volume, and Genschel and Seelkopf 2016, Chapter Three in this volume.

8. For an earlier account of the crisis of the fiscal state, see O'Connor 2001.

markets. According to the externalities argument in defence of an IFTT, a financial transaction tax ensures that those transacting on markets bear the costs their interactions impose on third parties. According to the public-goods argument in defence of an IFTT, a financial transaction tax ensures that those transacting on financial markets share in the costs of providing a stable market system.

Third party costs: the externalities argument

A first argument in defence of an international financial transaction tax is simple and straightforward and can be embraced without subscribing to any particular conception of socio-economic justice: the imposition of an international financial transaction tax ensures that those transacting on financial markets bear the costs that their activities create for others.

Transacting on financial markets may give rise to costs that are not borne by any of the transacting parties. Often these costs arise as the unintended consequence of the uncoordinated activity of a large number of actors. The third party bearing the cost of the transaction(s) may be other participants in the international financial system or outsiders. One type of cost that may accrue to those who do not even transact on financial markets are the costs of financial and economic crises: low growth and unemployment adversely affect peoples' lives regardless of whether or not they have taken out a sub-prime mortgage, invested in a mutual fund or purchased a credit default swap. And citizens in least developed countries, who do not participate in the international financial system in any meaningful way, are also among those adversely affected by crises, for example, as a consequence of remittance payments going down.[9] Other costs of financial transaction are borne by non-transacting participants of the international financial system. For example, the exchange rate of a small country's currency may fluctuate for a number of reasons entirely independent of any of the activities of that country. To prevent its currency from collapsing, for example, the central bank may have to hold large amounts of foreign currency reserves, which has high opportunity costs. Instead of putting financial resources to productive domestic use, they have to be held by the central bank; and instead of receiving capital from the developed world, net capital actually flows from developing to developed countries.[10]

Two mechanisms explain how an IFTT would take care of these externalities. On the one hand, a tax would be a disincentive to engaging in the cost-inducing behaviour, thus limiting the number of externality-prone transactions and reducing the costs accruing to third parties.[11] Financial markets will, for example, become less volatile as a consequence of the tax and economic actors

9. According to the World Bank's *Migration and Remittance Factbook*, global remittance payments fell by 6 per cent from 2008 to 2009 (World Bank 2011).

10. See the phenomenon of role reversal in international finance as described in Prasad 2011.

11. One might worry that a low tax rate will not have the desired incentive effect. But even a very low tax rate will, in effect, turn out to be a much higher tax rate, given the frequency with which the targeted transactions are usually performed.

who suffer from price fluctuation, such as developing countries that need to engage in costly self-insurance, will be better off.[12] As originally put by James Tobin, an IFTT will be 'sand in the wheels' of international finance.[13] On the other hand, the tax would raise revenues to compensate those suffering from the externalities. In the case of domestic victims of economic crises, tax revenues could be spent in ways that benefit those adversely affected by them, for example, on welfare-state expenditure and macro-economic management. In the case of countries being adversely affected through currency fluctuation, tax revenues could be made available as low-interest loans for insurance purposes.[14]

Financial stability: the public goods argument

A second argument builds on the observation that the existence of a stable and well functioning international financial system is a public good: a financial transaction tax would be a way of sharing the costs involved in providing the public good fairly between those who benefit from it.[15] To see why the international financial system can plausibly be thought of as a public good, one ought to distinguish between two types of benefits associated with its existence. Participating in the international financial system, for example through transacting on financial markets, gives rise to important benefits: to borrow, to lend, or to hedge against risks comes with important benefits for individuals, firms and states. Lenders are relying on financial markets to earn a return on their savings; borrowers rely on financial markets to invest in and fund their activities; and there are welfare gains in the aggregate by putting financial resources to their most efficient use. These benefits that arise from making use of the market in particular ways do not satisfy the standard conditions of a public good (non-rivalry and non-exclusion). But there is a second, more indirect, benefit associated with the conditions that create and maintain markets. These conditions or goods which enable market interactions in the first place *are* non-excludable and non-rival. Market interactions presuppose a practice of market reliance, comprising background institutions, regulators, norms and expectations which create and maintain the option of interacting in a market.[16] Unfortunately, the provision of these market-enabling public goods comes with costs. There

12. See Wollner 2014: 19.
13. For more contemporary uses of that metaphor, see, for example, Eichengreen and Wyplosz 1995.
14. Note that I am not arguing that doing so would necessarily be the best use of tax revenues. Independent arguments will be needed to decide how tax revenues should be spent.
15. Figuring out what exactly a fair share would amount to will turn out to be tricky. At the same time, it seems uncontroversial that the financial sector is currently contributing nowhere-near enough and even critics of an IFTT admit that the financial sector should be taxed more (Dixon 2013). Any shift towards greater contributions by financial institutions would be an improvement in terms of fairness.
16. See James 2012 for the notion of market reliance in the context of trade.

are costs associated with maintaining financial markets as morally justifiable institutions, for example, through welfare-state provisions that compensate those losing out on the market.[17] And there are the costs of funding the institutions and interventions that secure the basic functioning of financial markets, including, for example, central banks, deposit insurance schemes, bailouts and so on. The problem that arises in this context is familiar from the provision of other public goods: individuals have a strong incentive to free-ride and to enjoy the benefits of the public good without contributing to its provision. Financial institutions like banks and funds interact on financial markets without doing their bit towards the maintenance of those institutions that enable their interaction, leading to a situation where there is not enough provision of the public good in question, the burden of provision is distributed unfairly, or both.[18]

And this is where the proposal of an international financial transaction tax comes in. Imposing a tax on transactions on financial markets addresses the problems associated with the observation that financial stability is a public good in two ways. First, an international financial transaction tax is itself a regulatory tool directly contributing to the stability of financial markets. Assuming that short-term speculative trading, in combination with 'herd behaviour' and so on, makes a financial system more volatile and less stable – and assuming that the tax curbs such behaviour by making speculative transactions less attractive – the tax contributes to the stability of the system. Second, one might see an international financial transaction tax as a contribution to the provision of public goods. Given that the good of stability is primarily provided by states, regulators and institutions, the funds raised by a transaction tax could be seen as a way of paying for the services provided by states and regulators. As the crisis of the fiscal state illustrates, those providing the public good of financial stability are underfunded. That they are underfunded is a function of both high spending to maintain the financial system, such as high public debt as a consequence of bailouts, and low revenues, for example, as a consequence of capital mobility and tax competition. Through its twofold effect, – the incentive effect and the revenue effect – an IFTT would help address both dimensions of the problem.

17. Note that a welfare state is not, technically, a market-enabling measure but, in virtue of its compensation effect, it enables markets as morally justifiable institutions. For the argument that certain types of market interactions are justifiable only if losers are compensated, see James 2012.

18. Two questions arise in this context. Why does my present argument not generalise into an argument about any type of market, thus undermining the special case for an IFTT? And why should one think that there is currently not enough of the relevant public good provided? My response to the first question is twofold. First, I am not opposed to the idea that additional taxes should be levied to ensure that participants in other markets should share adequately in the cost of providing them. Second, it could well be that the maintenance of financial markets is particularly costly, thus rendering an additional mechanism of sharing costs necessary. In response to the second question, I would argue that not enough of the relevant public good is provided currently, because financial markets are neither well functioning and stable, nor embedded in institutions that would render them morally justifiable.

3. The second set of arguments: domestic and global justice

Taxation is one of the primary tools for putting a conception of distributive justice into practice and international financial transaction taxation is no exception. An IFTT is a promising instrument for achieving justice because of its direct effect on the distribution of the benefits of economic co-operation and because of its impact on the ability of political institutions to realise the requirements of justice in practice. I shall argue that the direct distributive and the institution-enabling aspects matter on both the domestic and the global level. An international financial transaction tax is a policy instrument for enhancing domestic and global justice.

A twofold contribution: the domestic justice argument

What does justice require in the domestic context? There are number of different conceptions of social and distributive justice, including, most famously, Rawls's two principles of justice, a variety of luck-egalitarian conceptions, prioritarian principles, sufficientarian principles and so on. My arguments about the promise of an international financial transaction tax as an instrument for realising requirements of domestic justice remains neutral between these different conceptions of justice. There are two versions of this argument. First, because of its redistributive potential, an international financial transaction should be welcomed by anyone who believes that improving the situation of the worst-off in society or narrowing the gap between those who are better off and those who are worse off counts as an improvement in social justice. To be sure, the distributive effect of a tax structure can only be assessed by examining the combined effect of the revenue side and the spending side, that is, by looking at both the tax incidence and at how the tax revenue is spent.[19] I shall argue that a properly designed IFTT will be progressive in effect and have a redistributive effect. Second, an IFTT should be embraced by Rawlsians, luck-egalitarians, prioritarians and sufficientarians alike because its introduction would have a positive impact on the ability of political institutions to put any conception of justice into practice. Consider the latter aspect first.

The first version of the social justice argument turns on the ability of domestic political institutions to put a conception of distributive justice into practice. To ensure that the distribution of the benefits of economic co-operation meets the requirements of justice, the state has a number of its instruments at its disposal. It may, for example, rely on fiscal and monetary policy to provide public goods, redistribute wealth and income and macro-manage the economy. Three preconditions underpin the state's ability to use these instruments effectively: the state needs to generate revenue; it will have to be in a position where the revenue can actually be spent in the relevant ways; and using policy tools in the name of justice must not systematically conflict with other policy aims to which the state is committed. In this context, the international financial system is a double-edged sword. On the one hand, access to funding through the international financial system

19. See the argument of Murphy and Nagel (2002).

is important. The state may need to borrow on international financial markets in order to finance a fiscal expansion in times of crisis and maintain the provision of public goods when tax revenues are low. On the other hand, the dynamics of the international financial system as sketched above threaten the ability of the state to put justice into practice. The phenomenon of tax competition in a context of capital mobility, for example, creates problems for the revenue condition.[20] States find it increasingly difficult to generate revenue through the taxation of corporate activities. Economic and financial crises create problems with regards to the spending side. Instead of providing the goods needed to achieve justice, states have to bail out banks, comply with demands for austerity and so on. And capital mobility creates yet another problem for the effectiveness of fiscal and monetary policy. Countries with a fixed exchange rate, for example, cannot rely on monetary policy to realise justice:[21] instead of using monetary policy to lower interest rates during an economic crisis, these states will have to use monetary policy to defend their exchange rate. As a result of capital mobility and financial integration, policy instruments required for achieving justice at home become ineffective.

Levying a tax on international financial transactions would provide a threefold remedy, thus restoring the ability of the state to act on principles of justice. First, even a very low tax would raise billions in revenues and ameliorate the crisis of the fiscal state. Estimates for the US range from an annual revenue of $170 to $350 billion from a transaction tax.[22] Second, if it is true that an international financial transaction tax would render the international financial system more stable, for example by reducing volatility and proneness to crisis, its imposition would address the spending dimension of the problem as well. Very simply, not having to bail out banks will free up funds for achieving justice. And finally, the tax would allow states to effectively use the policy instruments relevant for delivering social justice. For example, a tax on international financial transaction will give states leeway to rely on expansionary monetary policy, that is, a low interest rate, by making it less attractive for capital to leave the country in order to earn a higher return at the world interest rate. The higher the tax rate, the more expensive it is for capital to move around and the greater the potential difference between the domestic and the world interest rate. Within limits, a transaction tax has the same effect as capital controls in providing states with the policy space need to deliver justice at home.[23]

The second argument emphasises the direct distributive impact that a properly designed international financial transaction tax might have: an international financial transaction tax may work to benefit the worst-off in society and narrow

---

20. One may wonder why the problems of tax competition and capital mobility should not matter in the same way for an IFTT as they do for an income tax. In Section Five I shall argue that they do not.
21. See Mundell 1963 and Fleming 1962.
22. The exact number will depend on whether the tax is levied on the full range of financial assets, the associated impact on trade volumes, etc. See Baker *et al.* 2009.
23. For a discussion of 'policy space' and its significance, see Rodrik 2012.

the gap between rich and poor. There are three effects that matter. The first one concerns the impact of the tax on real economic activity; the second one is about the tax incidence; and the last one concerns spending. First, a tax would benefit the worst-off in society by dealing with the above-mentioned feature of financialisation. Here is how financialisation is relevant to questions of justice: a well functioning financial system improves the well-being of everyone, including the worst-off, by supporting the real-world economy, for example, through enabling investments in a company by funding initial public offerings (IPOs), presumably leading to additional growth and employment. But, as a consequence of excessive financialisation, financial resources are often used in ways that do not contribute to the production of goods and services. Instead of serving real production, financial resources are put to speculative use. An international financial transaction tax serves the purpose of re-channelling financial resources towards the real economy; as short-term speculative transactions become less attractive, investment in the real economy becomes more attractive. Assuming that investment in the real economy is better in creating benefits for the worst-off in society than speculation, by creating jobs for those who would otherwise be unemployed, for instance, an international financial transaction tax improves the situation of the worst-off.

Second, even a flat financial transaction tax will have a progressive effect and restore equity in the distribution of the tax burden. As argued above, because of the related phenomena of capital mobility and tax competition, labour is taxed more highly than capital, leading to a situation in which those with comparatively low incomes primarily from labour shoulder too large a share of the overall tax burden. An international financial transaction tax would, at least on most spending scenarios, counteract this asymmetry and, in effect, be highly progressive. Two mechanisms explain why. First, the worst-off in society generally do not own any financial assets and thus will never engage in the type of transaction subject to the tax. It is of course an open question on whom exactly the tax incidence would fall: would a tax on trading collateralised mortgage debt, for example, reduce the trader's profit or just increase the interest rate for the homebuyer?[24] But as the worst-off in society do not own, buy, or sell the assets taxed, there is no way in which the burden of the tax could be shifted on to them. And second, even among those who own financial assets, the better-off are likely to pay more. Only relatively large fortunes are actively managed in ways that involve frequent transactions. They will thus give rise to much of the overall tax revenue. Small fortunes, on the other hand, such as private savings in a bank account, which those worse off are likely to possess, for lack of relevant transactions will hardly ever be taxed.[25]

And finally, an IFTT will have a redistributive and progressive effect by spending tax revenues in ways that benefit the worse-off in society. Critics may argue that because the tax is redistributive and progressive only as long as the

24. I am grateful to Itai Grinberg for pressing this issue.

25. For a discussion of how fortunes of different sizes are managed, see, for example, Piketty 2014, chapter 12.

revenue is spent in the right way, that is, such that the combination of costs and benefits associated with the tax improves the situation of the worse-off relative to the better-off, my justice-based case for the tax remains inconclusive. But by bringing tax revenue under democratic control, the tax makes the use of resources amenable to considerations of distributive justice, which would not be the case if these resources remained in private hands. And even though the exact redistributive and progressive effect of an IFTT will depend on how exactly the revenue is spent, many, if not most of the plausible spending scenarios will turn out to have an overall redistributive and progressive effect.

A threefold contribution: the global justice argument

There is disagreement about how to think of justice beyond the nation-state. Some argue that global justice requires redistribution between globally worse-off and globally better-off individuals; some believe that international justice is primarily about protecting the sovereignty of nation-states; and still others are convinced that various aspects of the global order generate particular normative requirements in their own right.[26] I shall argue that from each of these points of view, an international financial transaction tax would be a welcome instrument of justice.

First, an international financial transaction tax would contribute to narrowing the gap between the rich and the poor, not just in a domestic context but also globally. To begin with, the revenue of an international financial transaction, or at least part of it, could be used to fight global poverty and alleviate the position of the worst-off.[27] But the regulative effect of the tax would also be to the benefit of the global poor. If it is true that an IFTT will curb the volatility of financial markets and reduce the frequency of crises, people in developing countries would benefit, for example because the phenomenon of role reversal and capital outflows would be contained and because the reductions in remittance payments associated with economic crises would not take place. And finally, international co-operation in collecting a tax could help build institutions on the domestic level that would be needed for a full blown fiscal and welfare state, the kind of state many developing countries currently lack but the existence of which would be crucial for economic development and for the well-being of the worse-off.[28]

Second, an international financial transaction tax would promote the sovereignty of states and thus maintain conditions of international background justice: circumstances under which states can interact with each other as free and

---

26. For advocates of these different positions, see, for example, Caney 2006, Rawls 1999 and Risse 2012.

27. Note that there might be a competition between this use and other uses talked about elsewhere in the argument of my paper. For a discussion of an IFTT as an instrument to fight poverty, see Brock 2008.

28. For the significance of institutions for economic development, see, for example, Rodrik 2007 and Acemoglu and Robinson 2012).

equal.[29] There are many ways in which the dynamics of the international financial system threaten the sovereignty of states. The crisis of the fiscal state undermines the state's ability to be in effective control of important domestic policies, to provide public goods and to manage its economic affairs. The sovereign-debt crisis of countries like Greece and Argentina undermines sovereignty by giving rise to external interference in domestic affairs, for example, in the case of the former by having the ECB and the IMF exercise effective budgetary control. There are two ways in which the imposition of an international financial transaction tax would take care of both these dynamics. First, the tax revenue would help coming to terms with the crisis of the fiscal state, provide funds for the provision of public goods and so on. Second, the crisis-mitigating effect of the tax would reduce the number of events requiring external interference by other states or international financial institutions. And third, the imposition of a tax on the exchange of financial instruments would reduce the bargaining power of the owners of capital, by making it more costly to move financial assets around. A financial transaction tax thus promotes effective sovereignty by reasserting the strength of the state *vis-à-vis* capital.

Finally, one might argue that the international financial system is a practice that, in virtue of its defining features, gives rise to its own internal normative requirements, which a financial transaction tax would then help to satisfy. In a nutshell, the argument is this: the international financial system and its institutions deliver important benefits but also constrain the agency of those who interact through it. Because of these constraints, the international financial system will have to be justifiable to its participants; and justification takes place by appeal to its participants' important interests, including autonomy and well-being interests. Choosing between different versions of the international financial system, a version including an international financial transaction tax would, in part for the reasons developed above, turn out to be more justifiable than a version without such a tax. Because of its effect on sovereignty, individual well-being and overall distributive justice, the introduction of an IFTT would improve the justifiability of the international financial system.

4. Alternative proposals and a twofold argumentative strategy

Why should the imposition of an international financial transaction tax be the instrument of choice for regulating global financial capitalism? Why not rely on a different type of tax? And why rely on taxation at all? There are two argumentative strategies one might employ in answering these questions. First, one could argue that an international financial transaction tax is superior to both other tax proposals and alternative policy measures. Second, one could pursue a more ecumenical strategy and explain how an international financial transaction tax coheres with and supplements alternative approaches. I shall offer a brief sketch of both these

29. This argument relies on the ideas of background justice (Ronzoni 2009) and effective sovereignty (Dietsch 2011).

approaches and argue that while an international financial transaction tax possesses distinct advantages over prominent alternative types of taxation, including a global wealth tax and a financial activities tax (FAT), it would feasibly and coherently supplement many of the reform proposals discussed in this volume.

Two alternative tax proposals have figured prominently in recent debates. While some have argued that a FAT, which would effectively work as a value-added tax for the financial sector levied on banks' profits, is preferable to a financial transaction tax (Dixon 2013); others have put forward the idea of a progressive tax on capital ownership (Piketty 2014) as key to addressing the perils of contemporary capitalism. I believe that an international financial transaction tax possesses distinct advantages over both these alternatives. These advantages play out in different dimensions.

First, an IFTT is superior to alternative proposals because it fares better in capturing normatively relevant considerations. Consider the alternative of the FAT. A tax raised on the basis of profits does not generate any revenue if no profits are made. A tax on the basis of transactions, on the other hand, generates revenue regardless of whether the transactions are profitable. Important considerations favour the latter tax over the former. Because those transacting on financial markets benefit from the good of there being a market practice in the first place, they should contribute to its provision irrespective of their economic success. Parties to a transaction are responsible for the transactions they undertake and they should bear the costs of their transactions, even if they turn out to be unsuccessful.

Second, one may invoke considerations of feasibility and effectiveness in support of an IFTT. Given that a large share of wealth is hidden in tax havens,[30] a tax on capital will be of limited use unless all tax havens co-operate fully.[31] An IFTT would avoid this complication: even wealth hidden in tax havens will have to be invested and managed to earn a return. As investing and managing wealth presupposes financial transactions, and plausibly assuming that wealth will rationally be invested in financial instruments beyond the jurisdiction of tax havens, an IFTT would succeed in targeting tax-haven wealth.[32]

A second response strategy is ecumenical. Instead of choosing between an IFTT and alternative policy strategies, several of these strategies could be embraced at once. There is no reason to think of the proposals as mutually

---

30. See Zucman 2013.

31. For pessimistic prospects, particularly in the context of mock compliance, *see* Woodward 2016, Chapter Five in this volume.

32. To come full circle, the feasibility argument would have to address a number of issues: why is international co-operation more likely to succeed in the case of a transaction tax, rather than in the case of an income or wealth tax? And why don't capital mobility and tax competition pose the same problem for the former that they pose for the latter? Convincing answers to these questions will emphasise the nature of the tax base: because it is the transaction associated with capital mobility that is taxed, capital mobility does not undermine the tax base. And because transactions rather than possession are taxed, implementing an IFTT will be informationally and administratively less demanding.

exclusive alternatives but one should see an IFTT as a feasible and coherent supplement to the proposals put forward in this volume. The first set of these proposals concerns increased transparency in tax governance, through domestic legislation like FATCA, for example, (*see* Grinberg 2016, Chapter Seven in this volume); through a financial secrecy index (*see* Meinzer 2016, Chapter Twelve in this volume); and through automatic exchange of information (*see* Hakelberg 2016, Chapter Six in this volume). In particular, the success of the latter should ground moderate optimism about the prospects of an IFTT. If powerful actors like the US can succeed in bringing about multilateral tax agreements against the interests of those who benefit from the *status quo*, the force of one of the main feasibility objections against an IFTT is greatly diminished. The second set of proposals discusses more ambitious forms of international tax co-operation, including the OECD's base-erosion and profit-shifting (BEPS) initiative (*see* Eccleston and Smith 2016, Chapter Eight in this volume) and an International Tax Organization (ITO) (*see* Rixen 2016, Chapter Fifteen in this volume). The latter might, conceivably, provide the institutional home for an IFTT. In addition to ensuring transparency, promoting tax harmonisation, monitoring compliance and settling disputes, the ITO might additionally be tasked with levying and administering an IFTT. And, finally, there are substantive proposals on particular tax policies, such as universal minimum corporate taxation (*see* Ronzoni 2016, Chapter Nine in this volume) and Unitary Taxation and Formula Apportionment (*see* Avi-Yonah 2016, Chapter Thirteen in this volume) in line with the membership principle (*see* Dietsch 2016, Chapter Eleven in this volume). I believe that an IFTT could coherently be endorsed in combination with any of these proposals. Note that there is one worry that advocates of this argumentative strategy will have to respond to: relying on many instruments at once, that is, different types of taxation, might lead to what one might call problems of over-regulation, such as double taxation. How could the ecumenical strategy be defended against this objection? I believe that a successful response will be based on two observations. First, the adequacy or permissibility of a tax (or a combination of taxes) is not to be assessed by local criteria governing the relationship between a tax base and tax rate but by examining the overall effect that a tax (or combination of taxes) has on the relevant scheme of co-operation or domain of activity it is intended to regulate.[33] Second, if a particular tax is required to address a problem within the wider scheme of co-operation or domain of activity, that tax may turn out to be justified, even if that tax base has been subject to taxation before. If a tax on the ownership of financial assets addresses problems of inequality and a tax on the transaction of financial assets contributes to the public good of enabling such transactions, both kinds of taxation may be justified, even though the same underlying asset is taxed twice. Arguing along these lines, advocates of the ecumenical strategy can embrace a variety of policy and tax proposals at once.

33. Again, see Murphy and Nagel 2002.

5. Conclusion

There are two sets of arguments in defence of an IFTT. The first one is about externalities and public goods: an IFTT would help to internalise the externalities that come with interacting in financial markets and ensure that those who benefit from the existence of an international financial system contribute to the costs of its provision and maintenance. The second one is about justice: an IFTT would play an important role in realising requirements of both domestic and global justice. If these arguments are sound, policy-makers should rely on an IFTT as an instrument of global tax governance and as a proposal for reforming the international financial system.

References

Acemoglu, D. and Robinson, J. A. (2012) *Why Nations Fail: The origins of power, prosperity, and poverty*, London: Profile.

Avi-Yonah, R. (2016) 'A proposal for unitary taxation and formula apportionment to tax multinational enterprises', in Dietsch, P. and Rixen, T. (eds) *Global Tax Governance: What is wrong with it and how to fix it*, Colchester: ECPR Press.

Baker, D., Pollin, R., McArthur, T. and Sherman, M. (2009) 'The potential revenue from financial transactions taxes', Centre for Economic and Political Research issue brief: http://www.cepr.net/documents/publications/ftt-revenue-2009-12.pdf (accessed 20 August 2015).

BIS (Bank for International Settlements, 2013a) 'Triennial Central Bank Survey. Foreign exchange turnover in April 2013: preliminary results': http://www.bis.org/publ/rpfx13fx.pdf (accessed 20 August 2015).

— (2013b) *Statistical release: OTC derivatives statistics at the end of June 2013*.

Brock, G. (2008) 'Taxation and global justice: closing the gap between theory and practice', *Journal of Social Philosophy* 39(2): 161–84.

Caney, S. (2006) *Justice Beyond Borders: A global political theory*, Oxford: Oxford University Press.

Clausing, K. (2016) 'The nature and practice of capital tax competition', in Dietsch, P. and Rixen, T. (eds) *Global Tax Governance: What is wrong with it and how to fix it*, Colchester: ECPR Press.

Dietsch, P. (2011) 'Rethinking sovereignty in international fiscal policy', *Review of International Studies*, 37(5): 2107–20.

— (2016) 'Whose tax base? The ethics of global tax governance', in Dietsch, P. and Rixen, T. (eds) *Global Tax Governance: What is wrong with it and how to fix it*, Colchester: ECPR Press.

Dixon, H. (2013) 'We can do better than the defunct financial transaction tax', *Financial Times*, 13 September: http://www.ft.com/cms/s/0/d7196aa0-1afa-11e3-b781-00144feab7de.html#axzz3hxKMBsug (accessed 20 August 2015).

Eccleston, R. and Smith, H. (2016) 'The G20, BEPS and the future of international tax governance', in Dietsch, P. and Rixen, T. (eds) *Global Tax Governance: What is wrong with it and how to fix it*, Colchester: ECPR Press.

Eichengreen, B. (2009) *Globalizing Capital: A history of the international monetary system*, 2nd edition, Princeton, New Jersey: Princeton University Press.

Eichengreen, B. and Wyplosz, C. (1995) 'Two cases for sand in the wheels of international finance', *Finance Economic Journal*, 105(428): 162–72.

Fleming, J. M. (1962) 'Domestic financial policies under fixed and floating exchange rates', *Staff Papers (International Monetary Fund)* 9(3): 369–80.

Genschel, P. and Seelkopf, L. (2016), 'Winners and losers of tax competition', in Dietsch, P. and Rixen, T. (eds) *Global Tax Governance: What is wrong with it and how to fix it*, Colchester: ECPR Press.

Grinberg, I. (2016) ‘Does FATCA teach broader lessons about international tax multilateralism?’, in Dietsch, P. and Rixen, T. (eds) *Global Tax Governance: What is wrong with it and how to fix it*, Colchester: ECPR Press.

Hakelberg, L. (2016) ‘Redistributive tax co-operation: automatic exchange of information, US power and the absence of joint gains, in Dietsch, P. and Rixen, T. (eds) *Global Tax Governance: What is wrong with it and how to fix it*, Colchester: ECPR Press.

Halliday, D. (2013) ‘Justice and taxation’, *Philosophy Compass* 8(12): 1111–22.

James, A. (2012) *Fairness in Practice: A social contract for a global economy*, Oxford: Oxford University Press.

Keynes, J. M. (1965) *General Theory of Employment, Interest, and Money*, San Diego, CA: Mariner Books.

Meinzer, M. (2016) ‘Towards an international yardstick for identifying tax havens and facilitating reform’, in Dietsch, P. and Rixen, T. (eds) *Global Tax Governance: What is wrong with it and how to fix it*, Colchester: ECPR Press.

Mundell, R. (1963) ‘Capital mobility and stabilization policy under fixed and flexible exchange rates’, *Canadian Journal of Economics and Political Science* 29(4): 475–85.

Murphy, L. and Nagel, T. (2002) *The Myth of Ownership*, Oxford: Oxford University Press.

O’Connor, J. (2001) *The Fiscal Crisis of the State*, Piscataway, New Jersey: Transaction Publishers.

Palley, T. I. (2007) ‘Financialization: what it is and why it matters’, Levy Institute working paper 525: http://www.levyinstitute.org/pubs/wp_525.pdf (accessed 20 August 2015).

Piketty, T. (2014) *Capital in the Twenty-First Century*, Cambridge, Massachusetts: Harvard University Press.

Prasad, E. S. (2011) *Role Reversal in Global Finance*, National Bureau of Economic Research working paper 17497, Cambridge, Massachusetts: National Bureau of Economic Research.

Rawls, J. (1999) *The Law of Peoples* with *The Idea of Public Reason Revisited*, Cambridge, Massachusetts: Harvard University Press.

Reinhart, C. M. and Rogoff, K. S. (2009) *This Time is Different: Eight centuries of financial folly*, Princeton, New Jersey: Princeton University Press.

Risse, M. (2012) *On Global Justice*, Princeton, New Jersey: Princeton University Press.

Rixen, T. (2016) ‘Institutional reform of global tax governance: a proposal’, in Dietsch, P. and Rixen, T. (eds) *Global Tax Governance: What is wrong with it and how to fix it*, Colchester: ECPR Press.

Rodrik, D. (2007) *One Economics – Many Recipes: Globalization, institutions, and economic growth*, Princeton, New Jersey: Princeton University Press.

— (2012) *The Globalization Paradox: Democracy and the future of the world economy*, New York and London: W. W. Norton & Company.

Ronzoni, M. (2009) 'The global order: a case of background injustice? A practice-dependent account', *Philosophy and Public Affairs*, 37(3): 229–56.

— (2016) 'Tax competition between self-determination and global governance: what should and should not be globalized?', in Dietsch, P. and Rixen, T. (eds) *Global Tax Governance: What is wrong with it and how to fix it*, Colchester: ECPR Press.

Streeck, W. (2014) *Buying Time: The delayed crisis of democratic capitalism*, Brooklyn, New York: Verso Books.

Tobin, J. (1978) 'A proposal for international monetary reform', *Eastern Economic Journal* 4(3–4): 153–59.

von Weizsäcker, J. and Darvas, Z. (2010) 'Financial transaction tax: small is beautiful', European Parliament: http://bruegel.org/wp-content/uploads/imported/publications/external_FTTParliament_110110.pdf (accessed 20 August 2015).

Wollner, G. (2014) 'Justice in finance: the normative case for an international financial transaction tax', *Journal of Political Philosophy* 22(4): 458–85.

Woodward, R. (2016) 'A strange revolution: mock compliance and the failure of the OECD's international tax transparency regime', in Dietsch, P. and Rixen, T. (eds) *Global Tax Governance: What is wrong with it and how to fix it*, Colchester: ECPR Press.

World Bank (2011) *Migration and Remittances Factbook 2011*: http://data.worldbank.org/data-catalog/migration-and-remittances (accessed 19 February 2015).

Zucman, G. (2013) 'The missing wealth of nations: are Europe and the U.S. net debtors or net creditors?', *Quarterly Journal of Economics* 128(3): 1321–1364.

Chapter Fifteen

Institutional Reform of Global Tax Governance: A Proposal

*Thomas Rixen**

It is widely accepted that the current system of international taxation is deficient. As has been shown in Part One of this volume, the current principles and rules of apportioning the tax base between countries do not function properly because they are prone to manipulation by taxpayers. The result is an unfair international tax system. Tax competition among states and tax-base-shifting across different jurisdictions undermine revenue-raising capacity and lead to an unjust differentiation of tax burdens among groups of taxpayers. The contributions in Part Two show that the current policies pursued by the G20 and the OECD, while certainly representing progress, are still insufficient to address these problems. Thus, in Part Three, some of the guiding principles for reform have been proposed and discussed, whereas in Part Four specific policies and institutions in line with those principles are presented.

This chapter contributes to this last task. I will be less preoccupied with specific policies to regulate harmful tax competition, however, but rather wish to discuss their institutional preconditions. My aim is to answer the question: what are the optimal international institutions in the area of direct taxation? In line with the basic claim of new institutional economics or functional, liberal institutionalism (as the same basic insights are referred to in international-relations research), any efficient solution must meet certain functional requirements that derive from the specific strategic structure of the problem. In this chapter, I discuss the functional requirements of a solution to the problem of international tax competition and then derive a detailed institutional design from these requirements. I thus engage in an exercise of positively informed, normative institutional design.

The strategic structure, however, merely provides necessary conditions for the institutional design. There will often be several institutions satisfying those conditions (cf., for example, Snidal 1985: 923). In order to distinguish between different possible institutions, I introduce additional normative considerations that relate to the notions of background justice and fiscal self-determination

* I am grateful for helpful comments and suggestions from Reuven Avi-Yonah, Peter Dietsch, Patrick Emmenegger, Philipp Genschel, Lukas Hakelberg, Anja Jacobi, Ronen Palan, Inga Rademacher, Richard Woodward and participants in the workshop on International Tax Competition and Financial Secrecy at the University of St Gallen, November 2014.

(tax sovereignty).[1] As I argue below, preference should be given to those institutional solutions that leave national tax sovereignty untouched to the largest extent possible. However, safeguarding effective national tax sovereignty actually requires rather strong institutions, which restrict nation states' tax-policy choices in significant ways. The seeming paradox inherent in these two sentences will be resolved below.

Tax competition can be understood as an asymmetric prisoner's dilemma. An institution that supports a cooperative solution under this strategic structure needs to be global and inclusive in membership and it needs strong monitoring and enforcement mechanisms. I argue that an International Tax Organization (ITO)[2] could successfully carry out these tasks. It would, for one, function as a multilateral forum for governments to negotiate the concrete rules, thus replacing the mode of bilateralism and clubs so far prevalent in international taxation. Second, and even more important, it should entail a legalised dispute-settlement procedure very similar to that of the World Trade Organization (WTO), in which countries can be forced to abandon tax policies that constitute harmful tax competition.

There are a number of calls for an international tax organisation. These provide discussions of various issues and describe different tasks for such an organisation. Some focus mainly on the task of collecting and disseminating information (Tanzi 1999); others focus on the under-representation of developing countries at the current focal institution, the OECD (Horner 2001; United Nations 2001; TJN 2012). Finally, Sawyer's proposal (2009) restricts itself to the issue of Advance Pricing Agreements (APAs) and does not consider what tasks an ITO could take on in international taxation more generally. None of these contributions, however, try to rigorously derive the specific design and tasks of such an organisation from the functional requirements that international taxation and tax competition entail. The present chapter wants to close this gap and aims to integrate all of the functions and aims that are voiced in the existing literature in one institutional solution.

The chapter is structured as follows: first, I briefly revisit why tax competition is problematic. From this discussion, I derive one set of principles for the regulation of tax competition. After that, I introduce the basic elements of rational design and discuss the strategic structure of tax competition, to derive the functional requirements of successful co-operation. This serves to derive a second set of

1. The implied distinction between functional and normative requirements is shaky. One could rightfully object that functional requirements also have an underlying normative foundation – efficiency. Likewise, respecting the normative demands of sovereignty may also be a functional requirement, since it affects the feasibility of an institution. Nevertheless, differentiating between the two may be defended on the ground that efficiency is a 'thinner' value than sovereignty; the latter has its normative foundations in 'thick' values such as self-determination and, ideally, democracy.

2. Some commentators have suggested that this choice of abbreviation is unfortunate, since it is identical to that of the failed predecessor institution to the GATT/WTO, the International Trade Organization. While that is true, at the same time, other potential names such as IFO (International Fiscal Organization) or WTO (World Tax Organization) are also problematic, because they can be confounded with existing IOs. In contrast, an ITO does not currently exist.

principles underlying my proposal. While the principles derived in Section 1 rest on a normative political theory of background justice, those in Section 2 rely on a positive theory of rational action. In Section 3, I provide a detailed discussion of the institutional design of the International Tax Organisation (ITO). Section 4 addresses potential objections that could be raised to the proposal. Finally, in the conclusion, I consider how far the ITO differs from the current institutional trajectory of international taxation, in order to assess the feasibility of my proposal.

1. The problems

In this section, I briefly rehearse why tax competition needs to be regulated. I first recapitulate what the effects of tax competition are on the revenue and structure of tax systems and will then focus on why these effects are normatively undesirable. Both issues have been discussed in detail in Parts One and Three of this volume and elsewhere (for example, Rixen 2011b). Nevertheless, a brief recapitulation of the normative basis of the negative verdict on tax competition is necessary, because it provides the grounds for giving preference to those institutional solutions that leave national tax sovereignty untouched to the largest extent possible.

What are the effects of tax competition?

Under conditions of a globalised and liberal economy, tax bases, most importantly mobile capital, will be free to shop around for the best tax treatment.[3] The result is that national tax policies become interdependent and governments engage in tax competition, that is, the interactive tax-setting by independent governments in a noncooperative, strategic way. We can distinguish between 'virtual' and 'real' tax competition.

Virtual competition refers to tax evasion and avoidance by taxpayers. While they differ with respect to the legality of the respective activity, they share the characteristic that it is only the financial capital that is booked elsewhere. The taxpayer remains in the residence state or the state of production, which, according to generally accepted principles of international taxation, should provide the economic nexus that gives rise to taxation. Due to a lack of enforcement capabilities in the case of evasion and dysfunctional rules in the case of corporation taxes, however, the state of residence or production cannot tax the income. The amount of funds hidden in tax havens for purposes of tax evasion is estimated to be at least 8 per cent of global private wealth, about €5.8 billion (Zucman 2013), and evidence of paper-profit-shifting by MNEs through techniques such as transfer-pricing manipulations and thin capitalisation is also abundant (*see* Clausing's overview 2016, Chapter Two in this volume). Importantly, under virtual competition, taxpayers and foreign states collude, as I argue below, in an illegitimate way. Taxpayers behave as free-riders; they enjoy public goods and services in their country of residence or production but escape taxation. On the

3. This subsection is a shortened and modified version of section 3.1 in Dietsch and Rixen 2014a.

flipside, the behaviour of governments trying to attract foreign tax base under virtual competition is best understood as 'poaching' (OECD 1998; *see also* Dietsch 2016, Chapter Eleven in this volume).[4]

By contrast, under 'real' tax competition, taxpayers actually have to relocate to enjoy lower taxes. Countries compete for foreign direct investment (FDI) in the form of real business activity via tax levels. Examples include the relocation of a production site to incur a lower tax burden. The decision to relocate such real economic activity depends on various factors, such as the level of education of the workforce, the costs of labour and the quality of infrastructure. But the effective tax burden also plays a role. Empirical studies come to the conclusion that lowering effective tax rates increases the inflow of FDI (de Mooij and Ederveen 2008, *see also* Clausing 2016, Chapter Two in this volume). Attracting economic activity by lowering the effective tax rate may be called luring. While it does not entail free-riding, luring is also illegitimate under certain conditions (Dietsch and Rixen 2014b; *see also* Dietsch 2016, Chapter Eleven in this volume).

Both kinds of tax competition have consequences for public finances. In OECD countries, nominal corporate tax rates have been lowered from an average of 50 per cent in 1975 to 23.4 per cent in 2014 and nominal top personal income tax rates from 70 per cent to 43.6 per cent (OECD 2015). These rate cuts were refinanced by broadening the bases on which taxes are applied ('tax-cut-*cum*-base-broadening'). As a result, tax revenue as a percentage of GDP has so far remained stable – though at least for the corporation tax this may actually be a negative result, as revenues should have increased given the increase in the number of incorporated businesses and higher profitability (*see* Clausing 2016, Chapter Two in this volume). The situation is different in developing countries, largely because they lack the administrative capacity to pursue base-broadening policies to counter-finance the nominal rate cuts that they undertook. They experienced revenue losses in the era of tax competition.

While the effect on tax revenue varies with the stage of development of countries, the distributive consequences do not. In both developed and developing countries, the distribution of the tax burden among different kinds of taxpayers has changed. For one, there is an effect within the business sector: highly profitable MNEs benefit, while nationally organised small and medium-sized enterprises are more heavily burdened. Second, the tax burden is shifted from capital to labour. This is also visible in the general trend to increase indirect taxes, such as consumption taxes. Last but not least, due to the 'backstop' function of the corporate for the personal income tax, a lower corporate tax rate often spills

4. One may dispute the appropriateness of the term 'poaching' as a metaphor for all kinds of virtual tax competition. Many would maintain that one attribute of poaching is illegality, whereas virtual tax competition, as described, involves (illegal) tax evasion as well as (legal) tax avoidance. My usage of the term should be understood so as to not necessarily imply illegality. It is, however, intended to characterise profit-shifting as illegitimate. Thus, the insistence on this term underlines our demand to make it illegal.

over into a flatter personal income tax structure.[5] Overall, both developed- and developing-country governments felt compelled to pursue less redistributive polices than they would otherwise have pursued (for a more detailed discussion of these matters with further references, *see* Rixen 2011a).

In sum, tax competition negatively affects the revenue-raising capacities of governments and exacerbates existing inequalities.

Tax sovereignty and two principles of background justice

But why is that a problem? In short, the answer is that the policy changes just described are not legitimately chosen by the governments involved but forced upon them by the pressures of tax competition (*see* Ronzoni 2016 and Dietsch 2016, Chapters Nine and Eleven in this volume). In order to develop this point, Peter Dietsch and I have elsewhere argued that tax competition in its current form violates the condition of background justice (Dietsch and Rixen 2014b). In a world divided into states – irrespective of the question of whether such a world is ideal or not – the minimum requirements of background justice are that states must be able to '(1) exercise sovereignty over their territory, (2) regulate justice-relevant socioeconomic dynamics, and (3) interact as free and equal with one another' (Ronzoni 2009: 457). Under increasing economic globalisation, the background conditions under which states interact with each other change and, in order for the three conditions to continue to hold, it is necessary to set up international institutions to ensure these conditions (Ronzoni 2009). All three of the conditions for fair and just interactions of states relate to different aspects of a state's sovereignty or self-determination, which is the basic normative foundation of the institutional design proposed here.

More precisely, background justice requires what has been called *de facto sovereignty* and can be distinguished from *de jure sovereignty* (Bull 1977: 8; Palan 1998: 628–9; Rixen 2008: 26–9). *De jure* tax sovereignty can be defined as the 'legal freedom of action' (Keohane 1993: 91) to impose taxes, that is, it merely relates to the formal legal authority to decide upon, implement and enforce tax policies. *De facto* sovereignty, in contrast, goes beyond a merely formal right and can be defined as the ability to effectively achieve the desired goals of tax policy, such as efficiency or equity (*cf.* Keohane 1993). Thus, it relates to the actual real-world capability to pursue policy goals.

The relationship between *de jure* and *de facto* sovereignty is not straightforward. On the one hand, *de facto* sovereignty depends on *de jure* sovereignty. Only if the government of a state is formally authorised to determine tax policy can it be in a position to actually achieve its policy goals. On the other hand, whereas *de jure*

5. The spill-over occurs if the nominal corporate tax rate on retained profits is aligned with the top personal income tax rate. If the corporate rate were lower than the personal income rate, then individuals would have an incentive to hide their income behind a corporate veil – incorporating themselves and re-categorising their income as corporate. In order to make such tax avoidance unattractive, policy-makers often aim at the alignment of the two rates.

sovereignty can only be constrained by formal, legal measures, *de facto* sovereignty can also be constrained by social, material or other factors – globalisation and tax competition, for instance. Importantly, it may be the case that states possess full *de jure* sovereignty but lack *de facto* sovereignty.

This is the case in the area of international taxation. In particular, tax competition is characterised by a situation in which the very fact that states possess *de jure* sovereignty and use that sovereignty to compete for capital undermines their *de facto* sovereignty. The result is the seeming paradox that in order to regain *de facto* sovereignty under conditions of internationally integrated markets, governments have to give up some of their *de jure* sovereignty, by pooling it with other states or by delegating it to an international organisation. Effective protection of self-determination requires limits on self-determination.[6] Only through this can they overcome the collective-action problem inherent in tax competition. Depending on the particular problem structure, this may require different governance structures – and turn out to be more or less difficult.[7]

All this implies that states must not give up all of their *de jure* sovereignty. While an analysis of the specific policy problem to be solved is required (and provided below) to determine how much or which parts of *de jure* sovereignty states have to pool or delegate, it is clear that a state cannot command any *de facto* sovereignty if there is no *de jure* sovereignty left. Of course, being sovereign in a *de jure* sense should not be an ultimate goal of governments but only a means to achieve their policy goals. But it is assumed that, as long as it leads to good outcomes in terms of *de facto* sovereignty, it is preferable to leave their *de jure* sovereignty intact. In other words, the maxim is to internationalise as much *de jure* sovereignty as necessary but as little as possible.

There are two reasons for this maxim. First, it is most in line with the requirements of democracy. The main reason why we care for sovereignty or self-determination of nation states is that this self-determination is carried out in a democratic way. While there are certainly undemocratic states on the one hand and rudimentary forms of international democracy on the other hand, I take it that democracy in a rich sense does (so far) only exist within nation-states. Domestic democracy, however, can only be meaningful if the demos has (i) the formal authority to decide about relevant issues (*de jure* sovereignty); and (ii) those choices can actually matter to achieve the desired policy goals (*de facto* sovereignty). Given the partially complementary and partially competitive relationship between *de jure* and *de facto* sovereignty, the proposed maxim aims at an optimal balance of the two. Second, and relatedly, there are feasibility arguments for this maxim. Irrespective of how one evaluates the desirability of a world state (or several regional ones), states are unlikely to disappear any time soon and to delegate all

6. This is, of course, a well known and widely accepted principle of domestic liberal societies: individual freedom must be constrained if it endangers the freedom of others. We have to constrain freedom adequately in the defence of freedom.

7. This is the usual perspective of neo-liberal institutionalism on the issue of national sovereignty and effectiveness (*cf.* e.g. Keohane and Nye 2000: 19–22; Raustiala 2003: 856–62).

of their power to tax to a supranational entity (for more on the issue of feasibility, *cf.* Dietsch and Rixen 2014a).

In Dietsch and Rixen 2014b, we argue that there are two principles that provide the required constraints on *de jure* sovereignty and would, if put into practice safeguard nation-states' *de facto* sovereignty. Thus, they are the principles from which a globalisation-proof understanding of tax sovereignty could be developed. First, the *membership principle* demands that all natural and legal persons should be liable to pay tax in the state of which they are a member. This principle is compatible with the internationally accepted, but laxly enforced, principles of residence taxation for individuals and taxation at source for multinational enterprises (MNEs). If implemented, individuals and multinationals would no longer be able to free-ride on generous public services and infrastructure in one country while paying their taxes elsewhere. The membership principle would curb virtual tax competition and governments' poaching of foreign tax bases. The membership principle should be rather uncontroversial because it merely amounts to the requirement of non-discriminatory tax treatment of all members of a nation-state.

Second, the *fiscal policy constraint* states that real tax competition is illegitimate when it is both strategically motivated and leads to a reduction in the aggregate level of fiscal self-determination of other states. Strategic intent is given if a government implements a tax reform with the aim to attract foreign FDI. A tax reduction is not strategic if it would also have been chosen in the counterfactual absence of an FDI inflow. The requirement of maintaining the aggregate level of fiscal self-determination is violated if one country's tax-policy choices constrain several other countries' ability to set taxes as they wish, for example, compelling them to lower their corporation tax even though they would not have done so absent the policy-move of the other country. A policy is considered illegitimate only if both conditions are met. This principle is likely to be more controversial, as it attempts to balance the tax sovereignty of involved countries against each other. Notice that the principle does indeed constrain a nation's self-determination. Not all interdependence between countries' tax systems is ruled out. A policy that is not strategic but nevertheless compels other countries to lower their taxes is legitimate, as is a policy that is strategic but does not constrain other countries in their policy choices. The intuition behind this is that *some* fiscal interdependence is the price to be paid for economic globalisation.

Besides the differentiation between *de jure* and *de facto* sovereignty, it is useful to further differentiate *de jure* sovereignty into *legislative* and *administrative* sovereignty. Legislative sovereignty is the authority to make tax policy; that is, to design tax laws. Administrative sovereignty is the authority to implement and enforce these laws, that is, to collect taxes (Rixen 2008: 28; for the same distinction with different terminology, see Cnossen 1996: 77; McLure 1997: 35–6). This distinction is useful because, as we will see in the next section, it is likely that the functional requirements of global tax governance allow for delegating or pooling legislative and administrative sovereignty to different degrees.

2. Institutional design and the functional requirements of global tax governance

In this section, I determine what the functional requirements are for successful co-operation against harmful tax competition. I first give an overview of the basic elements of rational institutionalism and then turn to the strategic structure inherent in tax competition in order to derive the required institutional design.

Basics of institutional design

The basic contention of the (normative) theory of rational institutional design is that an institution should be designed in such a way that it guarantees collectively optimal outcomes.[8] It starts from the assumption that actors are self-interested or even opportunistic (self-interest with guile) and boundedly rational. In order to achieve a collectively optimal outcome, they have to come to a cooperative agreement that sticks. The task of the institutional designer is to devise mechanisms that sustain co-operation under these conditions (*cf.* for example, Williamson 1985, 1996).

We can distinguish between different stages of co-operation, at which different kinds of co-operation problems arise and require institutional solutions. In the *ex ante* phase the task is to agree on what the issue of co-operation is. The problems involved at this stage are mostly issues of bargaining. In the *ex post* phase, the task is to make sure that the parties involved will actually stay in line with the agreement, that is, do not cheat on each other. In reality, the *ex ante* and *ex post* phases of co-operation interact, because parties already consider possible *ex post* problems in the *ex ante* phase of co-operation. This means that there is a need to distinguish between (empirical) enforcement and bargaining phases and (analytical) bargaining and enforcement problems (Williamson 1985; Kreps 1990; Fearon 1998).

This basic distinction can be further refined by reference to the ANIME scheme of Abbott and Snidal (2009), which is simply a variant of the well known policy-cycle and consists of the following stages of the co-operation process (Figure 15.1).

1. At the **A**genda-setting stage, the issues to be put on the institution's agenda must be decided or, in other words, what are the objects of co-operation?
2. In **N**egotiations, parties develop the rules which are then laid down in an agreement. At this stage, the main problems concern questions of a distributive nature: who gets what? Likewise, as stated above, actors also have to agree on mechanisms that ensure the effectiveness of the three *ex post* tasks.

---

8. Rational institutionalism is often used as positive theory that postulates that the functional requirements inherent in different strategic structures *are* reflected in the resultant institutional design. Whether or not, and under what conditions, such a postulate makes sense is, of course, a controversial matter (even among rational institutionalists). In any case, the normative line of argument pursued here, that the functional requirements *should* be reflected in the institutional design, is far less controversial.

Figure 15.1: Stages of co-operation

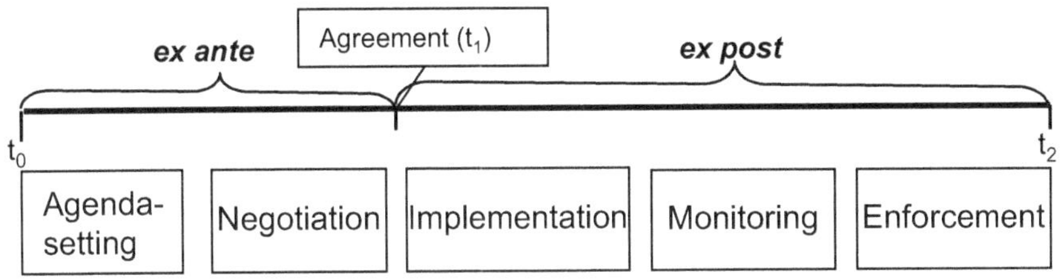

3. After an agreement has been made it needs **I**mplementation. The most important question to be answered is: who is responsible for implementing the agreement? In order to ensure that the agreement is actually put into practice, there is a need for
4. **M**onitoring compliance, to verify whether all actors actually play by the rules they agreed to.
5. Finally, there may be a need for **E**nforcement, that is, sanctions must be imposed on non-complying actors to bring them into line with the agreement.

Policy issues exhibit different strategic structures. The interest or actor constellations can be differentiated in a stylised way and different co-operation problems can be derived from them. From the nature of the co-operation problem, the institutional design required for a cooperative agreement is then derived in a functionalist manner. For example, overcoming a prisoner's dilemma situation requires strong enforcement measures, whereas coming to agreement in co-ordination games may simply require certain supporting functions in the *ex ante* phase, such as the provision of information or focal points so that the negotiation process is speeded up (Stein 1982: 302–3; Koremenos *et al.* 2001: 787–8). In the next section, I turn to a description of the co-operation problems inherent in international taxation.

Functional requirements of co-operation against international tax competition

Determining the strategic structure of a policy issue requires careful analysis of the underlying problem and the relevant actors' interests. Since this work has been done elsewhere (for example, Rixen 2008: 30–54, 156–61; Dehejia and Genschel 1999; Bucovetsky 1991) it is well established that the problem of international tax competition exhibits the strategic structure of an *asymmetric prisoner's dilemma*. States can individually benefit from undercutting each other's taxes to attract foreign capital but, if they all engage in this behaviour, the outcome is collectively damaging. However, the incentive to under-tax is different for big and small countries (in terms of population). For big-country governments, since their domestic tax base is relatively large compared to the attracted foreign tax base, tax competition may lead to national welfare losses. While they may individually profit from undercutting other countries, it is collectively preferable for them to come to a cooperative agreement to curb tax competition. Small-country governments, since their domestic tax base is small compared to the foreign tax base, can overcompensate the potential welfare loss of lower taxes with the inflow of tax base from other countries. Thus, small countries oppose collective agreements to abolish tax competition.

Overcoming an asymmetric dilemma is very demanding because of the strong conflicts of interest and the individual incentives to defect from a cooperative solution. Big countries would first have to overcome the dilemma among themselves – they are in a symmetric dilemma game – and then collectively get tax havens (always small countries) into the agreement. Overcoming the symmetric dilemma is difficult enough but easier than overcoming the asymmetric dilemma, since tax havens, as the winners from tax competition, are reluctant to agree to co-operation. The fact that the two games are nested within each other makes this a very hard problem to overcome.

Specifically, the cooperative solution has to meet the following requirements (*cf.* Rixen 2008: 46–8, with references to the relevant theoretical literature): First, as is well known, prisoner's dilemma situations can be overcome if actors use a strategy of reciprocity and the shadow of the future is long enough (Axelrod 1984). This insight provides a *prima facie* case for durably institutionalising any efforts to solve the problem. Building a formal intergovernmental organisation (IGO), and joining it, implies a commitment (if only a mild one) to the cooperative effort. Second, any agreements have to apply to all countries worldwide. Under the assumption that financial capital is perfectly mobile, it would, in theory, suffice to undermine the effectiveness of co-operation if only one country remained outside and did not effectively commit to the agreement. In this sense, the international tax base is a common-pool resource that can be depleted. This means that co-operation should be multilateral and encompassing, so that no country can get a free ride and exploit co-operating countries. Third, especially in a situation with many players, it is costly to identify defectors and thus target retaliatory action at the right country. Because of that, an institutional solution needs effective monitoring mechanisms to provide assessments of (non-)compliance with the agreement. Fourth, the cooperative agreement must be enforceable. Given the individual incentives to defect, there must be mechanisms to punish non-compliant states effectively.

3. Institutional design of the International Tax Organization

This section describes the design of an International Tax Organization (ITO) that meets the functional requirements set out in Section 2 and is in line with the normative requirements of protecting *de facto* sovereignty (the membership principle and the fiscal policy constraint developed in Section 1). I first briefly discuss the goal and purpose of the ITO before I turn to a detailed discussion of its institutional design. The second subsection focuses on general aspects such as the ITO's bodies and membership. After that, I turn to the specific functions the organisation needs to fulfil along the policy process (ANIME scheme). The third subsection details the competences and structure in the *ex ante* phase of co-operation and the fourth subsection turns to the *ex post* phase.

The ITO's mission and purpose

My aim here is not to describe in detail the specific policies that should be adopted by the ITO. For one, potential candidates have been laid out in previous chapters (*see*, for example, Grinberg 2016, Avi-Yonah 2016 and Wollner 2016, Chapters Seven, Thirteen and Fourteen in this volume) and elsewhere (TJN 2012; Dietsch and Rixen 2014b). Also, the specific content of the policies is not the topic of this chapter. That should ultimately be left to the negotiations and deliberations of member-states within the ITO. However, since the main purpose of this chapter is to zoom in on the institutional preconditions of a solution to the problem of tax competition, it is helpful to identify policies that fulfil the functional and normative requirements. It serves to illustrate the ITO's mission and purpose.

First, governments have to abolish all rules that make it impossible for other countries to enforce the membership principle. Thus, strict bank-secrecy regulations, the supply of other deliberately non-transparent legal constructs and the refusal to exchange information with other tax administrations have to be ruled out, under the membership principle. The requirement of transparency should be implemented through a system of multilateral automatic exchanges of information (*see* Grinberg 2016, Chapter Seven in this volume). Note that an international agreement on automatic information-exchange would only require states to pool their *administrative* sovereignty – national tax administrations help each other in enforcing[9] their country's tax policies. This suffices to stop the tax-evasion part of virtual tax competition (mostly, personal portfolio capital).

The matter is different with respect to the tax-avoidance part of virtual tax competition, which likewise violates the membership principle. Here, transparency is not enough. Ultimately, profit-shifting by multinational companies is possible because the rules for apportioning the tax base to different countries are vulnerable to (legal) manipulation. As Avi-Yonah (2016, Chapter Thirteen in this volume) and others (for example, McIntyre 2004; Rixen and Uhl 2007) have argued – and this is the second policy the ITO could pursue – a solution to this problem would be unitary taxation with formulary apportionment (UT+FA). This would require governments to agree on a common and consolidated corporate tax base. This, however, means that all governments have to give up some of their *legislative* sovereignty, as they could no longer determine the tax base entirely as they wish.

9. Note that this refers to the enforcement of national tax laws by the national administration *vis-à-vis* taxpayers. It is not about the enforcement of an international agreement to exchange information automatically or any measure of tax co-operation (to which we turn below).

This point can be generalised for all tax-avoidance practices. As tax avoidance/tax-planning always relies on differences between national tax systems, the solution, even if it were a different one from UT+FA, will always require some co-ordination of tax bases and/or rates, that is, (partial) restrictions of legislative sovereignty.

Third, in addition to these policies that put the membership principle into practice, it is necessary to define rules in line with the fiscal policy constraint. Defining such rules is likely to be a difficult and controversial undertaking, because the criteria – aggregate amount of fiscal self-determination and a government's strategic intent – are difficult to observe and operationalise. Most importantly, the fact that intentions are unobservable invites hypocrisy. It is possible for governments to misrepresent their intentions, attributing any national tax reforms to the legitimate preferences of their citizens even if, in reality, the government merely pursues the strategic aim of attracting foreign tax base. In order to avoid hypocritical political discourses and long but futile attempts to distinguish honest from dishonest representations of intentions, the institutionalisation of the principle should, as much as possible, rely on objectively observable proxies. Is there scientific evidence that the policy adopted would have beneficial effects in terms of efficiency and/or equity on the domestic economy, other than the inflow of foreign tax base? It is clear that data on capital flows, economic-growth rates or distributive results are readily available and could be used to derive rules. Reference to these indicators is routinely made in all kinds of debates on policy design; international fiscal policy is no exception in this respect. Nevertheless, given the many factors that affect economic outcomes and the complex relationships among them, controversies over the right interpretation of these data are likely. As described below, what is needed in case of controversy is a judicial or quasi-judicial system in which disputes among governments over tax policy can be settled.

In addition to these considerations, one very simple and (uncontroversial) rule can be formulated: all forms of preferential tax regimes (ring-fencing) must be abolished. The only plausible explanation for such discriminatory arrangements is strategic intent to lure in foreign capital. As to its consequences, preferential tax regimes will generally not have a positive effect on the aggregate amount of fiscal self-determination but rather a negative one. Thus, overall, the third set of rules should basically state the principle of the fiscal policy constraint, mention potential indicators on how to operationalise the principle and explicitly rule out all kinds of preferential tax treatments for foreigners.

The ITO's bodies, membership and general functions

The ITO should consist of three main bodies. First, it should feature an *assembly*, in which the principles and rules of international taxation can be negotiated and defined by the representatives of member-states. More precisely, membership status and voting rights are granted only to state governments and the officials of (dependent or semi-sovereign) territories that possess independent tax jurisdiction.[10] Societal interest-groups, such as NGOs, business or labour representatives, would not enjoy voting rights but should be allowed observer status and access to delegates, as is increasingly the case in IGOs (Tallberg *et al.* 2013).

Given that it is a functional requirement that the rules apply to all countries, because otherwise co-operation would be undermined by outsiders, it is a requirement of democracy (all affected interests should participate in collective decisions on the issue) that all states are *members* of the institution and have a say in developing its policies. This is not only a matter of fairness, as has been argued by tax-justice activists for a long time (for example, TJN 2012) but also one of effectiveness. This claim may at first appear counterintuitive: from the perspective of effectiveness, it could be argued that an organisation that is not fully inclusive would be preferable. With fewer and a more homogeneous group of states, it could be easier to reach an agreement with more bite, which might, afterwards, be adopted by non-members. However, given the strategic structure of tax competition, it is unlikely that any outsiders to the agreement would voluntarily adopt the policies. Thus, given that some kind of pressure has to be exerted upon the current winners of tax competition, be it negative (sanctions) or positive (incentives), this is much easier to achieve if the respective jurisdictions are actually at the negotiation table. The development of the OECD's harmful tax competition project lends some support to this argument. While one might rightly point out that tax havens watered down the substance of the agreements, they did at least have to commit to something, instead of remaining fully unrestricted in their policies (*cf.* Rixen 2008; Sharman 2006). As is often the case in IGOs, the membership assembly might meet at the level of heads of governments or ministers (usually once or twice a year) and at the level of the heads of national delegations to the organisation, who may meet on a weekly or monthly basis. In addition to this, the assembly could also form committees or working-groups to address specific topics in greater detail and prepare specific proposals to be discussed and passed by the assembly.

Second, there should be a *secretariat* that provides administrative and other services for the organisation. The secretariat and the member-states (that is, the assembly) would have a principal–agent relationship. The member-state principals

10. This is actually more controversial than it may initially appear. One may, for example, reasonably question the legitimacy of the tax sovereignty of some of the UK's 'crown dependencies'. In most of these territories, Britain has wide powers that it could use to disallow or change their harmful tax and secrecy legislation. But Britain has generally chosen not to exercise its powers because these jurisdictions serve as useful satellites for London as a financial centre (TJN 2013). It could thus well be an item on the agenda of the ITO to revoke tax sovereignty from such (at best semi-sovereign) territories. If it were revoked, they would lose their membership and, from then on, be represented by the country under whose tax jurisdiction they fall. However, as long as they enjoy tax sovereignty, such territories should be at the negotiation table, as I argue in the following paragraph.

delegate tasks to the secretarial agent.[11] The tasks performed by the secretariat would include providing information to all members about the agenda of meetings, writing protocols, preparing the texts of formal decisions and also helping in the implementation of policies. All these tasks are discussed in more detail in the following two sub-sections, concerning subsequent stages of co-operation.

One function of the secretariat that is pertinent to all stages of co-operation, however, is the provision of *information* on all issues of taxation relevant to the ITO's work. The organisation should collect data on member-states' tax systems, innovative tax reforms or administrative solutions in different countries and so on. Such information is important because it provides a solid ground for discussions in the ITO and it also helps to diffuse innovation across countries. This may be particularly helpful for developing countries. In this respect, the OECD can serve as a model, as it provides its members with this kind of information. The new organisation would do the same for its more inclusive membership. The secretariat should be staffed with international public servants who command expertise in fiscal and tax matters and are formally independent of their own states. As in most IGOs, citizens from all member-states should be adequately represented in the secretariat.

Third, as developed in more detail below, there should be an independent *dispute-settlement body* that can settle disputes between member states in a (quasi-)judicial manner.

Ex ante: *agreeing on the rules of the game*

The decision-rules and procedures of the institution need to be specified. The first requirement follows directly from what has just been said about membership. All members of the assembly must be able to cast a vote in agenda-setting and negotiation.

Agenda-setting: in principle, every member-state should be allowed to propose agenda items. Additionally, the secretariat, staffed with experts who constantly observe developments in international taxation, should also have the right to propose items. However, in order not to congest the agenda with hopeless initiatives, there should be a minimum number of countries whose support is needed to put an item on the agenda. On the other hand, the threshold should not be so high that minority rights are not protected. A reasonable threshold, which is used in national parliamentary settings and some IGOs, is 20–25 per cent.

Negotiation and agreement: in terms of decision-rules on the actual agreement, consensus is appropriate for the ITO as well. As has been shown, this is the decision-rule that is most common in IGOs. Even those IGOs that allow

11. Governments can, in principle, veto agents' actions, should they use the discretion that comes with delegation in ways not wanted by the principals. However, a renunciation of delegated tasks will only be possible if the member-states agree collectively on this. It should not be possible for an individual government to disempower the agent only because it alone was negatively affected by it. On the other hand, consensus decision would be dysfunctional, too, because it would give too much power to veto-players. Simple majority voting seems to be appropriate in this respect.

(qualified) majority decisions usually decide by unanimity in practice (Blake and Payton 2014). This does not preclude shifting to (qualified) majority voting in the future, should global economic integration proceed and countries become willing to further integrate their tax policies over time.

Of course, negotiations about international tax rules, as in other intergovernmental contexts, will entail tough bargaining, coalition-formation, issue-linkages and side-payments. While there is no need for formal regulation of these real-world aspects of all negotiations, their existence shows that the process of negotiation needs to be structured so that it allows enough (but not too much) time for all these activities. Agreeing on appropriate procedural rules can be left to the delegates in the assembly. Implementing those procedural rules should be the task of the assembly's chair-holder. The chair could be filled by member-state delegates on a rotating basis.

Ex post: *putting the rules of the game into practice*

What would it take to effectively implement, monitor and enforce the new rules of international taxation on which governments have agreed?

Implementation of the rules should be a national matter. In line with the general stance of my argument, taxes can, in general, be collected from citizens by their national tax administrations. Accordingly, it should be up to national parliaments, governments and administrations to honour the agreements made and implement the respective rules. It would, however, be conceivable that developing countries, which may, in some cases, lack the administrative expertise and capacity to implement the rules, are granted administrative assistance. This task could be taken on by the secretariat of the ITO, which could advise national tax administrations. It would also be conceivable for the organisation to fund a programme of continuous knowledge-transfer to developing countries. The secretariat could, for example, offer training programmes for tax administrators in developing countries. The WTO secretariat, for instance, also provides assistance to developing countries.

Monitoring is a different matter. Given the individual incentive to defect on the cooperative agreement, there is a need for very strict monitoring rules. Mere self-reporting is insufficient because of the incentive to overstate actual compliance. While it is certainly true that members of the institution have an incentive to monitor each other's compliance because they do not want to be taken advantage of, it is also clear that it is useful to institutionalise an orderly and independent monitoring procedure. Members may, depending on their own situation or position, either be overly critical or too lax in their evaluation of others' policies. A functional monitoring mechanism should (a) channel the allegations of member-states observing each other and (b) provide independent reporting on compliance. Monitoring should thus be carried out by the secretariat. There should be routine missions of a secretarial monitoring team to all member countries, to inspect whether and how the rules are implemented 'on the ground'. The monitors must be allowed access to all relevant information.

In addition to these scheduled monitoring missions, the inspectors should also have the authority to make unheralded on-site inspections. This way they can objectively establish (non-)compliance. Absent such strict monitoring, 'mock compliance' (*see* Woodward 2016, Chapter Five in this volume) is to be expected.

Monitoring can also play an important role in improving implementation, even in those countries willing to comply. One could envisage the monitoring team preparing regular country-reports on implementation and tax policy in general (in this regard, the WTO, with its trade-policy reviews, could once again serve as a model). The reports would be published and all member-states would have access to them. While this would create peer pressure and thus help in enforcement, it could also, in the first instance, be viewed as an instrument for the diffusion of administrative innovation.

Enforcement: since the structure of tax competition is such that every individual government has an incentive to deviate from the collectively desirable rules, there is a need for an effective enforcement mechanism. This requires a largely independent authority that is accepted by all member-states. The ITO should rely on legalised enforcement, modelled after the WTO's dispute-settlement procedure, to satisfy this requirement.[12]

The procedure could be as follows. If either the ITO's independent monitors find or another member-state makes a valid complaint that the tax practices of a state violate the rules, for example, because it is not exchanging all the tax information that it should or because a national tax reform violates the fiscal policy constraint, the defecting state is asked to comply with the rules within a specified time. If it does not, member-states affected by this non-compliance can commence the formal dispute-settlement procedure, which involves a quasi-legal assessment of the case before a Dispute Settlement Panel (DSP) made up of three or five independent international tax experts, who assume a role similar to judges.[13] The panel has to come to a ruling on the case. If a state's policy is found to be in violation of the rules, the panel estimates the damage done and authorises targeted sanctions of the same magnitude by the offended countries against the offender, should the policy in question not be repealed within a specified time limit. All members vote on the panel report (ruling). Importantly, however, the report can only be rejected if such a decision is unanimous. This is highly unlikely since, at the least, the state which 'won' the dispute would not agree to reject it. Thus, the panel report is of a quasi-judicial nature. Since parties to a dispute know that there is effective enforcement of decisions in the dispute-settlement procedure, it can be expected that they will resolve many cases in consultation. This procedure has the advantage of avoiding excessive litigation and leaves room for political

12. For a description of the WTO dispute-settlement process, see, e.g. Zangl 2008.

13. To be sure, in the WTO, the panels are not really independent, but they are forced to act as if they were independent because otherwise their decisions would run the risk of ending up before an Appellate Body, which is a truly independent body (Zangl 2008: 830–1).

negotiations and decisions but, at the same time, ensures effective enforcement of agreements.[14]

Such a legalised procedure, which relies, to a large extent, on the expertise of international tax lawyers, will, over time, help to clarify the relative vagueness of the fiscal policy constraint discussed above. In order to come to a ruling, the DSP would have to legally interpret the fiscal policy constraint. Over time, these interpretations will fill gaps in the rules drafted by the assembly and thus specify the rules, or even create new rules by setting precedents.[15]

One difficulty discussed above in the application of the fiscal policy constraint is the need to assess actors' real intentions. In this regard, it is worth noting that doing just that is the everyday business of courts. This is not only true in domestic criminal law but also holds for international law. For example, in applying the genocide convention, courts, like the International Court of Justice (ICJ) or the International Criminal Court (ICC), or tribunals have to assess the intentions of the alleged offender. The WTO is another case in point. Under the rules on non-tariff trade barriers, policies with protectionist effect are generally prohibited. However, if a country pursues a policy with the intention of protecting consumers' health and safety and can prove its good intentions, an exception to the rule of non-protectionism is granted. As in our proposal, the WTO institutionalised this rule by focusing on the observable implications of countries' intentions. A government has to provide valid scientific evidence of the claimed adverse effects on consumers' health and safety (Zangl 2008: 840–1).

4. Potential objections to the proposal

In this section, I discuss six potential objections to the proposed ITO, which can be grouped in two categories. The first is concerned with the question whether we really need a new organisation; the second takes issue with the design of the proposed organisation.

Do we really need a new organisation? This objection could be raised in at least three different ways, each emphasising an alternative institutional solution. First, one might argue that the OECD has served as the most relevant forum of international tax governance for the last five decades and it has developed a lot of expertise in the area. It should thus continue to do the job, albeit with expanded functions and competence. This is unconvincing because, for one, the OECD as an organisation does not have global scope. While it could

14. It may be argued that leaving room for political negotiations is undesirable as it would open up the door for bribery and power politics. However, the potential recourse to a legalised procedure should ensure that any negotiated agreement outside the formal process should actually be in line with the spirit of the rules of the ITO.

15. Technically speaking, the dispute-settlement procedure provides a solution to the problem of uncertainty and the resultant incompleteness of contracts (Williamson 1985: 70–1). Contract theory maintains that, under these circumstances, parties 'agree *ex ante* not so much on what will be done in each particular contingency as they do on the procedure by which future contingencies will be met' (Kreps 1990: 119). The proposed dispute-settlement procedure serves this purpose.

invite non-OECD countries to join the cooperative effort – and does in fact in its Global Forum on harmful tax competition – there would always remain a status difference between (core) OECD member-states and (invited) other countries. More importantly, the OECD as an organisation is not restricted to a single field but is active in many social and economic policy areas. It does not have any enforcement capacity in any of those fields (including taxation) but the organisation derives its recognition and authority from its neutral and professional expertise (*cf.* Woodward 2009; Sharman 2006). Granting enforcement powers and judicial review to the OECD in taxation would not fit the organisation's tradition and image and would undermine its credibility as a knowledge-broker.

Second, it could be argued that we do not need a new tax organisation because the issue could be dealt with under the auspices of the WTO. Most importantly, it has been argued that direct taxation already falls within the jurisdiction of the WTO (*cf.* Slemrod and Avi-Yonah 2002; Daly 2005).[16] The WTO has, indeed, ruled certain instances of tax breaks as incompatible with international trade law. For example, in a panel report on the case of *Boeing* v. *Airbus*, some of the tax breaks allowed by the state of Washington and the US government were ruled to be a form of export subsidy that is not allowed under WTO rules.[17] Likewise, the panel ruled that the US foreign-sales corporation (FSC) legislation and its successor, the Extraterritorial Income Exclusion Act (ETI), violated international trade law (Zangl 2008). While it is thus true that certain harmful tax practices could be eliminated on the basis of WTO law, trade law is not sufficient to adequately address all relevant problems of international tax competition. For the WTO to get involved, the tax policy must have a distorting effect on international trade flows. Very often, this is not the case. For example, it would be hard to argue that individual capital-tax evasion has an effect on the flow of goods and services among countries. Also, typically, trade distortions are caused by preferential tax regimes. Absent preferential treatment, it is difficult to see how a distortion can result. Thus, generalised tax competition will not cause trade distortions and thus the WTO could not rule on such competitive moves by governments.

Third, one might argue that such a big and inclusive institution is not needed at all. The largest share of investment is, ultimately, made in industrialised or emerging economies (even though it may be routed through several tax havens), because this is where a decent return can be earned. Since this group of countries is relatively small, it may be feasible to co-ordinate the imposition of a withholding tax on investment income without a new institution. Co-ordination would be necessary because, otherwise, countries would experience capital flight amongst each other. The introduction of a 35 per cent withholding tax on all investment

16. Indirect taxation, most importantly tariffs but also other non-tariff trade barriers, have, of course, always been within the WTO's jurisdiction.

17. See https://www.wto.org/english/tratop_e/dispu_e/cases_e/ds353_e.htm (accessed 7 April 2015) for a summary of the case and the findings.

income, for example, would make sure that the income is taxed at least once. If an investor proves that he/she has reported the income to his residence country, the tax would be refunded (Avi-Yonah 2008). A natural international forum for devising this policy might be the G20. The problem with this proposal is that it underestimates the severity of the enforcement problem. The current evidence on tax competition suggests that informal co-ordination on certain policies cannot be achieved or, if it is achieved, remains toothless, as governments do not properly implement the agreements.

The second set of concerns deals with the design of the proposed organisation. First, it could be argued that the judicial nature of the procedure hollows-out national political decision-making. Some of the decisions are transferred from democratically accountable political leaders to experts who lack democratic accountability and legitimacy. One line of this criticism, additionally, accuses these experts of a neo-liberal bias, aiming to constitutionalise free markets to protect them from state intervention in the name of social justice (for example, Höpner and Schäfer 2012; Gill and Cutler 2014). These are important concerns. But I believe they can be refuted by two counter-arguments. For one, the *status quo*, with its hollowing-out of effective fiscal sovereignty through tax competition as described in Section 1, is even more problematic in this respect. Although it formally guarantees democratic accountability, *de facto*, this is not the case. Conversely, while the ITO with its legalised enforcement may reduce the scope of fiscal policy issues for which there is direct democratic accountability, it would make sure that there is effective democratic choice within this restricted realm. Further, the principles and rules of the ITO do not have a liberalising or 'dis-embedding' effect. Rather, they aim at 're-embedding' the market into political and legal rules, to cushion its adverse social effects.

Second, it could be argued that the inclusion of rather strict enforcement mechanisms undermines progress on the front of creating new and improved rules against tax competition. Goldstein and Steinberg (2009) make such an argument with respect to the WTO. In short, they submit that the increasing difficulty the WTO has in concluding new trade agreements and further liberalising international trade is partly due to the fact that all governments are cautious about passing new agreements because, given strong enforcement, they will be truly bound by them. Before, agreement on new rules was easier to achieve, as actors enjoyed more 'wiggling' room in implementation. On the basis of this argument and considering the general state of play on international taxation, characterised by a lack of agreement on the issue of tax competition, one could argue that strict enforcement mechanisms could undermine progress on the front of developing new rules against tax competition.

This is an important argument. It does not, however, dispute the functional need for enforcement mechanisms. It merely points to the inevitable side-effects on the negotiation phase. Proponents of this argument would not jump to the conclusion that dispensing with strong enforcement mechanisms altogether could solve the problem. After all, as the argument implies, a lack of enforcement merely results in a lack of compliance. Thus, this argument could usefully be interpreted, I would argue, as a consideration on the timing of the introduction of the enforcement mechanism. It may be worthwhile to consider launching the institution without the legalised dispute-settlement procedure, adding it only after governments have come to develop more areas of consensus in the course of their ongoing deliberations. Such phasing-in of different design features would resemble the transition from GATT to WTO in international trade law.

A related, but much broader critique might claim that it is a bad idea to use the WTO as a role model. Has it not just been shown that the organisation is dysfunctional, as it is incapable of delivering a new trade agreement? While this criticism has intuitive appeal, it cannot withstand closer scrutiny. While it is true that we currently see stalemate in international trade negotiations, this is unlikely to be due to design flaws in the WTO. First, international trade liberalisation is already very far progressed, so negotiations on the few remaining barriers to trade are particularly hard. But overall, the track record of the GATT/WTO is still positive. Second, in recent years there has been a proliferation of bilateral and other preferential trade agreements (PTAs) that provide an alternative road to liberalisation that involves fewer concessions for many countries. It does, however, come at the price of welfare-diminishing trade diversions. So, while such PTAs may be second-best solutions, they are the result of countries pursuing their individual interests at the expense of the common good. If anything, the lesson to be learnt here is that while countries are reluctant to conclude agreements under the umbrella of the WTO, the world would be better off if they did.

5. Conclusion: where does the proposal differ from the current trajectory?

Is the creation of an ITO politically feasible? In order to evaluate this, I compare the institutional design features of my proposal with those of the current trajectory of global tax governance.

In Rixen 2008, I show that the soft governance that has characterised international tax policy for many decades is a functionally adequate solution to the problem of double-tax avoidance (DTA). DTA is a co-ordination game with a distributive conflict. A bilateral approach, supported by the OECD disseminating information and shared practices that all have an interest to follow, can well accommodate countries' preferences. The institutions needed to deal with this problem do not have to be equipped with enforcement capabilities. The nature of the problem is such that it can be handled by mere 'interface regulation' while preserving national *de jure* sovereignty. As the economy becomes more global, however, this setup enables the related phenomena of tax evasion and avoidance and tax competition. As discussed in this chapter, these issues exhibit the institutionally more demanding structure of an asymmetric prisoner's dilemma. While it is obvious that the governance structure is undergoing changes in response to the fundamentally altered international tax game, these adaptations are still incomplete and do not meet the functional requirements of the new strategic structure (see also Genschel and Rixen 2015).[18]

Three observations on the current institutional trajectory characterise this governance gap. First, while it is true that there is a move towards multilateralism in the fight against tax evasion, it is not fully global and inclusive of all states. For example, the recent agreement on automatic exchange of tax information, which is an important step forward, was signed by only fifty-one countries. Second, while it can be observed that the OECD and its members are increasingly willing to exert pressure on tax havens, they still rely on informal instruments such as naming and shaming or, less often – but FATCA is an example – blunt power politics (*see* Hakelberg 2016, Chapter Six in this volume). So far, there has not been an attempt to institutionalise formal enforcement mechanisms. Third, it is true that states are increasingly willing to share their *administrative* sovereignty in order to regain *de facto* control over their tax policies. Administrative co-operation and information-exchange with other governments has been considerably strengthened. However, they are hardly willing to delegate or pool their *legislative* sovereignty, the authority to make national tax policy. According to the argument put forward in this chapter, while this is not a problem as long as the particular issue can be effectively addressed by administrative co-operation, there are strong indications that the effective regulation of harmful tax competition in the field of business taxation requires a sharing of legislative sovereignty, that is to say, partial harmonisation of national tax laws. This, however, is not so far forthcoming, as the recent stalemate in the fight against corporate tax avoidance within the G20 illustrates. In short, international tax law has to become harder and more multilateral and involve the partial transfer of legislative sovereignty.

These three stylised shortcomings lead me to conclude that the ITO proposed here would indeed be something *qualitatively different* than the existing institutional trajectory and, consequently, that governments are currently unwilling to establish an ITO. However, both the existence of the WTO and the experience of changes in international tax governance that were considered utopian only three years ago (most importantly on automatic information-exchange) suggest that it is feasible. While this will require a lot of political investment, the prospect of resurrecting domestic and international tax justice should make this investment worthwhile.

18. In Rixen 2008 and 2011b, I argue that the lack of adaptation has two causes. First, since DTA is a co-ordination game, the process becomes self-reinforcing: actors do not wish to endanger the co-ordinating function of the regime that they had established long before tax competition became virulent. Second, governments are unable to resolve the asymmetric prisoner's dilemma, because of conflicts of interest between big and small countries and powerful business influences on all governments. Consequently, governments only achieve gradual, indirect and incomplete reforms of the international tax system.

References

Abbott, K. W. and Snidal, D. (2009) 'The governance triangle: regulatory standards institutions and the shadow of the state', in Mattli, W. and Woods, N. (eds) *The Politics of Global Regulation*, Oxford: Oxford University Press, pp. 44–88.

Avi-Yonah, R. S. (2008) 'A coordinated withholding tax on deductible payments', *Tax Notes* 119: 993–6.

— (2016) 'A proposal for unitary taxation and formulary apportionment (UT+FA) to tax multinational enterprises', in Dietsch, P. and Rixen, T. (eds) *Global Tax Governance: What is wrong with it and how to fix it*, Colchester: ECPR Press.

Axelrod, R. M. (1984) *The Evolution of Co-operation,* New York: Basic Books.

Blake, D. J. and Payton, A. L. (2014) 'Balancing design objectives: analyzing new data on voting rules in intergovernmental organizations', *Review of International Organizations* 10: 1–26.

Bucovetsky, S. (1991) 'Asymmetric tax competition', *Journal of Urban Economics* 30(2): 167–81.

Bull, H. (1977) *The Anarchical Society: A study of order in world politics*, New York: Columbia University Press.

Cnossen, S. (1996) 'Company taxes in the European Union: criteria and options for reform', *Fiscal Studies,* 17(4): 67–97.

Daly, M. (2005) *The WTO and Direct Taxation*, WTO Discussion Paper No. 9, Geneva: https://www.wto.org/english/res_e/booksp_e/discussion_papers9_e.pdf.

Dehejia, V. H. and Genschel, P. (1999) 'Tax competition in the European Union', *Politics & Society,* 27(3): 403–30

de Mooij, R. A. and Ederveen, S. (2008) 'Corporate tax elasticities: a reader's guide to empirical findings', *Oxford Review of Economic Policy,* 24(4): 680–97.

Dietsch, P. (2016) 'Whose tax base? the ethics of global tax governance', in Dietsch, P. and Rixen, T. (eds) *Global Tax Governance: What is wrong with it and how to fix it*, Colchester: ECPR Press.

Dietsch, P. and Rixen, T. (2014a) 'Redistribution, globalisation, and multi-level governance', *Moral Philosophy & Politics,* 1(1): 61–81.

— (2014b) 'Tax competition and global background justice', *Journal of Political Philosophy,* 22(2): 150–77.

Fearon, J. D. (1998) 'Bargaining, enforcement, and international co-operation', *International Organization,* 52(2): 269–305.

Genschel, P. and Rixen, T. (2015) 'Settling and unsettling the transnational legal order of international taxation', in Halliday, T. C. and Shaffer, G. C. (eds) *Transnational Legal Orders*, Cambridge: Cambridge University Press, pp. 154–84.

Gill, S. and Cutler, A. C. (2014) *New Constitutionalism and World Order*, Cambridge: Cambridge University Press.

Goldstein, J. and Steinberg, R. H. (2009) 'Regulatory shift: the rise of judicial liberalization at the WTO', in Mattli, W. and Woods, N. (eds) *The Politics of Global Regulation*, Princeton, New Jersey: Princeton University Press pp. 211–41.

Grinberg, I. (2016) 'Does FATCA teach broader lessons about international tax multilateralism?', in Dietsch, P. and Rixen, T. (eds) *Global Tax Governance: What is wrong with it and how to fix it*, Colchester: ECPR Press.

Hakelberg, L. (2016) 'Redistributive tax co-operation: automatic exchange of information, US power and the absence of joint gains', in Dietsch, P. and Rixen, T. (eds) *Global Tax Governance: What is wrong with it and how to fix it*, Colchester: ECPR Press.

Höpner, M. and Schäfer, A. (2012) 'Embeddedness and regional integration: waiting for Polanyi in a Hayekian setting', *International Organization* 66(3): 429–55.

Horner, F. M. (2001) 'Do we need an international tax organization?' *Tax Notes International,* 24 (October 8): 179–87.

Keohane, R. O. (1993) 'Sovereignty, interdependence and international institutions', in Miller, L. B. and Smith, M. (eds) *Ideas and Ideals: Essays on politics in honor of Stanley Hoffmann*, Boulder, CO: Westview, pp. 91–107.

Keohane, R. O. and Nye, J. S. (2000) 'Introduction', in Nye, J. S. and Donahue, J. D. (eds) *Governance in a Globalizing World*, Washington, DC: Brookings Institution Press, pp. 1–41.

Koremenos, B. *et al.* (2001) 'The rational design of international institutions', *International Organization* 55(4): 761–99.

Kreps, D. M. (1990) 'Corporate culture and economic theory', in Alt, J. and Shepsle, K. A. (eds) *Perspectives on Positive Political Economy*, Cambridge, Cambridge University Press, pp. 90–143.

McIntyre, M. J. (2004) 'The use of combined reporting by nation states', *Tax Notes International* 35 (September 6): 917–48.

McLure, C. E. (1997) 'Tax policies for the XXIst century', in International Fiscal Association (IFA) (ed.) *Visions of the Tax Systems of the XXIst Century*, The Hague: Kluwer Law International, pp. 9–52.

OECD (1998) *Harmful Tax Competition: An emerging global issue*, Paris: OECD: http://www.oecd.org/tax/transparency/44430243.pdf

— (2015) *OECDiLibrary Statistics*: http://www.oecd-ilibrary.org/statistics (accessed 5 March 2015).

Palan, R. (1998) 'Trying to have your cake and eating it: how and why the state system has created offshore', *International Studies Quarterly* 42(4): 625–44.

Raustiala, K. (2003) 'Rethinking the sovereignty debate in international economic law', *Journal of International Economic Law* 6(4): 841–78.

Rixen, T. (2008) *The Political Economy of International Tax Governance*, Basingstoke: Palgrave Macmillan.

— (2011a) 'Tax competition and inequality: the case for global tax governance', *Global Governance: A Review of Multilateralism and International Organizations* 17(4): 447–67.

— (2011b) 'From double tax avoidance to tax competition: explaining the institutional trajectory of international tax governance', *Review of International Political Economy* 18(2): 197–227.

Rixen, T. and Uhl, S. (2007) *Europeanizing Corporate Taxation. Regaining national tax policy autonomy*: http://library.fes.de/pdf-files/id/04750.pdf (accessed 31 August 2015).

Ronzoni, M. (2009) 'The global order: a case of background injustice? A practice-dependent account', *Philosophy & Public Affairs,* 37(3): 229–56.

— (2016) 'Tax competition: a problem of global or domestic justice?', in Dietsch, P. and Rixen, T. (eds) *Global Tax Governance: What is wrong with it and how to fix it*, Colchester: ECPR Press.

Sawyer, A. J. (2009) *Developing a World Tax Organisation: The way forward,* Birmingham, UK: Fiscal Publications.

Sharman, J. C. (2006) *Havens in a Storm: The struggle for global tax regulation,* Ithaca, New York: Cornell University Press.

Slemrod, J. and Avi-Yonah, R. (2002) '(How) should trade agreements deal with income tax issues?', *Tax Law Review* 55: 533–54 and also Michigan research paper #01-008: http://papers.ssrn.com/sol3/papers.cfm?abstract_id=285345 (accessed 31 August 2015).

Snidal, D. (1985) 'Coordination versus prisoner's dilemma: implications for international co-operation and regimes', *American Political Science Review* 79(4): 923–42.

Stein, A. A. (1982) 'Coordination and collaboration – regimes in an anarchic world', *International Organization* 36(2): 299–324.

Tallberg, J. *et al.* (2013) *The Opening Up of International Organizations. Transnational access in global governance*, Cambridge: Cambridge University Press.

Tanzi, V. (1999) 'Is there a need for a world tax organization?', in Razin, A. and Sadka, E. (eds) *The Economics of Globalization: Policy perspectives from public economics*, Cambridge: Cambridge University Press, pp. 173–86.

TJN (Tax Justice Network, 2012) *Tax Us If You Can*, 2nd edition: http://www.taxjustice.net/cms/upload/pdf/TUIYC_2012_FINAL.pdf (accessed 27 March 2013).

— (2013) 'Narrative report on United Kingdom': http://www.financialsecrecyindex.com/PDF/UnitedKingdom.pdf (accessed 10 March 2015).

United Nations (2001) *Report of the High Level Panel on Financing for Development* [the Zedillo Report]: http://www.un.org/en/ga/search/view_doc.asp?symbol=A/55/1000 (accessed 21 June 2006).

Williamson, O. E. (1985) *The Economic Institutions of Capitalism*, New York: Free Press.

— (1996) *The Mechanisms of Governance*, Oxford: Oxford University Press.

Wollner, G. (2016) 'International financial transaction taxation, public goods and justice', in Dietsch, P. and Rixen, T. (eds) *Global Tax Governance: What is wrong with it and how to fix it*, Colchester: ECPR Press.

Woodward, R. (2009) *The Organisation for Economic Co-operation and Development (OECD)*, Abingdon, Oxon and New York: Routledge.

— (2016) 'A strange revolution: mock compliance and the failure of the OECD's international tax transparency regime', in Dietsch, P. and Rixen, T. (eds) *Global Tax Governance: What is wrong with it and how to fix it*, Colchester: ECPR Press.

Zangl, B. (2008) 'Judicialization matters! A comparison of dispute settlement under GATT and the WTO', *International Studies Quarterly* 52(4): 825–54.

Zucman, G. (2013) 'The missing wealth of nations: are Europe and the U.S. net creditors or net debtors?', *Quarterly Journal of Economics* 128(3): 1321–64.

Index

www.ingramcontent.com/pod-product-compliance
Lightning Source LLC
LaVergne TN
LVHW011907200926
848484LV00002B/551

* 9 7 8 1 7 8 5 5 2 1 2 6 3 *